PARASITES OF OFFSHORE BIG GAME FISHES OF PUERTO RICO AND THE WESTERN ATLANTIC

PARASITES OF OFFSHORE BIG GAME FISHES OF PUERTO RICO
AND THE WESTERN ATLANTIC

Ernest H. Williams, Jr.
and
Lucy Bunkley-Williams

Sportfish Disease Project
Department of Marine Sciences
and
Department of Biology
University of Puerto Rico
P.O. Box 5000
Mayagüez, PR 00681-5000

1996

Cover drawing: Atlantic blue marlin with magnifications of parasites found on this host in Puerto Rico. Cover by Ms. Gladys Otero

Published cooperatively by the Puerto Rico Department of Natural and Environmental Resources , P.O. Box 5887, Puerta de Tierra, San Juan, PR 00906; and the University of Puerto Rico, Mayaguez, PR 00681

Funding provided by the Department of Natural and Environmental Resources with Sportfish Restoration Funds, Federal Aid Projects F-28 and F-35 (U.S. Fish and Wildlife Service) and the University of Puerto Rico, Mayaguez.

The content of this book is the sole responsibility of the authors and does not necessarily reflect policy of the Department of Natural and Environmental Resources or the U.S. Fish and Wildlife Service.

Printed by Antillean College Press, Mayaguez, PR 00681
First printing 1.5 M, 1996

Library of Congress Catalog Card Number 96-86468

ISBN 0-9633418-2-0

Suggested citation:
> Williams, E. H., Jr. and L. Bunkley-Williams 1996. Parasites of offshore big game fishes of Puerto Rico and the western Atlantic. Puerto Rico Department of Natural and Environmental Resources, San Juan, PR, and the University of Puerto Rico, Mayaguez, PR, 382 p., 320 drawings.

Key Words: Fish parasites, big game fishes, parasite ecology, parasite evolution, fish diseases.

CONTENTS

4

REVIEWERS

The following people gave generously of their time and expertise to immeasurably improve the accuracy and timeliness of this book. We deeply appreciate their efforts.

We thank Drs. John M. Grizzle, Department of Fisheries and Allied Aquacultures, Auburn University, USA; Robert J. Goldstein, Robert J. Goldstein & Associates, Inc., Raleigh, North Carolina, USA; and Ms. Carol J. Sanner-Kendall, Girdwood, Alaska, USA, for reviewing the manuscript of this book. For reviewing portions (parasite, associates and disease sections), we thank Drs. Jan H. Landsberg, Florida Marine Research Institute, St. Petersburg, Florida, USA (protozoans); Thomas G. Rand, Department of Biology, St. Mary's University, Halifax, Nova Scotia, Canada (fungus); Landsberg (Cnidaria); Delane C. Kritsky, Idaho State University, USA, and Sherman S. Hendrix, Department of Biology, Gettysburg College, Pennsylvania, USA (copepod worm); Fuad M. Nahhas, Department of Biological Sciences, University of the Pacific, Stockton, California, USA, and William G. Dyer, Department of Zoology, Southern Illinois University, Carbondale, Illinois, USA (flukes); R. J. G. Lester, Department of Parasitology, University of Queensland, Australia and Peter Speare, Australian Institute of Marine Science, Townsville, Australia (tissue flukes); Kritsky and Hendrix (gillworms); Janine N. Caira, Department of Ecology and Environmental Biology, University of Connecticut, USA, Goldstein and Ian Beveridge, Department of Veterinary Science, University of Melbourne, Parkville, Victoria, Australia (tapeworms); Abul K. M. Bashirullah, Instituto Oceanografico, Universidad de Oriente, Cumana, Venezuela and Niel L. Bruce, Zoologisk Museum, Kobenhavns Universitet, Kobenhavn, Danmark (roundworms); Omar M. Amin, Institute of Parasitic Diseases, Phoenix, Arizona, USA (spiny-headed worms); Kenneth G. McKenzie, "Yugen", Wagga, New South Wales, Australia (seed shrimp); George W. Benz, Tennessee Aquarium, Chattanooga, Tennessee, USA and William E. Hogans, Huntsman Marine Science Center, Atlantic Reference Center, St. Andrews, New Brunswick, Canada (copepods); Benz (fish lice and barnacles); Bruce (isopods); Bruce B. Collette, Systematics Laboratory, NOAA/NMFS, National Museum of Natural History, Washington, District of Columbia, USA (fish associates); William D. Swink, Search Coordinator for Pathogens and Parasites of Lampreys, Great Lakes Fishery Commision, Lake Huron Biological Station, Millersburg, Minnesota, USA (lampreys); John A. Plumb, Department of Fisheries and Allied Aquacultures, Auburn University, Alabama, USA (bacteria and viruses); John C. Harshbarger, Registry of Tumors in Lower Animals, Department of Pathology, George Washington University Medical Center, Washington, District of Columbia, USA (tumors, abnormalities and conditions); and Collette (hosts). The reviewers made useful corrections and additions to the book, but any mistakes or irregularities are the responsibility of the authors.

INTRODUCTION

The purpose of this book is to serve as a fish parasite guide for sport fishermen, commercial and tour-guide fishermen, fishery biologists, ecologists, scientists, and anyone interested in the health and welfare of big game fishes. We hope it will encourage the study of the interrelationships between fishes and their intimate parasite partners around Puerto Rico and throughout the Atlantic.

Big game fishes are important sportfishing and food resources. Many of their fish parasites attract the attention of fishermen because they are large, abundant and always on particular host species. The health of these fishes, and the humans who enjoy catching and eating them, is of great concern. The environments of many coastal areas have deteriorated and there is little agreement about how much of this environmental damage has spilled over into the open ocean. The abundance and diversity of big game fish parasites might be used as an indicator of environmental changes. Many parasites are useful as biological tags for tracing stock movements, mixing, migrations and other aspects of the biology of big game fishes. They can also provide readily available examples of many invertebrate phyla which can be used for classroom examinations.

The present knowledge of parasites of big game fishes is at the most basic level, describing species, but the interrelationships between big game fish parasites and their intermediate and final hosts are as complex and intricate as food webs described by ecologists. It is extremely difficult to study the parasites and diseases of live oceanic, fast-moving fishes. Hook and line fishing selects for healthy fishes because sick fishes seldom bite lures or baits. Debilitated fishes in the open sea are quickly eaten, or sink, and seldom wash ashore. Still, we can assume that parasites and diseases cause as many problems for these big game fishes as they do for fishes in more easily examined habitats. A study found that the presence of one species of parasite reduced the yield of a big game fishery by about one fifth. We estimate that somewhere between one third to one half of all big game fish resources are lost due to disease. We need to understand the workings of diseases throughout the ecosystem if we are to have any hope of recuperating losses due to diseases. Unfortunately, we lack complete knowledge of these processes in a single fish, or even of a single disease organism! Most big game fishes are either already overexploited, or are soon to be over fished. As dolphin, greater amberjack and other big game fishes are raised in captivity, we are beginning to discover their deadly parasitic, bacterial and viral diseases. We cannot afford to ignore manageable problems that have the potential to double the stocks of big game fishes We hope that this book will serve as a beginning to better understand these forces in the ecology of big game fishes.

No one before has had the opportunity to make an overview of an entire ecological mix of parasites of the dominant predators of an ocean system. We discuss some trends and relationships, but too little information exists for a complete analysis of this system. Even though many big game fishing tournaments are held every year, there is an incredible lack of published information and basic knowledge about parasites of big game fishes. Much confusion has been caused by the difficulties in identifying these parasites. We hope this book will solve that problem and will allow fisherman and amateur scientists to make contributions to our knowledge of big game fishes. It is a world of great to little mysteries--all worthy of exploration.

The information included in this book comes from our long-term, original observations on big game fishes in Puerto Rico, the West Indies, Gulf of Mexico, Atlantic coast of North America, and from published records in a scattered, often obscure and contradictory literature. Fishes examined in this work were collected by hook and line in fishing tournaments in Puerto Rico from 1974 to 1996 and in Dauphin Island, Alabama, from 1967 to 1974; or by individual sport fishermen and scientists (see Acknowledgments). Some of the barracuda, mackerels and jacks were speared by the authors using skin and scuba diving equipment; or collected with nets by Department of Natural and Environmental Resources (DNER) personnel. There was no attempt to make systematic collections. Parasites were either removed from freshly caught hosts and preserved immediately, or organs and tissue samples removed and placed in plastic bags surrounded by ice for laboratory examinations within 24 hours.

We recognize 39 species of offshore big game fishes in the western Atlantic. Three (Atlantic bonito, chub mackerel, frigate tuna) have not been reported off Puerto Rico and 3 others only occur further south (serra Spanish mackerel) or north (Atlantic mackerel, Spanish mackerel) than our island. They were included to provide a more complete analysis of these otherwise rather homogenous, and wide-ranging, groups of fishes and parasites.

We identify and define 273 species on/in these fishes from the western Atlantic. Each parasite species is illustrated and descriptions of its diagnostic characters, records, geographic range, location in host and length are always presented; and, usually to occasionally, name, life history, ecology, associations, host specificity, damage to host, detection, harm to humans, preparation for study, treatment and significance to sport fishing are discussed. The damage parasites cause in big game fishes has rarely been documented histologically (in tissue sections), therefore we have estimated potential damage based on number and size of parasites, known pathological changes caused by similar infections, and our own experience. No genius is required to predict that superinfections will harm a host, but our other interpretations may be less certain. Most families and genera of parasites are not discussed as groups except for a few that have a series of similar species. In these cases it was more efficient to discuss their similar characters rather than repeating this information with every species.

Methods are suggested to avoid the spread of diseases. Diseases of big game fishes (other than parasites) are noted. The importance of parasites, their use as environmental indicators, controlling and avoiding fish parasites and the effects of fish parasites on humans are discussed. Damaging and dangerous parasites are described, and methods to protect human health are explained. The

Host Summaries and Host-Disease Checklists include the complete classification of these fishes and a list of the diseases we found on each host from the western Atlantic and parasites on these fishes worldwide.

We hope you will use this book as your guide to the parasites of big game fishes. Within the drama of big game fishing lies a play-within-a-play of the parasites and associates of these great fishes. We look forward to receiving reader input concerning these fascinating creatures. - - - Good fishing!

DEFINITIONS AND CONVENTIONS

We tried to avoid the use of scientific jargon, but some scientific terms must be used for the sake of conciseness, clarity or continuity. These terms are either defined where they appear, in each section explanation or below.

Levels of infections for microscopic parasites (protista) were estimated from skin or fin scrapings or gill clippings viewed with a compound microscope. Five medium power (100X) fields were averaged to establish parasite levels shown in the box at right. The very light category can be less than 1 because the value was taken from 5 fields. These categories were also used to express the number of metazoan parasites per host (or average of 5 hosts when possible).

Levels of Infection
very light = <1
light = 1-5
moderate = 6-50
heavy = 51-100
very heavy = 100+
superinfection = 1000+

Frequency of Infection
always = 100-99%
almost always = 98-90%
usually = 89-70%
frequently = 69-50%
commonly = 49-30%
often = 29-10%
occasionally = 9-1%
rarely = <1-0.1%
very rarely = <0.1-0.01%
almost never = <0.01%

Numbers-per-host is only one dimension of parasite occurrence. Determining how often they are found associated with a host species requires more examinations, but is more meaningful. The terms we use to describe the frequency of infection is shown at the left.

Most fish have some parasites that are so characteristic of the host that the fish could be identified from its parasites alone. These "characteristic" parasites almost always or always occur in the host. "Primary" parasites frequently to usually occur in the host. Characteristic parasites evolved in concert with the host, while primary parasites may have evolved with or may be less correlated with the host. Recognizing characteristic and primary parasites is important because they are more dependable indicators of the evolutionary relationships (phylogeny) and population parameters (biological tags) of the host than more casual parasites. Characteristic and primary parasites are usually specific to a species, genus or family of host(s). Approximately 100 specimens of a host (from different times and localities) must be examined for parasites to confirm its characteristic or primary parasites. Few hosts and parasites in this book are so well known. In many cases, we have speculated and used these terms with insufficient data. Further studies will be necessary to confirm or refute these projections. Less important categories are "**secondary**" **parasites** occurring occasionally to commonly in the host; and "**accidental**" **parasites** occurring rarely to almost never. Any of these terms can be used to describe multiple parasite species on a host (for example: characteristic parasite fauna).

The specificity of parasites has been variously defined. We prefer:

Host specific - The parasite is confined to one species of host, or occurs no more than accidentally in other hosts or in false or transfer hosts.

Almost host specific - The parasite is confined to one species of host, but rarely to very rarely occurs in others.

Dominant host - The parasite is characteristic of one host, and occurs no more than commonly in others.

Preferred host - The parasite occurs most often and/or in higher numbers in one host species.

Genus specific, Family specific, etc. - These terms can be used with similar definitions and gradations as above.

Habitat specific - The parasite usually to always occurs in hosts associated with a particular ecological niche or set of ecological conditions, and demonstrates no other host specificity.

No specificity - The parasite occurs in all available hosts with no discernable pattern of preference or abundance.

A number of different kinds of hosts have been defined and we coin a few new ones which seem to be important in the realm of big game fishes:

Accidental host - Sometimes called **Incidental host**. The parasite very rarely to almost never occurs in very light infections. Usually these parasites do not mature on or in the accidental host.

False host - Sometimes called **Temporary host**. The parasite occasionally to almost never occurs in very light to moderate infections in the stomach or intestine of the host. The host is a predator which has eaten a prey fish infected with this parasite. The parasite remains after the prey fish has been digested. It probably does not survive long in this inappropriate host. Another indication of prey transfer is parasites, that only occur in the <u>intestine</u> of prey fishes, but are only found in the <u>stomach</u> of predators.

Intermediate host - A different larval stage of a parasite infects each intermediate host. One or more intermediate hosts may be necessary to complete a life cycle.

Intermediary host - Many parasites and associates rest and feed on/in a host that is not appropriate as their final host. This mechanism allows them to survive longer to locate a final host. It is particularly important in oceanic habitats. This host is not an intermediate host because the parasites are not larval stages; and it is not a transport host because the parasites are not encysted.

Decoy host - An intermediary host on/in which parasites lie in wait to either ambush attach or penetrate the gut of predators that prey on their host. This mechanism appears to be well established in big game fishes. Possibly an abundance of intermediary parasites (or the reputation for having them) could protect prey organism from predation.

Transport host - Sometimes called **Reservoir host** or **Paratenic host**. An encysted parasite in an intermediate host is eaten by a predator that is not the correct final host. The parasite re-encysts in the inappropriate host and will develop into an adult only when this host is eaten by the proper final host. The ability to transfer among succeeding hosts increases the parasite's chances of reaching the correct host.

Describing the size of a parasite is useful. Too often terms such as "large" and "small" have been used without explanation. We define a scale of relative size from the perspective of fishermen or casual observers. If the unaided eye cannot see it, then it is "microscopic"; if it can be barely seen it is "minuscule"; a fingernail length is "moderate". We also define size in metric scale as shown in the box at right

Size of a Parasite	
microscopic =	<0.7 mm
minuscule =	0.7-3.0 mm
tiny =	3.1-7.0 mm
small =	7.1-12.0 mm
moderate =	12.1-20.0 mm
large =	20.1-40.0 mm
very large =	>40.0 mm

We provide a classification for each group of parasites. Classification groups organisms at different levels and is a method of sorting similar things close together and different things further apart. It allows us to guess what an unknown organism must be, just by knowing another organism in its group or by the general characters of the group. Most parasite classifications have been stable for decades to centuries, but advances in modern biology have brought about many exciting changes in the ways we classify parasites. We have attempted to choose the most recent and stable of these systems.

Some species of big game fish parasites have been named more than once because the characters used to separate species are sometimes difficult to interpret. As parasites become better studied, two or more similar forms that had been described as different species may be found to overlap in characteristics. Thus one species may be found to have more than one species name. Since a species can only have one name, the first name used (first description in the literature) is valid and the names published later are called synonyms. We only explain synonyms which have either been used until recently, or are important in understanding the biology or history of a parasite. Other synonyms can be found in the technical guides that we list.

Proper describing and naming of an organism allows us to correctly identify it time after time and to build up biological information about it. Otherwise we would be overcome with uncertainty, identifying organisms over and over, and starting from scratch each time. Indifferent or incomplete classification or taxonomy of big game fish parasites has drastically repressed knowledge of these important organisms. Certainty in absolutely identifying a parasite is the difference between knowing if a worm you noticed in your last piece of sushi at your boss's party can kill you; and in saving $100,000 worth of thawed filets because you can quickly prove the contaminating worms are harmless.

American Fisheries Society (AFS) approved common names (Robins et al. 1991) of western Atlantic big game fishes are used in the text with their scientific names listed in the Host Summaries. Fishes not occurring in the western Atlantic are not in the Checklists, but their AFS approved common names are used in the text and their scientific names appear with the first use of their common names. Organisms other than fishes are similarly identified in the text. Any common name can be matched with its scientific name by looking in the Index for the page number in bold face. Departures from AFS names are discussed in the Host Summaries. Parasite common names are not used except for a few that are generally accepted.

Samples of most of the parasites were deposited in the U.S. National Museum (USNM) and U.S. National Parasite Collection (USNPC) (see Acknowledgments). They are indicated in the text by one of those acronyms followed by their deposition number, or by the acronym alone where a deposition number was not received prior to publication of this book. Collection numbers for specimens deposited in the British Museum of Natural History (BMNH) and Museum of the Canadian Department of Fisheries and Oceans, Atlantic Reference Collection (ARC) are also listed.

PROTOZOA (PROTOZOANS)
MYXOZOA (MYXOZOANS)

Protozoa were once considered a single phylum in the Animal Kingdom. Later, they were classed as a subkingdom, containing a number of phyla, in the Kingdom Protista. Today they are classified among several phyla in 2 kingdoms. In this section, we examine protozoan parasites including members of the Phyla Sarcomastigophora (amoebas and flagellates) and Apicomplexa (coccidians) in the Kingdom Protista, and the Myxozoa (myxozoans) in the Phylum Cnidaria in the Animal Kingdom (Siddall et al. 1995). We list these forms adjacent to each other as they were traditionally presented.

As a group, protozoa are essentially complex, unicellular, microscopic organisms. They differ from the basic animal or plant cell by having additional morphological and physiological characteristics. Protozoa have one to several nuclei; multiple nuclei can be either identical or different. Flagellates usually have few, relatively long flagella for locomotion and one nucleus. Ciliates usually have many, relatively short cilia for locomotion and 2 types of nuclei. Coccidians have a group of specialized organelles forming the apical complex that is visible only by using the electron microscope. Reproduction may be asexual by binary fission, multiple fission, external budding or internal budding; or sexual by fusion, conjugation or autogamy. Myxozoans are characterized by producing multicellular spores with 2-6 external valves containing 1-6 (usually 2) polar capsules and 1-2 infective units. Polar capsules are essentially identical to the nematocysts (stinging cells) of cnidarians. Myxozoans have complex life cycles involving an intermediate host where sexual reproduction takes place. The spores produced from the intermediate host are infective to the fish host.

Protozoan lifestyles range from free-living through various forms of commensalism to parasitism inhabiting animals, plants, and even other protozoans. Amoebas, flagellates and ciliates live in a range of habitats from freeliving to parasitic, while all coccidians and myxozoans are parasites. Most consume solid food (holozoic) or fluid (saprozoic), but a few photosynthesize and make their own energy (holophytic or photo-autotrophic). Parasitic protozoa kill, mutilate and debilitate more people in the world than any other group of disease organisms. Protozoan parasites of fishes, however, are not known to infect humans but can directly transmit microbial diseases to other fishes. Protozoans sometimes kill marine or freshwater fishes in Puerto Rico (Bunkley-Williams and Williams 1994, 1995). Many free-living species occur abundantly in salt water here, consuming dead material in all habitats. Some of these can occur in fishes under certain conditions, but others are specific pathogens of fishes. In Puerto Rico, we have found protozoa to rarely parasitize the skin, fins, gills, and blood of marine fishes.

There are more than 65,000 described species of protozoa with half being fossil (useful in identifying oil deposits) and about 8800 parasitic species, including 2500 ciliates and 1800 flagellates. More than 1300 parasitize fishes.

In addition to the protozoans, there are almost 1200 species of myxozoans which parasitize fish. Protozoans and myxozoans vary in length from 1 μm to 7 cm or more, but most are 5-250 μm. Many thousands of species remain to be described and about one new species is described every day!

Popular Reference - "How to Know the Protozoa" (Jahn, Bovee and Jahn 1979).

Reference - Lom and Dyková (1992), Lee, Hutner and Bovee (1985).

Classification and Contents

Trypanosoma sp. of Saunders (1958)

This West Indian blood flagellate infects the young of a variety of marine fishes, including the offshore big game fishes that spend sufficient time inshore.

Name - This parasite remains undescribed but we assume that what we found is the same as that observed by Saunders (1958). It is possible that these records represent more than 1 species.

Diagnostic Characters - This flagellate has a single flagellum at one end, and swims freely in the blood (not inside blood cells).

Records - We found light infections in 1 of 8 crevalle jack, 2 of 10 great barracuda and in a variety of coral reef fishes from various localities around Puerto Rico. A light infection occurred in 1 of 137 great barracuda in the Florida Keys.

Geographic Range - West Indies.

Life History - Abundant in young fishes, but few remain in adult hosts.

Ecology - This blood parasite is limited to inshore fishes because it is transmitted by leeches, predominantly *Trachelobdella lubrica* (Grube), which do not occur on offshore fishes.

Location in Host - Free swimming in blood.

Length - Approximately 50.0 μm.

Host Specificity - There is a great variation in fishes infected in different localities which seems to be related to the availability of vectors. It can apparently infect any inshore fish. Crevalle jack is a new host for this parasite.

Damage to Host - More abundant in and probably more damaging to young fishes. Fishes infected by this trypanosome may not grow as quickly or as large.

Detection - Free swimming flagellates are easy to see in saline-diluted blood mounts viewed with a compound microscope.

Preparation for Study - A thin blood smear must be air dried on a microscope slide, fixed with 100% methyl alcohol, stained with Giemsa, and examined with the oil immersion lens of a compound microscope. Stained blood smears can be permanently mounted with commercial mounting medium and coverslips.

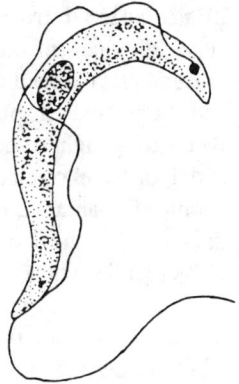

Haemogregarina bigemina Laveran and Mesnil

This cosmopolitan parasite of red blood cells infects a variety of fishes, including offshore big game fishes.

Name - The marine members of this genus, producing 2 or more elongate structures called gamonts per red blood cell, are called "schizohaemogregarines", and may represent a new genus. The wide geographic distribution and broad host choices of this parasite suggest that it could represent several species. However, its occurrence in

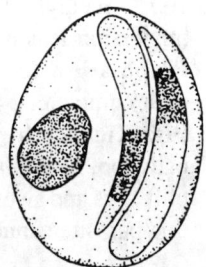

many wide-ranging big game fishes could provide an avenue for spreading a single species to the reported localities.

Diagnostic Characters - This parasite lives inside the cytoplasm of red blood cells. In each infected red blood cell, there are 2 gamonts that are slender at one end and clubbed at the other. Infected red blood cells are usually disfigured and the nucleus displaced by the parasites.

Records - Light infections occurred in 1 of 10 crevalle jack, 1 of 1 frigate tuna and 1 of 9 yellow jack in Puerto Rico; blue runner and great barracuda from Bimini, Bahamas; 2 of 46 bar jack, 1 of 3 dolphin and 2 of 16 great barracuda in Bermuda; and 2 of 17 Atlantic sailfish, 3 of 63 blue runner, 1 of 83 cero, 1 of 3 crevalle jack, 6 of 137 great barracuda, 8 of 37 greater amberjack and 1 of 62 king mackerel in the Florida Keys, USA. It possibly occurred in Atlantic mackerel from the northwest Atlantic (RTLA 4752), and has been reported in other fishes from Canada, Europe and the Pacific.

Geographic Range - Worldwide.

Life History - Most fish-blood protozoans are thought to be transmitted by leeches, but this haemogregarine is apparently transmitted by parasitic isopods. Slender free gamonts, and infective stages called oocysts and sporozoites were found in the gut of *Gnathia maxillaris* Montagu in Europe. Probably *Gnathia* sp. and other isopods parasitizing offshore game fishes act as vectors. In other species in the genus *Haemogregarina*, sporocysts arise in the oocyst. In *H. bigemina*, oocysts produce sporoblasts, which later segment into sporozoites around a residual body. In New Zealand fishes, a division also occurs in white blood cells.

Ecology - This haemogregarine is most numerous in younger fishes. It is found in both inshore and offshore fishes as are its isopod vectors.

Location in Host - It only infects red blood cells (except for the New Zealand form which has a stage in white blood cells).

Length - Gamonts 10.0 μm.

Host Specificity - This parasite occurs in a very great variety of inshore and offshore fishes. It appears to have little if any host preference.

Damage to Host - It is more abundant in and probably more damaging to young fishes. Fishes infected by this haemogregarine may not grow as quickly or as large.

Detection - Damaged red blood cells are difficult to see in saline-diluted blood mounts. A thin blood smear must be air dried on a microscope slide, fixed with 100% methyl alcohol, stained with Giemsa, and examined with the oil immersion lens of a compound microscope.

Preparation for Study - Stained blood smears can be permanently mounted with commercial mounting medium and coverslips.

Significance to Sport Fishing - Balao, *Hemiramphus balao* (Lesueur), and ballyhoo, *Hemiramphus brasiliensis* (Linnaeus), are used as live or fresh bait for billfishes and swordfishes. These fishes are often infected with *H. bigemina*, but this parasite cannot be transmitted directly to big game fishes.

Goussia clupearum (Thélohan)

This parasite lightly infects Atlantic mackerel.
Name - *Goussia cruciata* (Thélohan) may be a synonym.
Diagnostic Characters - This parasite is found in the liver of infected hosts. The spherical oocyst contains 4 ellipsoidal sporocysts, each with 2 sporozoites.
Records - It occurred in an Atlantic mackerel (RTLA 4422) from Maryland, USA; in Atlantic mackerel from France (RTLA 4689, 4699) and sardines from Europe, the Mediterranean and Pacific. A similar parasite *G. auxidis* (Dogiel) was found in the livers and spleen of almost all of 400 albacore from Australia, the Coral Sea, New Zealand, Tonga and the central south Pacific.
Geographic Range - Worldwide.
Life History - Older, larger fishes are more often infected (up to 90% of some herrings and sardines).
Associations - In specimens from France, it occurred with a bacteria *Mycobacterium* sp. (RTLA 4689, 4699).
Location in Host - The oocysts occur in liver parenchyma. (In a French specimen it was found in hepatic and renal granulomas.)
Length - Oocyst 18.0-25.0 μm; sporocyst 8.0-12.0 X 4.0-10.0 μm.
Host Specificity - It is almost family specific to herrings and sardines (Clupeidae) but occasionally occurs on Atlantic mackerel.
Damage to Host - Pathological changes include infiltration of macrophages (specialized white blood cells) around oocysts, necrosis (tissue death) and inflammation around oocysts and eventual encapsulation. In heavy infections up to 14% of the liver may be replaced by these parasites.
Significance to Sport Fishing - It appears to injure herrings and sardines more often than Atlantic mackerel, but heavy infections could limit stocks of these forage fishes, thus reducing the food available for big game fishes.

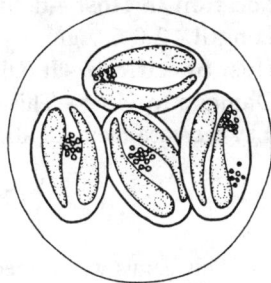

Haematractidium scombri Henry

This is a common but relatively harmless parasite in Atlantic mackerel.
Diagnostic Characters - It is found inside the red blood cells of the host fish and is smaller than the nucleus of the red blood cell. It has 1, sometimes 2, nuclei that appear dark in the light cytoplasm.
Records - It occurred in Atlantic mackerel from Maryland, USA (RTLA 4423); and off the coast of England. In the English specimens, 45% of the fish were infected, but only 5% of the red blood cells were affected.
Geographic Range - Northern Atlantic.

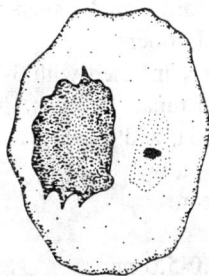

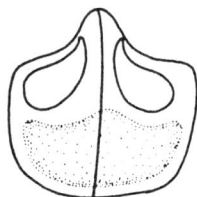

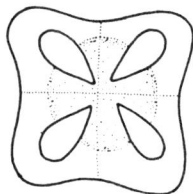

Location in Host - In the cytoplasm of red blood cells
Length - 2.0-6.0 μm.
Host Specificity - It only occurs in Atlantic mackerel.
Damage to Host - This parasite distorts the shape of the red blood cells and may increase their fragility and lyse them.

Genus *Kudoa* Meglitsch

This genus was named for a famous protozoologist, Dr. R. R. Kudo. It is important because most of the 37 described species (and all of the species discussed here) dissolve or liquefy fish muscles either while the host is alive or very soon after death. Thus they cause enormous economic loss.

The unique feature of these multicellular parasites is the polar capsules that contain a coiled spring-like filament that is extruded when stimulated. They may be used to attach to host tissue. The number and arrangement of these polar capsules and the shape of the spore are diagnostic for each species. Although the polar capsules are the dominant feature of this parasite, the sporoplasm (also called the infective unit) is the cell that infects the host.

Cysts can be seen in fillets held in front of a bright light. This process, called "candling", has historically been used to find defects and parasites in fishes. Cysts or small amounts of liquefied tissue can be mechanically removed from muscle, placed on a microscope slide with a drop of saline and gently squashed with a cover slip to release the spores. Spores or cysts can be preserved in 5% formalin. Muscle with cysts can be preserved in 10% formalin.

Kudoa clupeidae (Hahn)

The presence of this parasite in tunas makes them unsuitable for consumption. Liquefaction of flesh may occur after the fish is stored on ice.
Name - Possibly, *Kudoa* sp., which occurred in the muscle of approximately 1% of bluefin tuna from Tasmania, Australia (RTLA 2128), is this species.
Diagnostic Characters - Spores are rounded rectangular in apical view. They have a pointed apex when seen in lateral view. Trophozoites form spindle shaped masses that are easily seen in muscle fibers.
Records - The muscle was uniformly infected with 3-7 cysts per 10 cm^2 in an unidentified tuna, *Thunnus* sp. from New Jersey, USA (RTLA 2532); and bluefin tuna from the west coast of Africa.
Geographic Range - Atlantic Ocean.
Location in Host - Muscle.
Length - Spore 4.0-5.0 X 6.3-7.5 μm; cysts in muscle 2.0-5.0 mm.
Host Specificity - It is almost family specific to herrings and sardines (Clupeidae). The few records in scombrids may be accidental infections.

Significance to Sport Fishing - How often this parasite occurs has been employed as a biological tag to distinguish different stocks of fish.

Kudoa crumena Iversen and Van Meter

This protozoan heavily encysts in the muscles of Spanish mackerels off Florida and causes the flesh to rapidly deteriorate.

Diagnostic Characters - Spores are pouch-shaped, with 4 polar capsules and 1 infective unit (sporoplasm). Elliptical white pseudocysts are obvious in muscle.

Record - One in 9 Spanish mackerel from south Florida, USA, were found infected. Numerous cysts occurred in infected hosts, but few hosts were infected.

Geographic Range - Unknown.

Life History - The spores are probably inadvertently ingested by the fish host. In the intestine, the 4 polar capsules each eject a filament into the lining which holds the spore in place and makes an entry hole for its infective unit. This stage either reproduces in the epithelial cell or moves through the lymphatic or blood system to muscle tissue where it forms a pseudocyst, weakly encased by connective tissue of the host. Here, spores are produced which either escape when the host dies or are attacked and killed by the host (granulomatous inflammation). Pseudocysts are liberated either by digestion in the gut of a carnivorous fish or by host decomposition and are broadcast over the substrate.

Location in Host - Muscle.

Length - Spores 7.5 X 9.9 μm, filament 15.5 μm; cysts up to 2.6 X 1.7 mm wide. Lom and Dykova (1992) mistakenly used μm instead of mm for the size of the pseudocyst, making the macroscopic, spore-containing cyst smaller than the microscopic spores.

Host Specificity - It is only known from Spanish mackerel.

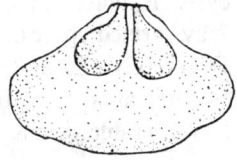

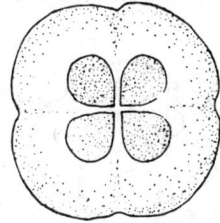

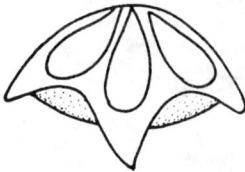

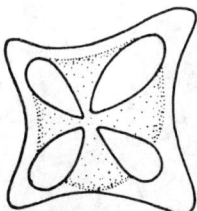

Kudoa histolytica (Perard)

This parachute-shaped protozoan liquefies the muscles of live Atlantic mackerel.

Name - The specific epithet, "histolytica", refers to its ability to liquefy the muscles of its hosts [from Greek "histos" = tissue, and "lytic" = dissolve].

Diagnostic Characters - The spore looks like a 4-pointed star when viewed from above, or a parachute when viewed from the side. It has 4 polar capsules.

Records - It occurs in Atlantic mackerel from the Atlantic and Mediterranean.

Geographic Range - Northern Atlantic and Mediterranean.

Location in Host - Muscle.

Length - Spores 4.0-5.0 X 6.3-7.5 μm.

Host Specificity - It is only known from Atlantic mackerel.

Damage to Host - Instead of being confined in host-produced connective tissue cysts, it liquefies the host muscle, turning it into a jelly-like mass containing fully formed spores.

Detection - Liquefied areas can be seen in muscle.

Significance to Sport Fishing - This important sport and food fish is made less desirable or unusable by this infection.

Kudoa nova Naidenova

These spindle-shape cysts infect a variety of fishes including bigeye tuna. It causes the flesh to rapidly deteriorate.

Name - This parasite was formerly confused with *K. clupeidae*.

Diagnostic Characters - Spindle-shaped cysts contain many plasmodia which form 1-8 spores each. Spores are pumpkin-shaped with 4 lobes and 4 polar capsules.

Records - It occurred in bigeye tuna off the Atlantic coast of the USA.

Geographic Range - Atlantic, Mediterranean and Black Seas.

Ecology - It is found in both oceanic and coastal areas.

Location in Host - Muscle.

Length - Spores 5.3-6.5 X 8.5-9.8 μm; cysts up to 7.0 mm.

Host Specificity - It occurs in a variety of fishes.

Significance to Sport Fishing - This parasite causes postmortem liquefaction of the muscle tissues of fishes. Bigeye tuna are made less desirable to unusable by this infection.

FUNGI (FUNGUS)

The fungal-like organisms that parasitize fishes were once thought to be simple and similar. These disease organisms are actually so diverse that they belong in 2, possibly 3, Kingdoms. *Paecilomyces* sp. (Rand, Bunkley-Williams and Williams 1997), the causative agent of tilapia-wasting disease (Bunkley-Williams and Williams 1995) is in the Kingdom Fungi; *Saprolegnia* spp., which causes problems in Puerto Rican and worldwide fresh and brackish water fishes, is in the Kingdom Protista; and *Ichthyophonus hoferi*, discussed below, is in an undermined Kingdom somewhere between the Animal and Fungi Kingdoms (Ragan et al. 1996). The name "fungus" comes from the Latin for "mushroom". The familiar mushrooms, lichens, yeasts and molds are in this kingdom. Fungi are the largest and the longest living organisms on earth. The forms found in fishes are not known to be dangerous to humans. Parasitic fungi might be useful in controlling some pest species. More than 100,000 species are known. They range from microscopic to more than 50 acres in size. They come in a variety of shapes and forms. Many resemble plants, but lack the green pigment chlorophyll. Elaborate modes of asexual and sexual reproduction occur. Most are spread by spores. Some fungi, including disease-causing forms, are called "imperfect" because they either lack sexual reproduction, or it has not been observed. Most fungi are free living, often feeding on decomposing materials (saprophytic). A few can alternate between saprophytic and parasitic existence. Others are completely parasitic (obligate parasites). Many organisms are infected by fungal-like organisms including big game fishes. A variety of marine fungi, including some that may harm humans, have been found in the marine waters around Puerto Rico, but none affect local fishes.
Popular Reference - "Fungal Diseases of Fishes" (Neish and Hughes 1980).
Reference - Rand (1996).

Classification and Contents

Ichthyophonus hoferi Plehn and Mulsow

This highly dangerous and destructive cosmopolitan organism kills and injures Atlantic mackerel, and possibly other big game fishes in the North Atlantic.
Name - The condition is commonly called "ichthyophonus disease". It was previously confused with a microsporidian protozoan *Ichthyosporidium gigan-*

teum (Thélohan), and called ichthyosporidium disease or ichthyosporidiosis. The wide range of habitats and hosts for this disease suggest that a number of similar fungal species may be involved.

Regan et al. (1996) erected a new group of fungal-like and extremely damaging parasites of aquatic organisms which includes *I. hoferi, Dermocystidium* spp. of fishes and amphibians, *Psorospermium haeckelii* of crayfish, and the "rosette agent" of salmonids. This unnamed Kingdom and/or Phylum was tentatively called "DRIP clade" and is phylogenetically at the divergence between the Animal and Fungi Kingdoms.

Diagnostic Characters - The cysts are usually spherical to irregularly shaped and opaque to translucent granular with thick, multilaminate walls. It sometimes germinates with single or multiple, branched or unbranched thalli extending into host tissues.

Records - Heavy infections occurred in Atlantic mackerel off the northeast coast of the USA and Europe. Random samples of Atlantic mackerel from sport fishing creel census conducted in New Jersey, USA, found 5% of apparently healthy fishes had light infections.

Geographic Range - Mass mortalities of marine fishes appears to be limited to the North Atlantic, but this disease is found worldwide in marine, brackish and fresh waters. Mass mortalities of cultured fishes have occurred in Japan and on the west coast of the USA.

Life History - The resting stage (cyst) containing a multinucleated cytoplasm is usually seen in the tissues of the host. More advanced cysts contain a few to hundreds of distinct nuclei. Endospores germinate in the cyst, and pseudopodia-like thalli extend out of the cyst and invade new host tissue (filamentous germination). Alternatively, the entire contents (plasmodium) of the cyst may move into the host tissues and occupy an area of 2-3 times the original volume of the cyst (plasmodial germination). Both methods produce new resting stages until the host tissues stop further development or the host dies. Resting cysts may leave the host through the digestive tract, gills and/or skin or *en masse* from dead and decomposing hosts. Mother cysts produce amoeboblasts which await being inadvertently eaten by a new host. Amoeboid bodies are released and penetrate through the intestinal wall into the blood and become resting cysts in the tissue in which they settle. Host death can occur in 1 month (acute) to 6 months (chronic).

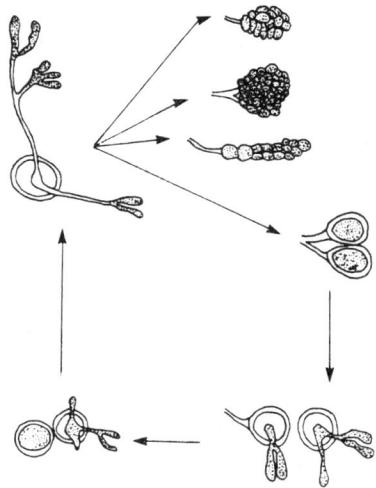

Ecology - This is an obligate parasite that grows best at 10°C but can grow between 3-20°C, but not at 30°C. It can continue to grow in hosts that it has killed. Atlantic mackerel on the east coast of the USA may be resistant to this disease, but can become infected and die during mass mortalities of Atlantic herring, *Clupea harengus* Linnaeus. Off Europe, mass mortalities of Atlantic mackerel have occurred without the stimulus of herring mortalities.

Location in Host - During mortalities of Atlantic mackerel, the kidney, spleen and other visceral organs were destroyed, but no external or muscle lesions were present. The disease is systemic, but attacks different tissues in different species of hosts.

Length - Cysts usually 10-300 μm.

Host Specificity - It can apparently infect almost any species of marine or freshwater fish and has also been reported in amphibians and copepods.

Damage to Host - Great losses have occurred in cultured fishes and in repeated mass mortalities in wild fishes. Mass mortalities may limit the populations of herrings in the western North Atlantic.

Detection - Multiwalled, spherical resting stage (quiescent) cysts are most easily seen in fish tissues. Death, emaciation and low body weight are seen in many cases.

Significance to Sport Fishing - This infection reduces the numbers, condition and vitality of at least 1 important big game fish.

Preparation for Study - It can be grown on Sabouraud's dextrose agar or glycerine-agar, both with 1% bovine serum added. Bacterial overgrowth can be reduced by adding 0.25 g/l each Streptomycin and Penicillin into the media before pouring the plates.

Disease Prevention - Fishes or even frozen or processed fish products from the north Atlantic or other areas of known infections should not be cleaned or processed in other regions where this disease could spread. Feeding infected tissues spreads and intensifies the disease in new hosts. Although this disease is assumed to be worldwide, it behaves quite differently in different regions. Different regional strains, or even species may occur, and should not be spread to other geographic areas.

22

PLATYHELMINTHES (FLATWORMS)

Flatworms form a phylum of soft-bodied, bilaterally symmetrical, flattened, worm-shaped animals. Usually each worm has a set of both female and male reproductive organs (hermaphroditic). They either have a primitive blind gut and a mouth, or absorb nutrients through their bodies. They respire through their skin and possess specialized cells that secrete ammonia waste products. There are about 20,000 species of flatworms including copepod worm, flukes, tissue flukes, gillworms, and tapeworms.

Classification and Contents

UDONELLIDEA (COPEPOD WORM)

The species below apparently represents a class of flatworms. No common name has been given to this animal, so we suggest copepod worm. This worm parasitizes fish-parasitic copepods. Some of these copepods, in turn, parasitize big game fishes! It has also been found on fish lice and fish-parasitic isopods. It superficially resembles a gillworm, but is so drastically different it must be separated. This distinction is based on the anatomy of the protonephridial excretory system. It also differs from gillworms by having a simple sac for an intestine and no hardened (sclerotized) attachment organs.

Classification and Contents

Udonella caligorum Johnston

This tiny parasite is seldom seen as an adult on parasitic copepods, but their eggs are occasionally found attached to the cuticle of copepods parasitic on big game fishes.

Name - Several genera and a number of species have been described, but all appear to be synonyms.

Diagnostic Characters - The cylindrical body has a posterior sucker-like attachment organ that is not divided into sections and is not armed with anchors, bars or spines.

Records - We found 1 on a male *Brachiella thynni* in a wahoo, 1 each on 3 *Euryphorus brachypterus* in a yellowfin tuna; and on *Caligus bonito* in a snapper from La Parguera, Puerto Rico. It has also been reported from a little tunny off Chesapeake Bay, USA; and yellowfin tuna in the Pacific.

Geographic Range - Worldwide.

Life History - This hyperparasite lives its whole life on parasitic crustacea. The elongate, pyriform operculate eggs are attached in clusters to the crustacean by an adhesive disk with a thread attached to the egg. The young hatch out of the egg and are capable of attaching to the crustacean (no free swimming, ciliated larval stage). They possess both male and female organs but cross fertilize each other. This direct life cycle allows large numbers of them to build up and some copepods are "furry" with eggs.

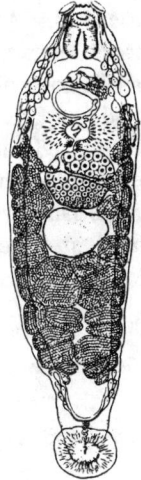

Ecology - This worm transfers from one copepod to another when these crustacean parasites are mating (a sexual disease of copepods). It has been found on free swimming parasitic copepods captured in plankton nets.

Associations - Usually found attached on a great variety of caligoid copepods, but has been reported on other genera of copepods; a fish louse, *Argulus* sp.; an isopod, *Livoneca vulgaris* Stimpson; and on the gills of host fishes.

Location in Host - Eggs are usually attached to the posterior part of a copepod, immature worms attach to the lateral margins of the carapace, and adults to the central and lateral parts of the carapace. Most worms are on copepods that parasitize the gills and mouth of fishes. One of our specimens occurred in a cavity beneath the pectoral fin of a wahoo.

Length - 1.1-2.3 mm

Host Specificity - This worm does not appear to prefer any particular fish species, but does prefer flat, round crustacean parasites, particularly copepods in the genus *Caligus*. *Brachiella thynni* is a new, and unusually shaped, host for this worm, and wahoo is a new fish host.

Significance to Sport Fishing - This worm may feed on parasitic copepods instead of the fish host, and certainly covers these crustacean parasites with eggs that are probably detrimental. Oddly enough, this parasite may harm other parasites and may actually benefit the fish host.

DIGENEA (FLUKES)

Flukes or digeneans (formerly called digenetic trematodes) form a class of flatworms. Flukes reproduce as adults and again as larvae, hence the name "digenetic" or 2 births. They cause serious and fatal diseases in many animals including humans. Bilharzia (*Schistosoma mansoni* Sambon) in humans is found in Puerto Rico. Flukes are important fish parasites with fishes serving both as intermediate (grubs) and final hosts (flukes). More than 9000 species have been described. Adults range in size from <0.2 mm to >10 cm. One of the largest, *Hirudinella ventricosa*, occurs in the stomach of local wahoo. Flukes usually look like typical flatworms with a mouth in the anterior region, and a blind gut and reproductive and other organs in the trunk region. Unlike generalized flatworms, many have 2 sucker-like holdfast organs. One is located near the mouth (oral sucker) and the other is usually in the middle of the worm on the same (ventral) side (ventral sucker or acetabulum). Great differences in shape, size and orientation of structures occur in different species. The internal organs illustrated in the adjacent drawing can be seen if worms are placed in saline wet mounts and viewed with a compound microscope.

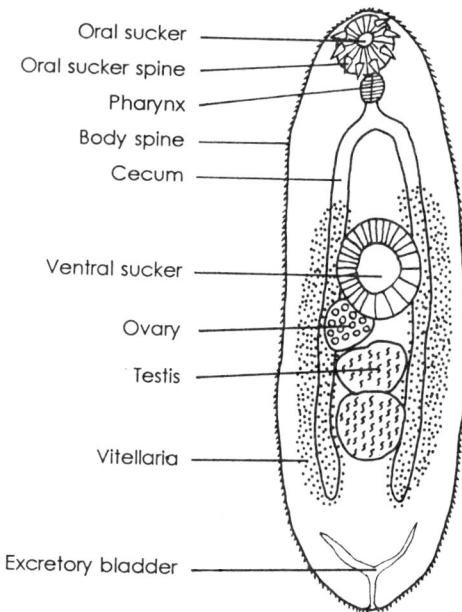

Flukes have a complex life cycle usually with 2-3 intermediate hosts, possible transfer hosts and a final host. In a typical life cycle, eggs from the body of the fluke pass out the intestine of the final (definitive) host. The eggs are either eaten by the first intermediate host or hatch into a swimming ciliated larva (miracidium) that infects the first intermediate host, usually a snail. Once inside the snail the miracidium transforms into a sporocyst. Each sporocyst asexually produces many larval parasites (rediae) which in turn produce many swimming infective larvae (cercariae) that leave the snail. The cercariae infect the second intermediate host, encyst, and become metacercariae. If the appropriate final host eats this infected host, the metacercariae are digested out of the cyst and become adult flukes. There are many variations in the life cycle especially in the asexual phases. Each fluke has both female and male reproductive systems (hermaphroditic). Self fertilization is possible in some flukes but cross fertilization usually occurs.

Flukes are permanent parasites in most marine fishes, and in many fresh-water fishes, amphibians, reptiles, mammals and birds. Larval stages occur in a variety of invertebrates and vertebrates. Flukes usually occur in either the intestine, stomach or mouth, or occasionally lungs and other organs. Larval forms occur in almost any tissue. Sometimes predator hosts temporarily support flukes digested from prey (false hosts), but these soon pass out of the predator.

Didymozoids or tissue flukes belong in the digenea but their exact position and relationships are not clear. The classification will not be resolved until the life cycles and early life cycle stages are studied. We consider them separately after the flukes.

Popular Reference "How to Know the Trematodes" (Schell 1970).

Classification and Contents

Hirudinella ventricosa (Pallas)

This giant worm is the only fluke which has frequently been brought to us by fishermen. A pair of these stomach worms is almost always found in wahoo around the world, and less consistently in most tunas and dolphins.

Name - This giant fluke is so well known by sport fishermen that it has been given common names: "giant stomach worm", "giant fish stomach worm" and contracted and wrinkled flukes are called "walnut worms". Because of its great variability both in size and shape, this worm has been called by at least 39 scientific names. The name *H. marinum* Garcin was first proposed for this fluke in 1730. It has been rejected as the name of this worm because it was used before Linnaeus set up the present system of scientific names. *Hirudinella ventricosa* is the only valid species in the genus, thus the 14 other species names still in use are actually synonyms.

Diagnostic Characters - This small to very large fluke is unmistakable in the stomach of wahoo. It is a fleshy worm that varies in size and shape, with extended worms the size of a mans finger and contracted ones about the size of a walnut. Smaller worms are still massive but they are capable of contorting into

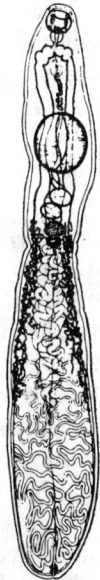

many shapes. It is brown to pinkish in color. The 2 suckers are easily seen and are close together on the anterior end of the worm.

Records - We found 1 in an albacore, 1-4 in 23 of 40 Atlantic blue marlin, 1 in a blackfin tuna, 1-3 in 16 of 40 dolphin (USNPC 84887), 1-4 in 3 of 6 little tunny, 3 in a longbill spearfish, 1-2 in 3 of 8 skipjack tuna, 2-4 (usually 2) in 15 wahoo (USNPC 77758-60) from various localities around Puerto Rico; 3 in 2 of 5 dolphin, 1 in a little tunny, 2 in each of 4 wahoo; and 4 in 1 of 2 yellowfin tuna from Dauphin Island, Alabama, USA. It occurred in a little tunny in the Gulf of Mexico off Mexico; and 19 in 1, and 2 in 3 of 13 wahoo from Bermuda. One to 6 occurred in 8 of 36 white marlin off Delaware and Maryland, USA (USNPC 80328) and 1-8 in 62 of 303 swordfish from the northwest Atlantic (ARC 2318); and in albacore, Atlantic blue marlin, Atlantic bonito, Atlantic sailfish, chub mackerel, little tunny, bluefin tuna, skipjack tuna, swordfish and yellowfin tuna from the Gulf of Mexico and Atlantic coasts of USA. This worm occurred once each in a pilotfish off the Canary Islands; in a great barracuda from the Atlantic, and a king mackerel from Brazil, but these may have been accidental infections. We also found it in wahoo from the central Pacific. It also occurs in black marlin and frigate tuna from the Indo-Pacific. In 14 localities across the Pacific, an average of 0.4 (0.0-1.1) worms occurred in 878 skipjack tuna. Less than 1% of the skipjack tuna off Florida had this worm, but 40% of those off Brazil, 7% off West Africa, 21% off the Marquesas in the Pacific, and 34% off Hawaii were infected.

Geographic Range - Worldwide.

Life History - Adults occur over a broad range of sizes. It feeds on blood, thus the gut of the parasite is usually filled with black, digested blood. Eggs are relatively small for the size of this worm. Studies have suggested that larger eggs occur in larger worms, but others have found egg size to be rather erratic.

Ecology - Wahoo, particularly those shorter than 160 cm, almost always have a pair of these giant worms in their stomach. Two wahoo longer than 160 cm, off La Parguera and off Mona Island had 3 and 4 worms. Other hosts are more variable in the occurrence and numbers of this parasite.

Associations - We examined 13 dolphin collected off La Parguera, Puerto Rico, for total parasites. Five of these fish had 2-3 of these worms, and thousands of other flukes in their stomachs. However, there was no obvious relationship between these worms and other species of flukes.

One worm was found in a 10 mm long 2 mm wide stomach ulcer of an albacore from Desecheo Island. The relationship between stomach ulcers and stomach parasites in big game fishes is not certain. We have seen injuries to the stomach lining of wahoo caused by these worms, but could not be certain that these were not caused after the death of the host.

Location in Host - Stomach.

Length - 8.5-100.0 mm. Live worms may extend to 170 mm.

Host Specificity - Wahoo is the preferred host of this parasite, both by being almost always present, and by achieving a consistently large size in this host. It is a characteristic parasite of wahoo and a primary parasite of Atlantic blue marlin, dolphin, little tunny and possibly other scombrids. It is a secondary parasite of other scombrids and billfishes. Blackfin tuna, frigate tuna and longbill spearfish are new hosts for this parasite.

Damage to Host - These very large worms cause wounds by penetrating the stomach lining to feed on blood and absorb a considerable amount of blood. Fortunately, few worms occur per host. Usually only 1 or 2 of the worms present in the stomach of a host are very large. Some mechanism of the parasites or the hosts appears to regulate both the numbers and sizes.

Preparation for Study - The thick skin (tegument) of this parasite protects it from acid and churning food particles in the stomach, but makes the penetration of chemicals more difficult and preparations more likely to contract or distort. Specimens that have been partially damaged by long contact with stomach acid, after the death of the host, are particularly difficult to prepare. Worms removed from the stomach can be kept alive temporarily in a small amount of saline held in a refrigerator until preserved.

Significance to Sport Fishing - The wounds they produce and sheer size must have a negative, if unstudied, impact on big game fishes. They have also been used as biological tags.

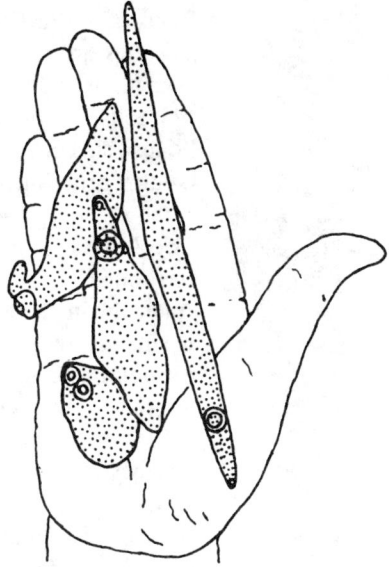

Bathycotyle coryphaenae Yamaguti

Geographically widespread, but little studied, this parasite of dolphin attaches in the gills, an unusual location for flukes.

Name - Burnett-Herkes (1974) reported *B. branchialis* Darr in dolphin, but we suspect it was this fluke.

Diagnostic Characters - This moderate-sized, elongate fluke has the ventral sucker located on a projection from the body. The oral sucker is smaller than the ventral sucker and moderately separated from it (more than 2, less than 3 ventral sucker diameters). There is a hood-like lobe that hangs over the oral sucker and the ventral sucker is enclosed by a fold of the body wall. No tail is present.

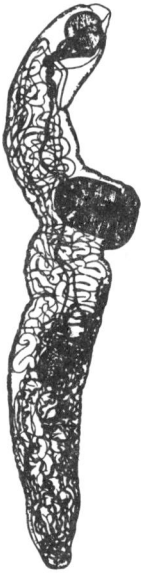

Records - We found 1-10 in 12 of 40 dolphin from various localities around Puerto Rico; and 1 in 1 of 5 dolphin from Dauphin Island, Alabama, USA. From 1-14 occurred in 75 of 125 dolphin from the Straits of Florida; and in this host from Louisiana, USA; and Japan.

Geographic Range - Worldwide. Our collections are the first in the Caribbean and northern Gulf of Mexico.

Life History - It does not parasitize the smallest dolphin but was found in fish from 12.1-138.4 mm in standard length. It gradually increases in numbers in larger fish and may thus accumulate over time.

Associations - The numbers of this fluke were positively correlated with the numbers of *Caligus productus* and *Euryphorus nordmanni* on the gills of dolphin, which suggests that they may, in some way, aid each other in parasitizing this host.

Location in Host - Attached to gill filaments.

Length - 13.0-24.0 mm.

Host Specificity - This worm only occurs on dolphin, but not often enough to be a characteristic parasite.

Damage to Host - Moderate infections may injure dolphin.

Brachyphallus parvus (Manter)

This fluke parasitizes a variety of hosts including a few big game fishes.

Name - This parasite has, at various times, been placed in the genera *Brachyphallus*, *Lecithochirium* and *Sterrhurrus*, but this peculiar worm does not appear to fit well in any described genus. The name *Lecithochirium parvum* was used for this worm in the records from Curaçao and Jamaica.

Diagnostic Characters - It is a microscopic to minuscule, elongate fluke with the body either bulging around the ventral sucker or with the ventral sucker on a projection off the body. The oral and ventral suckers are moderately (approximately 1 ventral sucker diameter) separated. A short tail is usually withdrawn into the body. The oral sucker is more than 1/3 and less than 1/2 the diameter of the ventral sucker. The vitellaria are reduced to 2 compact, lobate masses just posterior of the ovary, and the testes are one in front of the other with the anterior one partially underneath the ventral sucker. Overstreet (1969) found considerable variation in specimens of this fluke. The tail may be extended or not, with the ceca extending into the tail or not, the testes may be in contact or separated, the sizes of the oral sucker and ventral sucker and ratios of these sizes varied, sizes of the eggs varied. He

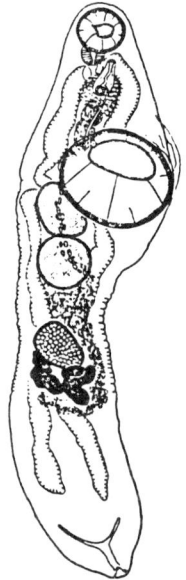

found that the small size of this worm, pre-acetabular pit, weakly-developed cirrus sac and low number of postovarian coils of the uterus, were consistent characters that allowed this worm to be identified.

Overstreet (1969) also pointed out that this species lacks the deep striations (cuticular plications) on the sides of the body that are characteristic of this genus, and placed it in *Lecithochirium*. Yamaguti (1970) stated it could not go into *Lecithochirium* because it lacks a prostatic vesicle characteristic of this genus. He did not address the striations question directly, but added "usually" to that character in the genus diagnosis.

Records - It occurred in little tunny from La Parguera, Puerto Rico (USNPC 39403); 2 in 1 of 3 crevalle jack, 2 in 1 of 18 horse-eye jack and 2 in 1 of 8 yellow jack from Jamaica; and 1 in a greater amberjack from Curaçao. It was found in 1 of 3 little tunny from Dry Tortugas, Florida, USA (USNPC 37018); in 1 of 2 blue runner from south Florida; and in frigate tuna and yellowfin tuna from the western Atlantic.

Geographic Range - Western Atlantic.

Associations - The fluke, *Lecithochirium texanum*, occurred with this worm in a little tunny examined in the Dry Tortugas.

Location in Host - Stomach.

Length - 0.5-1.2 mm.

Host Specificity - This worm appears to have little host preference.

Dinurus scombri Yamaguti

This stomach fluke is found worldwide in little tunny.

Name - The name, quite appropriately, refers to the family of the hosts.

Diagnostic Characters - This is a tiny, elongate fluke with the oral and ventral suckers close together and approximately the same size. The tail is less than 1/3 of the total body length. The tubular mass of vitellaria is confined in the midbody and does not nearly reach the tail.

Records - We found 2-3 in 2 of 5 Atlantic sailfish from various localities around Puerto Rico; 2 in a longbill spearfish from Aguadilla, Puerto Rico; and in a little tunny from Dauphin Island, Alabama, USA. One occurred in 1 of 3 little tunny from the Dry Tortugas off Florida, USA; and in chub mackerel, frigate tuna and other scombrids from Japan.

Geographic Range - Worldwide. Our collections are the first in the Caribbean and northern Gulf of Mexico.

Location in Host - Stomach.

Length - 3.6-4.8 mm.

Host Specificity - This worm is family specific to scombrids, but insufficient information is available to assess its individual host preferences. Our records in Atlantic sailfish and longbill spearfish may

represent false hosts resulting from these predators eating scombrids. These 2 billfish species are also new hosts for this parasite.

Dinurus tornatus (Rudolphi)

This large and impressive fluke occurs in the stomach of dolphin around the world. We found harmful superinfections in Caribbean dolphin.

Name - Traditionally, 4 species, *D. barbatus* (Cohn), *D. breviductus* Looss, *D. longisinus* Looss and *D. tornatus*, are recognized in the stomach of dolphin. Dawes (1968) suggested that these worms were 1 species. We struggled to separate these forms, but found that the characters used to separate the species intergrade and are not mutually exclusive. We conclude that only 1, highly variable, species of this genus occurs in dolphin. *Dinurus coryphaenae* Yamaguti and probably *D. hippurus* Nadakal, Kappikarayil and Jacob are also synonyms.

Diagnostic Characters - This is a highly variable, minuscule to large, elongate fluke with the oral and ventral suckers close together. The oral sucker is less than 1/2 to 2/3 the diameter of the ventral sucker. The tail is more than 1/3 to more than 1/2 of the total body length. Deep striations (cuticular denticulations) occur on the sides of body. The egg filled uterus extends into the tail and often 1/2 way down the tail. The intestinal ceca extend to the end of the tail. The winding vitellaria extend from the posterior body into the tail.

Records - We found 3-2805 in 40 dolphin from various localities around Puerto Rico (USNPC 39404-6,84882-4); 1 in 1 of 3 bar jack from Cabo Rojo, Puerto Rico (USNPC 85292); and 100-200 in 5 dolphin from Dauphin Island, Alabama, USA. It also occurred in dolphin and pompano dolphin from Cuba; more than 200 in a dolphin from Bimini, Bahamas; 1-3 in 3 dolphin from Curaçao; in 3 of 6, 1 of 6, and 2 of 6 dolphin from the Dry Tortugas, Florida, USA; in dolphin and pompano dolphin from Louisiana and North Carolina; in dolphin from Brazil; in Atlantic bonito and skipjack tuna in the western Atlantic; more than 200 in each of 2 dolphin from the Pacific coast of Panama; and in other scombrids in the Pacific.

Geographic Range - Worldwide.

Life History - Metacercaria occur in the skin and muscle of herrings, possibly other fishes, and in pelagic crustacea.

Ecology - The superinfections we found in the Caribbean have not been recorded elsewhere. Possibly, infections are more severe and damaging to dolphin in the Caribbean than in the Gulf of Mexico or Atlantic coasts of North and South America. Manooch, Mason and Nelson (1984) failed to find this fluke in 2632 dolphin collected along the Gulf and Atlantic coasts of the USA from Texas to North Carolina. A very heavy infection of 250 flukes was reported in a dolphin from India.

Associations - We found 5-2805 worms in 13 dolphin from off La Parguera. Hundreds of other parasites occurred with this parasite, but none showed any correlation with the numbers of this worm.

Location in Host - Stomach.

Length - 2.0-22.5 mm.

Host Specificity - This fluke is a characteristic parasite of dolphin and probably pompano dolphin. It appears to prefer dolphins to scombrids by having higher numbers and occurring in greater frequency. Some records from scombrids may represent false hosts from dolphin prey and/or misidentifications of *D. euthynni* Yamaguti or *D. scombri*. Bar jack is a new host for this parasite.

Damage to Host - Superinfections of this worm must damage and limit the growth of this commercially and recreationally valuable fish. Encysted metacercariae cause "black-spot disease" in herrings from Argentina.

Ectenurus lepidus Looss

This parasite is found worldwide in the stomach of jacks and other fishes.

Name - *Ectenurus americanus* (Manter), *E. virgulus* Linton and *E. yamaguti* Nahhas and Powell appear to be similar to this worm and may be synonyms.

Diagnostic Characters - It is a minuscule to tiny, elongate fluke with the oral and ventral suckers close together. The oral sucker is less than 1/2 the diameter of the ventral sucker. The tail is more than 1/3, but less than 1/2 the total body length. Deep striations (cuticular denticulations) occur on the sides of body. The uterus containing eggs extends into the tail; that the intestinal ceca stop well short of the end of the tail; and that the winding vitellaria are confined in midbody and do not extent to the tail.

Records - One occurred in a blue runner, 2 each in 2 of 3 crevalle jack, 1 in 1 of 4 greater amberjack, an unknown number in 18 horse-eye jack and 1-2 in 2 of 8 yellow jack from Jamaica; 2 in 1 of 19 yellow jack from Belize (USNPC 74267); 1-19 occurred in 52 bar jacks from Bermuda; and 3 in 1 of 2 yellow jacks from the Dry Tortugas off Florida, USA. Despite extensive examinations of these same hosts in Puerto Rico, we have not seen this worm. It has also been reported in Atlantic bonito, rainbow runner and a variety of other fishes throughout the western Atlantic.

Geographic Range - Worldwide.

Associations - In 52 bar jacks from Bermuda infected with this worm, 10 had double infections with *Alcicornis carangis*, 7 with *Prosorhynchus pacificus*, and 10 had triple infections with all 3 flukes.

Location in Host - Stomach or gills. Flukes in the gills have been reported by several authors, and probably indicate this worms' ability to leave dead fishes.

Length - 0.9-4.8 mm
Host Specificity - This parasite has been reported from a wide variety of fishes, but it may prefer jacks. In Bermuda, it is a characteristic parasite of bar jack.

Hemiurus appendiculatus (Rudolphi)

This fluke occurs in a great variety of fishes but seldom in big game fish.

Diagnostic Characters - A microscopic to tiny, elongate fluke with a short tail that is deeply embedded into the body. The oral and ventral suckers are rather close together, but separated by more than 1 width of the ventral sucker. The oral sucker is less than 1/2 as large as ventral sucker. Deep striations (cuticular denticulations) occur on the sides of the entire body.

Records - One occurred an in Atlantic mackerel and 2 in a banded rudderfish, *Seriola zonata* (Mitchill), (USNPC 8327) from Massachusetts, USA. Also reported in a variety of fishes from the temperate Atlantic from Europe to the north Atlantic coast of USA and Canada, Mediterranean and Black Sea.

Geographic Range - Northern Atlantic, Mediterranean and Black Sea.

Location in Host - Stomach.

Length - 0.4-4.5 mm.

Host Specificity - This fluke appears to have little host preference as it occurs in a great variety of inshore fishes. The 1 report from an Atlantic mackerel may have been an accidental infection or a false host.

Lecithochirium microstomum Chandler

This fluke occurs worldwide and has generalized host preferences. It is often found in big game fishes.

Name - Manter (1947) thought that this fluke was similar, if not identical, to *L. magnaporum* Manter which occurs in a variety of Pacific big game fishes. We consider it a synonym. Yamaguti (1971) thought it was similar to and often confused with *L. priacanthi* Yamaguti, but did not synonymize them.

Diagnostic Characters - It is a minuscule to tiny, bullet-shaped to oval fluke with the oral and ventral suckers well separated (more than 1 ventral sucker diameter). A moderate (approximately 1/3 of total body length) tail is usually not withdrawn into the body. The oral sucker is approximately 1/3 the diameter of the ventral sucker. The vitellaria are reduced to 2 compact, lobate masses just posterior of the ovary; that the testes are side-by-side diagonally, in contact and slightly separated from the ventral sucker; and that the uterus with eggs extends to the end of the intestinal ceca and both extend into the tail.

Records - Two occurred in 1 of 4 greater amberjack from
Jamaica; and 6 in 1 of 3 pompano dolphin from Pass-a-Grille,
Florida, USA. It was also found in skipjack tuna from the
Pacific coast of Mexico, frigate tuna from Hawaii and in a
variety of Pacific big game fishes.

Geographic Range - Worldwide.

Life History - Pearse (1949) found a "young" fluke in a clam,
ponderous ark, *Noetia ponderosa* (Say), from North Carolina
and suggested that it was this worm.

Location in Host - Stomach.

Length - 2.8-4.8 mm

Host Specificity - This fluke probably prefers Atlantic
cutlassfish, *Trichiurus lepturus* Linnaeus, since this fish has the
heaviest infections (up to 250), but it occurs in a variety of
fishes.

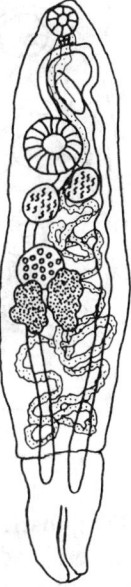

Lecithochirium texanum (Chandler)

This tiny stomach fluke parasitizes Atlantic
bonito, little tunny and other fishes in the Gulf of
Mexico.

Name - *Sterrhurus texanus* C. is a synonym and *Lecithochirium*
sp. of Overstreet, 1969 may be a synonym. Manter (1947)
suggested that this worm was a synonym of *S. imocavus* Looss
which was named in a tuna, *Thynnus* sp., from Egypt.

Diagnostic Characters - It is a minuscule to tiny, elongate fluke
with an ventral sucker that is relatively large and almost as wide
as the body. The tail is relatively short and less than 1/5 of the
body length. The ovary is widely (more than 4 diameters)
separated from the testes.

Records - It occurred in an Atlantic bonito from Texas, USA;
and heavy infections in 3 little tunny from the Dry Tortugas off
Florida, USA.

Geographic Range - Gulf of Mexico.

Associations - *Brachyphallus parvus* occurred with this worm in
a little tunny examined from the Dry Tortugas.

Location in Host - Stomach.

Length - 1.9-3.6 mm.

Host Specificity - This worm is possibly family specific to scombrids.

Lecithochirium sp.

This new fluke occurs in low numbers in a variety of fishes in Puerto Rico
including black jack and king mackerel.

Name - This worm is a new species which we are in the process of describing.
Siddiqi and Cable (1960) apparently assumed this worm was *L. microcercus*
(Manter) because it occurred in the same host in the Dry Tortugas off Florida,

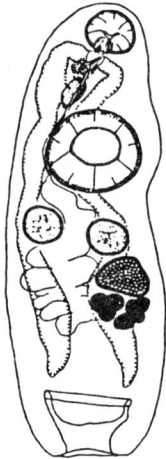

USA, and in Puerto Rico (USNPC 39402). We followed their lead and identified a series of specimens from Puerto Rico with the aid of their illustration. Only in preparing this book did we examine the original description and illustrations of *L. microcercus*. The Puerto Rican worms are similar to *L. microcercus*, but differ by having a genital pore that opens posterior to the oral sucker instead of on top of it [as Manter (1947) emphasized], widely separated (almost 1 testis diameter apart) testes instead of closely spaced almost touching testes, testes that are separated from the ventral sucker by approximately the diameter of a testis instead of being under the ventral sucker, a uterus that does not extend posteriorly passed the vitellaria instead of beyond the ends of the ceca and to the posterior end of the worm, and a uterus that is confined between the ceca instead of winding around and beyond the ceca.

Diagnostic Characters - A microscopic to minuscule, bullet-shaped fluke with the oral and ventral suckers moderately (less than 1 ventral sucker diameter) separated, and a short tail that is withdrawn into the body. The oral sucker is about 1/2 the diameter of the ventral sucker. The vitellaria are reduced to 2 compact, lobate masses just posterior of the ovary, the testes are side-by-side, widely separated (by approximately 1 diameter), widely separated from the ventral sucker, and the uterus with eggs is confined in the field between the intestinal ceca and does not extend posterior of the vitellaria.

Records - Two occurred in a black jack from Mona Island, 1 in 1 of 6 king mackerel from La Parguera, Puerto Rico.

Geographic Range - Unknown.

Location in Host - Stomach.

Length - 0.6-1.0 mm.

Host Specificity - Apparently this fluke has little host preference as 1-10 (average 3.4) flukes occurred in 12 fish specimens of 12 fish species in 9 families and 6 orders of fishes.

Lecithocladium excisum (Rudolphi)

This small, but distinctive, stomach fluke is a dominant parasite of Atlantic mackerel. It may be more abundant in the cooler water areas, but occurs throughout the world in a variety of hosts.

Name - *Ectenurus* sp. of Linton, 1910, *L. excisiforme* Cohn, *L. gulosum* (Linton), and *Paradinurus manteri* Perez-Vagueras, are synonyms, and *L. harpodontis* Srivastava is similar and may also be a synonym.

Perez-Vagueras (1958) described a new genus and new species, *P. manteri*, from a single, 11.2 mm long, worm from the stomach of a Cuban great barracuda. His specimen was unusual in having a body that inserted into the tail, instead of a tail that inserted into the body. Otherwise, this worm is identical to *L. excisum* in size, shape and arrangement of organs. The identical and distinctive oral sucker and egg sizes (20-22 x 10-12 μm) in both of these forms make a particularly compelling argument that they are the same. The genus *Paradinurus* is a synonym of *Lecithocladium*.

Perez-Vagueras (1958) and Yamaguti (1971), who accepted this new genus, were apparently not aware that Linton (1910) described and illustrated this worm as *Ectenurus* sp. Linton also noted and illustrated that the body inserted into the broader tail in 2 worms, but a tail that was more narrow than the body in a third worm. Thus the main character used to distinguish genus *Paradinurus* actually varies within the species.

Diagnostic Characters - The distinctive, elongate oral sucker is shaped like a scallop shell with a wide anterior and more narrow posterior. The oral sucker is larger than the ventral sucker and they are separated by approximately 1 width of the ventral sucker. This elongate fluke has a tail that is more than 1/3, but less than 1/2 of the total body length. Weak striations occur on the sides of the body. The pharynx is tubular. The intestinal ceca extend to near the end of the tail. The winding vitellaria and the egg-filled uterus extend into the tail.

Records - One occurred in a great barracuda from off Havana, Cuba; in chub mackerel from Brazil; 3 immature worms in a frigate tuna from the Dry Tortugas off Florida, USA; 2 in an Atlantic mackerel (USNPC 8377), and 1-17 (average 6.3) in 20 chub mackerel (USNPC 8375-6) from Woods Hole Massachusetts, USA. It is found in Atlantic mackerel and chub mackerel throughout the cooler waters of the north and possibly in the south Atlantic; and immature worms in bluefin tuna off Europe.

Geographic Range - Worldwide.

Life History - Immature forms of this fluke are found in a great variety of false hosts.

Ecology.- This parasite may occur more abundantly in temperate and cooler waters. There are records from south Florida, the northern Gulf of Mexico, both sides of the Atlantic, Baltic, Mediterranean, Black Sea, Pacific Ocean, Japan and New Zealand, but only 1 from the tropics.

Location in Host - Stomach.

Length - 6.0-15.0 mm. These worms are about half as long when the tail is retracted into the body. Immature worms are 1.0-5.9 mm.

Host Specificity - Atlantic mackerel is the dominant host of this parasite in the Atlantic, but it also occurs in a variety of other fishes. It may be a characteristic parasite of Atlantic mackerel, and is at least a primary parasite.

Parahemiurus merus (Linton)

This tiny fluke has generalized host preferences, but has only infected big game fishes in Jamaica.

Name - *Hemiurus sardiniae* Yamaguti is a synonym.

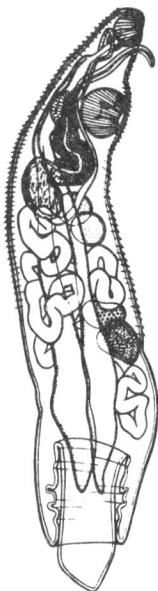

Diagnostic Characters - It is an elongate fluke with a short, deeply invaginated tail. The oral and ventral suckers are close together but separated by about 1 width of the ventral sucker. Deep striations (cuticular denticulations) occur on the sides from the oral sucker to 2/3 of the way down the body. The uterus with eggs either does not extend into the tail or just barely does, and that the intestinal ceca extend into the tail. Vitellaria are reduced to a rounded lump near the ovary.

Records - One occurred in a blue runner, 2 in 1 of 3 crevalle jack, 1 in 1 of 4 greater amberjack, and 4 in 3 of 18 horse-eye jack from Jamaica. Despite extensive examinations of these same hosts in Puerto Rico, we have not seen this worm in any of these hosts. It did occur in light infections in other fishes from Puerto Rico (USNPC 39398). This worm was found in Indo-Pacific sailfish from Japan. We found 1 *Sterrhurus* sp. in a great barracuda from Okinawa, Japan (USNPC 79985), that could possibly be this worm. It is also found in a variety of others hosts from the Dry Tortugas and throughout the western Atlantic, the Gulf of Mexico, Brazil, Pacific northwest coast of USA, Ecuador, and Japan.

Geographic Range - Worldwide.

Location in Host - Stomach.

Length - 1.4-3.5 mm.

Host Specificity - This fluke appears to have little host preference as it occurs in a broad range of hosts.

Sterrhurus musculus Looss

This tiny fluke has a worldwide distribution and a broad range of hosts including crevalle jack.

Name - *Lecithochirium floridense* (Manter); *S. floridense* M.; *Separogermiductus zeloticus* Travassos, T. de Freitas and Buhrnheim and *Sterrhurus zeloticus* (T., T. and B.) appear to be synonyms.

Diagnostic Characters - It is a bullet-shaped fluke with the oral and ventral suckers less than 1 ventral sucker width apart. The oral sucker is approximately 1/3 the width of the ventral sucker. The tail is usually extended from the body, but can be contracted into the body, and is more than 1/3, but less than 1/2 the total body length (when extended). The compact and rounded lobe of vitellaria is posterior to the ovary. The testes are touching or slightly separated, side-by-side on a slight diagonal, just posterior to or slightly under the ventral sucker. The egg-filled uterus

does not extend to the end of the intestinal ceca or into the tail. The intestinal ceca either do not extend into the tail or just barely do so.

Records - Found in 1 of 3 crevalle jack from Biscayne Bay, Florida, USA, and from Brazil; and in great barracuda in the Gulf of Mexico off Mexico. It occurred in a variety of fishes from Puerto Rico, Curaçao and Jamaica, but not in big game fishes. It is known throughout the western Atlantic, eastern Atlantic off Europe, Mediterranean, Black Sea, and Japan in the western Pacific.

Geographic Range - Worldwide.

Location in Host - Stomach.

Length - 1.0-2.1 mm.

Host Specificity - This fluke apparently has little host preference since it occurs in a great variety of fishes. Its rarity in great barracuda suggests that this is a false host.

Tetrochetus coryphaenae Yamaguti

This is a common and abundant parasite in dolphin around the world.

Name - This worm was placed in a new genus, *Paratetrochetus* Hanson, because it has a distinctive structure around the pharynx, but this character was not sufficient to distinguish a genus. *Tetrochetus aluterae* Hanson is a synonym, and *T. macrorchis* Yamaguti may be a synonym.

Diagnostic Characters - This is a minuscule to small, elongate fluke with the ventral sucker attached on a projection from the body. The oral sucker and ventral sucker are close together and of similar size. No tail is present.

Records - We found 1-41 worms in 8 of 13 dolphin examined off La Parguera (USNPC 84885), in this host and wahoo from Puerto Real and Mona Island, Puerto Rico; and 5 in 1 of 5 dolphin from Dauphin Island, Alabama, USA. It has also been found in dolphin, filefishes and puffers from Curaçao, Netherlands Antilles; Bimini, Bahamas (4 in a dolphin); Jamaica; Mexico; and Louisiana, USA, in the Atlantic; and Panama and Japan in the Pacific.

Geographic Range - Worldwide.

Ecology - It occurs in both offshore pelagic and inshore fishes, and thus must have a broad range of tolerances and intermediate hosts.

Associations - A variety of other worms occurred in the stomach and intestine of dolphin with this host, but we found no apparent interaction between this fluke and other parasites in the 13 dolphin we analyzed for total parasites.

Location in Host - Intestine.

Length - 2.3-7.8 mm.

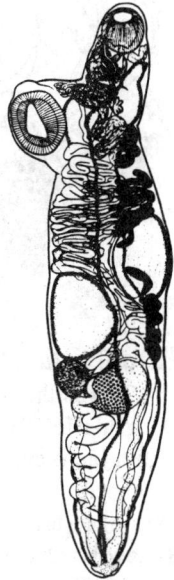

Host Specificity - This worm largely occurs in dolphin and filefishes. This is a peculiar pattern considering that these 2 families of fishes are not closely related. It is a primary, but not a characteristic parasite of dolphin. The single records in wahoo from Puerto Rico and a porcupinefish, *Diodon hystrix* Linnaeus, from Jamaica probably represent false or accidental hosts.

Mabiarama prevesiculata Freitas and Kohn

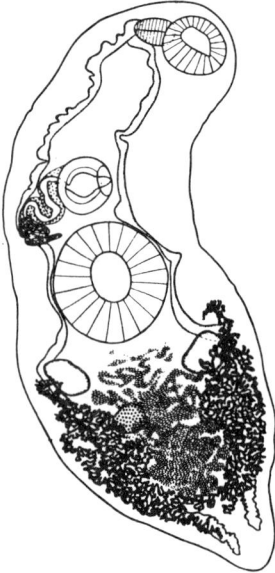

This peculiar worm was described from cobia in Brazil.

Name - A new family, Mabiaramidae, and new genus was based on this unusual worm.

Diagnostic Characters - This small, stout worm has an ventral sucker that is separated from the oral sucker by more than 1 diameter of the ventral sucker, and is approximately twice as large as the oral sucker. The oral sucker and cecal bifurcation attach almost directly to the pharynx. The ceca are irregular in outline and extend to the posterior end of the worm. The vitellaria are confined to the lateral margins of the posterior body.

Records - This fluke occurred in cobia from Brazil.

Geographic Range - Unknown.

Location in Host - Stomach.

Length - 6.9-11.9 mm.

Host Specificity - Unknown.

Paradeontacylix sanguinicoloides McIntosh

This is the only blood fluke known from big game fishes.

Diagnostic Characters - It is a uniformly wide, elongate worm with a blunt anterior end and pointed posterior end. The ceca are X-shaped. The middle of the body is filled with 2 long irregular rows of testes.

Records - One occurred in a greater amberjack off Miami, Florida, USA (USNPC 34329).

Geographic Range - Unknown.

Location in Host - Blood vessels of gills.

Length - 3.2 mm.

Host Specificity - Unknown.

Damage to Host - Two similar species from Asia cause mass mortalities of greater amberjack in aquaculture in Japan.

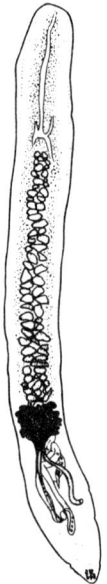

Tergestia laticollis (Rudolphi)

This highly ornamented small fluke has distinctive "dreadlocks". Its variability, worldwide range, and broad host preferences have caused much confusion.

Name - Yamaguti (1970) suggested that the only difference between this fluke and *T. pectinata* (Linton) was the sizes of the eggs, yet he listed overlapping ranges of egg size for these 2 species (Yamaguti 1971). We also struggled to separate these species, but now we recognize 1 definable species rather than 2 that are so similar that they confuse the experts. *Tergestia acuta* Manter, *T. pauca* Teixeira de Freitas and Kohn, *T. pectinata* and *T. selenei* Amato are synonyms of this highly variable fluke.

Diagnostic Characters - This minuscule to tiny fluke has relatively large, distinctive, tentacle-like papillae surrounding the oral sucker. Muscular folds are visible in the sides of the neck. The ventral sucker is relatively large and occupies more than 1/2 of the body width.

Records - Ten occurred in 1 of 3 bar jack from off Cabo Rojo (USNPC 85463), 12 in 1 of 2 bar jack (USNPC 85940) and in little tunny from La Parguera, Puerto Rico (USNPC 39332). One was found in a blue runner, 1 each in 3 crevalle jack, 9 in 5 of 18 horse-eye jack and 1-3 in 4 of 8 yellow jack from Jamaica; 1 in 1 of 4 bar jack, 4 in 1 of 2 blue runner, 1-6 in 3 of 4 horse-eye jack from Bimini, Bahamas; 2 in 1 of 4 horse-eye jack from Curaçao; 7 in 1 of 8 yellow jack from Belize (USNPC 74189); 2 in 1 bar jack from Bermuda; and in a little tunny in the Gulf of Mexico off Mexico. One occurred in 1 of 3 crevalle jack from southern Brazil and from Florida, USA; in 1 of 2 blue runner from south Florida, and Alligator Harbor and Tampa Bay, Florida; in a frigate tuna, 3 little tunny, skipjack tuna and 2 yellow jack from the Dry Tortugas, Florida; 6 in a bullet tuna from Woods Hole, Massachusetts, USA (USNPC 8190); and in chub mackerel and skipjack tuna from the Atlantic coast of the USA. Five were found in a rainbow runner from the Pacific coast of Costa Rica; and in chub mackerel from Japan. We found it in a variety of other fishes in Puerto Rico and Okinawa, and it has been reported from the Black Sea, North Sea, Mediterranean, eastern and western Pacific.

Geographic Range - Worldwide.

Life History - We found 2 immature specimens encysted in the heart of a gray angelfish, *Pomacanthus arcuatus* (Linnaeus), from La Parguera, Puerto Rico. These flukes differed from this species by having longer, lanceolate muscular lobes around the oral sucker and a smaller ventral sucker which was in the posterior half of the body. Possibly these structures change as the worm develops since we have found no other species in this genus in Puerto Rico.

Location in Host - Intestine.

Length - 0.9-5.4 mm.   The cysts in the heart of a gray angelfish were 218 μm, and the encysted worms were 188 μm.

Host Specificity - This worm has no host preference and occurs in a wide variety of big game fishes and other fishes.

Damage to Host - The cysts in the heart caused little tissue damage and no noticeable host response.

Family Bucephalidae

These tiny flukes are distinct because they do not have anterior mouths surrounded by an oral sucker. The "oral" sucker is replaced with a more elaborate "rhynchus" with folds, caps and tentacles. The name means big (bu) head (cephalo). The mouth is on the ventral side, usually somewhere in the middle third of the body. The intestinal ceca are reduced to little more than a small oval sack which can easily be mistaken for an ovary or testis in wet mounts. This family seems to occur most frequently in inshore fishes. Thus infections in the inshore wandering jacks, barracuda, and Spanish mackerels are understandable, but those in little tunas and bonitos are more difficult to explain.

These worms are rather important in big game fishes, possibly dispropor-tionately so. This may be related to some aspects of the ecology or behavior of near-shore big game fishes. The plasticity and variability of some of these worms has caused much confusion in the literature which we have probably not been entirely successful in resolving. Some flukes are host specific to big game fishes, but few occur with regularity, and none qualify as characteristic parasites.

The rhynchus should be examined in live flukes when possible. The definitive shape and structures may change in dead or improperly preserved samples. These flukes are almost too small to attract the interest of sport fishermen but hold a wealth of information for the eco-parasitologist.

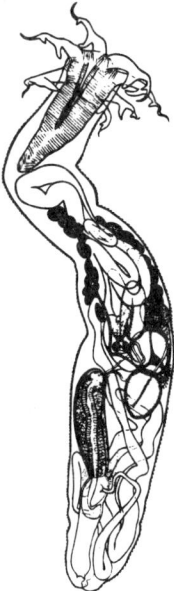

Alcicornis carangis MacCallum

This fluke may damage West Indian jacks. It has oddly shaped tentacles on the anterior end..

Name - Siddiqi and Cable (1960) correctly identified this fluke in Puerto Rico, but Nahhas and Cable (1964) described it as *A. siddiqii* based primarily on the larger and more developed rhynchus in larger worms. Very likely a bigger fluke has a larger, more developed rhynchus. We do not consider these differences sufficient to distinguish a new species when so little is known about this fluke. The rhynchus was redescribed in detail by Rees (1970).

Diagnostic Characters - It is a minuscule, elongate worm with a distinctive wedge-shaped, relatively large, elongate rhynchus with 7 tentacles. Each obvious tentacle has 2 side branches of different sizes. The mouth opens approximately in mid-body.

Records - Four occurred in 1 of 2 bar jack from La Parguera (USNPC 85464-5), 10 in a bar jack from Puerto Real (USNPC 39302), 22 in a blue runner from La Parguera (USNPC 85941), and more than 100 in a horse-eye jack from Humacao, Puerto Rico (USNPC 82997). Three were found in a bar jack from Curaçao (USNPC 60249); in bar jack from Cuba; 1-2 in 2 of 8 yellow jack from Jamaica; 1-40 in 40 of 52 bar jack from Bermuda; and "moderate numbers" in a bar jack from the New York Aquarium that was collected from Key West, Florida, USA.

Geographic Range - West Indies.

Associations - See *Ectenurus lepidus*.

Location in Host - Stomach or intestine (bar jack). We found 100 flukes in the pyloric ceca of a horse-eye jack.

Length - 0.9-2.5 mm.

Host Specificity - This parasite may be genus specific (*Caranx*), or family specific to jacks. The high numbers in horse-eye jack and lower ones in bar jack, could suggest that horse-eye jack might be the preferred host. This parasite appears to be a secondary parasite of both hosts. Horse-eye jack was a new host (Bunkley-Williams, Dyer and Williams 1996).

Damage to Host - The very heavy infection of more than 100 worms in the pyloric ceca could easily stunt or injure the host.

Significance to Sport Fishing - If it is restricted to the West Indies, this fluke might have some potential as a temporary biological tag.

Bucephalopsis arcuata (Linton)

This fluke may be a characteristic parasite of Atlantic bonito and important in other big game fishes.

Name - This species was briefly placed in the genera *Bucephaloides* and *Prosorhynchoides*. *Bucephalopsis scomberomorus* (Corkum) appears to be a synonym.

Diagnostic Characters - This minuscule to tiny, oval fluke has a relatively small, simple rhynchus. Ear-like anterior projections of the body occur on either side of the rhynchus. The eggs do not occur in the anterior part of the body. The positions of the testes and ovary vary considerably. This worm is very similar to *Bucephalopsis longicirrus*, with which it has often been confused, but it varies by having an excretory bladder than extends anterior of the pharynx.

The encysted form is usually yellow, but may be silver. Older cysts turn brown.

Records - Two occurred in 1 of 2, and 6 in 1 king mackerel from La Parguera, Puerto Rico (USNM). One was found in a king mackerel from Jamaica and 1 in 1 of 2 of this host from Curaçao.

It also occurred in 2 cero from south Florida, USA; in 3 of 11 king mackerel and 11 of 33 Spanish mackerel from Louisiana, USA (USNPC 70983); 1100 in 15, 500 in 15 (USNPC 8170), 36 in 3, 22 in 5, and 18 in 4 Atlantic bonito, and 5 encysted in 1 of 12 Atlantic mackerel, from Massachusetts, USA; in Atlantic bonito, king mackerel, Spanish mackerel, crevalle jack, and a few other fishes from North Carolina, Florida and Texas, USA. Various reports of this fluke from great barracuda were misidentifications of *Bucephalopsis longicirrus*.

Geographic Range - Western Atlantic (not confirmed from the Atlantic coast of South America).

Life History - These flukes probably enter the liver through the bile duct and become enclosed in host generated, connective tissue cysts.

Location in Host - Pyloric ceca, stomach and intestine; encysted in connective tissue cysts in the serous coat of the pyloric ceca and liver.

Length - 1.3-3.1 mm; cyst 3.0 mm.

Host Specificity - This fluke may be a characteristic parasite of Atlantic bonito, but reports and records are too incomplete to be certain. It also occurs in a variety of other fishes, including many big game fishes.

Damage to Host - The many hundreds of encysted flukes, that have been reported in each liver of some Atlantic bonito, could injure this host. The very heavy infections of gut flukes, that have frequently been reported from this host, must also be injurious.

Bucephalopsis longicirrus Nagaty

This worm is a worldwide parasite of barracudas.

Name - This fluke has been placed in the genera *Bucephaloides* and *Prosorhynchoides*.

Diagnostic Characters - It is a minuscule, elongate fluke with a relatively small, simple rhynchus. Ear-like anterior projections of the body occur on either side of the rhynchus. The eggs are not found in the anterior part of the body. This worm is very similar to *B. arcuata*, with which it has often been confused, but varies by having an excretory bladder than does not extend anterior of the pharynx.

Records - This worm occurred in great barracuda from Mona Island (USNPC 39306); in 5 of 11 from Louisiana, USA; 1 to more than 100 in 3 from Bimini, Bahamas; 1 in 1 of 6 from Curaçao; 3 in 2 of 3 from Jamaica; Atlantic coast of Panama; Dry Tortugas and south Florida, USA. It has also been reported in another species of barracuda from the Red Sea.

Geographic Range - Worldwide.

Associations - It occurred with *B. longovifera* and *Rhipidocotyle barracudae* from the Dry Tortugas; and with *B. longovifera* in 4 fish from Louisiana.

Location in Host - Pyloric ceca and intestine.

Length - 0.7-1.3 mm.
Host Specificity - This parasite is genus specific to barracuda (*Sphyraena*).

Bucephalopsis longovifera Manter

Great barracuda commonly have this parasite throughout the West Indies.

Name - The species name is for the unusually elongate egg ("longovi"=long egg, "fera"=bearing). This fluke has been placed in the genera *Bucephaloides* and *Prosorhynchoides*.

Diagnostic Characters - This microscopic to minuscule, oval fluke has a relatively small simple rhynchus. Relatively large elongate eggs are distributed throughout the body.

Records - One occurred in 1 of 3 great barracuda from Jamaica, 2 in 1 of 6 from Curaçao, in 8 of 15 from the Dry Tortugas, Florida, USA; and in 5 of 11 from Louisiana, USA.

Geographic Range - West Indies and Gulf of Mexico.

Life History - Manter (1940b) noted and figured the odd-shaped, and highly variably eggs of this worm.

Associations - See *Bucephalopsis longicirrus*.

Location in Host - Pyloric ceca and intestine.

Length - 0.6-1.0 mm.

Host Specificity - This worm only occurs in great barracuda.

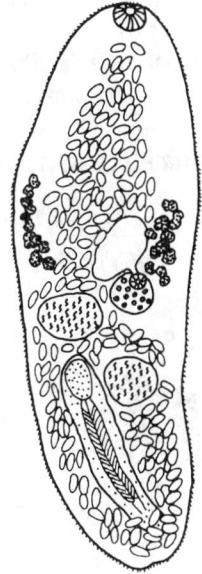

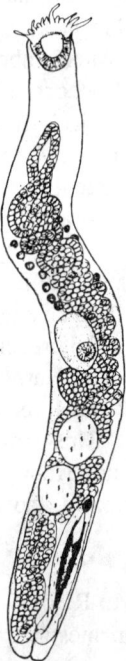

Bucephalus gorgon (Linton)

This fluke of amberjack has numerous distinctive tentacles around the anterior end.

Name - The name "gorgon" is a name for the Medusa, a mythological creature with snakes for hair that turned men to stone. The original specimens of *Gasterostomum gorgon* Linton were lost, the original description of the species was incomplete, and Linton often grouped multiple species under a single name, thus we cannot be certain what species his name actually represented. His renamed *Nannoenterum gorgon* (Linton 1940) (USNPC 8185) appears to be this fluke.

Diagnostic Characters - It is a minuscule to tiny, elongate worm with a rhynchus appearing like a relatively large oral sucker with 22 moderate-sized tentacles on the anterior end. The tentacles on each worm vary in size.

Records - This worm occurred in 7 of 8 greater amberjack and 1 of 3 banded rudderfish, from Louisiana, USA; and in a greater amberjack from North Carolina, USA; and 9 in 1 and

89 in 3 greater amberjack from Woods Hole, Massachusetts, USA (USNPC 8185).
Geographic Range - Atlantic and Gulf coasts of USA.
Location in Host - Anterior intestine.
Length - 1.6-3.3 mm.
Host Specificity - This parasite is genus specific (*Seriola*). It may be a characteristic parasite of greater amberjack.

Bucephalus varicus Manter

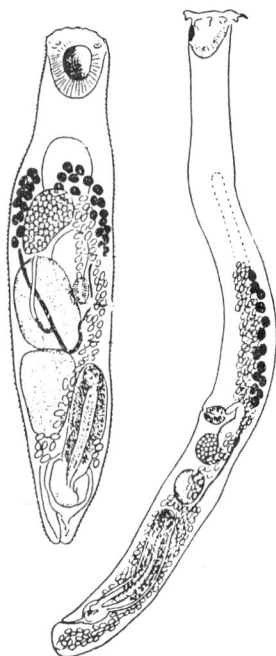

This worldwide parasite of jacks has some interesting distributional gaps.

Name - The name is appropriate as this fluke appears to be highly variable. *Bucephalus polymorphus* of Nagaty, 1937, and Caballero, Bravo-Hollis and Grocott, 1953 and *B. pseudovaricus* Velasquez are synonyms, and *B. solitarius* Kohn appears to be a synonym. This fluke needs to be redefined and refigured.

Diagnostic Characters - The rhynchus is relatively large with 6-7 relatively large tentacles on the anterior end. The tentacles are often not protruded, resulting in knob-like structures around the anterior sucker. Slight pressure on live specimens may cause the tentacles to protrude.

Records - One occurred in 1 of 2 bar jack, 3 in 2 of 3 crevalle jack, 2 in 1 of 4 greater amberjack, 1-3 in 12 of 18 and 1 in 1 of 3 horse-eye jack, and 1 each in 2 of 8 yellow jack from Jamaica; 1 in 1 of 4 bar jack, more than 300 in 1 of 2 blue runner, 12 to more than 300 in 4 horse-eye jack from Bimini, Bahamas; 25 in a yellow jack from Grand Cayman, Cayman Islands (USNPC 82471); 3-75 in 4 horse-eye jack (USNPC 74241) and 8-35 in 8 yellow jack (USNPC 74240, 74282) from Belize. It was found in 5 of 6 bar jack, 1 of 6 horse-eye jack and 1 of 2 yellow jack from the Dry Tortugas, Florida, USA; in 1 of 2 blue runner, and 3 crevalle jack from south Florida; in blue runner and crevalle jack from Alligator Harbor, Florida; and in 1 bar jack, 2 of 6 blue runner, 6 of 20 crevalle jack and 1 horse-eye jack from Louisiana, USA; and blue runner from Brazil. This worm possibly occurs in greater amberjack and in jacks and other fishes from the Pacific coast of Panama; Baja California, Mexico; the Red Sea; Okinawa, Japan; and the Philippines.
Geographic Range - Worldwide.
Ecology - This fluke is displaced by *Alcicornis carangis* in Puerto Rico.
Location in Host - Pyloric ceca, occasionally in the stomach or intestine.
Length - 0.9-2.0 mm

Host Specificity - This parasite largely occurs in jacks, particularly those in the genus *Caranx*, but not exclusively enough to be family specific. It may be a secondary parasite of most of the jacks listed above.

Rhipidocotyle baculum (Linton)

This is a rather variable tiny fluke of western Atlantic Spanish mackerels that has, until recently, been called by 4 names.

Name - This fluke and *R. adbaculum* Manter are very similar in size, shape and host preferences (the name "adbaculum" means similar to "baculum"). They are never reported together, although they occur in the same hosts in the same localities. The uncertainty about their identity has caused them to be measured and partially redescribed so many times that they can now be seen to be synonyms. *Prosorhynchus stunkardi* Siddiqi and Cable, described from an unidentified mackerel in Puerto Rico, is also a synonym (Bunkley-Williams, Dyer and Williams 1996). We also see little reason to distinguish the very similar *R. quadriculata* Kohn, described from serra Spanish mackerel in Brazil.

Diagnostic Characters - This minuscule to tiny, elongate fluke has a muscular rhynchus covered with a pentagonal, beret-shaped, flat hood. The pharynx is smaller than the rhynchus and is located approximately in mid-body.

Records - Four occurred in a cero from La Parguera, Puerto Rico (USNPC 81642); 1 in 1 of 2 king mackerel from Curaçao; and 8 in 1 of 2 cero from Belize (USNPC 74242). It has also been reported in 1 of 3 cero, 1 Spanish mackerel and 2 of 3 king mackerel from the Dry Tortugas, Florida, USA; in 2 king mackerel and 1 of 2 Spanish mackerel from south Florida; and 1 in 1 of 33 Spanish mackerel from Louisiana, USA; it is common in Spanish mackerels from South Carolina, USA; and occurs in Spanish mackerel from the northeast Gulf of Mexico and Massachusetts, USA; and serra Spanish mackerel from Brazil.

Geographic Range - Western Atlantic.

Ecology - It infects both inshore and offshore species of Spanish mackerels.

Location in Host - Pyloric ceca and intestine.

Length - 0.7-4.5 mm.

Host Specificity - This parasite is genus specific to western Atlantic Spanish mackerels (*Scomberomorus*). Serra Spanish mackerel is a new host.

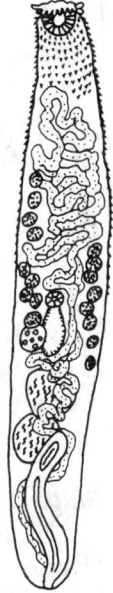

Rhipidocotyle barracudae Manter

This tiny fluke, found in great barracuda, has an oddly restricted distribution in south Florida, Cuba and the Bahamas. It might be useful as a biological tag.

Diagnostic Characters - It is a minuscule, elongate fluke with a muscular rhynchus without papillae but covered with a pentagonal, beret-shaped, flat-hood with 5 lobes. The pharynx is smaller than the rhynchus and located posterior to mid-body.

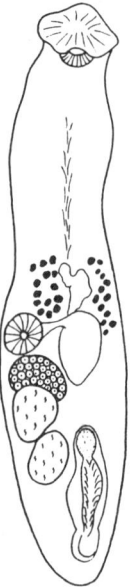

Records - Three occurred in 1 of 7 great barracuda from Belize (USNPC 74243); 1 of 2 from Eleuthera and Nassau, Bahamas; from Cuba and the western Gulf of Mexico off Mexico; and 1-7 in 7 of 8 and 2 of 15 from the Dry Tortugas, Florida, USA. There are no records from the northern Gulf of Mexico or the Caribbean. We have not seen it in Puerto Rico.

Geographic Range - Northern West Indies and southern Gulf of Mexico.

Associations - See *Bucephalopsis longicirrus*. Manter (1940b) found 1 fluke infected with "very minute microorganisms filling the parenchyma in the pharynx region."

Location in Host - Intestine and pyloric ceca.

Length - 1.2-1.8 mm.

Host Specificity - Only occurs in great barracuda.

Significance to Sport Fishing - If the distribution of this parasite is as restricted as our records suggest, then it might be useful as a biological tag.

Rhipidocotyle capitata (Linton)

This fluke occurs in little tunas around the world.

Name - Linton (1940) described *Gasterostomum capitata* before Manter (1940b) described *R. nagatyi*. Both names are synonyms. *Rhipidocotyle angusticollis* Chandler described in Atlantic bonito from Texas, USA (USNPC 36786) appears to be a synonym.

Diagnostic Characters - This minuscule, elongate fluke has a muscular, bowl-shaped rhynchus covered with a pentagonal, flat-hood. The pharynx is smaller than the rhynchus and is located posterior to mid-body.

Records - This worm occurred in little tunny from Puerto Rico (USNPC 39301). Nine were found in 3 little tunny from the Dry Tortugas off Florida, USA; 1 of 6 little tunny and 2 of 11 king mackerel from Louisiana, USA; in an Atlantic bonito and numerous little tunny from Texas, USA; 17 in a bullet tuna (USNPC 8172) and little tunny (USNPC 36707) from Massachusetts, USA; and 3 adults and a larva in a frigate tuna from Hawaii, USA.

Geographic Range - Worldwide.

Life History - A fusiform larva was figured by Yamaguti (1970).

Location in Host - Intestine.

Length - 1.1-2.2 mm; larvae 0.9 mm. The flukes in Pacific frigate tuna were smaller (1.3-1.5 mm) than those from Atlantic bullet tuna (1.1-2.2 mm).

Host Specificity - This worm could be almost tribe specific to little tunas. King mackerel and Atlantic bonito may be false hosts.

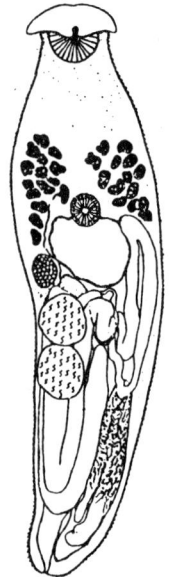

Coitocaecum extremum (Travassos, Frieitas and Bührnheim)

This fluke was found in chub mackerel from Brazil.

Name - *Nicolla extrema* Travassos, Frieitas and Bührnheim is a synonym. Thatcher (1993) returned it to genus *Nicolla*, but did not refute the transfer to *Coitocaecum* by Yamaguti (1971).

Diagnostic Characters - It is a minuscule, oval worm with a rather small ventral sucker that is larger than the oral sucker and located anterior to mid-body. It appears rather dark in color because the vitellaria extend throughout much of the body. The relatively large eggs are confined to mid-body. The testes are relatively large. The intestinal ceca join posteriorly forming a loop.

Records - Reported in chub mackerel from Brazil.

Geographic Range - Unknown

Location in Host - intestine.

Length - 1.4-2.1 mm

Host Specificity - It was reported in 2 other species of fishes.

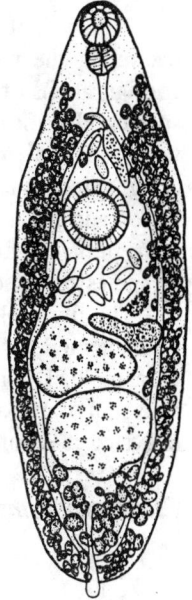

Neolepidapedon retrusum (Linton)

This fluke has only been found in chub mackerel

Name - This worm has been placed in the genus *Lepocreadium*. *Acanthocolpoides pauloi* Travassos, Freitas and Bührnheim appears to be a synonym.

Diagnostic Characters - This is a minuscule, elongate fluke with a relatively small ventral sucker, which is approximately the same size as the oral sucker, and is in the anterior 1/3 of the body. The vitellaria surround the intestinal ceca and extend from the posterior end to near the ventral sucker. The rhomboidal testes are in the posterior 1/3 of the body.

Records - One to 4 occurred in 2 chub mackerel from Woods Hole, Massachusetts, USA (USNPC 8273-4); and in a chub mackerel from Brazil.

Geographic Range - Western Atlantic.

Location in Host - Intestine.

Length - 1.1-3.2 mm.

Host Specificity - This worm is only known from chub mackerel.

Genus *Stephanostomum* Looss

Members of this genus possess distinctive spines in 2-3 uninterrupted rows encircling the mouth (circumoral spines). The variations on numbers and configurations of these spines would seem to provide ample diversity for easy species identifications, unfortunately, there is much variation in these spines within species. Manter (1947) discovered clusters of smaller, possibly regenerating, spines that appeared to be replacing missing and abnormal spines. Such losses and replacement with increased numbers of spines could contribute to some of the confusion about the number of spines in each species. The numbers of spines reported for the following species is the total count of all rows.

The life cycles of a few species have been deciphered and can be used as possible models for the remaining species. Redia, located in the digestive gland of a mollusk, produce cercariae which escape and infect fishes where they encyst in tissues as metacercariae. We have found metacercariae of these flukes encysted in coral reef fishes from Puerto Rico (USNPC 82967).

Stephanostomum coryphaenae Manter

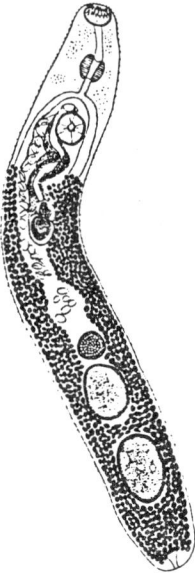

This small fluke is found in dolphin from the warmer-water portion of the western Atlantic. It might be of use as a biological tag.

Diagnostic Characters - It is a small, stocky fluke with 36 circumoral spines. The oral and ventral suckers are separated by more than 3 diameters of the ventral sucker and are approximately the same size. The vitellaria do not extend anteriorly to the ventral sucker. The pharynx is not near or in contact with the bifurcation of the intestinal ceca.

Records - We found 2-13 worms in 4 of 13 dolphin from off La Parguera, Puerto Rico (USNPC 84886); and in dolphin from the Mona Passage (USNPC 39339). It has also been reported from this host from Bimini (1 in 1), Curaçao (1 in 1 of 3), Brazil and the Dry Tortugas off Florida, USA.

Geographic Range - West Indies and Atlantic coast of South America to Brazil.

Ecology - This worm appears to be restricted to the warmer-water regions of the western Atlantic. What ecological mechanisms are involved in maintaining this distribution would be fascinating to explore.

We found this fluke in a porkfish, *Anisotremus virginicus* (Linnaeus), from a shallow, inshore seagrass bed habitat adjacent to Isla Magueyes, La Parguera, Puerto Rico (USNPC 77726). It has previously been found only in offshore, pelagic habitats.

Associations - This fluke occurred with a variety of other worms in dolphin from Puerto Rico, but did not appear to be interacting either negatively or positively with any other parasite.

Location in Host - Stomach, intestine and rectum.
Length - 2.0-5.1 mm.
Host Specificity - This worm only occurs in dolphin, but does not occur consistently enough to be a characteristic parasite of this host. The 3 flukes we found in a porkfish were probably an accidental infection.
Significance to Sport Fishing - If the apparently restricted distribution of this fluke is correct, it might be of some use as a temporary biological tag in identifying dolphin that move north into the Gulf of Mexico or up the Atlantic coast of the USA.

Stephanostomum ditrematis (Yamaguti)

This elongate fluke parasitizes jacks and rarely barracuda around the world. It is so variable that many synonyms have been named.
Name - It was originally described from a surf perch in Japan. Subsequently, it was found in jacks all over the world. This worm could represent a complex of 2 or more similar species.

Stephanostomum cubanum Perez-Vigueras, *S. filiforme* Linton, *S. longisomum* Manter, *S. manteri* Perez-Vigueras, and *S. microcephalum* Perez-Vigueras are synonyms of this fluke. *Stephanostomum ghanense* of Fischthal, 1977 (USNPC 74281) appears to be this worm.

This worm has been found in 3 great barracudas and described as a different species each time. Linton (1910) described it as *Distomum* sp. from Bermuda; Perez-Vigueras (1942) as *Monorchistephanostomum gracile* from Cuba; and Yamaguti (1970) as *S. kawalea* from Hawaii. The new genus, *Monorchistephanostomum* Perez-Vigueras, was erected because the single worm available had only 1 testis (monorchism). Parasitic worms that normally have 2 testes are sometimes found with a single testis (Williams 1976). Overstreet (1969) noted a specimen of the similar *Stephanostomum sentum* with a single testis. Yamaguti (1971) synonymized this genus with *Stephanostomum*.

Diagnostic Characters - This small, elongate fluke usually has 36 (rarely 32-50) circumoral spines. The oral and ventral suckers are separated by approximately 3-4 diameters of the ventral sucker, and the oral sucker is smaller than the ventral sucker. The vitellaria do not extend anterior to the ventral sucker. Eggs are relatively large and confined between the intestinal ceca. The testes are separated by approximately 1-3 of their lengths.

Records - We found 8 in a crevalle jack from Ponce, Puerto Rico (USNPC 83023). It has also been reported in a bar jack and rainbow runner from Cuba; 1 in a blue runner, 2 in 1 of 3 crevalle jack, 4 in 3 of 18 horse-eye jack and 3 in 2 of 8 yellow jack from Jamaica; in an unidentified jack from Curaçao; 2-5 in 3 of 4 horse-eye jack from Bimini; 2-3 in 2 of 4 horse-eye jack (USNPC 74208) and 1-6 in 8 yellow jack from Belize (USNPC 74207,

74281, 74283); in 1 of 6 bar jack and 1 of 6 horse-eye jack from the Dry Tortugas off Florida, USA; and in 1 of 2 blue runner and 2 of 3 crevalle jack from Biscayne Bay, Florida; 1 in 1 of 15 blue runner (USNPC 8204), 1 in a crevalle jack (USNPC 8203), and 5 in 1, and 28 in 3 greater amberjack (USNPC 8202) from Woods Hole, Massachusetts, USA. It has also been reported in rainbow runner and other jacks from the Pacific.

One occurred in a great barracuda from Cuba; 3 in 1 from Bermuda; and 2 in another species of barracuda from Hawaii, USA (USNPC 63734).

Geographic Range - Worldwide.

Ecology - It appears to occur rarely in Puerto Rico. We have examined more than 100 specimens of jacks, but have only seen this fluke once. We examined 45 great barracuda in Puerto Rico and 2 from Alabama, USA, but did not find this rather distinctive and obvious worm.

Location in Host - Intestine.

Length - 3.2-19.0 mm (3.2-15.0 mm in jacks; 12.5-19.0 mm in barracudas).

Host Specificity - This worm is almost family specific to jacks. It does not occur consistently enough to be a primary parasite of any host. The low numbers that rarely occur in barracudas suggest that these are false hosts that temporarily obtain these worms by eating jacks. The greater length of these worms in barracuda may only be an artifact of how seldom they have been measured in any fish.

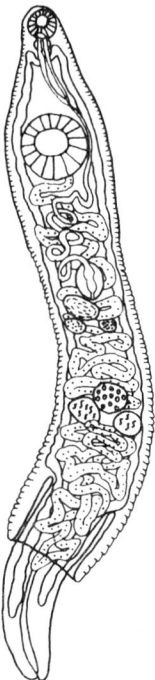

Stephanostomum imparispine (Linton)

It occurs in cobia from the Atlantic coasts of the USA.

Name - *Distomum valdeinflatum* Stossich of Linton is a synonym.

Diagnostic Characters - This tiny to small, elongate fluke has 33-34 circumoral spines. The oral and ventral suckers are separated by less than 3 diameters of the ventral sucker, and are approximately the same size. The vitellaria do not extend anterior to the ventral sucker. The pharynx is in contact with the intestinal ceca bifurcation. The ovary and testes are in contact.

Metacercariae are in globular cysts often containing yellowish to greenish fluid. Dark pigment sometimes coats the cysts.

Records - Five occurred in a cobia from off Madeira Beach, Florida; off St. John's Pass, Florida, USA; and an unstated number of adults in 2 of 3, and 1 metacercaria in 1 of 6 cobia from Beaufort, North Carolina, USA.

Geographic Range - Atlantic and Gulf coasts of USA.

Life History - Its metacercariae encyst in a variety of intermediate fish hosts.

Location in Host - Intestine. Metacercariae encyst in mesenteries, liver and other internal organs.

Length - 4.5-10.0 mm; metacercaria 0.6-2.4 mm.

Host Specificity - The adult worm only occurs in cobia and is probably a secondary parasite of this host.

Stephanostomum megacephalum Manter

This fluke occurs in jacks from warm waters throughout the New World.

Name - The name "megacephala" refers to the large oral sucker. *Stephanostomum belizense* Fischthal is a synonym.

Diagnostic Characters - It is a tiny, elongate fluke with 24-32 circumoral spines with a slight gap in the 2 rows. The oral and ventral suckers are separated by more than 3 diameters of the ventral sucker. The oral sucker is larger than the ventral sucker, and the ventral sucker is separated from the body by a projection of the body. The vitellaria do not extend anterior to the ventral sucker. The pharynx is elongate and near to the bifurcation of the intestinal ceca.

Records - Four occurred in 1 of 18 horse-eye jack from Jamaica; 1-10 in 5 of 8 yellow jack from Belize (USNPC 74282-3, 74163); 1 in 1 of 6 horse-eye jack from the Dry Tortugas off Florida, USA; and in 2 of 3 crevalle jack from Biscayne Bay, Florida. It was also found in other jacks from the northern Gulf of Mexico; tropical west Africa and the eastern Pacific.

Geographic Range - Atlantic and eastern Pacific tropics and subtropics.

Associations - One fluke occurred with numerous *S. ditrematis* in a horse-eye jack from the Dry Tortugas; and 1 of each species occurred in a Pacific jack from White Friars, Mexico and San Francisco, Ecuador.

Location in Host - Intestine.

Length - 1.1-3.3 mm.

Host Specificity - This worm is family specific to jacks. Only 1 unconfirmed record exists of a host other than a jack.

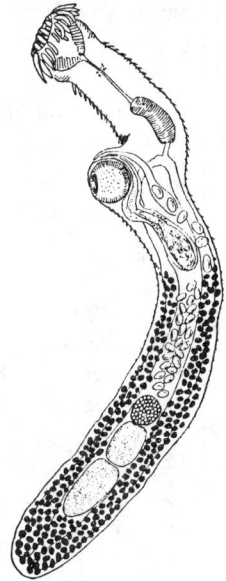

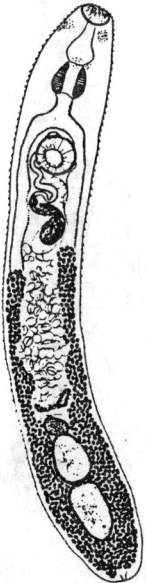

Stephanostomum sentum (Linton)

This fluke prefers inshore, benthic hosts, but parasitizes big game jacks in Puerto Rico and Jamaica.

Diagnostic Characters - This minuscule to tiny, elongate fluke has 36 circumoral spines. The oral and ventral suckers are separated by more than 3 diameters of the ventral sucker, and the oral sucker is smaller than the ventral sucker. The vitellaria do not extend anterior to the ventral sucker. The pharynx is near the bifurcation of the intestinal ceca.

Records - We found 1 in a crevalle jack (USNPC 81579) and 12 in a horse-eye jack (USNPC 83014) from La Parguera, Puerto Rico. One was found in 1 of 18 horse-eye jack from Jamaica.

Geographic Range - West Indies.

Location in Host - Intestine.
Length - 1.9-3.8 mm.
Host Specificity - This fluke is found in a variety of fishes. It appears to occur more often in grunts, porgies and mojarras and is only a secondary parasite of jacks.

Tormopsolus filiformis Sogandares-Bernal and Hutton

This worm occurred in cobia from the Gulf coast of Florida.
Name - The name means hair-like (filum=hair).
Diagnostic Characters - This long slender, tiny worm has relatively tiny and widely spaced oral and ventral suckers.
Records - Five occurred in a cobia from St. John's Pass, Florida, USA (USNPC 39003).
Geographic Range - Unknown
Location in Host - Rectum.
Length - 4.8-5.7 mm.
Host Specificity - Only reported from cobia.

Tormopsolus orientalis Yamaguti

This worm parasitizes amberjacks around the world.
Name - *Tormopsolus hawaiiensis* Yamaguti is a synonym.
Diagnostic Characters - This elongate, tiny to small worm has an oral sucker that is close (less than 1 ventral sucker width) from the ventral sucker and about 1/2 the size of the ventral sucker. The testes are elongate oval-shaped, not touching, and are in the posterior part of the body. The vitellaria do not extend to the ventral sucker.
Records - One occurred in a greater amberjack from Curaçao; and 2 in 1 and 1 each in 2 of 5 lesser amberjack from Bermuda. Also reported from another species of amberjack in the eastern Pacific; an unknown amberjack, *Seriola* sp., and greater amberjack in Hawaii; and greater amberjack and yellowtail in Japan. Silas (1962) suggested that "bonito" or Atlantic bonito had erroneously been reported as a host of this worm from Bermuda, but this record refers to the common name "bonito" that Linton (1907) used for lesser amberjack.
Geographic Range - Worldwide.
Location in Host - Pyloric ceca and intestine.
Length - 4.3-7.5 mm.
Host Specificity - This parasite is genus specific to amberjacks (*Seriola*).

Pseudopecoeloides carangis (Yamaguti)

This is an oddly shaped stomach worm of jacks around the world.

Diagnostic Characters - This slender fluke has an ventral sucker on a distinct peduncle or projection from the body. The peduncle is close to the anterior end of the body. The oral sucker is relatively large and larger than the ventral sucker.

Records - One occurred in a bar jack and 1 in a blue runner from Curaçao; 1 in 1 of 2 bar jack from Jamaica and in 1 of 6 bar jack and 1 of 3 yellow jack from the Dry Tortugas off Florida, USA. It has also been reported from various jacks in the Pacific.

Geographic Range - Worldwide.

Location in Host - Intestine.

Length - 1.2-5.0 mm.

Host Specificity - This parasite is family specific to jacks. A record from a barracuda in the Philippines could represent a false host.

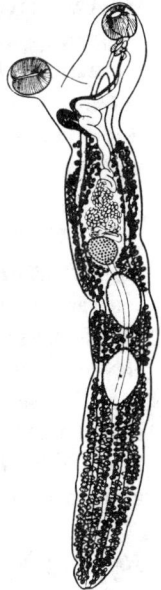

Cetiotrema carangis (MacCallum)

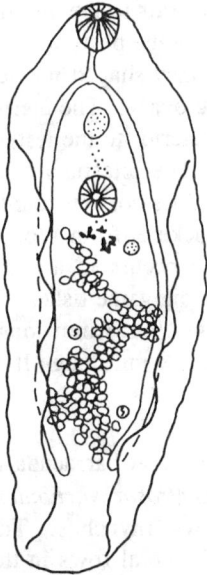

This is an obscure urinary tract parasite of jacks.

Name - MacCallum (1913) described *Distomum carangis* and Yamaguti (1971) changed it to *Gorgoderina carangis*, thus placing it in a genus of frog flukes. Manter (1947) described *Phyllodistomum carangis* and Manter (1970) changed it to *Cetiotrema carangis*. These 2 forms are synonyms, but had not been compared previously. It is not the same as *Pseudopecoeloides carangis* (Yamaguti).

Diagnostic Characters - This small worm has thin lateral margins that often fold over onto its body. The oral and ventral suckers are approximately the same size and are separated by more than 3 diameters of the ventral sucker. The eggs are relatively large.

Records - One occurred in 1 of 6 bar jack from the Dry Tortugas off Florida; and 4 in a blue runner from Woods Hole, Massachusetts, USA.

Geographic Range - Atlantic coast of the USA.

Location in Host - Urinary bladder or ureter. MacCallum (1913) reported this worm from the rectum, but this location is adjacent to the urinary bladder and contamination could have occurred in the dissection.

Length - 8.1-13.0 mm.

Host Specificity - Possibly genus specific to jacks (*Caranx*). Yamaguti (1971) incorrectly stated that MacCallum's host was "*Carangis*".

Detection - Manter's specimen was washed from the body cavity of the host, but presumably came from the urinary bladder. This organ is seldom examined. It is often difficult to locate when damaged during the dissection process or not inflated.

Miscellaneous Flukes

Aponurus laguncula **Loss** - This worm was found in a chub mackerel from southern Brazil. It has a ventral sucker about twice as wide as the oral sucker. The suckers are separated by about 1 width of the ventral sucker and both are elevated from the body by short peduncles. The vitellaria are in 7 distinct lobes posterior of the ovary. This parasite also occurs in the stomach of a variety of marine fishes from Florida and Louisiana, USA; Brazil; and the Mediterranean. It is 0.5-1.3 mm long. A single record in this rather well examined host suggests that this parasite may have been an accidental infection or in a false host.

Brachyphallus crenatus **(Rudolphi)** - Atlantic mackerel is a false or accidental host for this parasite. It is a minuscule to tiny, elongate fluke with a short tail that is deeply embedded in the body. The width of the tail is approximately 1/2 of the body width. The oral and ventral suckers are approximately the same size and are separated by 1-2 diameters. The body is covered with conspicuous cuticular serrations. The 2 testes are just posterior to the ventral sucker, round and arranged diagonally. The oval ovary is in the posterior 1/2 of the body. The vitellaria are formed into 2 roughly kidney-shaped masses indented into 2 and 3 partial lobes, and are posterior to the ovary. The uterus fills the body from just posterior to the vitellaria to just posterior to the testes, and then 1 tube passes anterior almost to the pharynx. The intestinal ceca extend almost to the posterior end of the tail, but the uterus does not extend into the hindbody or tail. One fluke occurred in an Atlantic mackerel from Woods Hole, Massachusetts, USA (USNPC 8348). This parasite occurs in a great variety of fishes worldwide, but has been noted in no other big game fishes. It occurs in the stomach and intestine of host fishes and is 0.9-4.0 mm long. Immature worms in the alimentary tract of fishes are 0.2-0.8 mm long It is habitat specific to the near-shore environment.

Bucephalopsis attenuata **(Siddiqi and Cable)** - Great barracuda is a false host for this fluke. This species was placed in genus *Prosorhynchoides*. It is a minuscule, elongate fluke with a relatively large, oval rhynchus. The eggs are relatively large. The vitellaria are arranged in 2 lateral rows in the anterior part of the body. Five flukes occurred in 1 of 10 great barracuda from La Parguera, Puerto Rico. This parasite has only been found in Puerto Rico. It occurs in the intestine of the host and is 0.6-1.1 mm long. Great barracuda is probably a false host which obtained this worm by eating the normal host, Atlantic bumper, *Chloroscombrus chrysurus* (Linnaeus). Great barracuda was a new host record for this fluke, although this was not noted by Dyer, Williams and Bunkley-Williams (1985).

Bucephalopsis gracilescens (Rudolphi) - The identity of this worm is

not clear as this species name may have been used for several different species in the western Atlantic. This fluke was placed in the genera *Bucephaloides* and *Prosorhynchoides*. It is a minuscule, oval worm with a relatively large, oval rhynchus. The relatively small and numerous eggs are distributed throughout the body. The vitellaria occur in 2 bunches on either side of the rhynchus. One immature worm occurred in 1 of 13 crevalle jack from North Carolina, USA. It has also been reported in frigate tuna from the Mediterranean. It is 0.5-1.7 mm long. Crevalle jack was probably a false host.

Bucephalus confusus Velasquez - This is a confusing and common

parasite of many species of fishes that may only accidentally infect Spanish mackerel. *Nannoenterum baculum* Linton is a synonym, but *Rhipidocotyle baculum* (Linton) is not the same species. The rhynchus of this worm has a relatively large sucker with 20 relatively short tentacles on the anterior end. The rather large, circular vitellaria are in 2 lateral rows of 12-18 follicles each in the middle 1/3 of the body. The 2 testes are in the posterior 1/3 of the body. The uterus extends from the testes to 1/2 the distance between the anterior end of the vitellaria and the rhynchus. One occurred in a Spanish mackerel and many other fishes from Woods Hole, Massachusetts, USA, and has not been found elsewhere. This worm occurs in the intestine of the host, and is 1.6-4.3 mm long. This worm may be an accidental parasite in Spanish mackerel; or Spanish mackerel may be a false host. The preferred or dominant host appears to be northern sennet, *Sphyraena borealis* DeKay, with many infections of up to 460 per host (USNPC 8180).

Claribulla longula Overstreet - Great barracuda is a false host for this

fluke. It is a minuscule, elongate worm with a relatively large and distinctive funnel-shaped or cup-shaped oral sucker. The ventral sucker is widely separated from the oral sucker, a little anterior of mid-body and much smaller than the oral sucker. Overstreet (1969) suggested that the single specimen he found in a great barracuda from Biscayne Bay, Florida, may represent an accidental infection. It is only known from south Florida. This worm is usually found in the pyloric ceca, but a few occur in the upper intestine. It is 0.9-2.7 mm long. This worm is host specific to bonefish, *Albula vulpes* (Linnaeus). Great barracuda was a false host resulting from this predator eating a bonefish.

Genolopa brevicaecum (Manter) - This grunt fluke is probably only

found in big game fishes that are false hosts. It has also been placed in genus *Paraproctotrema*. This elongate to oval worm has a relatively large, cup-shaped oral sucker. The oral sucker is approximately twice as wide as the ventral sucker. The genital opening, anterior to the ventral sucker, is not armed with spines. The 2 compact bunches of vitellaria are lateral, in approximately the middle of the worm, and the single testis occurs laterally just posterior to one of the bunches of vitellaria. The uterus occupies most of the hind body. Two occurred in 1 of 8 (Nahhas and Carlson 1994) and 17 in 2 yellow jack (Nahhas and Cable 1964) from Jamaica; and in 1 of 3 yellow jack from the Dry Tortugas off Florida, USA. It is distributed throughout the New World tropics/subtropics. This worm occurs in the intestine of the host and is 0.6-0.9 mm long. It is probably family specific to grunts (Haemulidae). The 2 records in 2 or 3 yellow jack may be false hosts due to predation on grunts.

Lasiotocus truncatus (Linton) - This grunt fluke is probably only found in big game fishes that are false hosts. It has also been placed in genus *Proctotrema*. This oval worm has a relatively large, cone or funnel-shaped oral sucker. The oral sucker is approximately 4 times as wide as the ventral sucker. The genital opening anterior to the ventral sucker is armed with spines. The 2 compact bunches of vitellaria are found laterally and approximately at the middle of the length of the worm, and the single testis occurs in the middle of the body just posterior to the vitellaria. The uterus occupies most of the hind-body. This fluke occurred once in a bar jack from Bimini, Bahamas. It is only known from Bimini and the Dry Tortugas off Florida, USA. This worm occurs in the pyloric ceca of the host and is 0.7-1.0 mm long. This parasite is probably family specific to grunts (Haemulidae). The single record in a bar jack may be a false host due to this predator eating grunts.

Lecithaster confusus Odhner - Atlantic mackerel is a false host for this parasite. It is an elongate, tear-drop shaped, minuscule fluke with no tail and relatively large suckers. The oral sucker is about 1/2 the size of the ventral sucker. The ventral sucker is about 1/2 as wide as the greatest width of the body. The 2 testes are side-by-side and posterior to the ventral sucker. The ovary has 4 obvious lobes and is median posterior to the testes. The vitellaria has 7 lobes and is in the middle, posterior to the ovary. It occupies less than 1/3 of the width of the posterior body. The uterus fills the hindbody posterior to the ventral sucker. *Lecithaster gibbosus* (Rudolphi) has also been found in Atlantic mackerel but off Europe in the eastern Atlantic, in bluefin tuna from the Mediterranean, chub mackerel in the Pacific, and in a variety of other fishes worldwide. It occurs on the Atlantic coast of the USA, but has not been reported from western Atlantic big game fishes. It differs from *L. confusus* by having a short tail, a larger asterisk-shaped, 7-lobed vitellaria that fills the entire hindbody and covers the ceca. The ventral sucker is smaller and is approximately 1/3 of the greatest body width of the worm. Eight and 10 *L. confusus* occurred in 2 Atlantic mackerel from Woods Hole, Massachusetts, USA (USNPC 8361). It is found in the northern Atlantic and Mediterranean. The first intermediate host is a marine snail and the second is a copepod. The metacercaria in copepods develop into adult flukes in the intestine of fishes that eat infected copepods. Adult flukes are 0.5-1.5 mm long, and immature worms in the fish intestine vary from 0.2-0.6 mm long. This parasite is family specific to herrings (Clupeidae). The record from an Atlantic mackerel was a false host.

Lecithochirium monticellii (Linton) - We found 1-20 of this fluke in 6 species of fishes in 5 families and 4 orders from Puerto Rico, but none occurred in big game fishes. If the egg sizes in this family are as narrow and precise as many experts claim, then this species with eggs 18-25 X 11-14 μm, must represent 2 or 3 species of flukes. Manter (1947) suggested that the original description of this worm probably included at least 3 species: (1) *L. branchialis* (Stunkard and Nigrelli), (2) *L. texanum*, and what we are now calling *L. monticellii*; and Overstreet (1969) added *L. microstomum* to this species-complex list, but suggested that *L. branchialis* may be the same as *L. microstomum*. Thus we cannot be certain which species of parasite this name indicated in the early records. It is a small, bullet-shaped fluke with the oral sucker and ventral sucker moderately (approximately 1 ventral sucker diameter) separated, and a short tail that is usually withdrawn into the body. The oral sucker is less than 1/3 the diameter of the ventral sucker. The vitellaria are reduced to 2 compact, oval masses just posterior of the ovary, the testes are side-by-side, separated by approximately 1/2 a testis diameter and separated from the ventral sucker by 1 diameter, the uterus with eggs does not extend to the end of the intestinal ceca or into the tail, and ceca either extend into the tail or do not. One fluke each may have occurred in 2 blue runner (USNPC 8350), 9 in a little tunny (USNPC 8353) from Woods Hole, Massachusetts, USA; and 2-3 in 2 of 6 cobia from Beaufort, North Carolina, USA. It also occurs in a variety of other fishes. It is found in the intestine of the host. The geographic range of this parasite is the western Atlantic. It is 1.0-5.4 mm long. Atlantic cutlassfish is the preferred host of this parasite because they are consistently more heavily infected (up to 240 flukes).

Lecithochirium priacanthi Yamaguti - In a checklist, Yamaguti (1970) lists this fluke as a parasite of rainbow runner from Hawaii, but does not mention it in the text.

Myosaccium opisthonema (Siddiqi and Cable) - This fluke was described from a herring in Puerto Rico (USNPC 39393). It was originally placed in *Neogenolinea*. It is elongate with an oral sucker about 1/2 the size of the ventral sucker. The 2 are separated by approximately 1 diameter of the ventral sucker. Striations on the body are obvious, the eggs are relatively large and confined posterior of the ventral sucker. Vitellaria are confined in 2 compact lobes just posterior of mid-body. We found 7 worms in a cero from Humacao, Puerto Rico (USNPC 83002), but this was probably a false or accidental host. Parasites in this genus are host specific or at least family specific to herrings and sardines (Clupeidae). Similar worms have been found in Florida and Japan, but this species is only known from Puerto Rico. It occurs in the stomach of herrings, but we found it in the intestine of the cero. This worm is 0.5-0.8 mm long.

Neolepidapedon belizense Fischthal - This species was described from 1 immature and one adult in 1 of 7 great barracuda from Belize (USNPC 74164), but this host is probably false or accidental. It is an elongate, tiny worm with a relatively large oral sucker, approximately the same size as the ventral sucker. The 2 suckers are separated by approximately 2 of their diameters. The first 1/3 of the body is covered with minute spines and contains both suckers. The oval testes are in the posterior 1/2 of the body and the ovary is anterior of the testes. The vitellaria extend from the posterior end to near the ventral sucker. It was 3.6 mm long and occurred n the pyloric ceca of the host.

Opechona orientalis (Layman) - This worm may indicate the migration of chub mackerel into the Atlantic. It was described from angelfish taken from the bilge tanks of a freighter - an excellent way to transport exotic fishes and parasites! This oval worm has a ventral sucker slightly larger than the oral sucker and separated from it by more than 3 of its widths. Both suckers are relatively small, but the eggs extending from the ventral sucker to the ovary are rather large. The vitellaria extend from near the ventral sucker to the posterior end, and the ceca also reach the posterior end. The testes are in the posterior 1/3 of the body, in tandem, and round to irregular rhomboidal in shape. This parasite occurs throughout the Pacific in various fishes but prefers chub mackerel as a host. A collection of this parasite in chub mackerel from southern Brazil and its apparent absence in the rest of the Atlantic could indicate that it was brought into the Atlantic by chub mackerel migrating from the Pacific. Yamaguti (1971) illustrated the more contracted specimens of Manter (1940a) from the Galapagos and Mexico, which were 0.7-1.0 mm long, but cited the lengths of more extended specimens (1.7-3.3 mm) from other localities.

Opecoeloides brachyteleus Manter - We found 1 worm in a bar jack from Aguadilla, Puerto Rico, but this appears to have been a false host. It is family specific to goat fishes (Mullidae) throughout the Caribbean and south Florida. It has a ventral sucker with 4 papillae, separated from the body on a peduncle. The oral sucker and pharynx are similar in size and the ventral sucker is slightly larger. The vitellaria and 2 rather large testes are confined in the hindbody. The uterus has rather large eggs and is confined between the testes and pharynx. It occurs in the intestine of its hosts, and is 1.0-2.3 mm long.

Opecoeloides vitellosus (Linton) - There is some uncertainty if this fluke was correctly reported by Linton (1901) from Atlantic bonito and Atlantic mackerel because these early records appear to have called several species of flukes by this name. This parasite has never subsequently been reported from these hosts. This slender fluke has an ventral sucker on a distinct peduncle or projection from the body. The peduncle is close to the anterior end of the body.

The oral sucker is smaller than the ventral sucker. The prepharynx is short, but the esophagus is long. The ceca extend to near the posterior end of the worm. The vitellaria fill the posterior 3/4 of the body. The testes are in tandem in the posterior body in between the ceca. One occurred in an Atlantic bonito and 2 in an Atlantic mackerel from Woods Hole, Massachusetts, USA. It occurs in fishes in Puerto Rico and Jamaica, but has not been found in big game fishes from the Caribbean. This worm is known from the western Atlantic. It occurs in the intestine and pyloric ceca of its hosts and is 1.0-3.4 mm long. It does not appear to have much host preference as it occurs in a great variety of fishes.

Opisthadena dimidia Linton - One to 12 occurred in 9 of 303 swordfish from the northwest Atlantic (ARC 2320). This was probably a false host since this worm appears to be genus specific to sea chubs (*Kyphosus*) in the western Atlantic and eastern Pacific. This worm has a relatively large ventral sucker that almost occupies the entire width of the worm. The sides of the worm bulge out around the ventral sucker. The ventral sucker is more than 3 times as large as the oral sucker, and the 2 are less than 1 ventral sucker width apart. The body is elongate. The testes and ovary are in the posterior 1/2 of the body, and the vitellaria are confined to 2 lobes in the hind-body posterior to the testes and ovary. It occurs in the intestine of its hosts and is 2.8-8.4 mm long.

Pinguitrema lerneri (Sogandares-Bernal) - We found 1 in a bar jack from La Parguera, Puerto Rico (USNPC 83011), but this was probably a false or accidental host. This parasite is apparently host specific to a mojarra (Gerreidae) in which it has been found from Puerto Rico and Florida, USA. *Pachycreadium lerneri* S.-B. and *Pinguitrema lobatum* Siddiqi and Cable are synonyms. It is an oval worm with a rather large, oval ventral sucker occupying about 1/3 to 1/2 of the body width just anterior of the middle of the body. Around the ventral sucker, the body covering is distorted into obvious oval wrinkles. The vitellaria surround the ceca from near the bifurcation to near the end of the worm. It occurs in the intestine and is 1.0-1.5 mm long.

Podocotyle chloroscombri (Fischthal and Thomas, 1970) - Yellow jack may be a false host for this parasite of Atlantic bumper. It is similar to *P. simplex* but differs by having its ventral sucker on a distinct peduncle. Two mature and 3 immature worms occurred in 1 of 8 yellow jack from Drowned Cays, Belize (USNPC 74238). It is 2.0-3.2 mm long and occurs in the intestine of its hosts.

Podocotyle simplex (Rudolphi) - This fluke may be only an accidental parasite of big game fishes. It is an elongate worm with the ventral sucker larger than the oral sucker and in the anterior half of the body. The pharynx is relatively large, the esophagus short, the ceca extend to near the posterior end of the worm, the vitellaria surround the ceca in the posterior part of the body, and the testes are in the posterior 1/2 of the body. This fluke was reported in

Atlantic mackerel from the Atlantic coast of Canada, but this may have been an accidental or a false host. It occurs in the intestine and pyloric ceca of its host, is 1.2-4.0 mm long and has been found in a variety of fishes.

Prosorhynchus pacificus **Manter** - This is a parasite of western Atlantic and eastern Pacific groupers (Serranidae). *Prosorhynchus atlanticus* Manter is a synonym. It has a rather large, long, cone-shaped rhynchus. The vitellaria are confined in 2 lateral rows in the anterior 1/2 of the body, and the uterus, with relatively large eggs, is confined in the posterior 1/2 of the body. One to 14 occurred in 17 of 52 bar jack from Bermuda, but this was probably a false or accidental host. This worm occurs in the intestine of its hosts, and is 0.7-1.7 mm long. See *Ectenurus lepidus* for associations.

Pseudolepidapedon pudens **(Linton)** - This fluke may have only accidentally occurred in a cobia. This oval fluke has an oral sucker smaller than the ventral sucker and separated from it by more than 2 diameters of the ventral sucker. A conspicuous "pit" occurs between the oral and ventral suckers. The prepharynx is short, the pharynx is almost as large as the oral sucker, the ceca are relatively thick and extend to near the posterior end of the worm. The vitellaria surround the cecal branches. The testes are in the posterior body, in tandem and occupy all the space between the ceca. The eggs are few in number and relatively large. A few eggs are present and the vitellaria are developed in immature worms in the intestine of the host. The ovary and testes in immature worms are approximately 1/2 the size found in adults. One fluke was found in 1· of 6 cobia from Beaufort, North Carolina, USA. It is only known from the Atlantic coast of the USA. This worm occurs in the intestine of its host and is 1.6-2.7 mm long; and immature worms are 1.2-1.4 mm. This parasite appears to be genus (*Paralichthys*), or family (Bothidae), specific to flatfishes or flounders. The single specimen of this fluke found in a cobia was small (1.3 mm), in poor condition, and possibly an immature worm. Cobia could be an accidental or a false host for this parasite.

Pseudopecoelus elongatus **(Yamaguti)** - One record in a horse-eye jack from Brazil could represent a false host. It has been reported in other fishes from Japan and Brazil. This worm is similar in general appearance to *Pseudopecoeloides carangis*, but lacks the distinct peduncle separating the ventral sucker from the body and the ventral sucker is larger than the oral sucker. It is 2.4-6.1 mm long and occurs in the intestine of its hosts.

Rhipidocotyle longleyi **Manter** - The great barracuda is a false host for this fluke that is usually found in deeper-water fishes. This minuscule to tiny, elongate worm has a muscular, bowl-shaped rhynchus covered with a flat pentagonal hood. The sucker around the mouth is smaller than the rhynchus and posterior to midbody. It occurs in deep-water (256-428 m) fishes off Florida and Japan. This worm was reported once in great barracuda from Florida,

USA. It probably occurs worldwide, but has only been confirmed from Florida in the Atlantic and Japan in the Pacific. This worm occurs in the intestine of its hosts, and is 1.7-3.7 mm long. These worms were obtained by the great barracuda feeding on deep-water fishes. A great barracuda, that one of our students caught-and-released on the way to a dive site, followed our submersible down to 300 m depth in the Bahamas. Thus this predator is capable of feeding on fishes at 256-428 m depths.

Stephanostomum aulostomi Nahhas and Cable - We found this fluke

in a bar jack, but it may be a false host. This is a tiny, elongate, fluke with 36 circumoral spines. The oral and ventral suckers are separated by more than 3 diameters of the ventral sucker, and the ventral sucker is approximately twice as large as the oral sucker. The vitellaria extend to the ventral sucker. The pharynx is almost in contact with the intestinal ceca bifurcation. Seven occurred in 1 of 2 bar jack from La Parguera, Puerto Rico (USNPC 85943). This worm occurred singly in a peculiar attachment position, between the stomach and the intestine, in 4 of 9 trumpetfish, *Aulostomus maculatus* Valenciennes, from Curaçao; but in the intestine in a bar jack. This worm is 5.5-7.0 mm long. Bar jack is a new host, but it may be a false or accidental one.

Stephanostomum dentatum (Linton) - This fluke was reported once from

cobia and pompano dolphin, but they are probably false or accidental hosts. *Cercaria dipterocerca* Miller and Northrup is the cercarial stage of this fluke. This is a minuscule, stocky fluke with 54-58 circumoral spines. The oral and ventral suckers are separated by more than 3 diameters of the ventral sucker, and are approximately equal in size. The vitellaria extend to the ventral sucker. The pharynx is in contact with the intestinal ceca bifurcation. One immature worm occurred in 1 of 6 cobia; and 2 immature in 1 of 3 pompano dolphin from Beaufort, North Carolina, USA. This fluke has been noted in a great variety of inshore fishes from the Atlantic and Pacific USA coasts and in the Caribbean. Redia inside eastern mudsnail, *Iyanassa obsoleta* Say, produce cercariae which escape and penetrate the pharyngeal region of Atlantic silversides, *Menidia menidia* (Linnaeus). The resulting encysted metacercariae become adults when the silversides are eaten by an appropriate final host. The adult fluke is found in the intestine of the final host and is 1.1-2.8 mm long. This is a generalized and widespread parasite of flounders and groupers. The worms described from pompano dolphin, as lacking oral spines (Linton 1905), were probably misidentified, and were inadequately described.

DIDYMOZOIDEA (TISSUE FLUKES)

These vivid and often spectacular worms are found encapsulated in the tissues of marine fishes, including big game fishes, but a few (probably of marine origin) infect freshwater fishes. These capsules (and the damage they cause) are frequently seen by fishermen but are rarely mentioned in general parasitology, and even many fish-parasitology, texts. Possibly more editors need to be taken big game fishing! No common name has been given to these worms so we suggest "tissue flukes". This name distinguishes tissue flukes encapsulated in the tissues of their hosts from the loose or free-moving flukes in the gut and other passages of fishes, and frees us from trying to pronounce "didymozoid". The scientific name is from "didymos" which means double or twin, and "zoë" for life. It refers to the characteristic 2 worms which usually occur in each capsule. The bright, usually yellow, color that makes these capsules so conspicuous is due to masses of eggs which occupy much of their bodies. Tissue flukes do not produce a cyst around themselves and are seldom enclosed in a heavy, host-produced capsule. Usually, they are surrounded by a thin connective tissue layer produced by the host, or occasionally there is no connective tissue. We use the term "capsule" to refer to the encapsulation of the worms in the tissue of the host.

Tissue flukes are not known to harm humans. Eggs of these worms from flyingfishes have probably been ingested by humans. Nikolaeva (1985) suggests that metacercariae in raw fish could adapt to humans or migrate through human tissues and become dangerous. Economically, tissue flukes in muscle tissue of fish may cause it to deteriorate more rapidly, and makes it less desirable for consumers. Heavily infected Atlantic mackerel flesh has to be discarded in processing, and wahoo in eastern Australia is undervalued due to its reputation for having large tissue flukes (a third are infected). Heavy to very heavy infections are routinely found in big game fishes. In the Indian Ocean, 100 or more capsules are found in every wahoo and half the tuna. Superinfections, up to 1167 capsules, have rarely been reported in tuna from the southern Gulf of Mexico. In contrast, in the central and eastern Atlantic, the highest infection reported from tuna was 148 capsules.

Approximately 200 species are known, and many probably await discovery due to their unusual and seldom examined locations in hosts. Ironically, a few of these 200 species are duplicate descriptions of the same worms (synonyms) due to their complexity, unavailability and difficulty in removing intact specimens. Encapsulated pairs of various species range from a few millimeters to the size of your fist. They are usually colored yellow or orange, but blue capsules occur in wahoo from Australia. Worms vary in length from a few millimeters to over 12 meters. In some species, the sizes of both capsules and worms vary between different tissues in the same fish. The body of the worm may be elongated, filamentous or ribbon-like, and intricately tangled, or divided into a narrow anterior and a broadly swollen posterior.

No complete life cycle is known. Release of eggs from encapsulated worms is accomplished annually in those from gills, ovaries, or other exposed locations. More deeply embedded or inaccessible worms may only release eggs after the death of the host and survive passage through the gut of the predator. In some cases, the capsule and surrounding tissue breaks down or ulcerates when the tissue flukes mature, releasing both eggs and adults. A non-ciliated miracidium with 2 or more circles of spines around the oral sucker hatches from the egg. Tissue fluke cercariae occur in plankton, and metacercariae in arrow worms, barnacles, copepods, krill, squids, small bony fishes and sharks. Very heavy larval infections in squid suggest that they are important intermediate hosts of the life cycle of many tissue flukes. Also, actively migrating, larval stages have been described in fishes. Juvenile stages may be found in a variety of hosts, but only those in the proper final hosts develop into adults, the rest act as transport hosts and are important in enabling parasites to reach their final hosts.

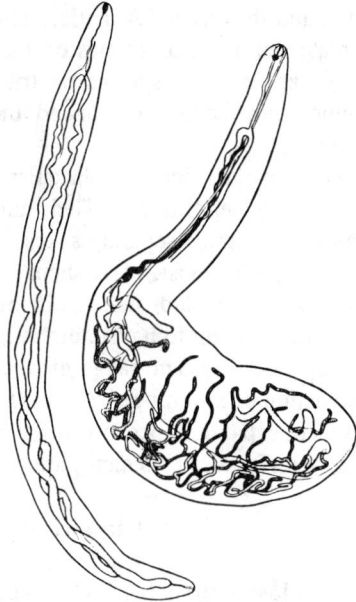

Larvae of *Didymocystis acanthocybii*.
from wahoo

All species are hermaphroditic (have both sexes in each worm), but often associate in pairs, one individual of which has female organs more developed and a smaller partner that has more developed male organs. Other pairs are fused to each other in the genital region. Presumably, the first worm to arrive at a site in the host becomes the "female" and the later arrival the "male". Usually a single male and female occur in each capsule, but 2-3 males may occasionally be found with a female. They encapsulate in the gills, skin, under scales, in connective tissue, muscle, fat, bone, teeth, eye socket (orbit), oral or nasal cavity, viscera, in the body cavity, vascular system or most any other tissue or organ. They are permanent or semi-permanent parasites in the final hosts. Most are assumed to survive for the life of the host or at least identifiable remains persist. Those in the gills or gonads may be lost each year.

Tissue flukes are found largely in tropical and temperate pelagic fishes, but also occur in some more sedentary fishes, such as groupers in Puerto Rico. Scombrids appear to be the preferred hosts with approximately 65% of tissue fluke species occurring in them. Approximately 100 species of fishes, including other pelagics, such as flyingfishes and ocean sunfishes, *Mola* sp., 8 species of barracuda (but not our great barracuda) and jacks, are infected. Two thirds of the big game fish species in this book are infected. Fewer species of tissue flukes occur in western Atlantic big game fishes compared to other warm-water regions (see Checklists). More tissue fluke species are reported from the Indo-

Pacific and the eastern Atlantic. This disjunct distribution may simply be due to greater numbers of studies on these animals in Japan, Hawaii and Europe, but, if many of these species are truly found in the eastern but not the western Atlantic, they could make good biological tags to document trans-Atlantic migrations.

Modern classifications place tissue flukes as a superfamily or a family in the Subclass Digenea (flukes). Their unique morphologies and habitats in the host, occasionally almost separate sexes, and life cycles possibly without a mollusk first intermediate host, make them worthy of superfamily status. Tissue flukes were once separated into their own subclass largely because they were incorrectly thought to have a direct life cycle. Even though schistosome flukes have separate sexes and sanguinicolid flukes possibly equally odd life cycles, the combination of differences still distinguish tissue flukes into a superfamily. We treat them separately because fishermen can readily distinguish these relatively large, colorful and abundant parasites of big game fishes.

Classification and Contents

Didymocystis acanthocybii Yamaguti

This worm occurs in the tissues of the head of wahoo, possibly around the world.
Name - Nigrelli (1939) described the same worm as *D. coatesi* Nigrelli. He was apparently not aware that it had been described the year before.
Diagnostic Characters - It usually occurs as rather large, lumpy orange to yellow masses on the gill arches, eye sockets or other tissues of the head. In worms removed from the capsule, the forebody projects from one end of the hindbody and is more than 1/2 the length of the hindbody. The hindbody is bulbous and bean-shaped.
Records - Two capsules occurred in 2 of 15 wahoo from Puerto Rico. One infected fish was from La Parguera and 1 from Arecibo, Puerto Rico (USNPC). Four and 38 capsules were found in 2 of 10 yellowfin tuna from the southern Gulf of Mexico. This parasite also occurs in wahoo on the USA Atlantic coast and in the Pacific.
Geographic Range - Worldwide. Our records are the first in the Caribbean.
Life History - Larvae (posttorticaecum) in fish are 2.4-3.0 μm long and 0.3-0.7 μm wide (see figures in Tissue Fluke introduction). Eggs produced by the larger larvae were slightly smaller than those in adults. Larval forms have been found in the tissues of the head of wahoos.
Associations - A very heavy infection of gillworms, *Neothoracocotyle acanthocybii*, also occurred on the fish from Arecibo. These may have affected the health of the fish, but probably did not otherwise interact with the tissue flukes.
Location in Host - It is encapsulated in the outer layers of gills, mouth, eye sockets and face; and in internal tissues of the head. We found capsules in the roof of the mouth (La Parguera), and gill filaments near the gill arch (Arecibo).
Length - Worm 2.8-23.0 mm (forebody 1.0-11.0, hindbody 1.8-13.0 mm), capsules 3.0-25.0 mm. Yamaguti (1970) found capsules and worms of different sizes in different tissues of the heads of wahoos in Hawaii.
Host Specificity - It only occurs in wahoo. The report of this parasite from yellowfin tuna (Nikolaeva 1968) requires further confirmation.
Detection - These capsules were obvious in the gills and mouth of the fish we examined. They should be equally apparent on the face and other exposed surfaces of wahoo, but may be less noticeable in other tissue of the head.

Preparation for Study - Careful dissection may be necessary to find hidden capsules and to ascertain which tissue was infected. Larval forms have been rinsed from dissected heads of wahoo.

Didymocystis scomberomori (MacCallum and MacCallum)

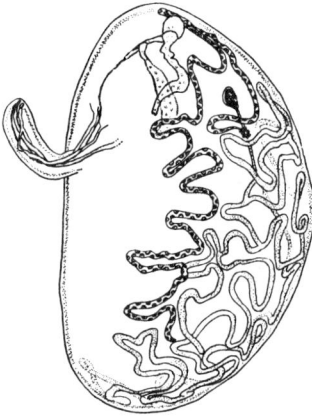

This potentially harmful parasite occurs as a bright mass in the gills and viscera of inshore, but not offshore, Spanish mackerels throughout the western Atlantic.

Name - It was originally placed in genus *Koellikeria*, and was refigured and redescribed by Overstreet (1969).

Diagnostic Characters - Capsules usually occur as rather large, lumpy orange to yellow masses. When removed from the capsule, the forebody projects from one end of the bulbous and bean-shaped hindbody and is less than 1/2 the length of the hindbody.

Records - We found 2-6 capsules in 7 of 30 cero from La Parguera (USNPC); more than 50-100 capsules in 2 of 3 cero off Humacao, Puerto Rico (USNPC 82966); and a few capsules in 2 serra Spanish mackerel from Cartagena, Colombia (USNPC). Twenty-five capsules were found in 2 Spanish mackerel and 1 of 2 cero from Biscayne Bay, Florida, USA (USNPC 71319); and 4 worms and 1 capsule in 2 Spanish mackerel from Woods Hole, Massachusetts, USA.

Geographic Range - Western Atlantic.

Life History - The capsules in the gills, intestinal wall and liver might suggest that larval forms penetrate the blood stream of the host and are transported to these sites.

Ecology - This worm has been found in all 3 species of western Atlantic, nearshore Spanish mackerels, but not in the more offshore king mackerel. Other parasites follow this same pattern (see Discussion).

The area in eastern Puerto Rico with the heavy infection rates is known to be contaminated with heavy metals and other pollutants (Tetra Tech 1992) (see *Hysterothylacium reliquens*). La Parguera in western Puerto Rico is less polluted. However, our data are too limited to make any environmental correlations.

Associations - A female-male pair of isopods, *Livoneca redmanii*, often occur in the gill chamber with the tissue fluke capsules. However, our limited statistical analysis seems to show no relationship between presence of the isopods and the capsules. In the fish with more than 100 capsules, heavy infections of encysted larval roundworms, *H. relinquens*, and tapeworms also occurred in the same areas of the gut.

Location in Host - It is encapsulated in the gills, usually in an arch, but occasionally in filaments; in the wall of the stomach or intestine; exceptionally, in the liver. Capsules were found in the liver only in the heavily infected cero. This may represent an unusual site only utilized in heavy infections. In some fish, the capsules were limited to the gills or the gut, but in others all sites were involved. This variation has not been explained.

Length - Worms 0.9-2.2 mm. Small capsules of a few millimeters occur in the intestinal wall and liver, but small to large ones up to 24.5 mm long and 12.0 mm wide are found on the gill arches.

Host Specificity - It is genus specific (Scomberomorus). Apparently it does not occur in king mackerel. This worm is a secondary parasite of Spanish mackerels. Serra Spanish mackerel is a new host.

Damage to Host - Heavy to very heavy infections of this worm had not previously been reported. The levels we found were probably sufficiently high to cause injury to the host. More study is needed to determine how often and under what condition heavy infections occur. An infection in the gills of Spanish mackerel from Florida, USA, produced a fibroblastic encapsulation (RTLA 4501).

Detection - The rather large, bright orange to yellow lumps on the gills or organs are obvious.

Harm to Humans - We have not hesitated to eat numerous cero we collected that were infected with this worm (possibly not an endorsement, as you might become horribly transformed like us into parasitologists!).

Significance to Sport Fishing - These large, obvious to spectacular lumps on the gills and guts of Spanish mackerel may offend fishermen cleaning their catch, but the worms are not known to harm humans.

Didymocystis thynni (Taschenberg)

This is a potentially damaging parasite of tunas and little tunas across the Atlantic.

Name - *Didymocystis reniformis* Ariola is a synonym.

Diagnostic Characters - Capsules appear as small, lumpy yellow masses. The forebody of the female is relatively short and shorter than the length of the hindbody. The oral sucker is relatively large and wider than 1/2 the width of the anterior expansion.

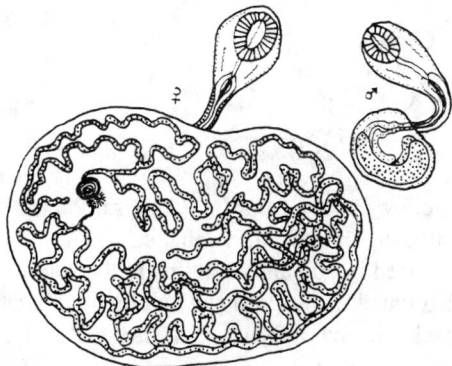

Records - Three to more than 70 capsules occurred in 2 little tunny from La Parguera, Puerto Rico. This parasite did not occur in 4 other little tunny we examined from Puerto Rico or 1 from the northern Gulf of Mexico off Alabama, USA. It also occurs in albacore, bluefin tuna and little tunny in the Mediterranean and bluefin tuna and skipjack tuna off Europe in the Atlantic.

Geographic Range - Atlantic and Mediterranean. Our records are the first in the western Atlantic.

Associations - Very heavy infections of 4 species of flukes occurred in the intestinal tracts of 2 little tunny with tissue flukes.

Location in Host - Most capsules occurred in the throat and 3 occurred in the wall of the anterior stomach of 1 little tunny; and 3 capsules occurred in the intestinal wall just posterior to the stomach of a second fish. This worm was previously reported encapsulated on the gills and inside the gill cover

Length - Worm 5.1-5.6 mm (forebody 2.6-2.8, hindbody 2.5-3.0 mm), capsules 0.7-13.0 mm (in throat 0.7-2.0, gills and gill cover 2.0-4.0, stomach 7.0-13.0 mm).

Host Specificity - It is family specific to scombrids.

Damage to Host - The heavy infection of this tissue fluke in combination with a very heavy infection of flukes in little tunny would probably be a sufficient parasite load to injure this host.

Detection - These small, bright yellow capsules are easily seen in the gills, gill cover or throat, but may be less obvious when more deeply embedded or in the intestinal tract wall.

Significance to Sport Fishing - The potential for damage to big game fishes makes further study of these parasites prudent.

Didymocystis wedli Ariola

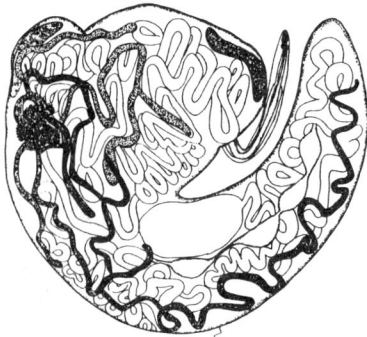

This is a potentially dangerous parasite of tunas, little tunas and mackerels around the world.

Diagnostic Characters - In worms removed from the capsule, the forebody projects from one end of the hindbody and approximately 1/2 the length of the hindbody. The hindbody is elongate with a 2 lobes on the front (bilobed anterior) and a twisted tail (spirally twisted).

Records - We found 17 capsules in 1 of 2 yellowfin tuna from La Parguera, Puerto Rico; and 26 in 1 of 2 yellowfin tuna off Dauphin Island, Alabama, USA. From 4-526 capsules (average 333) occurred in 10 yellowfin tuna in the southern Gulf of Mexico. This worm was also found in albacore and bluefin tuna in the Mediterranean, bluefin tuna, chub mackerel and skipjack tuna in the Pacific, and frigate tuna in India (BMNH 1981.6.9.5).

Geographic Range - Worldwide. Our collections were the first from the Caribbean and the northern Gulf of Mexico.

Location in Host - Gills filaments.

Length - Worm 4.8-5.6 mm (forebody 0.9-1.4, hindbody 4.5-5.1 mm).

Host Specificity - This worm is family specific (Scombridae) and almost tribe specific to tunas, but it also infects a little tuna and a mackerel.

Damage to Host - Nikolaeva (1968) reported hundreds of capsules of this worm and *Didymozoon longicolle* in yellowfin tuna which were also parasitized by heavy infections of 2-3 other tissue flukes (up to 1167 capsules). Superinfections are sufficient to stunt or injure these hosts and are rather alarming because few studies have targeted these parasites in the western Atlantic. We cannot be certain that damaging levels are not routine. "Large numbers" have also been reported in the gills of bluefin and skipjack tuna in Japan.

Didymozoon longicolle Ishii

This parasite is potentially damaging to tunas, little tunas and mackerels around the world.

Name - The *Didymozoon* sp. described from a chub mackerel by Linton (1940) was probably this worm.

Diagnostic Characters - Capsules are as small yellow, oval and elongate. In worms removed from the capsule, the forebody is elongate and narrow and the hindbody is cylindrical with a conical anterior end and a broadly rounded posterior end.

Records - Ten to 120 capsules (average 51) occurred in 6 of 10 yellowfin tuna from the southern Gulf of Mexico; 1-3 capsules in 2 chub mackerel from Woods Hole, Massachusetts, USA (USNPC 8389). It was also found in bluefin tuna, chub mackerel, skipjack tuna and yellowfin tuna in the Pacific.

Geographic Range - Worldwide. The 2 rather tenuous Atlantic records need to be confirmed with new collections.

Location in Host - Gills. It was reported in the skin of yellowfin tuna from the Gulf of Mexico.

Length - Worm 4.3-18.0 mm (forebody 0.8-3.8, hindbody 3.1-8.5 mm); capsule 3.0-5.0 mm.

Host Specificity - This worm is family specific (Scombridae).

Damage to Host - See *Didymocystis wedli*.

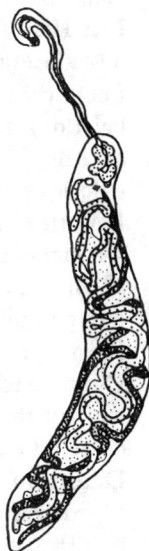

Colocyntotrema sp. of Nikolaeva

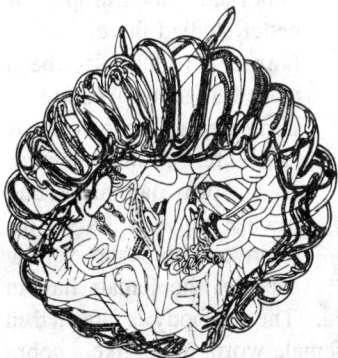

These bright orange globular capsules in the gills and internal organs are easily seen by fishermen, particularly when skinning sailfish. It is quite possible that this parasite damages billfishes.

Name - *Colocyntotrema auxis* Yamaguti was reported in frigate tuna in the Pacific, but this worm appears to be a different species.

Diagnostic Characters - Capsules appear as orange to yellowish, flattened oval masses, under the outer layer of organs. An elongated forebody projects from the globular hindbody when removed from the capsule.

Two identical worms in each capsule are fused at their posterior ends.

Records - A heavy infection of this worm occurred in 1 of 5 Atlantic sailfish caught off Arecibo, Puerto Rico (USNPC), but not in 2 from the northern Gulf of Mexico off Alabama, USA. It has also been reported from Atlantic sailfish and Atlantic blue marlin from the southern Gulf of Mexico. The unidentified tissue flukes associated with longbill spearfish stomach ulcers (see Other Diseases and Conditions) could be this worm.

Geographic Range - Northern Caribbean and southern Gulf of Mexico. Our collection is the first in the Caribbean. If its range is restricted, it might be of value as a biological tag.

Life History - This parasite may be transported by the circulatory system of the host since it is found both in the gills and internally.

Location in Host - More than 50 capsules occurred in the gills, 15 in the outer layer of the stomach and intestine, and 5 between the skin and body muscle in an Atlantic sailfish from Puerto Rico. This parasite was reported from the pyloric ceca of Atlantic sailfish and Atlantic blue marlin in the Gulf of Mexico.

Length - The capsules varied in size from 2-3 mm in the outer layer of the gut, 4-6 mm in the gills, and 5-8 mm under the skin. Whether these sizes were due to differences of nutrients available at different sites, or the duration of the different infections, could not be determined.

Host Specificity - It is possibly family specific to billfishes.

Damage to Host - The capsules were numerous enough to cause some impairment of the gills. The few capsules under the skin and on the gut probably cause little harm.

Detection - The orange oval capsules are obvious.

Significance to Sport Fishing - The potential of heavy infections injuring billfishes makes this parasite worthy of additional study.

Koellikeria bipartita (Wedl)

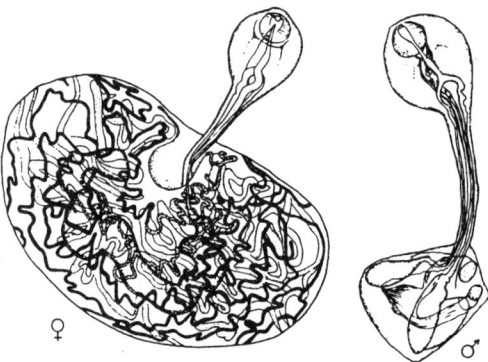

This Atlantic-wide parasite of tunas and greater amberjack, is either more important in Europe or better studied there.

Name - It has also been placed in genus *Wedlia*.

Diagnostic Characters - A larger female and smaller male worm pair are found in each capsule. In worms removed from the yellow capsule, the female has an elongate forebody with an expanded anterior end. The forebody is attached in the middle of the bean-shaped hindbody. The female worm looks like a cobra uncoiling from a basket. The smaller male has a similar forebody with a relatively short neck about as long as the anterior expanded region, but a relatively small, globular hindbody.

Records - One to 2 capsules occurred in 3 of 10 yellowfin tuna from the southern Gulf of Mexico; 4, 8 and 30 or more capsules in 3 bluefin tuna from Woods Hole, Massachusetts, USA (USNPC 8392); albacore, bluefin tuna and greater amberjack from the eastern Atlantic; and bluefin tuna and greater amberjack from the Mediterranean. It is either more abundant in Europe or less studied in the western Atlantic.

Geographic Range - North Atlantic and Mediterranean.

Location in Host - It is encapsulated in the wall of the intestine, pyloric ceca, gills, gill arches and skin of the head.

Length - Female 1.6-9.0 mm (forebody 0.4-0.6, hindbody 1.2-2.0 mm), male 2.9-9.0 mm (forebody 2.0-2.5, hindbody 0.9-1.4 mm), immature worm in a capsule 1.2 mm; capsules 3.0-9.0 mm. Capsules in the intestinal wall are smaller than those in the pyloric ceca.

Host Specificity - It is almost tribe specific to tunas, but is also found in greater amberjack.

Detection - Capsules in the intestine look like small yellow spots.

Koellikeria globosa Ishii

This marble-shaped parasite occurs worldwide in tunas and occasionally skipjack tuna and yellowtail.

Name - The name "globosa" aptly describes the spherical hindbody of the female. This worm had also been placed in genus *Wedlia*.

Diagnostic Characters - A larger female and smaller male worm pair are found in each capsule. The hindbody of the female is oval to round instead of bean-shaped and the oral sucker is relatively small. The male has a similar forebody, a neck longer than the expanded anterior, and a hindbody about the same size as the expanded anterior.

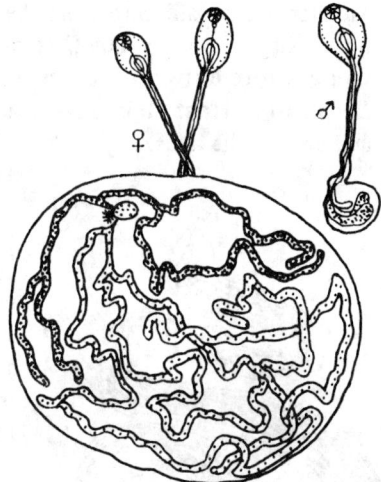

Records - Two to 87 capsules (average 20) occurred in 9 of 10 yellowfin tuna from the southern Gulf of Mexico; several capsules in 1 of 64 yellowfin tuna from west Africa; and in bluefin tuna, skipjack tuna and yellowtail from Japan.

Geographic Range - Worldwide.

Location in Host - It is encapsulated in the mouth, esophagus, intestine and pyloric ceca.

Length - Female 9.0-19.4 mm, male 6.6-8.0 mm; capsule 2.0-5.0 mm.

Host Specificity - It is almost tribe specific to tunas, but occasionally found in little tunas and jacks.

Koellikeria orientalis (Yamaguti)

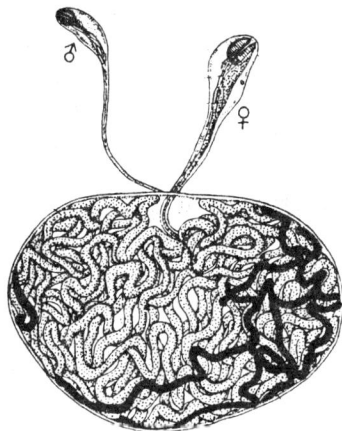

This is a worldwide parasite of tunas and occasionally skipjack tuna.

Name - This worm has also been placed in genus *Wedlia*.

Diagnostic Characters - A larger female and smaller male worm pair are found in each capsule. The female has an elongate forebody with an expanded anterior end. The forebody is attached in the middle of the bean-shaped hindbody. The female worm looks like a cobra uncoiling from a basket. The male has a similar forebody with a relatively long neck about 4 times the length of the anterior expanded region, but a relatively small bean-shaped hindbody.

Records - Fifteen capsules occurred in 1 of 10 yellowfin tuna from the southern Gulf of Mexico; in bluefin tuna from the Mediterranean; albacore from the eastern Atlantic; and bluefin tuna, skipjack tuna, yellowfin tuna from Japan.

Geographic Range - Worldwide.

Location in Host - It is encapsulated in the gills, esophagus, intestine, stomach and around the anus.

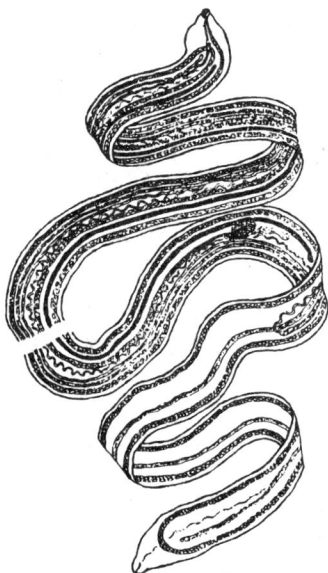

Length - Female 2.5-2.8 mm (forebody 1.6-1.8, hindbody 0.9-1.1 mm), male 2.0-2.4 (forebody 1.5-1.7, hindbody 0.5-0.7 mm); capsule 1.0-3.5 mm. Capsules in the gills and esophagus are larger (1.5-3.5 mm) than in the stomach and intestine (1.0-2.0 mm).

Host Specificity - This parasite is almost tribe specific to tunas, but has also been found in skipjack tuna.

Atalostropion sardae MacCallum

This is a strange and tangled worm.

Name - Yamaguti (1971) refigured pieces of this worm.

Diagnostic Characters - It occurs as a tangled mass of long, narrow, ribbon-shaped filaments in the tissues of fishes. Only the extreme anterior and posterior ends are shown.

Records - Four to 43 capsules (average 14)

occurred in 6 of 10 yellowfin tuna from the southern Gulf of Mexico; many hundreds in Atlantic bonito, and in 7 of 16 Atlantic bonito from Woods Hole, Massachusetts, USA (USNPC 36309).

Geographic Range - Unknown.

Location in Host - In connective tissues of yellowfin tuna, and under the mucous membranes in the mouth of Atlantic bonito.

Length - 140.0-190.0 mm, immature worms 50.0-70.0 mm (total adult lengths were estimated from pieces of worms).

Host Specificity - This worm may only occur in Atlantic bonito. More collections are needed to confirm its occurrence in yellowfin tuna.

Preparation for Study - Dissecting complete specimens from the tissues of the host is difficult, bordering on the impossible.

Nematobothrium pelamydis (Taschenberg)

These obvious, orange, often damaging gill capsules in Atlantic bonito are well known in the eastern Atlantic and Mediterranean. Their importance in the western Atlantic is more obscure.

Name - *Didymozoon pelamdis* Taschenberg, *N. sardae* MacCallum and MacCallum, *Unitubulotestis pelamdis* (T.) and *U. sardae* (M. and M.) are synonyms.

Diagnostic Characters - The orange capsules are oval and flattened. When removed from the capsule, worms are elongate with the anterior end much more narrow, but not distinctly set off as a forebody. The narrow anterior end is more than 4 times as long as wide.

Records - One to 6 capsules occurred in 6 of 13 Atlantic bonito, and, in a study especially designed to determine prevalence and intensity of this worm, 2-3 capsules were found in 83 of 100 Atlantic bonito from Woods Hole, Massachusetts, USA. It is found in this host from the eastern Atlantic off Europe, the Mediterranean and Black Sea.

Geographic Range - Northern Atlantic, Mediterranean and Black Sea.

Life History - These parasites do not infect larval or small fishes, but Atlantic bonito 25.0-42.0 cm long as well as adults are infected. One larva enters a gill lobe blood vessel, a second larva joins the first, they grow, distort the artery and elicit host tissue response to form a capsule in the artery and enlarge, forming a sacculated aneurism. The first larva to arrive becomes the "female" (female gonads predominate) and the second becomes the "male".

Metacercariae of this worm and *N. scombri* parasitize sprat, *Clupea sprattus* Linnaeus, and rarely 9 other species of Black Sea fishes. The number of these larval forms in sprat from the Black Sea have been monitored since 1950. From

1959 to 1961, 93.5% were infected with 1-116 metacercariae each. In 1975, the first of the final hosts of these tissue flukes, Atlantic bonito, became drastically reduced in numbers, and the second host, Atlantic mackerel, disappeared from the Black Sea. In 1977, only 1.0% of sprat were infected with 1 metacercaria each.

Location in Host - Capsules usually occur along the outer layer of the gill filaments, rarely in the viscera. Larval forms were found under the lining of the gill chamber.

Length - Adult worm 15.0-50.0 mm, immature worm encapsulated in the gills 18.0 mm, free juvenile 0.7-14.0 mm; capsule 7.0-12.0 mm (3.0-3.5 mm wide).

Host Specificity - It only occurs in Atlantic bonito. This worm can occur commonly in parts of the Mediterranean and Black Sea, but it is a secondary parasite of this host.

Damage to Host - Very heavy infections, possibly capable of injuring the host, have been reported in fish during their return migration from the Black Sea to the Sea of Marmara. In some studies, 64.8% of the fishes were infected with up to 10 capsules per gill arch. Although the blood flow in the gill filament is clearly impaired by larva settling in the artery, little host reaction was apparent. A small host, 20 cm long, with a heavy infection of 10 capsules per gill arch, had pale gill filaments.

Detection - The orange capsules are obvious on the gills.

Significance to Sport Fishing - This rather important parasite of Atlantic bonito is probably the best studied of the tissue flukes, but it has been ignored in the western Atlantic.

Nematobothrium scombri (Taschenberg)

This parasite has only been found once in the western Atlantic in a butterfish, but occurs around the world in big game fishes.

Name - It was previously placed in the genus *Didymozoon* (actually as the type species).

Diagnostic Characters - The pale yellow capsules are usually isolated, but sometimes occur in groups. Worms are elongate with the anterior end much more narrow, but not distinctly set off as a forebody. The narrow anterior end is approximately twice as long as wide.

Records - Seven worms occurred in a butterfish, *Peprilus triacanthus* (Peck), from Woods Hole, Massachusetts, USA (USNPC 8386); and in chub mackerel from southern Brazil. This parasite was also found in Atlantic mackerel from off Europe and the Mediterranean, chub mackerel from the Mediterranean, and chub mackerel and skipjack tuna from Japan.

Geographic Range - Worldwide.

Life History - Capsules usually contain 1 pair of worms, but may

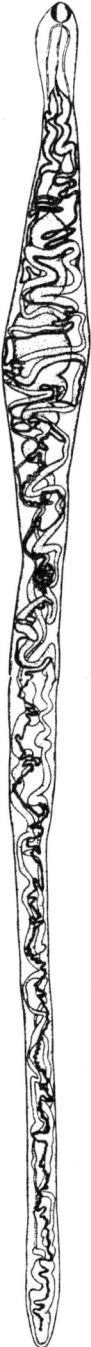

hold up to 16. See previous worm.

Location in Host - This worm occurred in the inner surface of mouth, gill cover or gill arches of mackerels, but in the intestinal wall of butterfish.

Length - Worms 15.0-65.0 mm; capsules 4.0-7.0 mm.

Host Specificity - It is almost tribe specific to mackerels. The record in a butterfish may have been an accidental host or a data-recording error.

Maccallumtrema xiphiados (MacCallum and MacCallum)

Capsules of this cauliflower-shaped worm may damage or deteriorate the muscle of swordfish.

Name - Yamaguti (1970) named a new genus in honor of the MacCallums based on their *Koellikeria xiphiados*. This worm has also been placed in the genera *Didymocystis* and *Wedlia*.

The genus *Makairatrema* Yamaguti was also based on a species, *Makairatrema musculicola* Yamaguti (=*Maccallumtrema musculicola*) from the ventral abdominal muscle of a billfish. We fail to see any adequate distinctions between these 2 genera and suggest that *Makairatrema* is a synonym of *Maccallumtrema*. This combines 2 rather similar species from the muscles of billfishes into 1 genus. This action seems justified by the overlapping characters of the 2 genera, and particularly in a family with too many genera for its number of species.

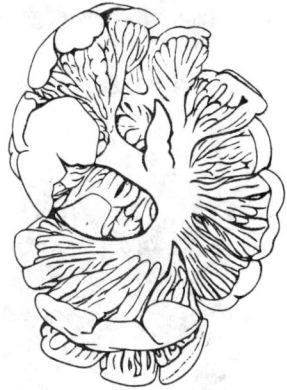

Diagnostic Characters - Capsules appear as large, ovid masses in the abdominal muscle. The capsule has extensions (vascular septa) that separate the hindbodies of the 2 enclosed worms. In worms removed from capsules, the forebody is attached in the middle of the hindbody, and the hindbody is cauliflower-shaped with lobes.

Records - Several capsules occurred in swordfish from Woods Hole, Massachusetts, and Hawaii, USA.

Geographic Range - Worldwide.

Location in Host - In the abdominal muscle in the upper (dorsal) flanks, the same muscle that is so commercially prized.

Length - Worms 17.0-29.5 mm (forebody 3.0-6.5, hindbody 14.0-23.0 mm), exceptionally 40.0 mm; capsule up to 50 mm.

Host Specificity - This worm only occurs in swordfish.

Detection - Larger, yellow capsules near the surface of the muscle are obvious as soon as the fish is skinned. Smaller, less developed (white instead of yellow) or more deeply embedded capsules may be less obvious.

Harm to Humans - Indirectly, the presence of these capsules could harm humans by causing the muscle tissue used as human food to deteriorate more rapidly than would be expected. Capsules should be picked out (mechanically removed) from swordfish steaks to prevent contamination and deterioration. In cases of heavy infections, it may be wise to cook the flesh as soon as possible. Cooking fresh infected steaks before freezer storage may be prudent.

Preparation for Study - Locating capsules without damaging them and dissecting out intact capsules and worms is a bit more of a challenge in muscle tissue than in dealing with capsules on the surface of other tissues. Sections of muscle, no more than a few centimeters thick, with capsules should be excised from freshly caught swordfish and placed in 10% buffered formalin (10 parts fluid for 1 part tissue).

Significance to Sport Fishing - This parasite should be of considerable interest to fishermen, seafood inspectors and seafood processors. Our almost utter lack of knowledge of this important problem is astounding.

Neodidymozoon macrostoma Yamaguti

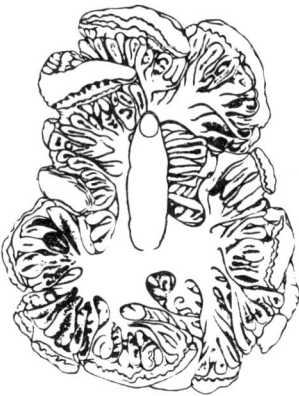

This worm is encapsulated on the gills of billfishes around the world.

Diagnostic Characters - It occurs in a relatively large, ovid flat capsule with host tissue intruding between the 2 worms. Worms removed from the capsule have a cauliflower-shaped hindbody with small slender forebody attached in the middle.

Records - One capsule occurred in 1 of 40 Atlantic blue marlin from various localities, 6 in a longbill spearfish from Aguadilla, and 1 in a white marlin off La Parguera, Puerto Rico. This parasite was described from Hawaii in Indo-Pacific blue marlin and 2 other billfish species.

Geographic Range - Worldwide. Our collections are the first in the Atlantic.

Location in Host - In the outer layer of the gill arch in our specimens; and reported previously in the connective tissues of the gill arch, and in fat and muscle around the gill chamber.

Length - Worm 11.0-25.5 mm (forebody 3.0-5.5, hindbody 8.0-20.0 mm); capsule up to 12.0 mm.

Host Specificity - This parasite is family specific to billfishes. Our hosts are new records for this parasite.

Detection - The larger capsules are obvious on the arches and in the gill chamber.

Miscellaneous Tissue Flukes

Atalostropion **sp. of Grabda.** - Grabda (1991) reported Atlantic mackerel from the Georges Bank in the northwest Atlantic with this worm intertwining between the muscle fibers and forming orange-colored centers. These parasites hinder commercial processing of Atlantic mackerel by ruining fillets. Fillets with worms were soft, watery and grayish in color. This worm may also be the tissue flukes found in connective tissue between the muscle bundles of Atlantic mackerel (RTLA 4503). This parasite is causing problems in a commercial fishery and should be defined and evaluated.

Didymozoon auxis **Taschenberg** - The *Didymozoon* sp. described from a bullet tuna by Linton (1940) could possibly be this worm. New collections will be necessary to resolve this question. Worms removed from the capsule have a distinctive, long, narrow body that is bent at a right angle. The forebody is elongate and narrow. One capsule possibly occurred in a bullet tuna from Woods Hole, Massachusetts, USA (USNPC 8388). It has also been reported from bullet tuna in the Mediterranean and frigate tuna from Japan. This parasite probably occurs worldwide. Capsules are found on the gills of hosts. Worms are 3.9-12.0 mm (forebody 0.8-1.8, hindbody 3.1-8.2 mm) long; capsule 4.0 mm. It is genus specific (*Auxis*).

Didymozoon minor **Yamaguti** - The name of this worm, found in skipjack tuna from Japan, was changed to *Didymozoon minus*, but most confusingly, both names are found in the literature and in parasite checklists.

Platocystis **sp. of Nikolaeva** - This worm apparently differs from *Platocystis alalongae* Yamaguti found in the skin of Pacific albacore. The flat capsule contains 2 worms. Worms liberated from the capsule have an elongate forebody attached to one end of a globular, semicircular (slice of watermelon-shaped) hindbody. Two capsules occurred in the connective tissues of 1 of 10 yellowfin tuna from the southern Gulf of Mexico.

MONOGENEA (GILLWORMS)

The name "monogenea" means born once, and refers to the simple life cycle. In heavy infections, they can kill captive fishes and occasionally wild ones. More than 1500 species have been described, but this is probably only a small percentage of those existing. Adults range from 30 μm to 20 mm in length and are translucent, cream or pink. Gillworms have a distinct attachment organ on their posterior end called a haptor (or opisthaptor) with hardened anchors or specialized clamps to pierce the epithelium and hold on to the host. Sclerotized marginal hooks often surround the haptor, and bars, disks, scales or spines may occur on or near the haptor. The head sometimes has eye spots and specialized holdfast organs. Many monogenean parasites of big game fishes have large suckers or numerous clamps adapted for holding on to these fast moving animals. Most reproduce by laying eggs that hatch ciliated larvae (oncomiracidia) and quickly mature and attach to the host. Since no stages on intermediate hosts are necessary, they can multiply rapidly. When intensive culture crowds fish together, most gillworm offspring survive and can quickly begin to kill fishes. Gillworms are permanent parasites in the gills, mouths or on the bodies of fishes. Some occur in the nares, pockets in the lateral line or rarely in the gut of fishes. Some species occur in the urinary bladder of fishes, frogs or turtles. They generally feed on mucus, epithelial cells or blood. Gillworms are common on fishes in all aquatic environments.

Popular Reference "How to Know the Trematodes" (Schell 1970).

Classification and Contents

Capsalidea - Capsalids

These relatively large, broad and flat gillworms attach to the host with a large, cup-shaped haptor on the posterior and 2 smaller suckers on the anterior of the worm. A microscopic pair of anchors are found on the haptor. Larger adult worms are easily visible on the host and small or developing worms can be found in wet mounts of skin scrapings or clippings of gills observed with a compound microscope. Absence in samples does not assure that fishes are free from these parasites. They attach to the skin, gills and inside the nares and mouth of big game fishes. Sometimes there may be so many worms on the skin that they appear to be the scales of the fish. They can be relaxed by freezing in sea water first, and fixed in 5% formalin.

Our examinations of adult wild fishes suggest that these worms usually do little physical damage. They can become a serious problem in hatcheries or net-pen culture, where fishes are crowded together, water quality is poor and water exchange rates are low, enhancing the accumulation of worms. In heavy infections, attachment causes skin or gill irritation and production of mucus. Fishes may exhibit flashing behavior and scrape their bodies on the sides of the tank or pen. Bacteria can enter damaged areas, further weakening the fish.

In netpen culture, plastic sheeting can be used to isolate individual pens for treatments using formalin. This is extremely labor intensive and time consuming. When the plastic is removed, fishes again become exposed to reinfection of parasites from wild sources. Increasing the water flow rate in hatchery situations may flush out early stages of gillworms in the water and slow their accumulation on the gills. It should be noted that no treatment will eliminate all parasites, some will always remain. Treatments reduce the numbers to tolerable loads for fishes. Local stocks should be developed for any marine fish enhancement programs rather than importing fishes to new areas where they may be more susceptible to local parasites or introduce new parasites to local wild stocks.

Only large gillworms (Order Capsalidea and Order Mazocraeidea) occur on big game fishes. Smaller gillworms (Order Dactylogyridea and Order Gyrodactylidea) dominate (in number of fish species infected and number of individual worms per host) in most other fishes and in most other habitats. Certainly larger fishes might be expected to have larger parasites, but this does not explain the total exclusion of these otherwise omnipresent forms. Some capsalids are less host specific than is usually found in the majority of gillworms which normally occur on one species or genus of host. Capsalids often occur on many species of hosts in one or more families of offshore game fishes. This ability is of great advantage in exploiting such highly dispersed and fast swimming fishes. A similar situation is found in some of the copepods parasitizing these fishes, obvious examples of parallel evolution. These worms probably do little harm but in large numbers they could cause the fish to stop feeding and thus become less susceptible to hook and line fishing.

Caballerocotyla manteri (Price)

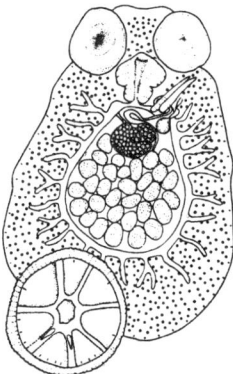

The relatively large suckers on the anterior end of this minuscule, and little known, worm look like a pair of spectacles. It occasionally occurs in low numbers on little tunny and wahoo. **Name** - It was originally placed in *Capsala*. **Diagnostic Characters** - This worm is elongate in body outline and the sucker-like haptor extends beyond the body outline. The cephalic suckers are large. The testes are all inside the cecal loop. **Records** - One occurred in a wahoo off La Parguera, Puerto Rico (USNPC 82585). Three were found in a little tunny from the Dry Tortugas, Florida, USA (USNPC 37228-9); and on this host from Chesapeake Bay and Woods Hole, Massachusetts, USA. **Geographic Range** - Western Atlantic (not confirmed form the Atlantic coast of South America). Our collection is the first from the Caribbean.

Life History - Justine, Lambert and Mattei (1985) described the shape and form of the spermatozoa, and Justine and Mattei (1987) spermatogenesis.
Location in Host - Gills. It occurred on the tongue of wahoo.
Length - 2.1-2.6 mm.
Host Specificity - It is probably host specific to little tunny and wahoo is a false host. It had not previously been reported from wahoo.

Capsaloides cornutus (Verrill)

This little known, worm occurs in the mouth of longbill spearfish and white marlin.

Diagnostic Characters - This oval worm has a sucker-like haptor divided into 7 large and 2 small, shallow depressions around the border and 1 in the middle. The haptor diameter is about 1/5 the length of the body of this parasite and only slightly extends past the body outline. It is pink when alive.

Records - Four occurred in a longbill spearfish from Aguadilla, Puerto Rico (USNPC). Light infections of this parasite have also been found in white marlin from Woods Hole, Massachusetts (USNPC 7178) and Block Island, Rhode Island, USA (USNPC 35136).

Geographic Range - Unknown. Our collection is the first from the Caribbean.

Associations - This parasite and *Tristomella laevis* were found in the mouth and on the gills of the longbill spearfish and *Capsaloides magnaspinosus* occurred in the nares of the same fish. Possibly these 3 parasites also co-exist in white marlin, but this requires confirmation.

Location in Host - Gills and mouth.

Length - 5.3-8.0 mm (white marlin); 4.3-5.5 mm (longbill spearfish).

Host Specificity - This parasite may be genus specific (*Tetrapturus*). Longbill spearfish is a new host for this worm, but this is not surprising since the fish has not previously been examined for parasites. Interestingly, this parasite was not found in 3 white marlin we examined in Puerto Rico, or in 2 from Alabama, USA.

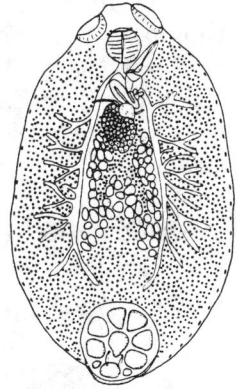

Capsaloides magnaspinosus Price

This wrinkled worm has rarely been seen because the nares of billfishes are seldom examined.

Diagnostic Characters - This tear-drop or pear-shaped (pyriform) worm has a sucker-like haptor divided into 7 large and 2 small shallow depressions around the border and 1 in the middle. The diameter of the haptor is 1/3 to 1/2 the length of the body of this parasite and is entirely within the body outline. The margins of the body are scalloped or crenelated and the worm is much thicker than *C. cornutus*. It is also pink in life.

Records - Three occurred in a longbill spearfish from Aguadilla, Puerto Rico (USNPC); and 3 in a white marlin from Woods Hole, Massachusetts, USA (USNPC 35648).

Geographic Range - Unknown. Our record is the first from the Caribbean.

Associations - See previous parasite.

Location in Host - Nares.

Length - 5.4-6.6 mm (white marlin); 4.3-5.5 mm (longbill spearfish).

Host Specificity - This parasite may be genus specific (*Tetrapterus*). Longbill spearfish is a new host for this parasite. Interestingly, this parasite was not found in 3 white marlin we examined in Puerto Rico, or in 2 from Alabama, USA.

Nasicola klawei (Stunkard)

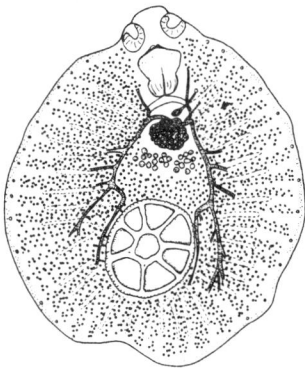

This round nasal worm is consistently found in yellowfin tunas and never in the similar bigeye. It may be used to distinguish these similar fishes.

Name - The genus name refers to the location in the nares. It has also been placed in genus *Caballerocotyla*. *Tristoma* sp. of Rossignol and Repelin, 1962 is a synonym; and *Capsala thynni* (Guiart) is probably a synonym.

Diagnostic Characters - This large, almost circular worm has a relatively small, sucker-like haptor divided into 7 relatively large depressions around the border and 1 in the middle. The haptor does not extend beyond the body outline. The anterior suckers are reduced and the pharynx is constricted in the middle.

Records - We found 4 in each of 2 yellowfin tuna from off La Parguera and Desecheo Island; and 4 in 1 blackfin tuna from Boqueron, but not in 1 from Aguadilla, Puerto Rico; and 1-7 in 2 yellowfin tuna from Dauphin Island, Alabama, USA. This worm has previously been reported in blackfin tuna and yellowfin tuna from Puerto Rico; and yellowfin tuna from the Bahamas, Venezuela; very light to light infections in albacore and yellowfin tuna from the Atlantic and Gulf coasts of the USA; the eastern Atlantic and from widely separated localities in the Pacific (USNPC 59865).

Geographic Range - Worldwide.

Location in Host - Nasal capsules. From 1-5 worms were found in each capsule, but usually 2 were present. It has rarely been reported from the gills or body where the worms were probably washed from the nares after the host died.

Length - 7.5-11.9 mm (yellowfin tuna); 8.2-10.9 mm (blackfin tuna). Bane (1969) reported the average and maximum lengths of 10.4 and 11.9 mm in 11 worms from yellowfin tuna (4 from Puerto Rico), and 9.6 and 10.9 mm in 30 blackfin tuna (from Aguadilla, Puerto Rico). He suggested that the difference in worm size was because blackfin tuna are smaller than yellowfin tuna and therefore the nasal capsules were smaller, restricting the growth of the worms inside. He also noted a correlation between the length of each worm and the length of its fish host.

Host Specificity - This worm is a characteristic parasite of yellowfin tuna. It appears to occur less often in blackfin tuna.

Significance to Sport Fishing - Bane (1969) suggested that since this worm always occurs in yellowfin tuna and never in bigeye tuna, the parasite could be used to distinguish these morphologically similar species of tuna.

Tristoma coccineum Cuvier

This parasite is more numerous on western Atlantic stocks of swordfish than the smaller *T. integrum*. The ratio of numbers of these 2 parasites reverses from the western to eastern Atlantic and may be used to identify these stocks.

Name - *Tristoma aculeatum* Grube and *T. papillosum* Diesing are synonyms.

Diagnostic Characters - This almost circular parasite has a sucker-like haptor divided into 7 large shallow depressions around the border and 1 in the middle. The haptor does not reach the posterior margin of the body. The numerous testes are confined to the intercecal area. The margins of the body have rows of minute spines radiating outward. If these rows are counted on one side, there are 43-54. This parasite is larger than the similar *T. integrum*.

Records - One to 79 (average 12.6) occurred in 264 of 303 swordfish (ARC 2322), and 233 (average 12.3) in 19 of 24 from the northwest Atlantic. It has also been found on swordfish from Woods Hole, Massachusetts (USNPC 4877, 7168, 35124, 35645-7), the Atlantic coast of Canada to Chesapeake Bay and the Mediterranean.

Geographic Range - Atlantic and Mediterranean.

Associations - see *T. integrum*.

Location in Host - Gills and gill cavity.

Length - 10.0-16.4 mm.

Host Specificity - This worm is only found on swordfish. It is a primary parasite of this host in the western Atlantic, but a secondary parasite in the eastern Atlantic. A record from smooth hammerhead, *Sphyrna zygaena* (Linnaeus), was probably accidental or erroneous.

Preparation for Study - Iles (1971) suggested that "deep frozen" worms do not contract and match the sizes reported in the literature. Those killed in formalin were 40% smaller due to contraction and distortion.

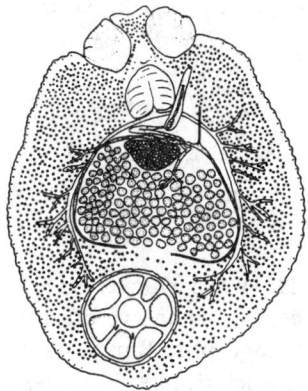

Significance to Sport Fishing - Iles (1971) reported that in the northwest Atlantic the abundance of this species is much higher than the similar *T. integrum*, but the opposite ratio of these 2 worms occurs on Mediterranean swordfish. She suggested that this relative abundance might be used as a biological tag to distinguish stocks of swordfish.

Tristoma integrum Diesing

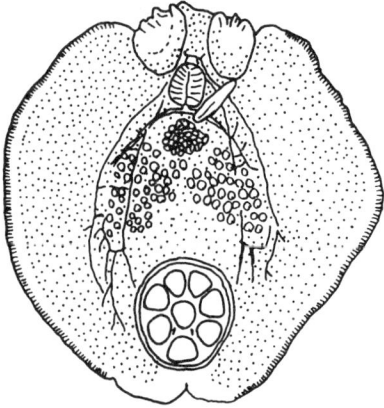

This parasite is more numerous on eastern Atlantic stocks of swordfish than the larger *T. coccineum*. The ratio of numbers of these 2 parasites reverses from the western to eastern Atlantic and may be used to identify these stocks.

Diagnostic Characters - This worm is similar to *T. coccineum*, but is smaller. The margins of the body have rows of minute spines radiating outward. If these rows are counted on one side, there are more than 300.

Records - One to 12 (average 3.0) occurred in 134 of 303 swordfish (ARC 2321), and 37 (average 3.7) in 10 of 24 from the northwest Atlantic. It has also been found on swordfish from the east coast of the USA and the Mediterranean.

Geographic Range - Atlantic and Mediterranean.

Associations - *Tristoma coccineum* occurred in 19, *T. integrum* in 10, and both worms occurred together in 7 of 24 swordfish from the northwest Atlantic.

Location in Host - Gills, between gill filaments.

Length - 5.8-12.0 mm.

Host Specificity - This worm is only found on swordfish and is a primary parasite in the eastern Atlantic, but a secondary parasite in the western Atlantic.

Significance to Sport Fishing - See previous parasite.

Tristomella laevis (Verrill)

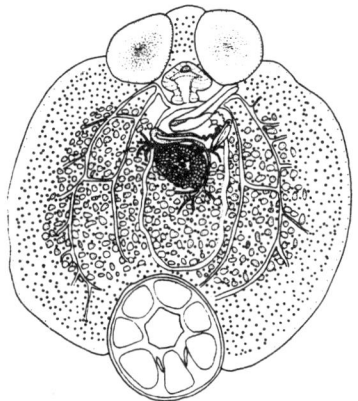

This worm attaches on any external surface of billfishes around the world.

Name - This parasite has also been placed in the genera *Capsala* and *Tristoma*. *Tristomum poeyi* Vigueras is a synonym. It was redescribed by Price (1938).

Diagnostic Characters - This parasite is circular in outline. The haptor is on the posterior portion of the body and extends past the body outline. The testes are numerous and occur outside and inside the

boundary of the ceca. The vitellaria extend nearly to the margin of the body.
Records - Six to more than 100 occurred on 40 Atlantic blue marlin from off
various locations around Puerto Rico (USNPC 81999-82003), 25-100 on 4 of 5
Atlantic sailfish from Arecibo, 55-70 on 2 of 3 white marlin from La Parguera,
and 3 on a longbill spearfish from Aguadilla, Puerto Rico. It has also been
found on white marlin from Havana, Cuba; and Block Island, Rhode Island,
USA (USNPC 7179); and billfishes from the eastern and southern Atlantic and
Indo-Pacific.

We have observed very heavy infections on freshly caught blue marlin, but
worms gradually fell off or were knocked off in handling, and were reduced to
moderate infections by the time the fish was examined at the dock. The
parasites of most big game fishes may be lost or reduced in numbers during
handling of the host, but this worm seems to be particularly vulnerable. Thus
the numbers per host reported may actually represent a small percentage of what
was on the live host.

Geographic Range - Worldwide.

Associations - This parasite was found in the mouth and on the gills of a longbill spearfish along with *Capsaloides cornutus*. *Capsaloides magnaspinosus* also
occurred in the nares of this fish. These 3 parasites are also found on the white
marlin and may co-exist on that host. *Tristomella laevis* was found alone on
Atlantic blue marlin we examined.

Location in Host - Body, gills and inside mouth. This worm is either a real
generalist in choosing attachment positions, or it moves or is washed into
different locations when the host is handled. Examination of freshly caught fish
by fishermen could explain this little mystery.

Length - 7.75-11.5 mm. Puerto Rican specimens were smaller (5.4-10.0 mm).

Host Specificity - This worm is a characteristic parasite of Atlantic blue
marlin. It is at least a primary parasite of Atlantic sailfish and white marlin.
This gillworm may be family specific to billfishes. Records from Atlantic and
Indo-Pacific swordfish, and Brazilian dolphin, and northwest Atlantic skipjack
tuna, appear to have been cases of accidental parasitism, erroneous
identifications, or contamination from billfishes. Atlantic blue marlin was
reported as a new host by Dyer, Williams and Bunkley-Williams (1992).

Significance to Sport Fishing - This is probably one of the most familiar
parasites for big game fishermen. It appears as soft, translucent-white, scale-
like attachments to the outside of billfishes. They are most numerous when the
fish is first boated but begin to fall off almost immediately. They may litter the
deck and wiggle among the mucus and blood. Many remain attached and some
move inside the gill covers to avoid desiccation. Probably, they do little harm
to the fish but very heavy infections may cause skin irritation.

Dionchus agassizi Goto

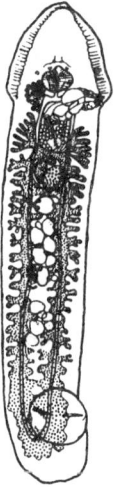

This worm occurs in cobia and remoras around the world. Its presence suggests that these fishes are related.

Name - *Dionchus rachycentris* Hargis was described in August, 1955; and *D. hopkinsi* Koratha in September, 1955, from cobia in the northern Gulf of Mexico (USNPC 54754). Both are synonyms of this worm. It was redescribed by Price (1938).

Diagnostic Characters - The haptor of this elongate parasite is formed into a sucker and has 2 stout, centrally placed anchors. The anterior portion of the worm is triangular in shape and has numerous cephalic glands that open along the lateral margins. This worm differs from the similar *D. remorae* because the 2 anchors on the haptor are larger than 1/4 the diameter of the haptor; and the blade of these anchors is shorter than their base.

Records - Two to 4 occurred in 3 cobia from Dauphin Island, Alabama; in light infections from Tampa Bay, Florida; Grande Isla, Louisiana; 8 worms in 4 of 9 cobia from Port Aransas, Texas, USA; and in this host from Australia. This worm also occurs on inshore remora, shark remora and spearfish remora around the world.

Geographic Range - Worldwide.

Associations - This worm and *D. remorae* occur on the gills of inshore remora together. The association of this worm with remoras and cobias suggests these 2 families are either related or the same (see Discussion).

Location in Host - Gill filaments.

Length - 3.0-5.1 mm (cobia); 0.8-3.7 mm (remoras). Cobia grow to a larger size than remoras, and larger worms on larger hosts is not surprising. The size of many parasites is directly related to the size of their host.

Host Specificity - This worm is probably a primary parasite of cobia, inshore remora, shark remora and spearfish remora.

Mazocraeidea

These worms have more complex haptors than capsalids. They can usually be easily seen with the naked eye. These worms have intricate attachment organs with a series of complicated clamps or suckers often on extensions of a complex haptor. They generally feed on blood. They produce few eggs and usually occur in low numbers on the host. They are largely marine. The few that do occur in fresh water are usually on hosts of marine origin. They do not increase in numbers rapidly, but since they feed on blood, they can severely damage their hosts with even slight increases in numbers. Usually big game fishes are not held in hatchery or culture conditions where worms can accumulate and cause problems. They could become a problem if culture for restocking of marine sport fish, as is being studied in Florida, is attempted.

These worms can be relaxed in dilute formalin solutions (1 part formalin to 4000 parts water) and cleared and mounted in glycerine jelly. Alternatively, they may be placed under a microscope coverslip on a slide and bathed in 5% formalin so that they are fixed flat. They can be stained and permanently mounted as described for flukes. Fishes infected with these worms can be treated with formalin as described for capsalids above.

Allopseudaxine katsuwonis (Ishii)

This distinctively triangular gillworm occurs on the gills of skipjack tuna around the world.

Diagnostic Characters - This worm is narrow anteriorly and broadens posteriorly. It has a short but broad haptor, slightly constricted from the body of the worm, and 24-27 clamps along the posterior border. It has 60-79 testes.

In the Indo-Pacific, *Allopseudaxinoides vagans* (Ishii) shares the gills of skipjack tuna with *A. katsuwonis* and may possibly be found in the Atlantic. The name *A. vagans* is from a former name (synonym) of skipjack tuna, *Katsuwonus vagans*. It is similar in size (6.0-7.0 mm) and general shape and organ arrangement, but differs from *A. katsuwonis* by having 13-15 clamps, and 30-35 testes. The clamps are also more complex possessing accessory sclerites.

Records - One occurred in 1 of 3 skipjack tuna from Arecibo, Puerto Rico (USNPC). It has also been found on this host in the north central and northwest Pacific. Lester (pers. comm.) found what was probably this worm and *A. vagans* on skipjack tuna from the southwest Pacific.

Geographic Range - Worldwide. Our collection is the first record of this parasite from the Atlantic Ocean.

Location in Host - Gill filaments.

Length - 7.0-8.0 mm.

Host Specificity - This worm only occurs on skipjack tuna and is probably a characteristic parasite of this host.

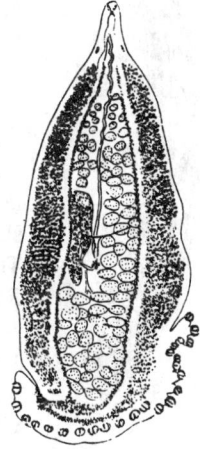

Allencotyla mcintoshi Price

This is a little-known gillworm on the well-known greater amberjack.

Name - It was once placed in genus *Heteraxine*.

Diagnostic Characters - The haptor is asymmetrical with a longer row of larger clamps and a shorter row of smaller ones. The space between the lateral rows of dark vitellaria (containing internal organs), is dumbbell-shaped with large numbers of eggs above and large numbers of testes below.

Records - Five occurred in greater amberjack off Miami, Florida, USA (USNPC 37730-1).

Geographic Range - Unknown.

Location in Host - Gill filaments.

Length - 8.0-10.0 mm.
Host Specificity - Unknown.

Cemocotyle carangis (MacCallum)

This elongate gillworm was thought to only occur in blue runner, but we have seen it on 3 other species of jacks.
Name - *Cemocotyle borinquenensis* is a synonym described from Puerto Rico by Price (1962) from a fish he identified as green jack, *Caranx caballus* Gunther, a Pacific fish which does not exist in Puerto Rico. He also redescribed *C. carangis*.
Diagnostic Characters - The anterior end of this parasite is wider than the "neck" and has 2 sucker-like organs in the lateral margins. The clamps on the haptor are in 2 rows, a short row with 11-14 clamps and a long row with 36 clamps. The genital opening is surrounded by spines.
Records - We found 1 in 3 of 15 bar jack; 1 in a blue runner; 1-15 in 5 of 9 crevalle jack (USNPC 82581, 85935); and 2 in 1 of 17 horse-eye jack from various localities around Puerto Rico; and 10 in a crevalle jack from Dauphin Island, Alabama, USA. Two occurred in a blue runner from Woods Hole, Massachusetts (USNPC 35170,37735); 4-13 in 2 from the New York Aquarium (USNPC 37737); 68 from Alligator Harbor, Florida, USA; and from Mexico.
Geographic Range - Western Atlantic. Our collections are the first in the insular Caribbean.
Life History - This worm was not in 22 immature crevalle jack (3-6 cm long) from 4 localities near Dauphin Island, Alabama. It may only parasitize adults.
Associations - Four species of gillworms occur together on jacks of the genus *Caranx*. The intensities of infection that we found on these fish are as follows:

LOCALITY:	Puerto Rico								Alabama
HOST:	bar jack			blue runner	horse-eye jack	crevalle jack			crevalle jack
NUMBER OF HOSTS:	4	2	1	1	4	3	1	1	1
GILLWORMS SPECIES:	NUMBER OF GILLWORM SPECIMENS PER HOST								
Cemocotyle carangis	-	1	1	1	-	1-4	15	3	10
Cemocotyle noveboracensis	-	-	-	-	1-2	1-2	-	2	15
Allopyragraphorus incomparabilis	1-3	3-4	2	3	1	1-4	2	1	15
Protomicrocotyle mirabilis	3	1-3	-	-	1-3	1-3	6	-	25

Location in Host - Gill filaments.
Length - 3.7-12.0 mm.

Host Specificity - This worm was thought to only occur in blue runner, but we have seen it on 3 additional jack species. It is genus specific (*Caranx*), and is a primary parasite of blue runner. In Puerto Rico it is also a primary parasite of crevalle jack and a secondary parasite of bar jack and horse-eye jack. Bar jack, crevalle jack and horse-eye jack are new hosts. An immature worm in a pompano, *Trachinotus carolinus* (Linnaeus), from the New York Aquarium was probably an accidental infection (USNPC 37742).

Cemocotyle noveboracensis (Price)

This parasite was thought to occur only in crevalle jack, but also occurs in horse-eye jack in Puerto Rico.
Name - It was redescribed by Price (1962).
Diagnostic Characters - This worm is shaped like an upright vacuum cleaner. It is similar to *C. carangis* but differs by having a larger number of clamps on each side of the haptor (43-57 and 15-17). Slightly more clamps were found on the long side in local specimens than had been reported previously.
Records - One to 6 occurred in 6 of 9 crevalle jack (USNPC 84688), and 1-4 in 8 of 17 horse-eye jack from localities in Puerto Rico. One to 5 worms were on 14 of 96 adult and 1-15 on 29 of 50 subadult crevalle jack from Venezuela; on crevalle jack from New York (USNPC 37738-41) and Florida, USA, and Mexico.
Geographic Range - Western Atlantic (not confirmed from the Atlantic coast of South America). Our collections are the first in the insular Caribbean.
Life History - This worm did not occur in 22 immature crevalle jack (3-6 cm long) from 4 localities around Dauphin Island, Alabama; or in 10 immature horse-eye jack (3-7 cm long) from 3 localities around Puerto Rico. It may only parasitize adults.
Associations - See *C. carangis*. This worm occurred with *Protomicrocotyle mirabilis*, *Allopyragraphorus incomparabilis* and *Cemocotylella elongata* in crevalle jack from Venezuela, but its numbers were only closely correlated with those of *C.elongata* (Bashirullah and Rodriguez 1992).
Location in Host - Gill filaments.
Length - Up to 4.5 mm.
Host Specificity - This worm was previously thought to only occur in crevalle jack, but we found it in this host and horse-eye jack from Puerto Rico (Bunkley-Williams and Williams 1995). It is genus specific (*Caranx*), a primary parasite of crevalle jack, and a secondary parasite of horse-eye jack.

Cemocotylella elongata (Meserve)

This worm has been found in crevalle jack from Venezuela and another jack from the Pacific coast of Panama.
Diagnostic characters - This parasite is similar to the 2 species of *Cemocotyle* described above. It differs by having fewer clamps on each side of the haptor

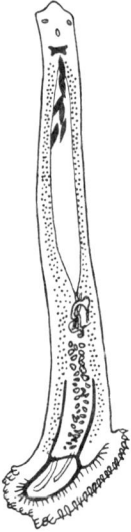

(24-25 clamps on one side and 4-5 on the other) and by lacking spines around the genital opening.

Records - One to 23 worms occurred on 57 of 96 adult, and 1-8 on 18 of 50 subadult, crevalle jacks from the east coast of Venezuela. It was described from a Pacific jack off Panama.

Geographic Range - Unknown.

Associations - This worm occurred with *Protomicrocotyle mirabilis*, *Allopyragraphorus incomparabilis* and *Cemocotyle noveboracensis* in crevalle jack from Venezuela, and its numbers were closely correlated with those of *A. incomparabilis* and *C. noveboracensis* (Bashirullah and Rodriguez 1992).

Location in Host - Gill filaments.

Length - 2.1-3.7 mm.

Host Specificity - It is a primary parasite of crevalle jack in the southern Caribbean.

Helixaxine winteri Caballero and Bravo-Hollis

This worm has both an unusual shape and distribution. Its distinctive haptoral clamps are situated on peduncles of tissue, and it has only been found from 2 Mexican states.

Diagnostic Characters - This small worm has a haptor that is curled and is nearly as long as the length of the worm. The clamps on the haptor are elongate in shape and are situated on small peduncles of tissue.

Records - Six occurred in an unstated number of horse-eye jack from Tuxpan, Veracruz and 13 in an unstated number of crevalle jack from Campeche, Campeche, Mexico.

Geographic Range - Unknown.

Ecology - Fewer jacks were collected from Campeche, but they had more worms. The infection levels could have been due to differences in habitat or season (June in Campeche, November in Tuxpan).

Location in Host - Gill filaments.

Length - 1.4-2.1 mm.

Host Specificity - Only known from crevalle jack.

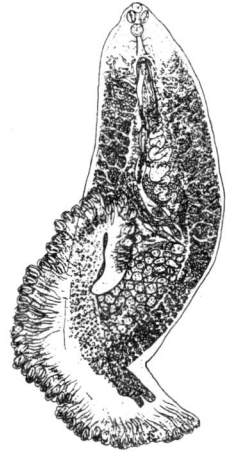

Allopyragraphorus incomparabilis (MacCallum)

This worm has a distinctive fish-tail-shaped haptor. It is found in the gills of jacks throughout the western Atlantic.

Name - *Allopyragraphorus hippos* (Hargis) only differs from *A. incomparabilis* in body size and extent of vitellaria. The smaller worms (2.9-3.3 mm) on which the description was based were probably less mature and had less developed vitellaria. We consider these 2 species to be the same. It was redescribed by Hargis (1957).

Diagnostic Characters - It has an S-curled, wedge-shaped (or fish-tail-shaped) haptor with 62-89 pairs of attachment clamps arranged in a double row. The clamps are not located on stalks. There are 56-75 testes.

Records - One to 5 occurred in 10 of 15 bar jacks from various localities around Puerto Rico (USNPC 85297, 85299), 1 in a bar jack from Desecheo Island, and 1-3 in 4 bar jack from Mona Island; 3 in a blue runner from La Parguera (USNPC 85942), and 1 in 1 of 2 blue runner from Aguadilla; 1-4 in 6 of 9 crevalle jack (USNPC 82580); 1 in 7 of 17 horse-eye jack from various localities around Puerto Rico. From 1-26 worms were found on 66 of 96 adult and 1-11 on 23 of 50 subadult crevalle jacks from the east coast of Venezuela. Five occurred in a bar jack from the New York Aquarium; this fish had been collected from Key West, Florida (USNPC 36528); 13 in 7 crevalle jack from Alligator Harbor, Florida, and 10 in 2 of 10 crevalle jack from Port Aransas, Texas, USA.

Geographic Range - Western Atlantic.

Life History - This worm did not occur in 22 immature crevalle jack (3-6 cm long) from 4 localities around Dauphin Island, Alabama; in 10 immature horse-eye jack (3-7 cm long) from 3 localities around Puerto Rico; or in 78 juvenile crevalle jack (fork length 4.0-11.0 cm) in Venezuela. It may only parasitize adults and subadults. Bashirullah and Rodriguez (1992) suggested that juvenile crevalle jack are found in inshore, shallow areas isolated from the adult jacks infected with gillworms.

Associations - See *Cemocotyle carangis* and *C. noveboracensis*.   It almost always occurred with *Cemocotylella elongata* on Venezuelan crevalle jack.

Location in Host - Gill filaments.

Length - 2.9-5.0 mm.

Host Specificity - This worm is a characteristic parasite of crevalle jack and horse-eye jack.   Too few collections are available to determine its status on other jacks. This parasite is genus specific (*Caranx*). Blue runner is a new host for this parasite. Bunkley-Williams and Williams (1995) reported horse-eye jack as a new host.

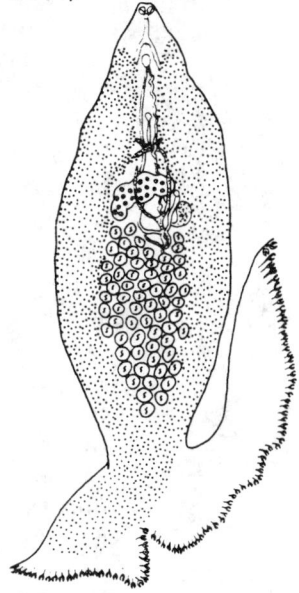

Hexostoma euthynni Meserve

This worm parasitizes the gills of 3 species of little tunas around the world.

Name - This worm has also been placed in genus *Neohexostoma*. *H. macracanthum* Fujii, *H. pricei* Koratha, and *N. kawakawa* Yamaguti are synonyms. It was redescribed by Millemann (1956).

Diagnostic Characters - This elongate worm is narrow at the anterior end and has a narrowed "waist" near the anterior 1/3 of the body. It has a haptor with 8 clamps, all equal in size, arranged in 2 rows along the lateral borders. The clamps have a distinctive X-shaped sclerite in the middle. Two pair of larval anchors can be seen on the posterior end between the rows of clamps. Rohde (1980) described the ceca of this worm.

Records - We found 1-2 in 3 of 6 little tunny from La Parguera, Puerto Rico (USNPC 82598); and 1 in a little tunny from Dauphin Island, Alabama. Two occurred in a little tunny from the Dry Tortugas off Florida (USNPC 36890), 3 in 1 from Louisiana, and from Chesapeake Bay; 4 in 2 of 10 Atlantic bonito from Port Aransas, Texas (USNPC 54761), USA. This worm has often been reported in little tunnies (*Euthynnus* spp.) from various localities in the Pacific including Hawaii, USA, (USNPC 63671, SY No. 172) and the Great Barrier Reef, Australia (USNPC 74151); and 4 in a yellowfin tuna from Hawaii.

Geographic Range - Worldwide. Our collections are the first in the Caribbean.

Location in Host - Gill filaments.

Length - 3.4-8.4 mm.

Host Specificity - This worm is almost genus specific (*Euthynnus*), and occurs in all 3 species in the genus (little tunny; kawakawa, *Euthynnus affinis* (Cantor); and black skipjack, *Euthynnus lineatus* Kishinouye). The single records of light infections in an Atlantic bonito and yellowfin tuna may have been accidental.

Hexostoma lintoni Price

This is a mysterious worm of Atlantic bonito.

Name - Linton (1901, 1940) called this worm *Hexacotyle thynni* Delaroche [now *Hexostoma thynni* (Delaroche)], and deposited 1 specimen (USNPC 9641). Price (1961) described the deposited specimen as a new species.

Diagnostic Characters - This elongate worm has a narrow anterior end. The haptor has 4 pairs of clamps arranged in a row along the posterior border. The middle 2 clamps are about 1/2 as large as the other 6 clamps. The clamps have a distinctive X-shaped sclerite in the middle of each.

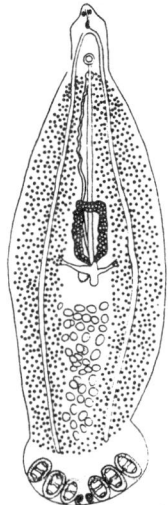

Records - One each occurred in 2 Atlantic bonito from Woods Hole, Massachusetts, USA (USNPC 9641).

Geographic Range - Unknown.

Location in Host - Mouth. Other species in this genus occur in the gills. This odd location also makes the validity of the worm questionable. Atlantic bonito could be a false host in which a worm was dislodged from a prey fish and attached in the mouth of this predator.

Length - 5.0-7.4 mm

Host Specificity - This worm has only been found in Atlantic bonito, but so rarely that it could be an accidental parasite.

Detection - Please look in the mouth of Atlantic bonito for this tiny to small worm, any collections will help resolve this mystery.

Protomicrocotyle mirabilis (MacCallum)

This asymmetrical worm is found from Chesapeake Bay to the Caribbean.

Name - This worm was redescribed by Koratha (1955b) and by Caballero and Bravo-Hollis (1965).

Diagnostic Characters - It has an elongate body with 4 small clamps which appear to be on the side of the body anterior of the broad haptor. The larval anchors are widely separated and located at the posterior border of the haptor.

Records - One to 3 occurred in 6 of 15 bar jack (USNPC 85298); 1-6 in 8 of 9 crevalle jack (USNPC 82534, 82663); and 1-3 in 11 of 17 horse-eye jack from various localities around Puerto Rico. One to 111 were found on 94 of 96 adult, and 1-39 in 48 of 50 subadult, crevalle jacks from the east coast of Venezuela. It has also been found in crevalle jack from Alligator Harbor, Florida; Texas; Chesapeake Bay, USA; and the west coast of Africa; and in horse-eye jack from Mexico.

Geographic Range - Atlantic.

Life History - This worm did not occur in 22 immature crevalle jack (3-6 cm long) from 4 localities around Dauphin Island, Alabama; or in 10 immature horse-eye jack (3-7 cm long) from 3 localities around Puerto Rico. It may only parasitize adults.

Associations - See *Cemocotyle carangis* and *C. noveboracensis*.

Location in Host - Gill filaments.

Size - Up to 5.5 mm long.

Host Specificity - This worm is genus specific (*Caranx*), and a characteristic parasite of crevalle jack. It is also a primary parasite of horse-eye jack, and a secondary parasite of bar jack.

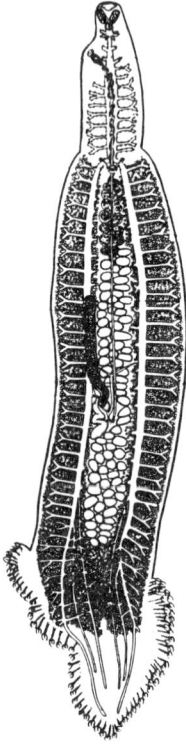

Pseudochauhanea sphyraenae Yamaguti

This arrow-shaped parasite occurs in light infections on the gills of great barracuda around the world.

Diagnostic Characters - The body is elongate, narrow anteriorly, and abruptly wider at level of vagina. The haptor is V-shaped with unequal rows of clamps, 28-50 on one side 27-37 on the other. No larval anchors are present on the haptor.

Records - We found 6 in a great barracuda from Mona Island; 3-6 in 23 of 33 from various localities around Puerto Rico (USNPC 86632); 1 in 1 from Great Inagua, Bahamas; and 3 in 1 of 2 from Dauphin Island, Alabama, USA (USNPC). It has also been reported from Key Biscayne, Florida, and Hawaii, USA (USNPC SY No. 16).

Geographic Range - Worldwide. Our collections are the first records in the Caribbean and the Gulf of Mexico.

Associations - It occurred on the gills of great barracuda in Hawaii with *Vallisiopsis sphyraenae* Yamaguti, but this second worm has not been found in the Atlantic.

Location in Host - Gill filaments.

Length - 4.4-10.0 mm.

Host Specificity - This worm is only found in great barracuda, and it is a primary parasite of this host.

Pseudaxine mexicana Meserve

This parasite, with a sombrero-shaped haptor, infects Spanish mackerels.

Name - The broad, wide haptor looks a bit like a Mexican sombrero. This shape plus a distribution largely on both sides of Mexico makes the name, "*mexicana*", appropriate. *Pseudaxine texana* Koratha is a synonym. It has also been placed in genus *Mexicotyle*.

Diagnostic Characters - It has a distinctive haptor with the simple anchors of the larva still present on one side and 37-56 clamps along the posterior border. The clamps sometimes appeared to curl around and form a double row on the side opposite the simple anchors.

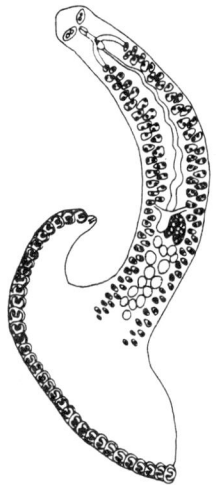

Records - We found 1 each in 7, and 2-4 in 2 of 35 cero from La Parguera (USNPC 82660); 1-15 in 9 of 14 king mackerel from various localities around Puerto Rico; and 9-20 in 2 of 4 king mackerel from Dauphin Island, Alabama, USA. This worm occurred in a king mackerel from Puerto de Veracruz, Veracruz, Mexico. It has been reported in Spanish mackerel from Florida, Louisiana, Texas (USNPC 54758), Chesapcake Bay, USA, and in other Spanish mackerels from the Pacific coast of Mexico.

Geographic Range - Western North Atlantic and the eastern Pacific. Our collections are the first in the Caribbean.

Associations - We found 1-4 *P. mexicana* with 1-11 *Thoracocotyle crocea* and 1-4 *Gotocotyla acanthophallus* in 3 cero; and 1 with 1 *G. acanthophallus* in 1 cero from Puerto Rico. Fifteen and 6 occurred with 6 and 25 *G. acanthophallus* and 1 and 2 *Scomberocotyle scomberomori* in 2 king mackerel; and 1-10 with 2-19 *G. acanthophallus* in 7 other king mackerel from Puerto Rico. Nine were associated with 18 *G. acanthophallus* and 1 *S. scomberomori* in a king mackerel from Alabama. On Spanish mackerels in Puerto Rico, *P. mexicana* and *G. acanthophallus* always occurred together when more than one worm was found. In 9 cero there was only a single worm.

Location in Host - Gill filaments.

Length - 1.9-5.5 mm; 3.0-5.0 mm (Puerto Rico); 3.8-5.5 mm (Alabama); 3.5-3.9 mm (Mexico).

Host Specificity - This worm is genus specific (*Scomberomorus*). It is a primary parasite of king mackerel and Spanish mackerel, but a secondary parasite of cero.

Neothoracocotyle acanthocybii (Meserve)

This gillworm with wrap-around clamps is found on wahoo around the world. The consistently heavy infections may damage this important sport fish.

Name - This worm was redescribed by Yamaguti (1968).

Diagnostic Characters - The haptor is wrapped around the elongate body. The 223-245 clamps occur in approximately equal rows.

Records - We found 10-60 in 15 wahoo from various localities around Puerto Rico (USNPC 82582); and 50-100 in 4 wahoo from Dauphin Island, Alabama, USA. It also occurs in this host from Chesapeake Bay, USA, and the Pacific.

Geographic Range - Worldwide. Our collections are the first in the Caribbean and the Gulf of Mexico.

Associations - It occurred in a wahoo with *Caballerocotyla manteri*.

Location in Host - These worms are consistently found near the distal ends of the gill filaments of the first 2 arches.

Length - 6.3-11.1 mm.

Host Specificity - It is only found on wahoo, and is a characteristic parasite.

Significance to Sport Fishing - A burden of 50-100 of these relatively large worms must damage this important sport fish. The effect of these consistently heavy infections should be studied.

Scomberocotyle scomberomori (Koratha)

This elongate worm with a fish-tail haptor very lightly infects the gills of Spanish mackerels.

Name - Originally placed in genus *Heteraxine*.

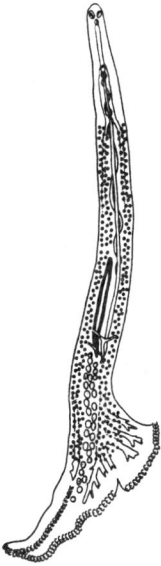

Diagnostic Characters - This elongate worm has a broad, fish-tail-shaped haptor with 2 uneven rows of 85 and 50 clamps. In the Puerto Rican worms, the long side had 84 clamps.

Records - We found 1-2 in 2 of 14 king mackerel from various localities around Puerto Rico; and 1 in 1 of 4 king mackerel, and 1 in each in 2 of 10 Spanish mackerel from Dauphin Island, Alabama, USA. It has also been reported in king mackerel and Spanish mackerel from Alligator Harbor (USNPC 37494) and Tampa Bay, Florida, and in Spanish mackerel from Port Aransas, Texas (USNPC 54757) and Chesapeake Bay, USA.

Geographic Range - Western Atlantic (not confirmed from the Atlantic coast of South America). Our collections are the first in the Caribbean.

Associations - One and 2 *S. scomberomori* were found with 15 and 6 *Pseudaxine mexicana* and 6 and 25 *Gotocotyla acanthophallus* in 2 king mackerel from Puerto Rico. One was associated with 9 *P. mexicana* and 18 *G. acanthophallus* in a king mackerel from Alabama.

Location in Host - Gill filaments.

Length - 5.5-6.5 mm.

Host Specificity - This worm only occurs on Spanish mackerel and king mackerel. It is genus specific (*Scomberomorus*), but occurs so infrequently and in low numbers that it is a secondary parasite of these hosts.

Thoracocotyle crocea MacCallum

This parasite is almost all haptor. It occurs, often sporadically, and usually in low numbers, on the gills of Spanish mackerels.

Name - It was redescribed by McMahon (1964). *Thoracocotyle paradoxica* Meserve is a synonym.

Diagnostic Characters - The haptor dominates the worm and looks like the skirt of a high-kicking dancer. It is actually one side of the body of this worm, with the 7 large testes appearing to be in the area of the "haptor". It has 2 rows of 17-21 clamps.

Records - We found 1 each in 16, and 11 in 1 of 35 cero from various localities around Puerto Rico (USNPC 82662). It also occurred in Spanish mackerel and king mackerel from Florida; 1 in 1 of 5 king mackerel from Beaufort, North Carolina; 10 in 1 from Grand Isle Louisiana, and 90 in Spanish mackerel from Chesapeake Bay; the New York Aquarium, USA; and Mexico.

Geographic Range - Western Atlantic (not confirmed from the Atlantic coast of South America). Our collections are the first in the Caribbean.

Associations - One to 11 were found along with 1-4 *Pseudaxine mexicana* and 1-4 *Gotocotyla acanthophallus* in 3 cero from Puerto Rico.

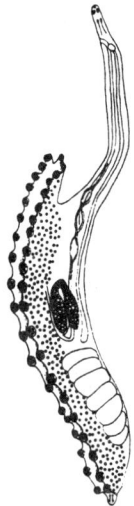

Ecology - This worm seems to occur sporadically, sometimes rarely and usually in low numbers. How this species survives under these conditions is a mystery.
Location in Host - Gill filaments.
Length - 1.0-4.5 mm.
Host Specificity - It is genus specific (*Scomberomorus*), but is at most only a secondary parasite of Spanish mackerels.

Gotocotyla acanthophallus (MacCallum and MacCallum)

This elongate worm with a long, V-shaped haptor occurs on the gills of Spanish mackerels in the western Atlantic.

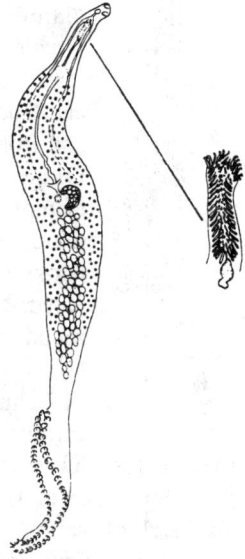

Name - *Microcotyle scomberomori* Koratha is a synonym.
Diagnostic Characters - This parasite has an extended "V" shaped haptor with an even number of clamps along each arm of the "V" and 60 testes in the posterior half of the body. The cirrus and genital atrium are armed with a series of spines of similar lengths in an arrangement that looks like the bristles of a test-tube brush and is characteristic of this worm.
Records - We found 1 each in 7, and 4 in 1, of 35 cero from La Parguera (USNPC 82661); 2-25 in 9 of 14 king mackerel from various localities around Puerto Rico (USNPC 82594, 86623); and 18-96 in 2 of 3 king mackerel from Dauphin Island, Alabama, USA. Heavy infections were reported in king mackerel and Spanish mackerel from Florida and Louisiana, and light to moderate infections from Port Aransas, Texas (USNPC 54756), and Chesapeake Bay, USA. This worm has also been reported in bluefish, *Pomatomus saltatrix* (Linnaeus), from the Atlantic coast of the USA.
Geographic Range - Western Atlantic (not confirmed from the Atlantic coast of South America). Our collections are the first in the Caribbean.
Associations - One to 4 *G. acanthophallus* occurred with 1-4 *Pseudaxine mexicana* and 1-11 *Thoracocotyle crocea* in 3 cero from Puerto Rico. Six and 25 *G. acanthophallus* were found with 15 and 6 *P. mexicana* and 1 and 2 *Scomberocotyle scomberomori* in 2 king mackerel; and 2-19 *G. acanthophallus* with 1-10 *P. mexicana* in 7 other king mackerel from Puerto Rico. Eighteen were associated with 9 *P. mexicana* and 1 *S. scomberomori* in 1, and 96 with 20 *P. mexicana* in another king mackerel from Alabama. On Spanish mackerels in Puerto Rico, *P. mexicana* and *G. acanthophallus* always occurred together when more than one worm was found. In 9 cero there was only a single worm.
Location in Host - Gill filaments.
Length - 3.3-7.0 mm. Published lengths were 5.5-7.0 mm, but our measurements were 3.3-6.2 mm (Puerto Rico) and 3.8-6.9 mm (Alabama).

Host Specificity - This worm is genus specific (*Scomberomorus*). It is a primary and possibly a characteristic parasite of cero, king mackerel and Spanish mackerel. Cero is a new host One recorded from a striped bass, *Morone saxatilis* (Walbaum), from the New York Fish Market, was probably accidental or erroneous.

Grubea cochlear Diesing

This oddly asymmetrical worm is found in the gills of Atlantic and chub mackerel.

Name - Linton (1940) described this worm as *Pleurocotyle scombri* (Gervis and van Beneden) and it and *G. pneumatophori* Price; *Grubea* sp. of Loftin, 1960; *Grubea* sp. of Rohde, 1984; and *Grubea* sp. of Wagner, 1975, are synonyms. Mamaev (1982) and Rohde (1987) redescribed this worm.

Diagnostic Characters - This is an elongate worm with 4 clamps on one side of the haptor and a single, smaller clamp on the other side. The sizes of clamps and the number of genital hooks vary among specimens from the same host and locality.

Records - It occurred in a blue runner from Florida, and 1 was found in a chub mackerel from Woods Hole, Massachusetts, USA (USNPC 8160). It was also found in Atlantic mackerel and 1-2 in 7 chub mackerel from Brazil; southwest Atlantic; Atlantic off Europe; 1-2 in 2 Atlantic mackerel from the Mediterranean; east, south and southwest coasts of Africa; and the eastern Pacific. Oddly, this worm does not occur in Great Britain (Dawes 1968). More than 1000 Atlantic mackerel of various sizes, examined at different times of the year, from southwest England had none of these worms. It apparently occurs sporadically and in very light infections.

Geographic Range - Atlantic and adjacent Indo-Pacific. Rohde (1987) summarized the distribution records of this worm.

Associations - In 100 Atlantic mackerel off Europe, only 3 were infected with this worm, but 40 had *Kuhnia scombri*.

Location in Host - Gill filaments.

Length - 7.5-15.0 mm.

Host Specificity - This worm is genus specific (*Scomber*) to the 2 Atlantic hosts, but is apparently replaced by *Grubea australis* Rohde in the third fish species of the genus, slimy mackerel, *Scomber australasicus* (Cuvier), in the Indo-Pacific. The single records in blue runner and eastern Pacific bonito, *Sarda chiliensis* (Cuvier), probably represent false or accidental hosts.

Kuhnia scombercolias Nasir and Fuentes Zambrano

It occurs sporadically and in low numbers in mackerels worldwide.

Name - This worm was confused with *K. sprostonae* until recently. *Kuhnia arabica* Mamaev and Parukhin is a synonym.

Diagnostic Characters - This is an elongate worm with 4 small clamps along each lateral border of the relatively small haptor that is not clearly separated from the body. It is similar to *K. sprostonae*, but differs by having anchors shorter than 50 μm and with bases shorter than the rest of the anchor, occurring on the gills instead of the pseudobranchs, and being slightly smaller. Rohde (1989) and Rohde and Watson (1985) studied the effect of geographic variation on the anchors, shape and size of this worm. It shows considerable variability in the lengths of the anchors and genital hooks.

Records - One to 2 occurred in 2 of 11 chub mackerel from the Gulf of Cariaco, Venezuela; and Brazil in the Atlantic, and on this host and slimy mackerel from the Indo-Pacific.

Geographic Range - Worldwide. Rohde (1989) summarized the known distribution records.

Associations - This worm is sometimes found with *K. scombri* on the gills. *Kuhnia sprostonae* also occurs on the pseudobranchs. There are always many more *K. scombri* than *K. scombercolias* on the gills.

Location in Host - Gill filaments.

Length - 1.1-1.4 mm.

Host Specificity - This worm is genus specific (Scomber), and occurs in 2 of the 3 species.

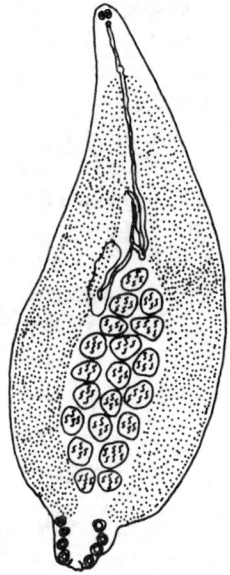

Kuhnia scombri (Kuhn)

This cosmopolitan parasite of mackerels is the best studied gillworm in big game fishes.

Name - This worm was redescribed by Price (1961) and Nasir and Fuentes-Zambrano (1983).

Diagnostic Characters - It is an elongate worm with 4 small clamps along each lateral border of the relatively small haptor that is distinctly separate from the body. Rohde (1991) and Rohde and Watson (1985) studied the effect of geographic variation on its shape and size, and Rohde (1987) variation in clamp sclerites.

Records - One to 2 occurred in 2 of 11 chub mackerel from the Gulf of Cariaco, Venezuela; and from southern Brazil. This worm was also found on Atlantic mackerel and chub mackerel from Chesapeake Bay; Newport, Rhode Island; off Cape Hatteras, North Carolina; and Woods Hole, Massachusetts, USA; Canada; the eastern and southwestern Atlantic; Mediterranean; and chub mackerel from the Indo-Pacific.

Geographic Range - Worldwide. Rohde (1989) summarized the known distribution records.

Life History - Euzet (1957) described the oncomiracidium that hatches from the egg, Llewellyn (1956) characterized the location on the gills and the larval development and Finlayson (1982) reported the reproductive processes of this worm.
Associations - See *Grubea cochlear* and *K. scombercolias*.
Location in Host - Gills at the base of the filaments. Llewellyn (1956) studied gill microecology, and Rohde (1991) and Rohde and Watson (1985) the effect of geographic variation and microhabitat.
Length - 1.3-6.6 mm. This worm becomes sexually mature at a length of 3.5 mm, but continues to grow.
Host Specificity - It is genus specific (Scomber), and occurs in all 3 species.
Damage to Host - Sproston (1945) and Llewellyn (1957) described the attachment of clamps on the gills of the host.

Miscellaneous Gillworms

Dionchus remorae (MacCallum) - This worm differs from *D. agassizi* because it has 2 anchors on the haptor that are smaller than 1/5 the diameter of the haptor. The blade of these anchors is longer than their base. One worm occurred on a crevalle jack from the New York Aquarium. Light to moderate infections were found on inshore remora worldwide. This parasite and *D. agassizi* occur together on the gills of inshore remora. This worm is probably a characteristic parasite of inshore remora. The record from crevalle jack was probably accidental and due to the artificial environment, although it has been reported from jacks in the Indian Ocean.

Kuhnia sprostonae Price - It may occur worldwide on mackerels (*Scomber* spp.), but it has not been found in the western Atlantic (see *K. scombercolias*).

Neobenedenia girellae (Hargis) - This highly damaging gillworm has been introduced into Hawaii, Hong Kong, Okinawa and throughout the main islands of Japan with introductions of greater amberjack for mariculture. It was first thought to be *N. melleni* (MacCallum), a dangerous worm from the western Atlantic. If *N. girellae* is introduced to the western Atlantic, big game fishes could be affected. The worm apparently lacks specificity.

Pricea minimae Chauhan - This worm was described from the gills of "*Thynus pelamys*" from Bombay, India. The host is usually thought to have been a skipjack tuna, but Silas (1962) suggested that this fish is almost never landed in Bombay, and the host must have been another scombrid.

Tristomella lintoni (Price) - This species was reported from the gills of a skipjack tuna caught off Woods Hole, Massachusetts, USA. It was described from a single immature specimen which was not in good condition (USNPC 4878). Despite the occurrence of this worm and "*Capsala laevis*" in checklists of western Atlantic skipjack tuna, we find no valid records of capsalids on this fish in our area. The specimen described by Price (1960) was probably the result of accidental infection and its status must remain uncertain.

Tristomella onchidiocotyle (Setti) - MacCallum collected an immature capsalid in the gills of a "*Thunnus thunnus*-horse mackerel" (=bluefin tuna) from Woods Hole, Massachusetts, USA (USNPC 35644). Price (1939) described this worm as a new species *Capsala maccallumi*, suggested that it was probably identical to *C. onchidiocotyle*, but listed the host as "little tunny" without explanation. The haptor of this worm extends beyond the body outline. Testes are numerous and extend beyond the field between the ceca. The anchors have a distinct hook on the end. It occurred on bluefin tuna in the Mediterranean and bigeye tuna off west Africa, probably on bluefin tuna off the Atlantic coast of the USA and throughout the Atlantic. This parasite occurs on the gills and is 2.6 mm long. It is probably genus (*Thunnus*) and tribe specific. This worm needs to be redescribed and more collections are needed in the western Atlantic to resolve the mystery of its distribution.

CESTODA (TAPEWORMS)

Tapeworms or cestodes form a large class of the flatworms or platyhelminths. The common name comes from the long series of body segments which resemble a tape measure. Most adult tapeworms look like long, flat cooked noodles. Most larval forms look like the tiny pieces of noodle that stick in the colander. A giant, broad tapeworm that lives in the body cavity of freshwater fishes in Europe is apparently routinely eaten by humans who mistake it for parts of the fish! Tapeworms can reduce growth and affect reproductive success of fishes. Some that infect humans occur as immature or larval forms in fishes. A small-boat fishery for tunas on the northwest coast of Puerto Rico was closed by the government because of reports of "wormy" flesh in these food fishes. When we were contacted to examine these parasites, we found that they were larval tapeworms, and recommended that the fishery be immediately reopened. We knew that previous experimental attempts to infect mammals with similar larvae failed because the parasites mature only in sharks and rays. The fishery was quickly reopened, averting major losses to local fishermen. We occasionally receive similar cases of wormy filets from individuals. People do not like seeing larval tapeworms moving around in the flesh of their fish, but those in Puerto Rican fishes are relatively harmless (particularly when cooked).

More than 5000 species of tapeworms are known. Adults range from less than a millimeter to more than 30 meters in length. Tapeworms usually consist of a chain of segments (proglottids) each with a set of female and male reproductive organs. The segments are continuously budded in the anterior portion of the body or neck, and enlarge and mature as they slowly move posteriorly. The scolex or "head" on the anterior end is usually armed with various combinations of suckers, hooks, bothridia (outgrowths), or bothria (sucking grooves) for attachment in the host intestine. Eggs escape through pores or a whole mature egg-filled segment may break off and pass out of the intestine. A successful tapeworm may produce millions of eggs over its lifetime.

Eggs or their hatched larvae (ciliated coracidia or unciliated hexacanth or oncosphere) are eaten by the first intermediate host (insect, crustacean or annelid) and become elongate procercoids. This host is subsequently eaten by a vertebrate (second intermediate host) and the larvae develop into partially differentiated plerocercoids or plerocerci. Plerocercoids can be passed from one host to another when an infected fish is eaten by another fish. Feeding infected viscera to fish therefore can greatly concentrate or increase the intensity of infection by these worms. We have seen this practice cause a superinfection in caged red hind, *Epinephelus guttatus* Linnaeus, in Puerto Rico, and in cage cultured fishes raised in the northern Gulf of Mexico. If viscera must be used as fish food, it should be cooked or frozen for several days to kill parasites. When the correct final or definitive vertebrate host eats the second intermediate host the adult tapeworms develop in the intestine.

Most tapeworms have both female and male sex organs in each proglottid. A few have separate sexes. They occur in all kinds of vertebrates and in all habitats around the world. All tapeworms are permanent parasites. The intestine of these worms has been lost thus food from the gut of the host is absorbed directly through the body wall. Few species of adult tapeworms are found in marine bony fishes and only 2 species occur in big game fishes. In contrast, many species of larval tapeworms are found in the intestinal tract, often in large numbers, and a few are encapsulated in the tissues of marine bony fishes including big game fishes. Most of these larval forms are found as adults in sharks or rays. A necropsy is necessary to find adults or larvae in the gut and encapsulated larvae in internal organs. Adult tapeworms can be relaxed in tap water until they no longer react to touch, and preserved in 5% formalin. Although some fish tapeworms can mature in humans, none of those in marine fishes infect people. We will consider the adult tapeworms first and the larval forms (*) second.

Reference - No recent guide to the species of tapeworms exists. "How to know the tapeworms" (Schmidt 1970) is a semi-popular guide to the genera and Schmidt (1986) is a more technical revision which includes lists of the known species. Khalil, Jones and Bray (1994) update the genera and higher classification of tapeworms, but do not list the species [see our review of this book (Williams and Bunkley-Williams 1995)].

Classification and Contents

_____
*Larval forms

Bothriocephalus manubriformis (Linton)

    This giant tapeworm infects billfishes around the world. Very heavy infections of hundreds of large worms damage these important sport fishes.

Diagnostic Characters - This is a very large parasite. It has an elongate scolex with an apical disk and long bothria which are open at the anterior and posterior ends. The egg-filled segments (gravid proglottids) are wider than long and notched in the middle of their posterior margin. The posterior margin overlaps the anterior margin of the next proglottid (craspedote condition).

Records - We found 2-4 in 8 of 40 blue marlin, 3-4 in 2 of 3 white marlin, and more than 100 in a longbill spearfish off Puerto

Rico, and more than 50 in an Atlantic sailfish, and more than 100 in a white marlin off Dauphin Island, Alabama, USA. Numerous adults occurred in 3 of 4 Atlantic sailfish off Miami, Florida; 108 in an Atlantic sailfish and 12-52 in 4 white marlin from the southern Gulf of Mexico; 4-463 in 33 white marlin off Maryland, USA (USNPC 80329); more than 50 in a blue marlin (USNPC 4711) and 50-77 in 2 sailfish from Woods Hole, Massachusetts, USA; and 1-12 (average 4.8) in 52 of 63 black marlin off Queensland, Australia.

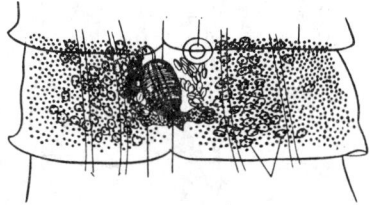

Geographic Range - Worldwide.

Life History - Tapeworms must live in the intestine for several years, to grow to 0.5-1.0 meters long. The preponderance of smaller worms suggests that competition of the adult worms or host immunity prevents most of these parasites from maturing.

Ecology - Fishes caught near shore have fewer immature tapeworms than those caught offshore suggesting that the last intermediate host in the life cycle may occur offshore.

Associations - Occasionally 3-5 tapeworms use the same perforation in the intestinal wall to penetrate and anchor their scolices in a capsule.

Location in Host - Intestine.

Length - Adults 130.0-1000.0 mm or longer (more than 1 meter); immature worm as small as 25.0 mm.

Host Specificity - It is family specific to billfishes. It may be a characteristic parasite of sailfishes and white marlin, but seems to occur more erratically in blue marlin. Many of the records in swordfish may be based on immature worms, or misidentifications, as some of the more careful and extensive studies have not found this worm in this host.

Damage to Host - Adult tapeworms have been blamed for retarded growth, weight loss and emaciation of billfishes. The effect of larval and immature worms has not been established, but they are much more abundant than adults in many cases. Four worms formed a deep pit in the anterior intestine of a white marlin from Puerto Rico.

Fistulicola plicatus (Rudolphi)

This characteristic parasite of swordfish must damage and limit the growth of this valuable fish.

Name - *Pseudeubothrium xiphiados* Yamaguti is a synonym. *Bothriocephalus truncatus* Leuckart and *Fistulicola xiphiae* (Gmelin) may be synonyms.

Diagnostic Characters - This is a very large parasite. The scolex has an apical disk and a rounded shallow bothrium on each side. The scolex may be replaced by an elongate and sometimes swollen pseudoscolex in worms embedded in the intestinal wall. Segments are short and have leaf-like lateral expansions.

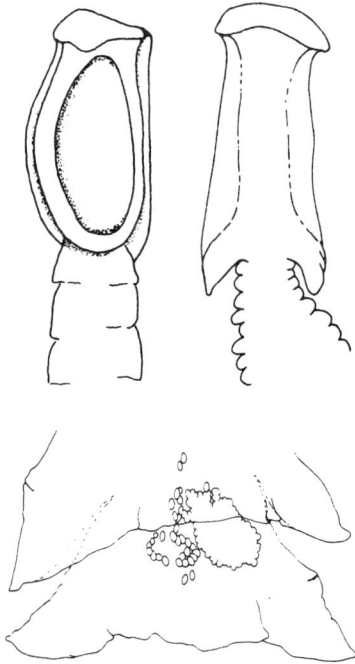

Records - Eight worms occurred in a swordfish off La Parguera, 1 in 1 off Guanica, and 6 in 1 off Humacao, Puerto Rico. One to 22 (average 5.5) occurred in 278 of 303 (ARC 2310), and 101 (average 4.2) in 24 swordfish from the northwest Atlantic; and 1-9 in 14 from Woods Hole, Massachusetts, USA (USNPC 4736, 8861).
Geographic Range - Worldwide.
Associations - Occasionally 3-5 tapeworms use the same perforation in the intestinal wall to penetrate and anchor their scolices in a capsule.
Location in Host - Intestine and rectum.
Length - Adult 75.0 mm to more than a meter.
Host Specificity - This parasite is only found in swordfish. It is a characteristic parasite of this host.
Damage to Host - Hogans et al. (1983) reported a maximum infection of 22 of these large tapeworms in a host. This should have been a sufficient parasite load to cause problems in a swordfish. However, they reported an average of 5.5 worms per host suggesting that few of these fish were this highly infected. Most perforations of the intestine occur in the rectum. Large thick host capsules are produced around the pseudoscolices of these worms. Even the tapeworms that do not penetrate the wall of the intestine produce irritation around their attachment positions. Blockage of the intestine by masses of these worms has been reported, but this needs to be confirmed.
Preparation for Study - Skillful dissection is necessary to obtain intact worms from capsules.

Larval Tapeworms

Almost all our knowledge about tapeworms concerns adults. The adult and larval forms of a tapeworm are seldom encountered in the same host species or even in the same scientific study, and larvae often share few features with the adult tapeworms. Thus, larvae are usually not mentioned or are considered only incidentally, incompletely and often erroneously. Few complete life cycles of fish tapeworms have ever been determined. Most larval forms in fishes have been "identified to species" by guessing which adult tapeworm the larvae resemble. These difficulties have caused larval forms to be under-identified (to class, order or genus), misidentified, or ignored completely. Thus the state of knowledge, is what could only be called "one hell of a confusing mess." We hope the following effort will be a framework to begin properly identifying these worms in big game fishes. Many more collections and examinations and much inspiration will be needed before we can understand the role larval tapeworms play in the health of these fishes.

Larval forms in big game fishes are third stage or plerocercoid larvae belonging to 4 orders of tapeworms. They fall into 2 categories: (1) those encapsulated in the tissues or body cavity, and (2) those in the gastrointestinal tract. A few plerocercoid larvae in the tissues are elongate unstructured *Bothriocephalus* spp. in simple capsules. But almost all are trypanorhynchid plerocerci with 4 hook covered tentacles in complex capsules composed of 3 layers: (1) an outer capsule produced by the host, (2) a blastocyst inside the capsule, and (3) a plerocercus larva inside one end of the blastocyst. A few capsules and/or blastocysts are so large and distinctive that they can be identified immediately to species. Unfortunately, most require careful measuring, dissection, and examination of the characters of each layer. The shape, thickness, color, location in the host, location of the blastocyst, and attachment of the capsule should be recorded and drawn. The capsule is dissected from the host tissue, placed in a container of saline, viewed with a dissection microscope and carefully opened to allow the blastocyst to escape. Some features are best seen while this form is alive and moving. The next step is to evert or pop out the scolex from the blastocyst. This requires experience, luck, or a large supply of capsules. Gentle pressure on the blastocyst with a blunt probe should pop out the scolex, but too much pressure may cause it to rupture into pieces. Either a "postlarva" with a tail (appendix) will separate from the blastocyst, or a "plerocercus" will evert on the end of the blastocyst, but remain attached. Larvae may be best seen in a wet mount viewed with a compound microscope. Some encapsulated larvae have ample characters to allow identification to species but many cannot be deciphered. In recently encapsulated larvae, characters may not be fully developed. Older capsules may contain dead larvae degenerated into dark, waxy masses or calcified and partially reabsorbed by the host. Mature postlarvae separate from capsules embedded in the outer layer of internal organs of fishes and are found free in the body cavity. Trypanorhynchid postlarvae and plerocerci have almost mature scolices similar to those found in the adult.

The second category of tapeworm larvae are those found free in the stomach and intestine of fishes. These postlarvae, plerocerci and capsules have been digested from invertebrates or fishes eaten by the host. Some of the larger larvae have distinctive attachment structures on the scolex that can be used to identify them to species. Unfortunately, the vast majority of these larvae are tiny tetraphyllid plerocercoids (see species summary) that are too indistinct to be identified to family, much less species. This tetraphyllid reputation for being difficult to identify is often and unjustifiably applied to all larval tapeworms in fishes. It has been used as an excuse to ignore this varied and fascinating group of parasites. These loose larvae in the alimentary canal of big game fishes are in false hosts. We do not know if they are quickly digested, pass out of the intestine, or if they remain longer and use big game fishes as intermediary hosts.

Most plerocercoid larvae have no specificity. Some are restricted to particular habitats or regions and show promise as biological tags to distinguish stocks of big game fishes and their migrations. If we knew more about their life cycles, they could potentially tell us what, when and where the fish ate, and possibly reveal a variety of other biological secrets.

We have attempted to distinguish larval tapeworms with obvious characters that can be seen with a hand lens or a dissection microscope. In some species, the hooks on the tentacles were used. This requires placing the larvae in wet mounts on microscope slides and viewing them with a compound microscope.

Larval tapeworms can be relaxed and preserved in steaming, 5% formalin; or relaxed in tap water and fixed in 5% formalin. Neither method assures that tentacles, important in the identification of trypanorhynchids, will always be fully everted so that their hooks can be seen. Lidocaine is used to evert the tentacles. The best insurance for success is to study many specimens.

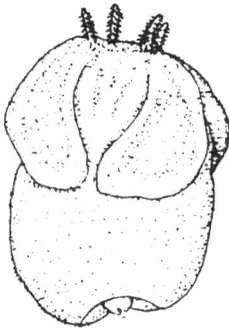

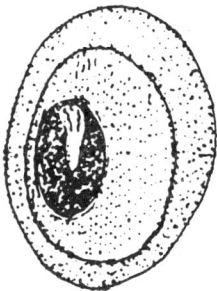

Nybelinia bisulcata (Linton)

This larval tapeworm is occasionally encapsulated in the stomach wall or is found as postlarvae in the intestine of big game fishes.

Diagnostic Characters - Most capsules are relatively small and oval and contain oval blastocysts. This worm has the characters of *Nybelinia* sp. listed below. The tiny tail is as long as wide and less than 1/4 the width of the body. Bothridia are broad, bean-shaped and longer than 1/2 the length of the body. Spine-like structures (microtriches) are visible on the margins of the bothridia. Tentacles are relatively short.

Records - One to 2 postlarvae occurred in 9 and 1-2 blastocysts in 3 of 40 Atlantic blue marlin and 1-3 postlarvae in 17 of 40 dolphin examined from various sites around Puerto Rico, and 14 and 27 capsules in 2 swordfish from off Guanica Bay, Puerto Rico. Capsules were very numerous in 3 of 5 dolphin off Miami, Florida; a few capsules and postlarvae in a cero, a few capsules in 1 of 8 cobia, 1 capsule in 1 of 15 crevalle jack, and 1 postlarva in a Spanish mackerel from Beaufort, North Carolina; 1-2 capsules occurred in 2 Atlantic mackerel and several capsules and a few postlarvae in 2 swordfish from Woods Hole, Massachusetts, USA. These larvae are more common in non-big game bony fishes, sharks and rays; and occasionally occur in squids.

Geographic Range - Possibly worldwide, but most records are from the U.S. Atlantic. Our collections are the first in the Caribbean.

Life History - The adult tapeworm occurs in sharks.

Location in Host - It is usually encapsulated in the stomach wall or on the sides of the stomach, and postlarvae are in the body cavity or in the intestine.

Length - Plerocercoid usually 0.4-1.2 mm, exceptionally to 20.0 mm, blastocyst 0.1-3.5 mm, capsule 0.2-4.8 mm.
Host Specificity - Atlantic blue marlin is a new host for this parasite.

Nybelinia lamonteae Nigrelli

A common larva in swordfish from the northwest Atlantic. Our records from Puerto Rico suggest that it may be more widespread and may occur in other hosts.

Diagnostic Characters - It has the characters of *Nybelinia* sp. below, but with fine spine-like structures (microtriches) visible along the margins of the bothridia. Tentacle sheaths are longer than the tentacles or the bulbs. Tentacle bulbs are more than 3 times as long as wide and are only slightly overlapped by bothridia.

Our specimens differ from the description of Nigrelli (1938) by having a bothridial area of the scolex that is rectangular, tentacle sheaths that curl near the bulbs, and a tail that is partially invaginated.

Records - One blastocyst occurred in a dolphin; and 1-2 postlarvae in 2 of 6 king mackerel from La Parguera, Puerto Rico (USNPC). One capsule was found in a swordfish from Nova Scotia, Canada; and 1-21 (average 2.8) postlarvae occurred in 154 of 303 swordfish from the northwest Atlantic (ARC 2314).

Geographic Range - Unknown. Our collections are the first in the Caribbean.
Life History - Nigrelli (1938) suggested that the adult of this worm could be *N. robusta* (Linton) which parasitizes rays and is encapsulated in shark remora.
Location in Host - These worms were found encapsulated in the mesenteries or as free postlarvae in the stomach.
Length - Plerocercoid 1.3-7.0 mm.

Host Specificity - Dolphin and king mackerel are new hosts.

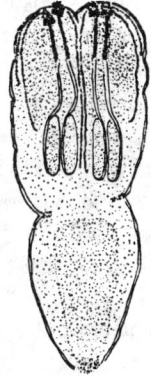

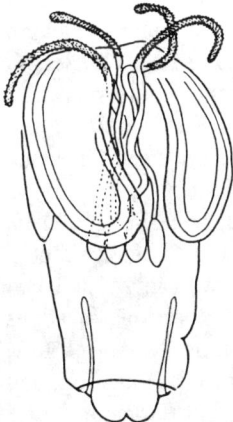

Nybelinia lingualis (Cuvier)

This larval tapeworm is occasionally encapsulated in the viscera or is found as postlarvae in the intestine of big game fishes.

Diagnostic Characters - This worm has all the characters of *Nybelinia* sp. listed below. The bothridia are bean-shaped and lack spines along the margins. Tentacle sheaths are approximately as long as the tentacles. Tentacle bulbs are about twice as long as wide and are largely covered by the bothridia.

Records - One blastocyst occurred in 1 of 2 skipjack tuna from off Arecibo, Puerto Rico (USNPC); and in swordfish from Woods Hole, Massachusetts, USA. The postlarvae occur commonly in bony fishes, sharks and rays.

Geographic Range - Possibly worldwide, but almost all records are European. Our collections are the first in the Caribbean.

Location in Host - Viscera (blastocysts) and intestinal tract (postlarvae).

Length - Postlarva 1.3-4.0 mm.

Host Specificity - Skipjack tuna is a new host.

Nybelinia sp.

Name - Several larval species are included under this name. In most cases, characteristics were not recorded and specimens were not deposited so they cannot be identified to species. Some of the larvae reported may have been the 3 species described above, but other species exist.

Diagnostic Characters - This postlarva has a short scolex and a short, usually invaginated tail. Four elongate bothridia are about 1/2 the length of the scolex. Tentacle bulbs extend posterior to the end of the bothridia. The posterior margins of the bothridia are free. The hooks are almost identical throughout the length of the tentacle. Extreme variations in shape typically occur.

Records - Six postlarvae occurred in 1 of 2 Atlantic blue marlin, 6-15 in 2 of 4 white marlin; 1-5 in 4 of 10 yellowfin tuna from the southern Gulf of Mexico; and 3-11 in 5 of 9 swordfish from the northwest Indian Ocean.

Geographic Range - Worldwide

Life History - The postlarvae are common in bony fishes and elasmobranchs.

Location in Host - Intestine.

Length - Postlarva 1.2-5.0 mm.

Tentacularia coryphaenae Bosc

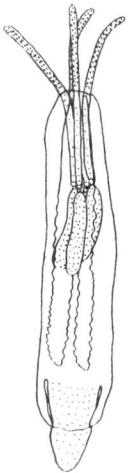

Larvae of this worm are encapsulated in a variety of big game and other bony fishes around the world.

Name - *Tentacularia bicolor* (Bartels) is a synonym.

Diagnostic Characters - This worm has all the characters of *Tentacularia* sp., noted below. In addition, the combined length of the tentacle sheaths and bulbs are about 1/3 to 1/2 the length of the bothridia. The bothridia vary from a uniform width throughout to tapering to a point on the posterior end.

Records - We found postlarvae in an albacore from Desecheo Island; 1-22 postlarvae in 25 and 1-3 blastocysts in 7 of 40 Atlantic blue marlin; 3 blastocysts in a blackfin tuna from Boqueron; 1-14 (average 6.1) postlarvae in 7 of 13 dolphin from La Parguera (USNPC); 1-100 blastocysts in 14 and 1 to many postlarvae in 22 of 40 dolphin from various localities around Puerto Rico; numerous blastocysts in 2 skipjack tuna from off Arecibo; 1 each in 1 of 3 wahoo from Boqueron, and 3 in a wahoo from Desecheo Island, Puerto Rico and 2-10 postlarvae in 3 of 5 dolphin from Dauphin Island, Alabama, USA. Numerous postlarvae were found in 2 of 5 dolphin and 1 of 2 king mackerel from Miami, Florida, USA; 1 capsule in 1 of 9 little tunny from Bermuda; 1 and few blastocysts in 2 of 6 Atlantic bonito; numerous capsules in a dolphin (USNPC 5483); and many in each of 4, 10 and 1 in 2, 3 in 1 (USNPC 4820), and 4 in 1 (USNPC 4829) swordfish from Woods Hole, Massachusetts, USA; swordfish off Nova Scotia, Canada; 1-7 postlarvae in 18 of 303 swordfish from the northwest Atlantic (ARC 2309); pompano dolphin from an unknown Atlantic locality; bluefin tuna, wahoo and yellowfin tuna off west Africa; chub mackerel, dolphin and skipjack tuna from the Pacific; and in a variety of other fishes and occasionally squids. Only 1 dead, encapsulated worm was found in 400 albacore from the southwest and south central Pacific.

Capsules of this worm are visible through the peritoneum in the wall of the body cavity and were counted in 1529 skipjack tuna from the southwestern Pacific. In 1017 of these fish collected from tropical areas, the numbers of capsules increased (0-18 worms) with increasing fish length (33-75 cm). In 512 fish collected from off New Zealand, the number of capsules in 45 cm fish was the same (N=7) as 45 cm fish collected from the tropics, but the number of capsules did not increase with increasing fish length (45-65 cm) (Lester, Barnes and Habib 1985). These data suggest that the fish off New Zealand originally came from the tropics when approximately 45 cm in length and remained there. It also suggests that the parasite must use a tropical intermediate host since no further infections were accumulated in the New Zealand fish.

Geographic Range - Worldwide. Our collections are the first in the Caribbean.

Life History - Adult tapeworms parasitize blue shark, *Prionace glauca* (Linnaeus), another offshore, pelagic fish, and dusky shark, *Carcharhinus obscurus* (Lesueur).

Associations - Three postlarvae used their tentacles to penetrate the tissues of another postlarval tapeworm, *Hepatoxylon trichiuri*, that occurred with them in the stomach of a swordfish. More records of these attacks would be useful in determining if these are routine aggressive acts or mere accidents. Host immunity and chemical effects of other parasites have been thought to control the numbers of worms in the intestine of at least mammalian hosts. The physical combat of hooked-tentacle duels for survival among these highly energetic worms might also be considered.

Location in Host - Blastocysts occur in the muscles, sides of the stomach and other organs. Postlarvae free from the blastocyst are found in the body cavity, stomach and intestine.

Length - Postlarva 1.3-9.5 mm, capsule up to 60.0 mm.

Damage to Host - Hard, calcified capsules covered the entire intestine and pyloric ceca of an Atlantic blue marlin from Puerto Rico. Three fresh capsules 40-60 mm long were also found in this fish. This larvae has been found associated with inflamed areas and ulcers in the stomach of swordfish.

Host Specificity - Plerocercoid larvae occur in a variety of fishes. The adult occurs only in sharks. Atlantic blue marlin and blackfin tuna are new hosts.

Significance to Sport Fishing - The capsule is easy to see through the peritoneum in the body wall of skipjack tuna, it lives for a number of years in the host, and is an excellent biological tag for discrimination of stocks and to indicate migrations.

Tentacularia sp.

Name - This name includes several larval species. In most cases, characteristics were not recorded and specimens were not deposited so they cannot be identified to species. Some of the larvae reported may have been *T. coryphaenae*, but other species exist.

Diagnostic Characters - This small to moderate-sized postlarva has a long scolex with a short tail. The scolex has 4 shallow, elongate, separate attachment grooves (bothridia) without free edges; and 4 short, retractile hook-bearing tentacles. The tentacle sheaths extend from bases of the tentacles and are relatively short, almost straight (not twisted), and do not extend beyond the posterior border of the bothridia. The hooks on the tentacles are almost identical (except that those at the bases of the tentacles are smaller) and closely spaced (homeoacanthous armature). Tentacle bulbs are banana-shaped and placed in the anterior 1/2 of the bothridial region.

Records - One larva occurred in a great barracuda from Jamaica; 2 in 1 of 2 Atlantic blue marlin, 7 in an Atlantic sailfish, 1 in 1 of 4 white marlin and 1 and 8 in 2 of 10 yellowfin tuna from the southern Gulf of Mexico, capsules in 29 of 45 yellowfin tuna from the northeastern Gulf of Mexico (USNPC 56909) and 5-8 larvae in 2 of 10 Indo-Pacific sailfish from the northwest Indian Ocean.

Geographic Range - Worldwide.

Life History - Adult tapeworms occur in sharks.

Ecology - The postlarvae are found in bony fishes (teleosts) in shallow, mid-water and continental slope habitats.

Location in Host - Blastocysts occur in the mesenteries, muscle and other viscera. Postlarvae occur in the body cavity, stomach and intestine.

Length - Postlarva 3.3-9.5 mm.

Host Specificity - The larvae appear to have no specificity. Adults of most species are specific to 1 or a few shark species.

Detection - Capsules in muscle or internal organs are difficult to find. Soft organs can be examined by squashing. In muscle cut into thin strips and held up to a light, capsules appear as opaque areas in the translucent flesh.

Hepatoxylon trichiuri (Holten)

Encapsulated larvae of this parasite occur commonly in swordfish and other fishes.

Name - Modern authorities apparently disagree if these worms represent 1 or several species (or if *H. squali* (Martin) or *H. trichiuri* is the type of the genus). We consider *Dibothriorhynchus attenuatus* (Rudolphi), *D. lepidopteri* Blainville, *D. xiphiae* MacCallum, *H. attenuatus* (Rudolphi), *H. grossus* Rudolphi, *H. stenocephala* (Guiart), *H. squali*, and *Hepatoxylon* sp. of Ward, 1962 synonyms.

These larval forms are in need of additional study and may be shown to represent different species. Yamaguti (1959) suggested that *H. stenocephala*, represented by a postlarva from an unidentified dolphin in the Atlantic, was a distinct species. Hogans et al. (1983) considered this form from swordfish to be *H. attenuatus*. Postlarvae have been divided taxonomically into long and short forms, but these shapes are apparently due to developmental changes instead of species differences.

Diagnostic Characters - Postlarvae are wrinkled all over except for the 4 bothridia. The tentacles are short, globular to conical, and vary from approximately as long as wide to twice as long as wide. Tentacular sheaths are about as long as the bulbs. Tentacular bulbs are more than 4 times longer than wide, and covered by the bothridia. The region containing the bothridia is less than 1/2 the length of the body. The postlarva varies greatly in shape and size.

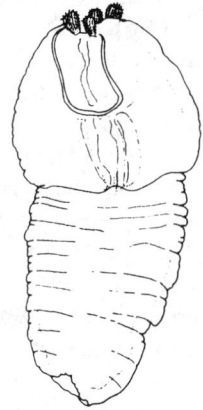

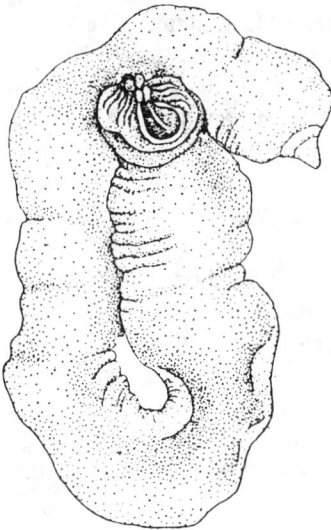

Records - We found 10-21 postlarvae in 15 of 40 dolphin from various localities around Puerto Rico, 5 and 8 capsules in 2 swordfish off Guanica Bay, Puerto Rico; and 1 postlarvae in 1 of 5 dolphin, and 3 in 1 of 4 wahoo off Alabama, USA. Capsules were present in 14 of 45 yellowfin tuna from the northeastern Gulf of Mexico (USNPC 56907); 1-24 blastocysts (average 3.4) in 178 of 303 swordfish from the northwest Atlantic (ARC 2313); 1 blastocyst in a large mass on the outer layer of the intestine, and 3 encapsulated on the outer layer of the gonads in 1 swordfish each; many blastocysts and postlarvae in 8, 40 in 1, 10 each in 2, 8 in 1, and 2 in 1 swordfish from Woods Hole, Massachusetts, USA (USNPC 7732); 23 postlarvae in a swordfish from Nova Scotia, Canada; postlarva in dolphin from Brazil and the Azores; capsules and postlarvae in albacore from the Mediterranean and the Pacific; and postlarvae in swordfish from the Baltic, eastern Atlantic and Mediterranean. The larvae of this parasite is also found in a variety of bony fishes, sharks and rays.

Geographic Range - Worldwide. Our collections are the first in the Caribbean.

Life History - Adults of this tapeworm are found in sharks.

Ecology - Unlike most larval forms in big game fishes, it is common offshore and inshore in the Atlantic. In a study of 400 albacore in the Pacific, it was abundant near Australia (38%) and western New Zealand (32-75%), but declined in the open Pacific (11-14%) and in the Coral Sea to the north (20%). This suggested that the intermediate host occurred in nearshore habitats (Jones 1991). **Associations** - One of 13 swordfish from Woods Hole was heavily infected with a tissue-embedding copepod (either *Pennella filosa* or *P. instructa*). The same fish had the heaviest infection of this larval tapeworm.

Location in Host - Blastocysts encapsulated on the outside of the stomach and viscera, and postlarvae were free in the body cavity or in the intestinal tract.

Length - Postlarva 7.5-70.0 mm; adults up to 400.0 mm. Linton (1924) found a 150.0 mm larva.

Host Specificity - Wahoo is a new host.

Significance to Sport Fishing - This parasite has been used as a biological tag to demonstrate how stocks of albacore migrate in the Pacific.

Eutetrarhynchus lineatus (Linton)

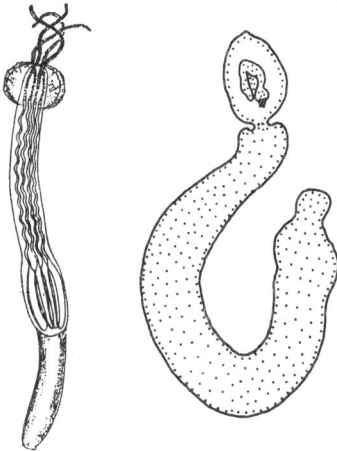

We solve a 75 year-old mystery by matching the larva from a big game fish with its adult.

Name - The larval species *Rhynchobothrius carangis* MacCallum, a mystery (species in question) for more than 75 years, is the larva of *E. lineatus*. *Rhynchobothrius* sp. of Linton (1908, Fig. 70) also appears to be a less mature specimen with the tentacle bulbs still bulging out the sides of the worm as they do in the larvae.

Diagnostic Characters - Blastocyst white with an orange yellow posterior. This moderate-sized postlarva has a long scolex and a tail. The scolex has 2 round bothridia, with free posterior borders, that project from the anterior end. The 4 tentacles are relatively long, tentacle sheaths are long and wavy or rippling, and tentacle bulbs are long and narrow. The body bulges out around the tentacle bulbs

Records - One capsule occurred in a crevalle jack at the New York Aquarium that had been transported from Key West, Florida, USA; 1 blastocyst in a green moray, *Gymnothorax funebris* Ranzani; and 1-7 adult tapeworms in 4 nurse sharks, *Ginglymostoma cirratum* (Bonnaterre), from the Dry Tortugas, Florida.

Geographic Range - Unknown.

Life History - Linton's (1908) and MacCallum's (1921) records are the only times the larvae of this worm has been collected and described. The rarity in fishes, single specimens in fishes, and the almost fishless diet of the final host, suggest that the larvae is usually encapsulated in an invertebrate that might be consumed by a nurse shark.

Ecology - The final host occurs in inshore, shallow habitats. Only big game fish that venture inshore would be exposed to its larval forms.

Location in Host - Both larvae occurred in the wall of the rectum.

Length - Postlarva 4.3-11.5 mm; adult 15.0-30.0 mm.

Host Specificity - Larvae are not specific since the 2 known specimens were found in different orders of fishes. The adult is host specific to nurse shark.

Otobothrium crenacolle Linton

The larvae of this tapeworm occurs in many big game fishes. Superinfections may damage the internal organs of these fishes.

Name - This species is sometimes spelled *O. crenacollis*.

Diagnostic Characters - The blastocyst is an amber colored, oval capsule without a caudal extension. Postlarvae have 2 short bothridia, a short tail, and a longer striated body. Tentacle sheaths are spiral, and tentacle bulbs are short, less than twice as long as wide, and reach the posterior margin of the body. The bothridia usually show a posterior notch, and have coma-shaped sensory pits on their margins. Usually 1 larva occurs in a capsule, but up to 3 have been found.

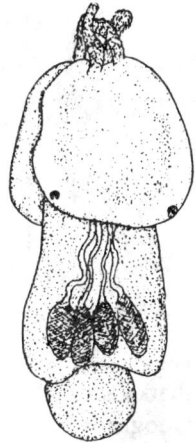

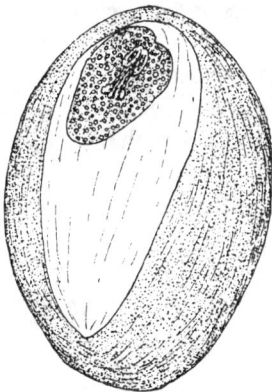

Records - Heavy infections of capsules occurred in dolphin and king mackerel and postlarvae in little tunny from Bermuda; a superinfection of capsules in a cero, and a very heavy infection of capsules in a dolphin from Beaufort, North Carolina, USA; a light infection of capsules in an Atlantic bonito, 1 postlarvae and a light infection of capsules in 2 blue runner, light infections of capsules in 4 cero (USNPC 5494), numerous capsules in a king mackerel, a few capsules in a swordfish and a light infection of degenerated capsules possibly of this worm in a white marlin (USNPC 5501) from Woods Hole, Massachusetts, USA. These capsules also occur in a variety of other bony fishes and sharks.

Geographic Range - Atlantic including the Gulf of Mexico.

Life History - Adults of this tapeworm occur in sharks.

Location in Host - Blastocysts are usually found in the wall of the stomach, less often on pyloric ceca and other viscera, occasionally in muscle. Postlarvae occur in the intestinal tract.

Length - Postlarva 0.3-2.4 mm, blastocyst 0.5-2.8 mm, capsule 1.5-7.0 mm.

Damage to Host - Superinfections of more than 100 capsules per 13 cm^2 of visceral surface occur.

Otobothrium dipsacum Linton

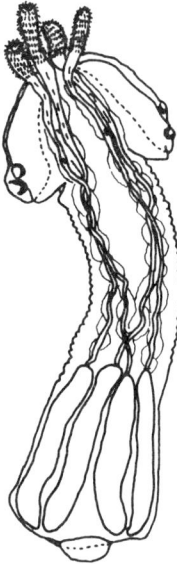

The larvae of this tapeworm is rarely encapsulated in big game fishes.

Diagnostic Characters - The rather large (up to 24 mm) capsule is ovoid, often darkly colored. The blastocyst is oval and has no tail. The postlarvae have 2 wide, short bothridia, a short tail, and a longer striated body. The tentacle sheaths are spiral. The tentacle bulbs are long, approximately 1/2 as long as the body, more than 4 times as long as wide, and reach the posterior margin of the body. The bothridia have a posterior notch, and oval sensory pits on the posterolateral margins.

Records - Three to 4 postlarvae occurred in 2 of 5 Atlantic sailfish, and 2-4 in 5 of 40 dolphin from various localities around Puerto Rico. Several postlarvae were found in 1 of 19 great barracuda off Miami, Florida; and 1 capsule in 1 of 2 swordfish from Woods Hole, Massachusetts, USA. This worm has also been found in Indo-Pacific sailfish. Blastocysts and postlarvae occur in other bony fishes, sharks and rays.

Geographic Range - Worldwide. Our collections are the first in the Caribbean.

Life History - The adult of this tapeworm occurs in sharks.

Location in Host - Blastocysts occur on the outer layers of the viscera. Postlarvae are free in the body cavity or intestine.

Length - Postlarva 2.5-4.5 mm, blastocyst 5.3-12.0 mm, capsule 7.5-24.0 mm.

Host Specificity - This parasite does not appear to be a very common parasite of swordfish. It did not occur in 303 swordfish examined in the northwest Atlantic. Atlantic sailfish and dolphin are new hosts.

Pterobothrium heteracanthum Diesing

These elongate, brown capsules are found in the viscera of Spanish mackerels and inshore fishes.

Name - *Pterobothrium filicolle* (Linton) is a synonym and *P. fragile* (Diesing) and *Synbothrium* sp. of Linton, 1900 may be. *Pterobothrium acanthotruncatum* Escalante and Carvajal, encapsulated in dolphin from Peru, appears to be a different species.

Diagnostic Characters - The elongate host capsules are brown. The "neck" of the blastocyst has a characteristic constriction just before the long, rather wide tail joins the bulbous head. When the plerocercus everts from the blastocyst, it has an elongate, slender scolex with 4 round bothridia mounted on characteristic projections from the scolex. Tentacles are long and are along side each bothridium at the end of each projection

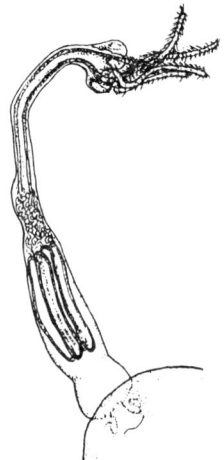

from the scolex. The tentacle sheaths are longer than
the tentacles and the tentacle bulbs, relatively straight
in the anterior, but irregularly curled near the tentacle
bulbs. The tentacle bulbs are elongate and fill much of
the width of the scolex and slightly bulge its width.
Tentacles have 5 hooks in the principal rows and
numerous smaller hooks.

Records - Numerous capsules occurred in a cero and
several in 1 of 2 Spanish mackerel from Beaufort,
North Carolina, USA; 1 capsule in a greater amberjack, numerous in 3 cero (USNPC 5486 and 5491), 3
to numerous in 2 king mackerel (USNPC 4792), and
numerous in 2 Spanish mackerel (USNPC 5487) from
Woods Hole, Massachusetts, USA.

Geographic Range - Worldwide.

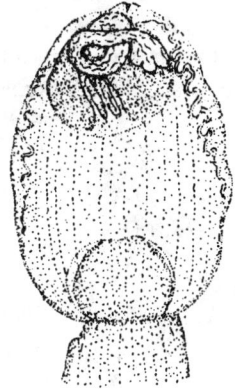

Life History - Adults are not known. The plerocercus
scolex remains attached to the blastocyst. It does not
separate and form a postlarva.

Ecology - Most of the known hosts occur in inshore
habitats. Spanish mackerels may become infected when
they feed inshore.

Location in Host - Encapsulated in the wall of the
stomach or intestine and in the outer layer of the liver,
ovary and other internal organs. Occasionally capsules are
deeply embedded in the liver.

Length - Plerocercus 4.4-6.4 mm, blastocyst 25.0-94.0
mm, capsule 3.0-10.5 mm. The length of the blastocyst
varied considerably, but the plerocercus is approximately
the same size in the longest and shortest blastocysts.

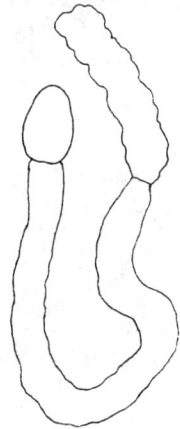

Host Specificity - The
occurrence of the plerocercus of this parasite in 3 of
the 4 species of western Atlantic Spanish mackerels
and no other big game fishes is apparently only a
coincidence.

Grillotia erinaceus (Van Beneden)

This parasite is encapsuled in inshore fishes and
occasionally big game fishes. Superinfections have
been reported and might injure Atlantic mackerel.

Name - *Rhynchobothrium imparispine* Linton is a
synonym. *Grillotia* sp. Nikolaeva, 1962 may be a
synonym.

Diagnostic Characters - The capsule is oval or
teardrop shaped and may be attached on a stalk.
Capsules sometimes occur in clusters. Younger

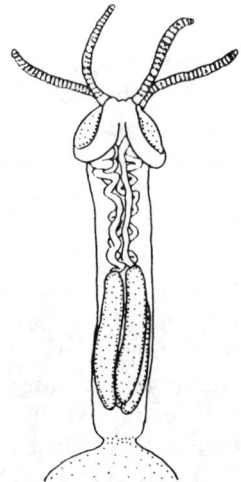

capsules are white to yellow, older ones brown to black. The blastocyst is oval to oblong, but does not have a bulbous end and a tail. The plerocerus attached to the blastocyst has a long narrow, scolex, with 2 short, round bothridia. The bothridia have thickened, raised rims, and the lateral and posterior margins are free. Tentacles, tentacle sheath and bulbs are all relatively long. Bulbs are elongate, more than 6 times longer than wide, and do not reach the posterior margin of the scolex. Sheaths are irregularly tangled. Tentacles have 4 hooks in the principle rows.

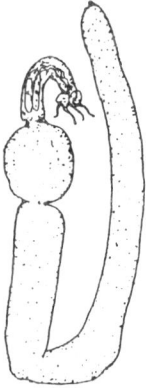

Records - One and a few cysts occurred in 2 of 31 Atlantic bonito; a superinfection in 1, numerous in each of 13, few to numerous in each of 23, a few in each of 6 and 1 in 1 of 32 Atlantic mackerel (USNPC 4743); and few in 5 swordfish from Woods Hole, Massachusetts, USA. Four, 6 and 170 plerocercoids of *Grillotia* sp. (possibly *G. erinaceus*) were found in 3 of 10 yellowfin tuna from the southern Gulf of Mexico. This parasite encapsulates in a great variety of bony fishes, sharks and rays. Eels and salmon carry this parasite from saltwater into freshwater habitats.

Geographic Range - Possibly worldwide, but most records are from the northern Atlantic.

Life History - The first intermediate host is probably a copepod. The second intermediate host is a fish. No free postlarvae occur in the life cycle. The adult is more common in skates and rays than in sharks. Parts of the life cycle were described by Ruszkowski (1932). A similar species, *G. angeli* Dollfus, survives for at least several years, if not the entire life of the host, in Atlantic mackerel in the Mediterranean and the Atlantic off Europe.

Ecology - The capsule is more common in inshore than offshore fishes.

Location in Host - Encapsulated in the outer layer of viscera, in the intestinal wall, or occasionally in muscle. Capsules are sometimes found in the intestinal tract after being digested out of prey fishes.

Length - Plerocercoid 4.2-7.0 mm, capsule 2.5-13.0 mm, exceptionally 22.0 mm.

Host Specificity - This parasite occurs in a great variety of fishes, but in few big game fishes. It only occurred in high numbers in Atlantic mackerel. The report from Atlantic bonito was of free capsules in the intestine digested out of other fishes. It does not appear to be a very common parasite of swordfish. It did not occur in 303 swordfish examined in the northwest Atlantic.

Damage to Host - Superinfections are probably injurious to the host. Infections of *G. branchi* Shaharom and Lester plerocercoids in the tissues of the

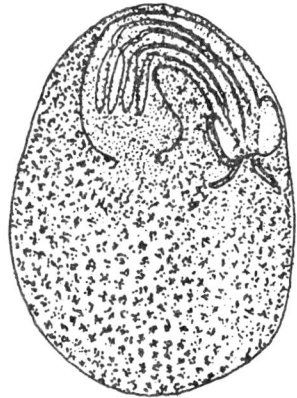

gill arches of Spanish mackerels in Australia and Malaysia caused inflammation, production of black pigment (melanization) and erosion of bone.

Comments - This is a common parasite in north Atlantic fishes and has been the subject of a large number of articles and a book (monograph) (Johnstone 1912).

Pseudogrillotia zerbiae Palm

Large spaghetti worms frequently wiggle out of highly prized greater amberjack fillets to the disgust of fishermen and cooks.

Name - The common name "spaghetti worm" is often used to describe its appearance in the flesh of fishes. *Pseudogrillotia* sp. of Deardorf, Raybourne and Mattis, 1984 is a synonym.

Diagnostic Characters - The blastocyst in the flesh of a fish is a long white worm with a bulbous "head" and a thick, string-like body. The plerocercoid larva has a scolex with 2 round bothridia. The tentacle sheaths are winding but not spiral.

Records - We found numerous worms in greater amberjack from Arecibo and Aguadilla, Puerto Rico, and in 10 off Panama City, Florida, USA. It has also been found in greater amberjack off Mississippi (BMNH 1995.3.20.1-2) and Hawaii; and in black marlin and jacks in Hawaii

Geographic Range - Worldwide. Our collections are the first in the Caribbean.

Location in Host - This worm is embedded in muscle. More are found along the spine and in the muscle towards the tail.

Length - Plerocercoid 23.0-25.0 mm, blastocyst 20.0-55.0 mm.

Host Specificity - It is possibly a characteristic parasite of greater amberjack. This parasite also occurs in rudderfish and could be almost genus specific (*Seriola*), or almost family specific to jacks. Rudderfish is a new host.

Detection - Actively moving worms can easily be seen when fillets are removed from freshly caught fish.

Harm to Humans - Large, live spaghetti worms wiggling in the flesh of greater amberjack have caused many

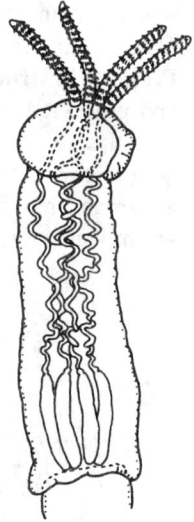

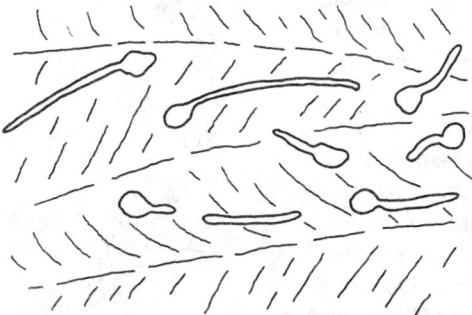

fillets to be needlessly discarded. This was not much of a problem 30 years ago when this big game fish was considered a "trash" fish, but now it has become a "highly prized" food fish. These worms do not harm humans. They have experimentally been fed to mammals and did not develop or cause harm. They are sufficiently large to be picked out of the flesh. If you are too squeamish to pick out or eat these worms, then avoid cutting fillets too close to the spinal column or too close to the tail. This technique will waste some fish muscle, but will avoid most of the worms. You might also refrain from showing these parasites to non-fishing spouses, if you want to be able to eat your catch!

Preparation for Study - These long worms are easily plucked from muscle and preserved. They make impressive classroom demonstrations of seafood parasites.

Significance to Sport Fishing - The problem of wormy flesh in greater amberjack has been impressing fishermen for the last 25,000 years but this worm was only described scientifically in 1995.

Molicola horridus (Goodsir)

This parasite rarely is encapsulated in muscle of swordfish.

Name - The genus was named for ocean sunfish (genus *Mola*). *Molicola uncinatus* (Linton) is a synonym.

Diagnostic Characters - The blastocyst is elongate, but does not have a bulbous anterior or a long tail. The plerocercoid larvae consists of a long scolex and a tail. The scolex is narrow and cylindrical except for the 4 short, broad bothridia which are wider than the neck. The tentacles are long, and the tentacle sheaths long and spiral. The tentacle bulbs are short, oblong, about 3 times as long as wide, and almost fill the width of the scolex. The tentacles have a ring of hooks at the base which contains the largest hooks.

Records - One blastocyst occurred in a swordfish from Woods Hole, Massachusetts, USA; and it commonly occurs in ocean sunfish, *Mola mola* (Linnaeus), a pelagic offshore fish.

Geographic Range - Worldwide.

Life History - The adult of this parasite has been listed in tapeworm guide books from the mysterious "*Vulpecula marina*" for more than 70 years although Linton (1924) calls it a "thrasher" [=thresher shark, *Alopias vulpinus* (Bonnaterre)]. Adults also occur in the pelagic and offshore blue shark.

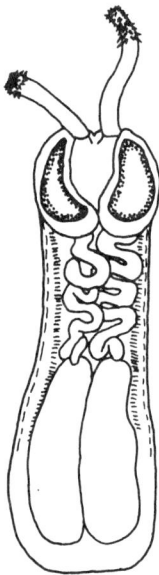

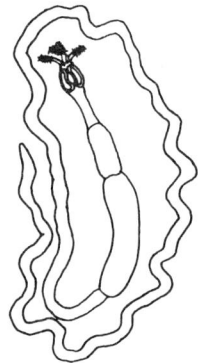

Ecology - Members of this parasite genus occur in offshore, pelagic habitats.
Location in Host - Blastocysts usually occur in the liver, but were found in the muscle near the spinal column of swordfish.
Length - Plerocercus 2.0 mm, blastocyst 89.0 mm.

Callitetrarhynchus gracilis (Rudolphi)

This parasite occasionally is encapsulated in a variety of big game fishes.
Name - This species was originally named from a plerocercoid larva in a bullet tuna or frigate tuna. *Tentacularia lepida* Chandler is a synonym.
Diagnostic Characters - The host capsule is bladder-like to elongate and usually white, but older capsules turn brown to blue-black and slightly iridescent. The postlarva has an elongate scolex, long tail, and 2 short, heart-shaped bothridia. The tentacle sheaths are tightly coiled. The tentacle bulbs reach the end of the scolex, do not occupy the entire width of the scolex, and are about 3 times longer than wide. The base of the tentacles does not have a ring of larger hooks.
Records - One to 2 postlarvae occurred in 7 of 40 dolphin from various sites around Puerto Rico; capsules were common in Spanish mackerel, 1-4 in 11 of 52 bar jack, 4 in 1 of 4 blue runner and postlarvae in bar jack from Bermuda; several capsules in 17 of 32 little tunny and/or skipjack tuna off Miami, Florida, USA. Two blastocysts were found in a dolphin and 1 in a pompano dolphin from Beaufort, North Carolina, USA; 1-20 capsules in 2 of 8 Atlantic mackerel, 1 capsule in a bluefin tuna, and 1 capsule in a blue runner, from Woods Hole, Massachusetts, USA; in bluefin tuna from the Mediterranean; yellowfin tuna from west Africa; bluefin tuna, chub mackerel, frigate tuna and Indo-Pacific sailfish from the Pacific; and in other fishes, particularly groupers and snappers.
Geographic Range - Worldwide. Our collections are the first in the Caribbean.
Life History - The adult occurs in sharks.
Location in Host - Blastocysts occurred in the wall of the stomach and intestine, or in the outer layers of the viscera.
Length - Postlarva 5.3-27.0 mm, blastocyst 6.0-30.0 mm, capsule 2.0-65.0 mm.

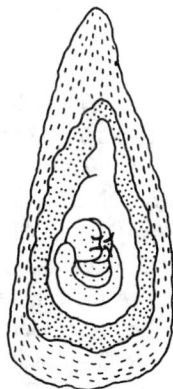

Lacistorhynchus bulbifer (Linton)

This parasite is occasionally encapsulated in a variety of big game fishes. It is more commonly found in inshore fishes.

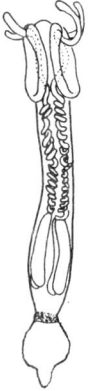

Name - *Lacistorhynchus tenuis* (van Beneden) was considered one worldwide species, but it has been shown to be a species complex with *L. tenuis* in Europe, *L. dollfusi* Beveridge and Sakanari in the Pacific, and possibly *L. bulbifer* in the western Atlantic. *Rhynchobothrium bulbifer* Linton is a synonym.

Diagnostic Characters - The host capsule is swollen on one end and has a tail on the other. The blastocyst has a tail that varies in length. The tentacles of the postlarvae emerge from the sides of the anterior end of each bothridium, instead of on top of the scolex. The postlarvae has a long scolex and a short tail. The 2 bothridia are elongate with raised rims. The tentacle sheaths are spiral, the bulbs elongate, and more than 4 times longer than wide. The scolex bulges around the tentacle bulbs.

Records - One and few capsules occurred in 2 Atlantic bonito; 12 in 1, few in 12 of 56, and 1 in 1 Atlantic mackerel; 1 in a bluefin tuna, 1 in a blue runner, several in a little tunny and 2 in a Spanish mackerel from Woods Hole, Massachusetts, USA; and in a variety of other fishes.

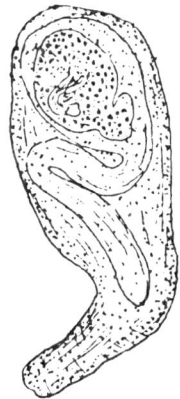

Geographic Range - Western Atlantic.

Life History - Coracidia of *L. dollfusi* were infective to copepods for 2 weeks, procercoids in copepods were infective to bony fishes for 4 weeks, eversible tentacles developed in the plerocercoids in 3 months, and worms in the final host began to form segments in 4 months at room temperature. Development and survival times are longer at lower temperatures. Other details of the life cycle have been reported by Young (1954) and Sakanari and Moser (1985a,b).

Ecology - Many of the final hosts for this tapeworm are smaller, inshore sharks. Thus the larval forms are more common in inshore fishes and are only occasionally found in big game fishes.

Associations - One capsule was associated with a capsule of *Koellikeria* sp., probably *K. bipartita*, in a bluefin tuna.

Location in Host - The larvae are encapsulated in the intestinal or stomach wall, in the outer layers of viscera, or occasionally free in the intestine, digested out of food items. They are also found encapsulated in the dorsal muscles of Atlantic mackerel.

Length - Postlarva 1.2-3.5 mm, capsule 1.5-4.5 mm.

Damage to Host - Five or more plerocercoid larvae of *L. dollfusi* developing into immature adults apparently killed young sharks. Infections kill 20-50% of the copepod intermediate hosts.

Dasyrhynchus giganteus (Diesing)

This spectacular capsule in the common and often caught crevalle jack deserves more attention.

Name - The genus is appropriately named for sting rays (genus *Dasyatis*). The *Dasyrhynchus* sp. of Overstreet, 1978 is the same as this worm (Overstreet pers. comm.). *Rhynchobothrium insigne* Linton is a synonym.

Diagnostic Characters - This large blastocyst has an oblong anterior and a long tail. The tiny postlarva has a long, narrow scolex which gradually expands in width from the front to the base, and has 2 short, inverted-heart-shaped bothridia. Tentacle sheaths are long and tightly coiled. Tentacle bulbs are long and narrow. The tentacles have 9 dissimilar hooks (5 larger and 4 distinctly smaller) in each principle row, rows of smaller hooks occur between principle rows, and a double file or chainette of closely spaced hooks is found on one side of each tentacle. The postlarvae of *D. variouncinnatus* (Pintner) is identical, but it only occurs in the Pacific.

Records - Blastocysts commonly infect crevalle jack in the northern Gulf of Mexico; 6 capsules in a greater amberjack off Miami, Florida; 1 postlarva each in 8, 2 in 1 and 3 in 1 of 303 swordfish from the northwest Atlantic (ARC 2414); 1 in a leatherjacket, *Oligoplites saurus* (Schneider), from Brazil, and other fishes from Florida, USA.

Geographic Range - Atlantic.

Life History - The adult occurs in several species of sharks.

Location in Host - Usually found encapsulated under the skin and in the muscle on the top of the head of crevalle jack, occasionally in other muscles. It is also found under the skin of leatherjacket and in the stomach of swordfish.

Length - Postlarva 5.0-18.0 mm, blastocyst anterior bulb up to 25 mm long.

Host Specificity - The larva may be family specific to jacks and the adult to requiem sharks (Carcharhinidae). The rarity and low numbers, and location in the stomach suggest that swordfish may be a false host.

Damage to Host - Six to 8 blastocysts on one side of the head occupy much of the muscle in this area, and may injure the host.

Detection - Most of the blastocysts occur in the head where they are seldom seen by fishermen as this part of the fish is seldom cleaned or opened. If the head is cut apart, these large white capsules are prominent.

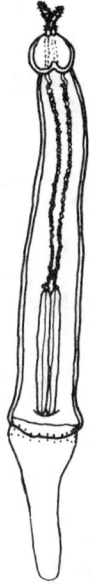

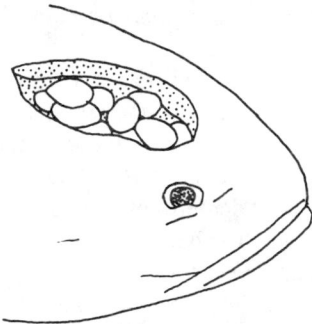

Gymnorhynchus gigas (Cuvier)

Larvae of this parasite are encapsulated in inshore and offshore fishes.

Diagnostic Characters - The plerocercus is attached to a large blastocyst with a long, thin tail. The 4 bothridia are elongate oval. The tentacles are relatively short and have long hooks with even longer hooks at the base. The tentacle sheaths are spiral. Tentacle bulbs are relatively short. The entacles have 9 hooks in each spiral row.

Records - One plerocercus occurred in 1 of 4 white marlin and 1-9 (average 4) in 8 of 10 yellowfin tuna from the southern Gulf of Mexico; and rarely in swordfish from Europe.

Geographic Range - North Atlantic.

Life History - The adult is not known.

Ecology - This parasite is encapsuled in ocean sunfish, rarely in swordfish, and commonly in yellowfin tuna. Many more records exist of this larva from inshore than offshore fishes.

Location in Host - Muscle (swordfish) and blood vessels (yellowfin tuna).

Length - Plerocercus 4.5-5.5 mm, blastocyst 24.0-125.0 mm.

Prosobothrium armigerum Cohn

This worm may only be an accidental parasite of big game fishes. Little is known about its postlarva.

Name - *Ichthyotaenia adhaerens* (Linton) and *P. japonicum* Yamaguti are synonyms.

Diagnostic Characters - The distinctive scolex has 4 relatively large, sucker-shaped bothridia which face forward (the circular flat faces are in the anteriormost plane). The suckers are cup-shaped from the sides (laterally) and are topped by circular disk-like pads. The spine-like structures (microtriches) that densely cover the neck of the adult are not apparent in the postlarva. The body of the postlarva is composed of a long narrow scolex and a short tail.

Records - One postlarva occurred in 3 of 40 Atlantic blue marlin from various localities around Puerto Rico.

Geographic Range - Worldwide. Our collections are the first in the Caribbean.

Life History - The eggs are clustered in groups of 24 within a cocoon.

Ecology - The adult of this tapeworm occurs in an offshore host, blue shark.

Location in Host - Intestine (postlarva).

Length - Postlarva 9.2 mm.

Host Specificity - Atlantic blue marlin is a new host.

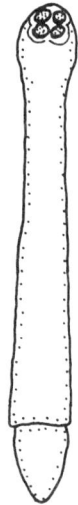

Ceratobothrium xanthocephalum Monticelli

This little known plerocercoid commonly occurs in swordfish.

Diagnostic Characters - The scolex is distinctive with 4 oval bothridia and relatively large, flat suckers on their anterior ends. The 2 posteriorlateral corners of the suckers are armed with large muscular protrusions. The bothridial area makes up more than 1/2 to the entire length of the postlarva.

Records - One to 99 postlarva (average 7.8) occurred in 112 of 303 swordfish from the northwest Atlantic (ARC 2315). It is also found in squids.

Geographic Range - Worldwide.

Life History - The adult of this tapeworm occurs in sharks.

Location in Host - Postlarva were found free in the intestine and rectum.

Length - Postlarva 1.1-1.8 mm.

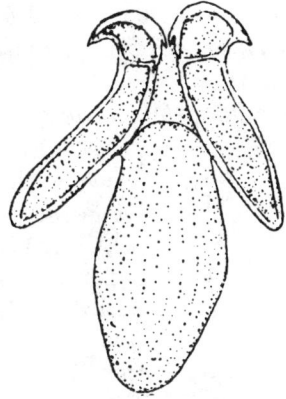

Pelichnibothrium speciosum Monticelli

This distinctive and widespread larva is encapsulated in tunas and other offshore pelagics.

Name - The status of this species is uncertain. *Phyllobothrium caudatum* Zschokke and Heitz and *P. salmonis* Fujita are synonyms.

Diagnostic Characters - The distinctive postlarva has a long body divided into a scolex with 4 bothridia and 5 suckers; a neck with obvious segments, and an unsegmented tail region. Four of the suckers are on the anterior ends of the bothridia, and 1 sucker is on the anterior end of the scolex (apical sucker).

Records - One to 2 postlarvae occurred in 5 Atlantic blue marlin, and 1-4 in 6 of 40 dolphin from various localities around Puerto Rico. It was also encapsulated in 27 of 45 yellowfin tuna from northeast Gulf of Mexico (USNPC 56913); in bluefin tuna from Europe and the Pacific and in blue shark, another offshore pelagic fish, other fishes in the Pacific, and squids.

Geographic Range - Worldwide. Our collections are the first in the Caribbean.

Life History - This parasite apparently uses squids and fishes as intermediate hosts for its plerocercoids. This is a useful strategy in the offshore realm where hosts may be isolated and sparse.

Ecology - Most of the known hosts of this parasite are offshore and pelagic which suggests it may be limited to this habitat.

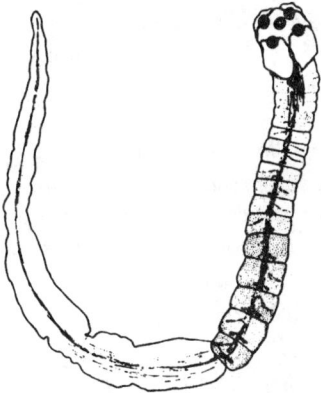

Location in Host - Encapsulated in the wall of the stomach, outer layer of the intestine or viscera.
Length - Postlarva 1.1-2.3 mm.
Host Specificity - Atlantic blue marlin and dolphin are new hosts.

Phyllobothrium delphini (Bosc)

This larva is found in the stomachs of swordfish, but is better known for forming large capsules in marine mammals.
Name - *Hydatis delphini* Bosc [=hydatid cysts of dolphins (mammal)]. It does not actually produce the dangerous hydatid cysts found in grazing land mammals. The species name has been treated as a larval-group name instead of a described species by some authors (Yamaguti 1959). *Phyllobothrium loliginis* (Leidy) from the stomachs of squids and swordfish may be a synonym.
Diagnostic Characters - When the plerocercus is everted from the bladder, the blastocyst is shaped like a cherry with a stem. The scolex and neck are about as long as the attached bladder. The scolex has 4 membranous bothridia with thickened margins that are puckered and crumpled. The bothridia are triangular and each has a prominent, cup-shaped sucker on its anterior apex. The anterior end of the scolex is capped with a broadly rounded raised rostellum containing an apical sucker, which may disappear before the larva becomes an adult.
Records - One to 102 capsules (average 7.0) occurred in 150 of 303 swordfish from the northwest Atlantic (ARC 2315).
Geographic Range - Worldwide.
Life History - The adult form of this larva could be *Phyllobothrium tumidum* Linton a parasite of great white sharks, *Carcharodon carcharias* (Linnaeus), (which eat marine mammals around the world) and a variety of other sharks.
Location in Host - Plerocercoids were found free in the stomach of swordfish and squids, but were encapsulated in the muscle of marine mammals.
Length - Plerocercus 26.0-34.0 mm, encapsulated bladder 12.0-18.0 mm.

Rhinebothrium flexile Linton

Blastocysts containing this distinctive, chandelier-shaped larva occasionally occur in big game fishes, but are found more often and in damaging numbers in inshore fishes.
Name - It has been placed in genus *Echeneibothrium*.
Diagnostic Characters - The blastocyst has a bulbous end containing the larva, a long string-like body and a smaller swelling on the posterior end. The postlarva removed from the capsule has a scolex with 4 elongate, oval bothridia on projections. The surface of each bothridium is divided in half by a long septum running down the middle, each half is then

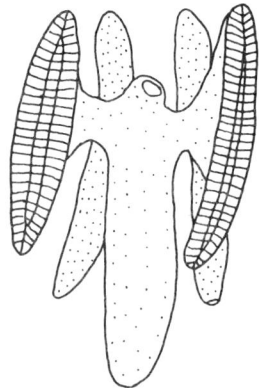

further subdivided into elongate segments (loculi) by smaller, muscular cross-septa.

Records - One to 14 postlarvae occurred in 12 of 40 dolphin from various localities around Puerto Rico. Numerous blastocysts occurred in 1 of 8 cobia from Beaufort, North Carolina, USA; and 1 capsule in a chub mackerel from Woods Hole, Massachusetts, USA. The *Rhinebothrium* sp. of Arandas-Rego and Santos, 1983 in chub mackerel from Brazil may be the same species.

Geographic Range - Worldwide. Our collections are the first in the Caribbean.

Ecology - The plerocercoid occurs more commonly and in much higher numbers in inshore bottom fishes than in offshore, big game fishes.

Location in Host - Encapsulated in intestine, liver and viscera.

Length - Postlarva 1.0-1.2 mm, blastocyst 8.6-21.2 mm.

Host Specificity - Encapsulated larvae occur in a variety of fish hosts, and the adults parasitize several species of rays. Dolphin is a new host.

Damage to Host - Very heavy infections injure the viscera of inshore fishes and could damage big game fishes.

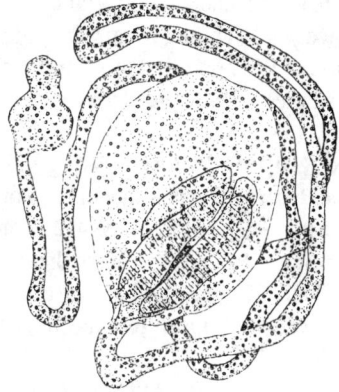

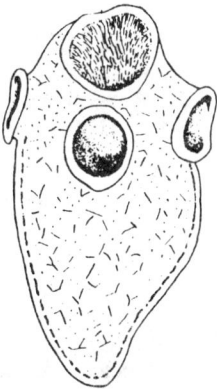

Tetraphyllid plerocercoid

These tiny, white, nondescript larvae occur in the intestine of all marine fishes. Superinfections may harm swordfish.

Name - Most plerocercoid larvae are undeveloped and cannot be identified beyond order. "*Scolex pleuronectis*" Mueller is a group name for these unidentifiable larvae. *Scolex polymorphus* Rudolphi and *S. delphini* Stossich are synonyms of this group name.

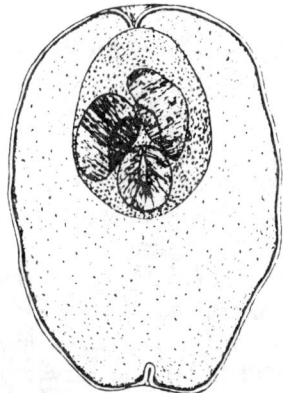

Diagnostic Characters - It is a simple, white conical shaped plerocercoid with a bulbous scolex and a tapering tail. The 4 bothridia have pleated margins on the scolex which are difficult to see. The suckers on each bothridium are obvious in wet mounts viewed with a compound microscope. A terminal sucker usually occurs on the apex of the scolex. Live worms are highly active, contracting and relaxing, and may invaginate the scolex into the body.

Records - These worms are found in all big game fishes and practically any fishes. We could list thousands of records, but this would be meaningless. For example, 1-1900 occurred in 277 of 303 swordfish in the northwest Atlantic (ARC 2412).

Geographic Range - Worldwide.

Location in Host - Intestine, stomach, pyloric ceca, bile duct and gall bladder.

Length - Plerocercoid 0.4-2.0 mm.

Damage to Host - Very heavy infections may block the bile duct or gall bladder. Large numbers in the stomach and intestine of hosts appear to have little effect. Superinfections have been reported in swordfish and in other fishes.

Bothriocephalus scorpii (Mueller)

This widespread parasite occurs in a variety of hosts, but rarely in big game fishes.

Name - Leeuwenhoek named this worm in 1722 before the present system of scientific names was established.

Diagnostic Characters - The immature worm has an elongate scolex with the lateral bothria becoming more shallow towards the posterior ends. The immature segments are as long as wide or longer. The plerocercoid is a flat, elongate worm that can only be identified by the presence of accompanying immature worms. More work is required before plerocercoid larvae of this genus can be easily identified to species.

Records - One immature and 1 plerocercoid occurred in 1 of 3 Atlantic mackerel from Woods Hole, Massachusetts, USA.

Geographic Range - Worldwide.

Location in Host - intestine.

Length - Immature 5.0 mm, plerocercoid 2.0 mm.

Host Specificity - Plerocercoids and immature worms occur in a wide variety of hosts.

Bothriocephalus sp. of Linton

The encapsulated larva occasionally occurs in big game fishes.

Name - The records below probably represent more than 1 species. Little effort has been made to distinguish these rather formless larvae. The records may include larvae of *B. manubriformis* and *B. scorpii*.

Diagnostic Characters - These plerocercoid larvae are flat, vase-shaped, flask-shaped or slender worms with calcarious bodies in their tissue. The scolex is simple, has 2 lateral grooves and is covered with minute spine-like projections (microtriches).

Records - One and a few encapsulated in 2 of 38 Atlantic bonito (USNPC 4785,6528), 1 to a few capsules in 8 of 192 Atlantic mackerel (USNPC 8890), 1 in a greater amberjack (USNPC 8891), and 5-12 capsules in 12 chub mackerel from Woods Hole, Massachusetts, USA.

Location in Host - These larvae were encapsulated in the mesenteries or outer layers of the viscera, in the wall of the stomach or intestine, or occasionally loose in the intestine where they were digested out of prey.
Length - plerocercoid 0.4-13.0, capsule 1.0-8.0 mm.

Miscellaneous Tapeworms

Bothriocephalus janikii **Markowski** - This worm was described from specimens collected from the stomach of a dolphin during the Discovery Cruise apparently in the south central Atlantic (2 latitudes and no longitude given?); and it was reported in the intestine of dolphin from the Bay of Bengal off India. Schmidt (1986) did not list this tapeworm.

Echeneibothrium **sp. of Nikolaeva** - The primary characteristic of this genus and its plerocercoid is the presence of 4, elongate, oval bothridia that are distinctly divided by ridges into longitudinal rows of 1 or 2 rectangular compartments. The whole bothridia resembles the sucker disks of remoras (genus *Echeneis*). Three capsules with plerocercoids occurred in 1 of 10 yellowfin tuna from the southern Gulf of Mexico and plerocercoids of *Echeneibothrium* sp. of Rego, Carvalho-V., Mendonca and Afonso-R., 1985, occurred in less than 10% of 80 Atlantic mackerel from Portugal. Adults usually occur in skates. This parasite has rarely been found in big game or any fishes. The normal intermediate hosts for the plerocercoids may be invertebrates, and fishes may be accidental hosts. More collections are needed to identify this form to species and to determine their importance in big game fishes.

Incompletely defined trypanorhynchid larval species - The species listed below have been named from big game fishes, but so few details were presented that they cannot be identified to genus or species. These names cannot and should not be used. They are only presented to prevent confusion, if they are seen in the literature. (1) *Bothriocephalus claviger* **Leuckart** - This worm has also been called "*Tetrarhynchus*" *claviger* (Leuckart), and is found in swordfish. (2) **Dasyrhynchidae of Ward (1962)** - Capsules were found in 21 of 45 yellowfin tuna from the northeast Gulf of Mexico (USNPC 56911). (3) *Dibothriorhynchus speciosum* **MacCallum** - Up to 20 capsules occurred in Spanish mackerel and many other fishes from Bermuda. Plerocercoids were 20.0-22.0 mm long. (4) *Rhynchobothrium ambiguum* **Diesing** - This worm was found in swordfish. (5) *Rhynchobothrium longispine* **Linton** - Several and 1 capsule in 2 of 11 Atlantic mackerel and 3 in 1 of 3 Spanish mackerel from Woods Hole, Massachusetts, USA; and possibly in cobia from Beaufort, North Carolina, USA. It is 0.8-3.8 mm long. (6) *Tetrabothriorhynchus scombri* **Diesing** - in Atlantic mackerel. (7) *Tetrarhynchus papillosus* **Rudolphi** - in dolphin. (8) *Tetrarhynchus scomber-pelamys* **Wagner** - in Atlantic bonito. (9) *Tetrarhynchus scomber-rocheri* **Wagner** - in bullet tuna or frigate tuna. (10)

Tetrarhynchus scomber-thynnus **Wagner** - in bluefin tuna. (11) *Tetrarhynchus thynni* **Wagner** - in tuna.

Pseudobothrium grimaldii **Guiart** - This adult (?) tapeworm was found out of the geographic range of this book in an albacore from the eastern Atlantic off the Azores. Both the genus and species are in question. We include it because: (1) the existence of this worm is not mentioned in modern guides to tapeworms and it is thus being forgotten; (2) few adult tapeworm species have ever been found in big game fishes and this worm could be very interesting; and (3) because we would like someone to find adult tapeworms in albacore. The description of this worm was inadequate to distinguish the genus or species. The body was badly contracted. It apparently had no attachment organs on the scolex. The posterior margin of the segment (proglottid) overlaps the anterior margin of the next proglottid (craspedote condition), and the posterior border has 10-12 pleats. It was about 55.0 mm long.

Sphyriocephalus **sp.** - This larval parasite could possibly be the same as *S. dollfusi* Bussierae and Aldrin which has been found in bigeye tuna in the eastern Atlantic. Postlarvae have a scolex that is thicker than wide and characterized by a deep bothridial cavity. The 2 ventral and dorsal bothridia are fused together around the cavity. The postlarva looks like a rather thick ping pong paddle. The tentacles emerge through the bothridia cavities and look something like cacti in a planter. The tentacles, tentacle bulbs and sheaths are all short. Two and 6 blastocysts were encysted in the viscera of 2 of 10 yellowfin tuna from the southern Gulf of Mexico and capsules occurred in 14 of 45 yellowfin tuna from the northeast Gulf of Mexico (USNPC 56908).

trypanorhynchid plerocercoid - Most of these plerocercoid larval forms in fishes can be identified, at least to genus, because the scolices are well formed and they have 4, distinctive, hook-covered tentacles. Some forms may lack characters for identification beyond order, particularly those that are less developed, badly contracted during preservation, or degenerated in capsules. The best way to resolve these identification problems is to obtain a larger series of specimens to find more mature plerocercoids in better condition.

NEMATODA (ROUNDWORMS)

Roundworms, threadworms or nematodes are a phylum. They, along with flatworms and spiny-headed worms, are sometimes called "helminths". Roundworms cause serious diseases and even death in humans. The recent popularity of Japanese raw-fish dishes has caused an increase in the number of fish-roundworm-related illnesses around the world. Modern refrigeration of fish catches has also allowed dangerous roundworms, that would have been discarded by quick cleaning, to migrate from the gut and mesenteries into the edible flesh. The unwise game of "live fish swallowing" has produced severe gastric distress in humans when roundworms from fish burrowed through the intestinal wall into the body cavity of humans. Treatment requires surgical removal. One case is known of a roundworm from the flesh of a Hawaiian jack penetrating a wound in the hand of a man cleaning the fish. The entry was painful and the worm could only be removed with surgery. More than 12,000 species are described of the more than 500,000 to 2 million that probably exist. They are one of the most abundant multicellular organisms on earth, both in total numbers of individuals and in number of species. Roundworms occur in such high numbers in almost all vertebrates and invertebrates that it has been suggested that the shapes of all living animals could be seen from space by merely seeing the mass of worms in each animal.

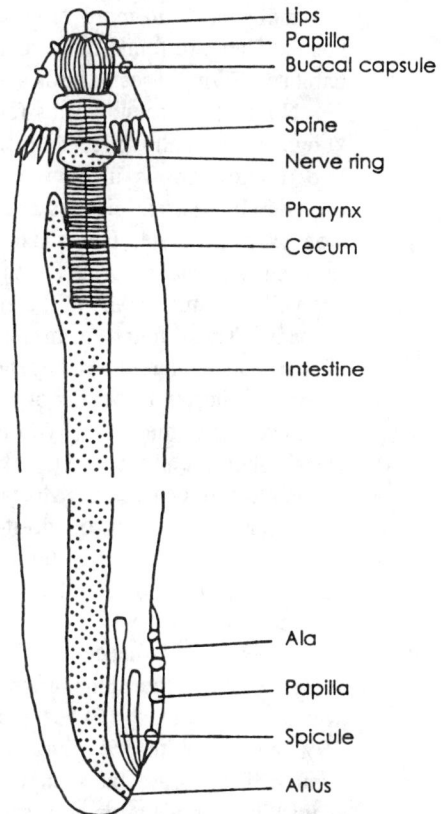

Lips
Papilla
Buccal capsule
Spine
Nerve ring
Pharynx
Cecum
Intestine
Ala
Papilla
Spicule
Anus

Most free-living forms are small to microscopic, but parasitic forms are large, up to 8 meters long. Roundworms, as the name implies, are circular in cross-section. The body is non-segmented, elongate and slender, often tapered near the ends, and covered with cuticle. Three to 6 lips surround the mouth. The digestive tract is complete. Musculature has longitudinal fibers. A pseudocoel (false body cavity) is present. A nerve ring is usually visible in the anterior end. Sexes are separate. The

male has a cloaca, a pair of chitinized copulatory structures (usually spicules), often with a variety of papillae, alae (long, thin flaps of cuticle), suckers in or on the posterior end. All of these male structures are important in identifying species. Eggs are released into the intestine of fishes, or through holes in the host skin in tissue-dwelling roundworms, into the water. Eggs may contain developed roundworms, while others are expelled while less developed. Some larvae are eaten by fishes and develop directly into an adult. Usually, larvae must go through 2-5 molts in 1 or more crustacean and/or fish intermediate hosts. They are found in all marine, freshwater and terrestrial habitats. Flying insects, birds and bats take them into the skies.

None of the roundworms found in Puerto Rican fishes are known to normally infect humans. Nevertheless, consuming live roundworms is ill advised as these parasites may cause considerable gastric distress or even penetrate the wall of the stomach or intestine. Humans in the continental USA have been infected with roundworms (anisakiasis) from raw skipjack tuna and yellowfin tuna. Any of the anisakids could potentially harm humans. Those found in the muscle of edible sport fishes are of particular interest as they are likely to be consumed by humans. Thorough cooking or freezing for several days kills all roundworms in muscle. If you must eat raw-fish dishes, make certain they are prepared by a professional chef who has been trained to avoid parasites. Most cases of anisakiasis in the USA have been the result of do-it-yourself preparations. The Japanese are thought to be the leading experts and demand the best quality fish, but they freeze most raw fish long enough to kill roundworms.

A necropsy is needed to find the larvae in the organs and mesenteries and the adults in the stomach and intestine. Round-worms can be relaxed in acetic acid and stored in a mixture of 70% ethanol with 5% glycerine. Adult roundworms from tissues of fishes are exceedingly delicate and tend to explode if placed in fresh water or preservatives. These small worms can be placed in a steaming 0.8% saline and 5% formalin solution. Once fixed (15 minutes for small worms up to 24 hours for large ones), worms can be rinsed in fresh water, and slowly transferred into gradually increasing concentrations of ethanol, until stored in a mixture of 70% ethanol and 5% glycerine.

Roundworms are usually examined in wet mounts. Semipermanent mounts may be prepared using glycerine jelly. In most larval species, identification to species is very difficult, but most genera can be determined. Study of the entire life cycle of a roundworm may be necessary to determine the species of larvae.

No treatment is possible for roundworms in the body cavity or tissues of fishes and is seldom necessary for intestinal roundworms. Worms that perforate the intestine of humans must be surgically removed.

Most roundworms in fishes are rather similar in shape. Thus the outlines of their entire bodies are not of much use in telling them apart. These worms are distinguished by relatively small structures on their anterior ends and on the posterior end of males. We illustrate a whole female *Hysterothylacium aduncum* here to show the general shape, but only illustrate enlargements of the anterior end and the posterior end of the male for each species described.

Reference - Anderson, Chabaud and Willmott (1974-83) is an excellent taxonomic guide to genera and higher classification of roundworms, and Bruce, Adlard and Cannon (1994) a taxonomic guide to species of fish-parasitic ascaridoids (anisakids and ascarids in big game fishes), but no general guide to all the fish roundworms has been crafted since Yamaguti (1961).

Classification and Contents

*Larval forms

Anisakis simplex Rudolphi

These tiny, inconspicuous worms cause severe pain, nausea, vomiting and can rarely kill humans. But this dangerous parasite can be easily avoided even in raw-fish dishes.

Name - This name has variously been used for a presumably single, widespread species in the northern Atlantic, similar species or any Anisakis sp. larva. We assume the "Anisapis sp." of Chen and Yang, 1973 in tunas off Taiwan was a typographical error for Anisakis sp.,

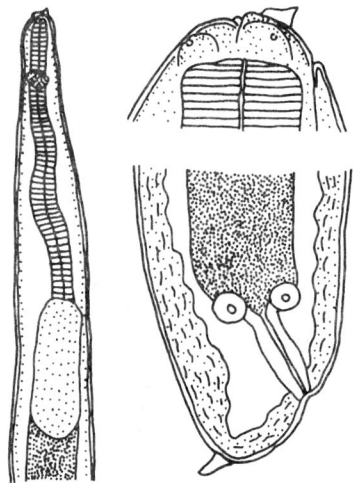

otherwise it would be a rather amusing roundworm. The disease this worm causes in humans is called "anisakiasis" or "sushi disease".

Diagnostic Characters - A cream-colored cyst encompasses the larvae which is coiled in a tight spiral (as are most other larval roundworms encysted in fish). When freed from the cyst, the anterior end of the worm has 3 relatively small, inconspicuous lips with an obvious, center off-set, forward projecting tooth (anteroventral projecting boring tooth). The relatively long esophagus is followed by a glandular region. There is no appendix or caecum. It has a bluntly rounded tail.

Records - One to 9 larvae occurred in 63 of 303 swordfish examined in the northwest Atlantic (ARC 2323). It has also been found in Atlantic bonito, Atlantic mackerel, skipjack tuna and yellowfin tuna off the northeast coast of the USA. This worm probably encysts in all big game fishes in this region. The larval *Anisakis* sp. reported in chub mackerel from southern Brazil may be this worm.

Geographic Range - Worldwide. It is well known in the North Atlantic from North America to Europe, and similar forms occur the north Pacific and in the cooler waters of the southern hemisphere.

Life History - Adults parasitize the gastrointestinal tract of dolphins (mammal), seals and whales. Eggs pass out of the intestine of the host. Second stage larvae escape from the egg in a few days. This free-swimming stage may be eaten by a crustacean transport host in which no development will occur, until this host is eaten by an appropriate intermediate crustacean or fish host, or it may be eaten directly by an intermediate host. The larvae, a few millimeters long, migrates to the hemocoel (crustacean) or mesenteries (fish), is soon encapsulated and develops into a third-stage larvae. When the appropriate marine mammal final host eat the intermediate host, the worm is digested out and develops into an adult. Third-stage larvae can infect humans. Larvae from Atlantic herring have been raised to adults in laboratory culture media without hosts.

Ecology - In the Atlantic it is limited to the colder regions (not in the Gulf of Mexico or the West Indies). However, in the Pacific it occurs from cold waters to tropical Hawaii and Australia.

Location in Host - These worms are usually found in the mesenteries around the gut and internal organs. Holding dead, fish, that have not been cleaned (eviscerated), on ice or under refrigeration allows these larvae to migrate into the flesh of the host.

A European herring fishery was converted from small boats with immediate cleaning practices to large vessels with refrigerated storage and shore processing. This gave the worms an opportunity to invade the flesh and widespread outbreaks of anisakiasis occurred in people consuming raw-herring dishes. Adequate freezing of the herrings before sale solved the problem.

Length - 11.2-34.5 mm.

Host Specificity - It is most common in inshore fishes and sometimes infects almost all fishes.

Damage to Host - Heavy infections of larvae in fishes can cause severe inflammation and death.

Detection - Once a fish is killed and held on ice, these larvae borrow out of their cysts and migrate into the muscle. These worms are relatively small and cream colored which makes them difficult to find in muscle. Studies have estimated that industrial techniques for detecting these and other larger worms in fish fillets can only find about half the worms.

Harm to Humans - Juveniles of this worm survive in refrigerated, iced, inadequately frozen, salted and pickled fish flesh. They penetrate the stomach of humans 1-12 hours after infected seafood is eaten, or may penetrate the intestine up to 14 days later. The penetrations usually cause sudden and severe pain in the upper stomach or abdomen. Usually nausea and vomiting are associated with the severe pain. Anisakiasis in the stomach can be diagnosed with an endoscope and the worms can be removed with biopsy forceps, if the surgeon is sufficiently skillful to catch these fast-moving and lively parasites. Worms that pass further down the intestinal tract cannot be so easily diagnosed and removed. In some cases penetration may occur without symptoms or with mild pain. Once the worms penetrate into the digestive tract wall or into other organs in the body cavity, diagnosis is more difficult as the symptoms causes by these parasites are similar to other, more common diseases. Immunological tests are available. Surgery may be necessary in some cases.

Experimental infections in monkeys are successful if the larvae enter an empty stomach, but not when the stomach contains food. This may explain the higher Japanese vs. Chinese infection rates, as raw fish is traditionally consumed in the beginning of the meal in Japan, but at the end in China (Williams and Jones 1976).

These worms can live for 51 days in vinegar, 6 days in 10% formalin (!), but only 2 hours in a home freezer (-20°C). Fish flesh should be frozen for 24 hours prior to being used in raw-fish preparations (Pinkus, Coolidge and Little 1975, Hilderbrand 1984). Larger and thicker fish may take longer to freeze and should be held 4-5 days in inefficient or over-filled freezers. This temporary freezing has very little effect on the flavor or texture of fresh fish, but kills dangerous roundworms. Thorough cooking kills all parasites.

Significance to Sportfishing - The larvae of this parasite may occur in sufficient numbers in Atlantic mackerel to injure, stunt or kill these fish. They are not known to occur in high numbers in other sport fishes.

This larvae has been evaluated as a potential biological tag for Atlantic mackerel and other fishes. Its abundance was used to show movement of albacore from New Zealand to the central south Pacific (Jones 1991).

Goezia pelagia Deardorff and Overstreet

This spiny burr of a parasite is more impressive in life than our drawings suggest. It is highly irritating and damaging to host fishes, but may be useful as a biological tag.

Name - The name "pelagia" means of the sea.

Diagnostic Characters - This worm has spines covering most of its body. It has over-hung lips on the anterior end, and a conical tail with a finger-like projection. Male spicules are approximately equal in length. Males have 12-19 pairs of papillae anterior of the anus; 2 pairs at the level of the anus, and posterior to the anus there are 4 pairs and the third pair is doubled (2 papillae jammed together in the row). The vulva of the female opens 29-55% of the total length of the worm from the anterior end.

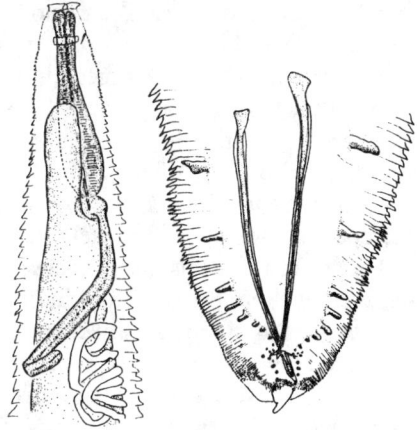

Records - Worms occurred in cobia (USNPC 75680-2) and other fishes off Alabama, Mississippi and Louisiana, USA.

Geographic Range - Northern Gulf of Mexico.

Ecology - These worms feed on both the blood of the host and partially digested food in the stomach of the host.

Associations - Several *Iheringascaris inquies* occurred in 1 capsule with this worm.

Location in Host - Free but firmly attached in the stomach or embedded and encapsulated in stomach wall.

Length - Female 3.6-14.5 mm, male 3.4-12.0 mm.

Host Specificity - This worm probably has little host preference, since the 3 host species are found in 3 families and 2 orders of fishes.

Damage to Host - Various amount of tissue penetration and host reaction occurred with encapsulated worms. Some worms in a capsule were degenerated. Extensive bacterial and fungal infections occurred inside the capsules. Inflammation and host reaction was limited to the area immediately around the capsules, and the capsules seemed to confine microbial infections and further worm penetration. Other worms in this genus have caused mass mortalities in fishes stocked in freshwater lakes. Some species elicit extensive host reaction. Deardorff and Overstreet (1980) suggested that these worms can detrimentally affect sport fishes.

Significance to Sport Fishing - This worm may be a good biological tag as it is easy to recognize, has a limited geographic range and survives in capsules for several years.

Hysterothylacium Ward and Magath

Many species of roundworms that have incorrectly been placed in the genera *Contracaecum* and *Thynnascaris* Dollfus (*thynnos*=tuna, *ascaris*=worm) belong in the genus *Hysterothylacium* (*hysteros*=after, *thylaco*=bag, and refers to the cecum). *Thynnascaris* was a marvelous name for parasites of big game fishes, especially tunas, but unfortunately it is not taxonomically correct for these worms. Deardorff and Overstreet (1981) resurrected and redescribed this genus, moved 55 species into it and detailed those species found in the Gulf of Mexico. Bruce and Cannon (1989) re-redescribed it and split off the new genus *Maricostula*. Bruce, Adlard and Cannon (1994) listed 65 species in Genus *Hysterothylacium*. The exact number cannot be determined as only a few of these species have been adequately described.

Larval forms of this genus encyst in fish and are similar in appearance to *Contracaecum* spp. larvae. They differ by having the excretory pore at the level of the nerve ring in *Hysterothylacium* spp. and near the lips in *Contracaecum* spp. Members of both genera have the offset boring tooth similar to *Anisakis* spp. larvae, but differ by having a distinct caecum. A complete life cycle is only known for *Hysterothylacium aduncum*, but the other species in big game fishes probably have similar cycles. Eggs are laid in the intestinal tract of the host and are shed into the environment. Second stage larvae 0.3-0.5 mm long hatch from the eggs. They can stay alive without a host from 2 weeks to several months. Once ingested by a copepod, the larvae grow to 0.4-0.7 mm long. A small fish may be able to serve as a host for this stage instead of a copepod. When the copepod is eaten by a fish, the second stage larvae is digested out of the copepod, penetrates the intestinal wall of the fish, and encapsulates and grows to 1.0-4.0 mm long. The process may be repeated several times in ascending sizes of fishes (transport host), if other fishes eat the infected fish before the larvae has sufficiently developed, or if the host eating the infected fish is not the appropriate final host. Eventually, the third stage larvae grows to 22 mm long and its intermediate host is eaten by the appropriate final host (or the larvae dies of "old age" or is finally overcome by the defenses of the host). In the gut of the final host, the larvae is digested out of its intermediate host, attaches in the stomach and develops into an adult.

Heavy infections of larvae in fishes can cause severe inflammation and death. Overstreet and Meyer (1981) found that a larval form of this genus, common in the northern Gulf of Mexico, was capable of penetrating the stomach and causing hemorrhage in monkeys that ingested these worms. The flesh of dolphins, Spanish mackerels, swordfish and tunas may become contaminated with this worm if they are not cleaned quickly. This is particularly true for uncleaned fishes held for hours on ice or under refrigeration. Most of these worms in the gut of the final host are either young, immature or larval forms. When the host dies these forms can easily penetrate the gut wall and pass into the flesh. These fish should be adequately frozen before being used in raw-fish dishes. These larvae occur in a great variety of invertebrates including commercial shrimp. Twelve hours in a home freezer (-20°C) kills these roundworms (Norris and Overstreet 1976), but more time may be necessary to kill these larvae in fish tissues. Thorough cooking kills all parasites.

Hysterothylacium aduncum (Rudolphi)

A general and widespread parasite of inshore fishes. Apparently a few adults and encysted larvae are transferred to big game fishes through feeding on inshore ones. Larval forms can infect humans.

Name - This species could be a complex of several similar species. *Hysterothylacium longispiculum* (Fujita) and *Thynnascaris adunca* (Rudolphi) are synonyms.

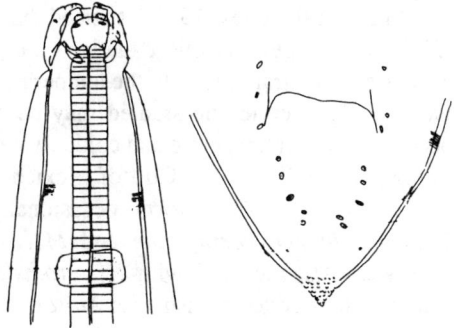

Diagnostic Characters - The alae begin just posterior to the lips. The lips are wider than long, lack interlabial grooves, are not indented in their sides, and taper toward the anterior margin. There is a deep constricted at the base of the lips. The tail gradually tapers and ends with a patch of small caudal spines (called "cactus-tail" by some authors). The cervical alae are narrow. Males have 2 pre-anal pairs of papillae, 2 pairs of papillae at the same level as the anus, and 5 pairs posterior to the anus. The spicules are approximately equal in length. The female has a vulva opening in the first 30-50% of the body length. The encysted, third stage larvae may be identified by the cactus tail.

Records - One to 21 worms occurred in 26 of 303 swordfish from the northwest Atlantic (ARC 2410); in Atlantic mackerel and white trevally off the Atlantic coast of the USA, in northern bluefin tuna off Europe, and in other jacks around the world. Encysted larvae were found in northern bluefin tuna and swordfish off Europe and in albacore in the southwest Pacific. Jones (1991) found larvae of this worm in 0-33% of over 400 albacore sampled from 13 locations in the tropical to temperate southwestern Pacific. High prevalence (27-33%) occurred in both tropical and temperate areas. Intensity increased with increases in host size. Adults and larvae have been reported from a great variety of fishes.

Geographic Range - Worldwide in temperate and cooler waters.

Life History - See description in the genus. Eggs hatch in 4-12 days. Larvae have experimentally developed in benthic polychaetes, planktonic copepods and fish fry, but are only commonly found in polychaetes in the wild. Sometimes as many as 13% of numerous polychaete species sampled are infected with 1, or rarely 2, larvae (once 150). Jones (1991) suggested that planktonic krill (euphausiids), plankton-associated hyperiid amphipods and squids were intermediate hosts in the southwest Pacific. More than 100 species of invertebrates in 7 phyla have been reported as intermediate hosts. This wide range of hosts may help to explain the great abundance and broad distribution of this parasite.

Ecology - It is usually found in inshore, benthic hosts. This parasite probably only occurs in offshore fishes that acquire them from eating inshore fishes. In

Europe it is the most common larval roundworm encysted in inshore fishes, occurring in almost every fish in some areas.

In contrast, Jones (1991) reported that this larval worm was more common (27-33%) in open oceanic situations east of New Zealand, than near island groups and Australia, in both the temperate and tropical regions of the southwest Pacific. The worms he studied may be a similar, but different species as it occurs strictly in temperate and colder waters in the Atlantic, and does not occur in the West Indies or the Gulf of Mexico.

Associations - This worm occasionally occurred in low numbers with *Hysterothylacium corrugatum* and *Maricostula incurva* in swordfish in the northwest Atlantic, and with *Hysterothylacium cornutum* in bluefin tuna off Europe. It encysted in fish with *Anisakis simplex* in the southwest Atlantic and probably does so in the north Atlantic.

Location in Host - Stomach.

Length - Female 16.0-94.0 mm, male 14.0-37.0 mm, third stage larva 5.9-21.6 mm (the cyst is smaller because the worms are coiled).

Host Specificity - It apparent has little host preference. This parasite has been reported from more than 100 fish species, although some of these records were probably in error. It is possible that big game fishes are only false hosts.

Harm to Humans - Williams and Jones (1976) document cases of human infection (eosinophilic granulomata) by larvae of this worm.

Significance to Sport Fishing - This worm apparently occurs only in cold-water areas. It might be useful as a biological tag of big game fishes moving into warmer regions. The adults may only survive a few months or a year, but encysted larvae should be available for a longer period of time. Jones (1991) was able to easily identify the encysted larvae in albacore in the southwest Pacific, but this biological tag was not diagnostic of movements in his study.

Hysterothylacium cornutum (Stossich)

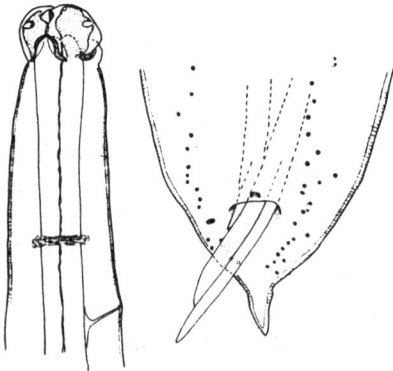

Light infections probably do little damage to tunas around the world. They do pose a threat to humans who eat these popular and pricey fish raw. **Name** - It was redescribed by Bruce and Cannon (1989). *Thynnascaris legendrei* Dollfus is a synonym.

Diagnostic Characters - The alae begin at the base of the lips. The lips are slightly shorter than wide. The tail is bluntly rounded with a prominent acute process. Males have 23-32 pre-anal papillae, 2 papillae at the level of the anus, and 9-13 (usually 9) papillae posterior to the anus. There are obvious striations (modified ventral annuli) across the body in the area of the papillae.

The spicules are approximately equal in length. The female vulva opens in the anterior 13.3-29.0% of the body length.

Records - One female and 2 males occurred in an albacore and 3 females and a male in blackfin tuna off Puerto Rico (USNPC). It has also been found in albacore, bluefin tuna and yellowfin tuna in the Atlantic; and these fishes and additional species of tunas in the Indo-Pacific. Deardorff and Overstreet (1982) found this worm in yellowfin tuna off Hawaii, but did not find it in 19 yellowfin tuna from the northern Gulf of Mexico. Ward (1962) also failed to locate it in 45 yellowfin tuna from this region. The *Contracaecum* sp. reported in the stomach and intestine of yellowfin tuna in the southern Gulf of Mexico by Nikolaeva (1968) could have been this worm.

Geographic Range - Worldwide. Our collections are the first in both the western Atlantic and the Caribbean.

Ecology - Pelagic, open ocean.

Location in Host - Stomach.

Length - Female 20.7-52.0 mm, male 19.6-29.4 mm.

Host Specificity - It is genus specific (*Thunnus*). Records from fishes other than tunas were other species of roundworms. Blackfin tuna is a new host.

Harm to Humans - The relatively new and expensive flying of fresh tunas into Japan from around the world, should provide an ample opportunity for these worms to contaminate the flesh.

Significance to Sport Fishing-If this worm occurs in the Caribbean, but not in the Gulf of Mexico; and in the northeast but not the northwest Atlantic, then it might be useful as a biological tag.

Hysterothylacium corrugatum Deardorff and Overstreet

This large parasite of swordfish occurs sparsely in the western Atlantic and eastern Pacific. Both the mystery of its unusual distribution and how it maintains such low numbers are worthy of investigation.

Name - The name "corrugatum" means ridged and refers to the modified annuli on the posterior, ventral surface of the male. This is a useful, but not exactly a unique character among these worms.

Diagnostic Characters - The alae begin just posterior to the base of the lips. The lips are distinctly longer than wide, are constricted in the middle, lack deep interlabial grooves and are not on peduncles. The tail gradually tapers. Males have 24-26 pairs of papillae anterior to the anus, 1 pair at the same level of the anus, and 4 pairs posterior to the anus. There are obvious striations (modified ventral annuli) across the body in the area of the papillae.

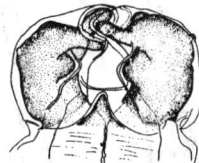

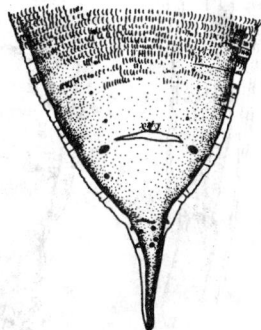

The spicules are approximately equal in length. The female vulva opens in the anterior 33.0-39.0% of the body length.

Records - A light infection occurred in 1 of 2 swordfish caught off La Parguera, Puerto Rico (USNPC); 6 females and 5 males in a swordfish from Miami, Florida (USNPC 75844-46); from Panama City, Florida, USA; up to 99 worms, but usually many fewer (mean 12.5), in 208 of 303 swordfish from the northwest Atlantic (ARC 2311); and in the eastern Pacific.

Geographic Range - Tropical to temperate western Atlantic and tropical eastern Pacific. Our collection is the first in the Caribbean.

Ecology - Pelagic, open ocean.

Associations - It occurred with *Maricostula incurva* in swordfish off Puerto Rico, south Florida, and in the northern Gulf of Mexico; and with *M. incurva*, *Hysterothylacium aduncum* and *H. reliquens* from the northwest Atlantic.

Location in Host - Stomach.

Length - Female 100.0-142.0 mm, male 26.0-50.0 mm.

Host Specificity - It only occurs in swordfish and is a secondary parasite.

Damage to Host - This large worm may stunt or injure swordfish particularly when it occurs in heavy infections of almost 100 worms. It may also contribute to severe injury to swordfish when they are superinfected with thousands of *Maricostula incurva*.

Significance to Sport Fishing - Parasites extract a heavy toll on this highly important sport and commercial fish. Their role in its ecology must be better understood. If the range of this worm is as restricted as our current knowledge suggests, then it might be of use as a biological tag.

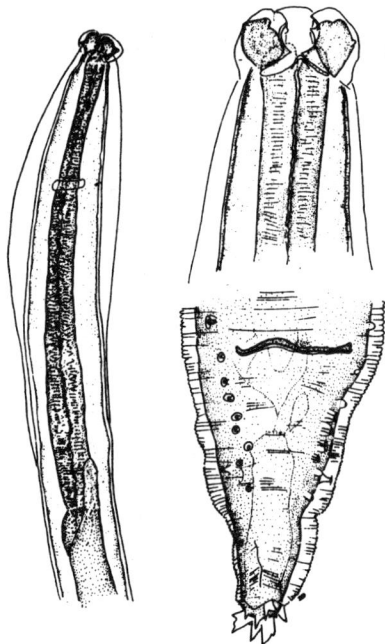

Hysterothylacium fortalezae (Klein)

This rather small worm occurs in low numbers in tropical and subtropical western Atlantic Spanish mackerels.

Diagnostic Characters - The alae extend the entire length of body and are prominently expanded into wings the anterior and posteriorly ends of the worm. The lips are as long as wide and have no interlabial grooves. A tuft of 12-14 projections occurs on the end of the tail. Males have 13-25 pairs papillae anterior to the anus, no papillae at the level of the anus, and 8 post-anal pairs. The female vulva opens in the anterior 30.0-38.0% of the body length.

Records - We found 1-2 in 3 of 35 cero and 1-5 in 8 of 9 king mackerel from La Parguera, Puerto Rico (USNPC); and 8-11 in 2 of 4 king mackerel and 2-24 in 3 of 9 Spanish mackerel from Dauphin Island, Alabama, USA (USNPC). This worm also occurred in Spanish mackerel from Florida and Mississippi, and in other inshore fishes from Mississippi, USA; and in king mackerel and serra Spanish mackerel from Brazil.

Geographic Range - Atlantic and Mediterranean. Our collections are the first in the Caribbean.

Location in Host - Stomach and intestine.

Length - Female 10.0-15.4 mm, male 12.0-23.4 mm, female fourth-stage larva encysted in fish 5.0-13.5 mm, third-stage larva 1.7-3.5 mm.

Host Specificity - Spanish mackerels are the preferred hosts, but it is not genus specific (*Scomberomorus*). Cero is a new host.

Hysterothylacium pelagicum Deardorff and Overstreet

A common, yet little known, stomach and intestinal parasite of dolphin around the world. More fish are parasitized by this worm in the tropics than in the temperate areas.

Name - The name "pelagicum" means of the sea. This species was confused with *Hysterothylacium cornutum* until it was separated by Deardorff and Overstreet (1982). It was redescribed by Bruce and Cannon (1989). *Ascaris increscens* of Linton and *Hysterothylacium* sp. of Deardorff and Overstreet are synonyms. *Contracaecum* [sp.] reported as extremely abundant in numerous dolphin stomachs caught off North Carolina by Rose (1966) was probably this worm.

Diagnostic Characters - The alae begin just posterior to the lips. The lips are shorter than wide, and have deep interlabial grooves. There is a tuft of 12-14 projections on end of the tail. Males have 36 pairs of papillae anterior of the anus, 3 pairs at the level of the anus, and 11-12 pairs posterior to the anus. It does not have body striations (modified ventral annuli) in the area of the papillae. There is a tiny round ball at the tip of the tail which looks like a nipple or a spinous process. The female vulva opens in the anterior 30-40% of the body length.

Records - We found 1-31 (average 5.8) in 23 of 40 dolphin from various locations around Puerto Rico (USNPC); and 1-20 in 2 of 5 dolphin from Dauphin Island, Alabama, USA. It also occurs in this host off the Gulf and Atlantic USA coasts from Texas to North Carolina, including the Florida Keys; and 1-35 (mean 10) were found in 19 of 33 dolphin from Hawaii. It has also been found in black marlin from the Pacific, but this could represent roundworms from dolphin consumed by this host.

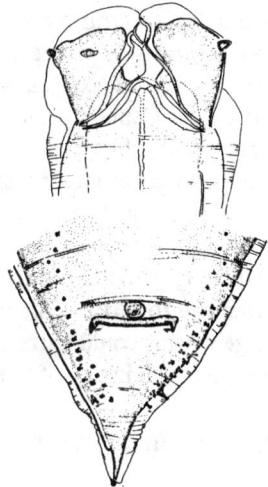

We identified all the gastrointestinal parasites in 13 dolphin collected off La Parguera, Puerto Rico. Twelve (92.3%) were infected with 1-12 males (average 1.6) and 1-44 females (average 11.9) of this roundworm. Manooch, Mason and Nelson (1984) examined the stomachs of 2632 dolphins in 10 sample areas from Texas to North Carolina, USA. They found 132 (5%) of these fish had from 1-100 of this worm, but most fish had few worms (mean 11). They also found more stomach parasites in larger fishes, but this was not apparent in our 13 fish. They only looked at stomachs, while we examined the entire tract. They also found few flukes, while we found more than 2800 in a single stomach. This suggests that Caribbean dolphin are much more heavily parasitized than those off the Gulf and Atlantic coasts of the USA.

Geographic Range - Worldwide. Our collections are the first in the Caribbean. It has been listed from the Caribbean in a summary article, but this was mistakenly based on the Gulf of Panama record (eastern Pacific).

Ecology - Pelagic, open ocean.

Associations - This roundworm occurred together with and in similar numbers to a fluke, *Dinurus tornatus*, in 13 dolphin we examined (The abundance of this roundworm was strongly positively correlated at a 99% confidence level with the presence of the fluke). Seven males and 4 females of *Maricostula makairi* Bruce and Cannon occurred with a male and 3 females of *H. pelagicum* in the stomach of a black marlin off Australia.

Location in Host - Stomach, pyloric ceca and intestine.

Length - Female 17.0-82.0 mm, male 28.0-67.0 mm.

Host Specificity - It is host specific and is a primary parasite of dolphin. Other big game fishes that eat dolphin are false hosts.

Damage to Host - The very heavy infections of more than 100 of these rather large worms could harm or at least stunt the growth of dolphin. They also contribute to the injury of this host when combined with superinfections of flukes.

Hysterothylacium reliquens (Norris and Overstreet)

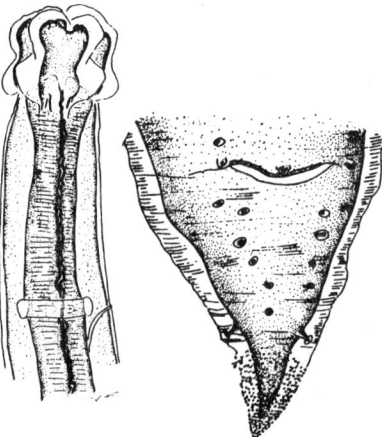

The adult of this worm is an incidental, uncommon and possibly temporary parasite obtained by big game fishes through eating inshore fishes, but the larvae is occasionally found in Spanish mackerels.

Name - The name "reliquens" refers to abandonment or the vacating of the host by these worms which pour out of the mouth, gills and anus, after the host is landed. It was placed in genus *Thynnascaris*.

Diagnostic Characters - The minute alae begin just posterior to the lips. The lips are longer than wide, constricted at their midpart, and lack interlabial grooves. The tip of the tail is covered with numerous minute spines. Males have 23-29 pairs of papillae anterior to the anus, no pairs of papillae at the level of the anus, and 4-5 pairs posterior to the anus with the third pair from the end doubled (2 papillae jammed together in the row). It does not have striations (modified ventral annuli) at the area of the papillae. Female vulva opens in the anterior 16-45% of the body length.

Records - We found heavy infections of larvae encysted in 2 cero from Humacao, but not in 33 other cero examined from various locations around Puerto Rico; and 7 in 1 of 4 king mackerel off Dauphin Island, Alabama. Larvae also encysted in Spanish mackerel from the northern Gulf of Mexico. One to 40 adult worms occurred in 14 of 303 swordfish from the northwest Atlantic (ARC 2411).

Geographic Range - Western Atlantic and eastern Pacific. Our collections are the first in the Caribbean.

Ecology - Fishes are infected in areas with salinities above 20 ppt but not above 35 ppt or hypersaline. The area in eastern Puerto Rico with the heavy infection rates is contaminated (see *Didymocystis scomberomori*).

Location in Host - Stomach and intestine. The third stage larvae are encysted in mesenteries and the outer layer of the stomach and intestine.

Length - Female 21.0-130.0 mm, male 25.0-40.0 mm, female fourth-stage larvae (encysted in fish) 8.7-22.5 mm, male fourth-stage larvae 14.0-22.0 mm, early fourth-stage larvae 4.3-9.2 mm.

Host Specificity - This adult occurs in a variety of inshore bottom fishes, but big game fishes may be false hosts. Encysted larvae occur in a variety of fishes including Spanish mackerels. Cero and king mackerel are new hosts.

Damage to Host - Heavy infections of encysted larvae may injure cero.

Iheringascaris inquies (Linton)

Heavy infections of this worm occur around the world in cobia.

Name - Deardorff and Overstreet (1980) resurrected and redescribed this genus. *Hysterothylacium shyamasundarii* (Lakshmi and Rao) and *Neogoezia elacateiae* Khan and Begum are synonyms of this worm.

Diagnostic Characters - The body is relatively narrow. The lips are as long as wide to wider than long, and do not have deep interlabial grooves. The tail is conical. Males have spicules that are approximately equal in diameter and length (20-25% of body length). There are lateral rows of 6 papillae in addition to the normal pre- and post-anal papillae and a medioventral preanal organ is present. Males have 25-29 pairs of papillae anterior to the anus, and 6 median

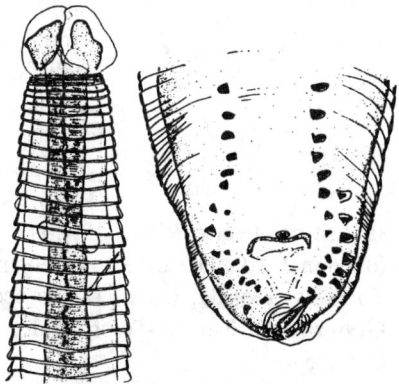

pairs posterior to the anus with third pair from the end doubled (2 papillae jammed together in the row). It does not have striations (modified ventral annuli) at the area of the papillae. The female vulva opens in the anterior 31-38% of the body length.

Records - Heavy infection of both sexes occurred in cobia from off La Parguera, Puerto Rico; and around the world. Overstreet in Shaffer and Nakamura (1989) noted that whenever a cobia is dissected, the stomach was found to be heavily infected with this roundworm.

Geographic Range - Worldwide.

Location in Host - Stomach and pyloric ceca.

Length - Female 14.0-50.0 mm, male 18.0-30.0 mm.

Host Specificity - It only occurs in cobia, and is a characteristic parasite of this host.

Damage to Host - Constant and heavy infections of this parasite must take a toll on the host. Overstreet (1978) reported that hundreds of worms occur in large cobia, and they occasionally cause ulcerated lesions at sites where several worms attach clustered together.

Maricostula histiophori (Yamaguti)

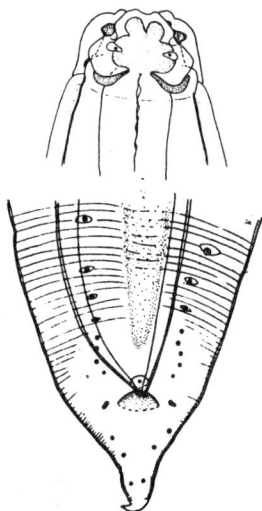

This is a cosmopolitan parasite of Atlantic and Indo-Pacific sailfish

Name - It was redescribed by Olsen (1952) and Bruce and Cannon (1989).

Diagnostic Characters - The alae begin at the lips. The lips are wider than long, indented 1/2 way up their sides, and have no interlabial grooves. There is a deep constriction at the base of the lips. The tail gradually tapers. Males have 14-17 pairs of papillae anterior to the anus, 1 doubled (2 papillae jammed together in the row) pair at the same level as the anus and 4 pairs posterior to the anus. There are crests (modified ventral annuli) in the area of the papillae. The female vulva opens in the anterior 26.7-56.8% of the body length.

Records - Two to 12 occurred in 4 of 6 Atlantic sailfish off Puerto Rico (USNM). A male and 1 female, and a female were found in 2 Atlantic sailfish off Panama; and 40 in an Atlantic sailfish off the Dry Tortugas, Florida, USA. It also occurs in Indo-Pacific sailfish.

Geographic Range - Worldwide. Our collections are the first in the insular Caribbean.

Location in Host - Stomach and intestine.

Length - Females 57.8-84.5, male 42.5-48.0, immature male 24.0-31.0 mm.

Host Specificity - Host specific to sailfish or genus specific to Atlantic and Indo-Pacific sailfish; depending on which host taxonomy you follow. The presence of this roundworm could be part of an argument for calling sailfish 1 species. It may be a characteristic parasite of sailfishes.

Damage to host - Iversen and Kelly (1974) found an intense granulomatous inflammatory reaction (or fibrous tissue in older infections) surrounding this worm in gastric ulcers. They suggested that the spines of prey fishes caused most ulcers but that nematodes may also be involved.

Maricostula incurva (Rudolphi)

It is a confusing and probably wide ranging and important parasite of swordfish.

Name - The identity of this worm has been confused and its biology obscured because redescriptions have either been based on *Maricostula histiophori* or on a mixture of different species.

Diagnostic Characters - The alae begin just posterior to the lips. The lips are wider than long, not indented in their sides, their anterior margin not narrowed and straight, and they have deep interlabial grooves. There is a deep constriction at the base of the lips. The tail gradually tapers, and the cervical alae are moderately wide. Males have 16 pairs of papillae anterior to the anus, 1 doubled (2 papillae jammed together in the row) pair at the level of the anus, and 4 pairs posterior to the anus. Crests (modified ventral annuli) occur in the area of the papillae, have a high profile, and overlap each other. The spicules are about 160% of the length of the ejaculatory duct. The female vulva opens in the anterior 25-40% of the body length.

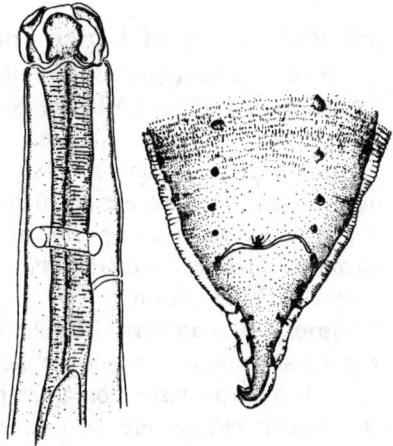

Records - More than 100 occurred in each of 2 swordfish off La Parguera, Puerto Rico; off St. Croix, U.S. Virgin Islands; from Cuba; off Miami, Florida, USA, up to 3038 (average 96.4) in 285 of 303 swordfish from the northwest Atlantic (ARC 2312); in the Adriatic, Baltic, Mediterranean, North Sea, and in the Pacific.

Geographic Range - Worldwide.

Life History - Hogans and Brattey (1982) suggested that larger worms, up to 16 cm, live for several years.

Associations - This worm occurred in combination with *Hysterothylacium corrugatum* in swordfish off Puerto Rico, Florida, in the northern Gulf of Mexico; and with *Hysterothylacium aduncum*, *H. corrugatum* and *H. reliquens* in the northwest Atlantic.

Location in Host - Stomach.

Length - Female 25.0-160.0 mm, male 17.0-34.0 mm. Linton (1897) reported worms up to 267.0 mm.

Damage to Host - This large worm may stunt or injure swordfish particularly when it occurs in heavy to superinfections of thousands of worms. They may also contribute to severe injury to swordfish when they are combined with very heavy infections of *Hysterothylacium corrugatum.*

Host Specificity - This worm is only found in swordfish and is probably a characteristic parasite. The few records of this roundworm from other fishes appear to have been other species.

Maricostula sp. of Bruce and Cannon

A characteristic parasite of white marlin that occurs less often in blue marlin throughout the western Atlantic. Superinfections damage billfishes and disgust fishermen.

Name - Bruce and Cannon (1989) distinguished this worm a new species, but did not name it. We are examining our samples from Puerto Rico to determine if this worm warrants description as a new species. The *Hysterothylacium incurvum* (or *Thynnascaris incurva*) reported by various authors from billfishes appear to be this worm.

Diagnostic Characters - The alae begin just posterior to the lips. The lips are wider than long, not indented in their sides, and have deep interlabial grooves. There is a deep constriction at the base of the lips. The tail gradually tapers, and the cervical alae are narrow. Males have 27-38 pairs of papillae anterior to the anus, 1 doubled (2 papillae jammed together in the row) pair at the level of the anus, and 4 pairs posterior to the anus. Crests (modified ventral annuli) occur in the area of the papillae, and are low profile and do not overlap each other. The spicules are about 60% of the length of the ejaculatory duct. The female vulva opens in the anterior 25-40% of the body length.

Records - We found 11 in a white marlin off Mayaguez, Puerto Rico (USNPC), and 100 each in 2 white marlin from Dauphin Island Alabama, USA; and 1-7 in 8 of 40 Atlantic blue marlin from various localities off Puerto Rico (USNPC). Up to 1787 occurred in each of 4 white marlin from the southern Gulf of Mexico; 300 worms in 22 white marlin off Destin, Florida to Orange Beach, Alabama, USA (USNPC 75843); and 6-741 in 36 white marlin from South Carolina, USA.

Geographic Range - Western Atlantic. Our collections are the first in the Caribbean.

Location in Host - Stomach and intestine.

Length - Female 25.0-69.0 mm, male 17.0-34.0 mm.

Host Specificity - This worm only occurs in billfishes and may be family specific. It is a characteristic parasite of white marlin, and a secondary parasite of Atlantic blue marlin. Atlantic blue marlin is a new host for this parasite.

Damage to Host - Superinfections of these worms must injure these hosts. Many of these worms quickly leave the host after it dies. Therefore, the numbers recorded in each fish may be a small percentage of the worms that existed in the live host and the damage greater.

Harm to Humans - These worms pouring out of infected marlin should be treated with caution. Splattering or wiping these parasites on your mouth or nose could cause a direct infection.

Significance to Sport Fishing - Heavily infected marlin shed these large roundworms from their mouths and gills after they are landed. This spectacle disgusts otherwise seasoned fishermen. It may cause perfectly safe and wholesome seafood to be unnecessarily discarded.

Oncophora melanocephala (Rudolphi)

This parasite sporadically occurs in yellowfin tuna and Atlantic and Mediterranean big game fishes.

Name - The name "melanocephala" means black head. A questionable species, *Oncophora neglecta* Diesing, was inadequately described from the gall bladder of a bluefin tuna in Europe.

Diagnostic Characters - It has a large, obvious, cuticulized buccal capsule that is shaped like a scallop shell and is golden in color. The ribs on the shell extend about half way down the capsule or less. The spines occur on the posterior 1/2 of the capsule. The capsule tapers and becomes more narrow before it attaches to the esophagus. The tridents which occur on either side of the buccal capsule are longer than the capsule and the center tine is shorter than the outer ones. The mature female has an enlarged posterior end.

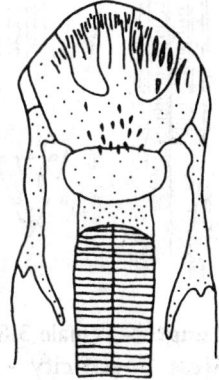

Records - Three occurred in an albacore from off Desecheo Island, Puerto Rico (USNPC), and 1-2 were found in 3 of 40 Atlantic blue marlin from various localities off Puerto Rico (USNPC). One was found in 2, and 7 in 1 of 10 yellowfin tuna from the southern Gulf of Mexico; 1-5 in 13 of 303 swordfish from the northwest Atlantic (ARC 2415); and in Atlantic bonito, Atlantic mackerel, bluefin tuna, bullet tuna and frigate tuna from the North Sea and Mediterranean.

Geographic Range - Atlantic and Mediterranean. Our collections are the first in the Caribbean.

Location in Host - Intestine.

Length - Female 111.0-150.0, male 10.5-12.6, immature female 14.2-16.1 mm.

Host Specificity - It may be family specific to scombrids. Atlantic blue marlin and swordfish are probably false hosts. Albacore and Atlantic blue marlin are new hosts.

Ctenascarophis lesteri Crites, Overstreet and Maung

This is a cosmopolitan and ever present parasite of the economically important skipjack tuna.

Name - It is named for the collector of this worm.

Diagnostic Characters - This parasite can be distinguished by the obvious spines on the body which are in broken combs instead of continuous rings.

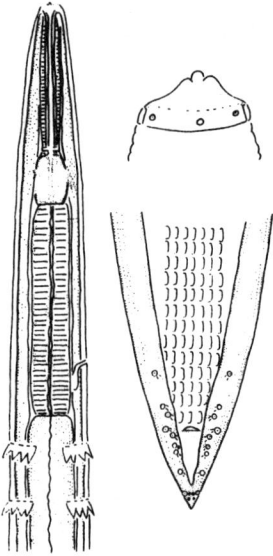

The only other member of the genus, *C. gastricus* Mamaev, appropriately occurs on another medium-sized big game fish, frigate tuna. It has only been reported in the Pacific, but we should be looking for it in this host in the Atlantic. *Ctenascarophis gastricus* differs from *C. lesteri* because the combs extend down 2/3 of the body length in the male and to the anus in the female, and it has a maximum of 32 instead of 8 spines per comb.

Records - Moderate infections occurred in 11 skipjack tuna from various localities around Puerto Rico (USNPC). Moderate to very heavy infections were found in 878 skipjack tuna from 14 sites across the Pacific.

Geographic Range - Worldwide.

Associations - This worm is always found with *Prospinitectus exiguus*.

Location in Host - Stomach.

Length - Female 3.8-5.7 mm, male 3.5-4.5 mm.

Host Specificity - It only occurs in skipjack tuna and is a characteristic parasite.

Prospinitectus exiguus Crites, Overstreet and Maung

This worm is a companion of the previous parasite species, and the little we know about their biologies is identical.

Name - The name "exiguus" means small or short and refers to the size of the body.

Diagnostic Characters - This parasite can be distinguished by the obvious spines on the body which are in continuous rings instead of broken combs.

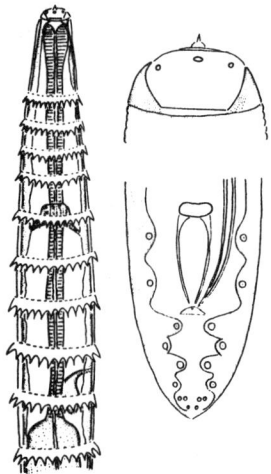

The only other member of the genus, *P. mollis* (Mamaev), occurs on another medium-sized big game fish, frigate tuna. It has only been reported in the Pacific, but we should be looking for it in this host in the Atlantic. *Prospinitectus mollis* differs from *P. exiguus* because its spines rings are interrupted rings, is less than half as long, has a proportionally longer esophagus, and fewer spines per ring (28-49 instead of 70-100).

Records - Moderate infections occurred in 11 skipjack tuna from various localities around Puerto Rico (USNPC). Moderate to very heavy infections were found in 878 skipjack tuna from 14 sites across the Pacific.

Geographic Range - Worldwide.

Associations - This worm is always found with *Ctenascarophis lesteri*.

Location in Host - Intestine especially near the pyloric ceca, and rarely in the stomach.

Length - Female 3.6-5.9 mm, male 3.6-4.0 mm.

Host Specificity - This worm is only found in skipjack tuna. It always occurs in this fish and is thus a characteristic parasite of this fish.

Significance to Sport Fishing - Skipjack tuna are economically important and abundant throughout much of the world. This worm and the previous parasite species occur abundantly in every skipjack tuna on Earth. Yet, these 2 parasite species were only recently recognized and described, and almost nothing is known about their biology. This situation is unfortunately indicative of the state of knowledge of big game fish parasites.

Miscellaneous Roundworms

Genus *Ascaris* Linnaeus - These roundworms occur as adults in terrestrial mammals and the larvae are not found in big game fishes. This genus name was used in the early literature for many larval forms found in these fishes, and poorly studied larval forms are still, although incorrectly, attributed to this genus.

Genus *Contracaecum* Railliet and Henry - Adults occur in fish-eating birds and marine mammals. All adult forms in fishes reported in this genus probably belong to the genus *Hysterothylacium*. Encysted larval forms in big game fishes may possibly belong in *Contracaecum*, but these are difficult to identify to species. Larval forms of members of this genus encyst in fish and are similar in appearance to *Hysterothylacium* spp. larvae. They differ by having the excretory pore at the level of the nerve ring in *Hysterothylacium* spp. and near the lips in *Contracaecum* spp. *Contracaecum clavatum* Rudolphi is a synonym of *Hysterothylacium aduncum*. *Contracaecum papilligerum* (Creplin) a larval form in Atlantic mackerel and bullet tuna in the Mediterranean is recognized as *Ascaris papilligera* Creplin by Bruce, Adlard and Cannon (1994).

Cucullanus carangis (MacCallum) - A 10.0 mm long, obviously immature, worm from the intestine of a crevalle jack at the New York Aquarium was described as *Dacnitis carangis*. Neither the description nor the illustration was sufficient to establish a new species. This name is best forgotten.

Cucullanus pulcherrimus Barreto - This worm was described from a black jack in Brazil, but has not been seen again in 75 years. Members of this genus are characterized by having relatively large broad mouths surrounded by a muscular pharynx with a club-shaped swelling posteriorly and no appendix. The male has a sucker anterior to the anus (preanal), 2 equal spicules and a shorter accessory piece (gubernaculum) and no caudal alae. The female has 2 ovaries and a vulva opening near midbody.

Cystoopsis scomber Zlatev - This worm occurred in the outer layer (conjunctiva) of the eye in Atlantic mackerel from the Black Sea, but has not been found in the Atlantic. This worm was described so poorly that it might be an encysted tissue fluke instead of a roundworm.

A very famous roundworm expert once screamed across a room, containing the bulk of USA parasitologists at an august national meeting, that she appreciated the "roundworm" specimens the poor fellow had sent her for identification, but if he could not tell a tissue fluke from a roundworm, then he did not belong at this meeting!

Ichthyostrongylus thunni Nikolaeva - This worm was named from yellowfin tuna in the southern Gulf of Mexico, but the status of this species and genus and even its Family or Order is uncertain.

Oncophora albacarensis Baudin-Laurencin - This worm was named from yellowfin tuna caught in the eastern Atlantic. It may not be very common as it was not seen by numerous other studies in the Atlantic. We should be looking for it in the western Atlantic.

Parascarophis galeata (Linton) - This worm is apparently a parasite of sharks that was accidentally introduced with prey into a pompano dolphin off North Carolina, USA. *Cystidicola galeatus* (Linton) and *Filaria galeata* Linton are synonyms. The head has a distinctive cap-like cuticular expansion which extends posteriorly further on one side (dorsal) than the other (ventral). The mouth has 2 long, thin front-to-back (dorsoventral) lips and 4 papillae. The mouth (buccal) cavity widens front-to-back (dorsoventrally) anteriorly and then becomes cylindrical. The esophagus is not distinctly divided into muscular and glandular portions. The tail is elongate, conical and ends in a blunt point. Numerous fragments were found in the stomach. Recorded from the Atlantic coast of the USA.

Philometra sp. - See *Philometroides* sp. below.

Philometroides sp. - We received a large fresh ovary of an Atlantic blue marlin caught off Puerto Rico that was so filled with squirming minute roundworms that most of its biomass was parasites. Raju (1960) reported 68,200 larval roundworms in the ovary of a Pacific skipjack tuna. All the eggs in the left ovary had been destroyed except the small transparent ones along the periphery. Fewer, but similar roundworms have been reported from the ovary of bigeye tuna and yellowfin tuna in the Pacific. Simmons (1969) found *Philometra* sp. and an unidentified spiruroid infecting the ovaries of approximately 90% of the mature skipjack tuna in the eastern and western tropical Atlantic Ocean. Young fishes lacking mature ovaries were not infected. The highest number of worms he found in a pair of ovaries was 75, and he found no obvious damage to the eggs. He also noted that the same 2 worms were found in skipjack tuna off New York, USA, and examined by Maybelle Chitwood (a famous roundworm expert). *Ichthyonema globiceps* Rudolphi, probably *Philometra* sp., was reported in the ovary of a Spanish mackerel from New Jersey, USA. All the worms reported above may not be the same species, but they all appear to be tissue-dwelling roundworms that were either larval or too undeveloped to identify. Superinfections of these worms destroy the ovaries. They must have a severe affect on the reproduction of these big game fishes.

The other, equally parasitized, ovary from our Atlantic blue marlin case was cooked and eaten by humans before they received our diagnosis. This apparently caused no obvious deleterious effects, as the dish received rave reviews for flavor, appearance and texture. This may be the only case known of an entire family basing an evening meal almost exclusively on fish-parasitic roundworms. These parasites are a mystery clearly in need of investigation.

A roundworm reported in the dorsal aorta of yellowfin tuna in Japan, has never been identified. It caused the vessel to thicken and become tough, and gave it a yellowish tint. Tissue roundworms have also been reported in the red muscle of bigeye tuna in the Pacific. Obviously, many tissue roundworms occur in big game fishes and are in need of study.

Porrocaecum paivai Silva-Motta and Gomes - This parasite was described from king mackerel from Brazil, but has been noted as poorly described or of uncertain status by subsequent authors. Adults in this genus parasitize birds, not fishes, thus the genus of this worm is also in question. The type material needs to be re-examined.

Prospinitectus mollis (Mamaev) - This worm has been found in frigate tuna and 2 species of little tunnies in the Pacific. Thus far it has not been found in frigate tuna or little tunny in the Atlantic, but we should be looking for it. *Spinitectus mollis* Mamaev, *Spinitectus palawanensis* Schmidt and Kuntz, are synonyms. See discussion of *Prospinitectus exiguus* for a comparison. Females are 11.0-15.4 mm and males 8.2-13.1 mm long.

Raphidascaris anchoviellae Chandler - This worm was described from striped anchovies, *Anchova hepsetus* (Linnaeus) [as *Anchoviella epsetus*] and reported in other fishes from Galveston Bay, Texas, USA (USNPC 39537-8). This species appears to have been described from immature males 4.0-5.8 and females 4.0-6.0 mm long and must remain questionable (species inquirenda) until it can be correlated with adult forms. Yamaguti (1959) listed "*Sphyraena*" as a host, but this appears to be an error.

spiruroids - See *Philometroides* sp. above.

ACANTHOCEPHALA (SPINY-HEADED WORMS)

These worms form a small phylum in the Animal Kingdom. The name "acanthocephala" means spiny headed. All spiny-headed worms are permanent parasites in the intestine of most vertebrates, including humans. Over 1000 species are known. Adult females vary from 1 mm to longer than 1 m, but are usually about 2 cm long. Males of the same species are typically smaller than females. They may be white, yellow, orange or red in color (*Pomphorhynchus lucyae* Williams and Rogers seems to absorb orange pigments from crayfish in the intestine of southeastern USA coastal fishes). They are bilaterally symmetrical and unsegmented. They attach in the gut of their host with a globular or cylindrical, protrusible, spiny proboscis. The proboscis pops out like an everting plastic glove, and the spines fold out and lock like a compact umbrella. Muscles invert the proboscis, and a hydraulic system (lemnisci) pop it back out. Some species have spines on the body as well. Sexes are separate, fertilization is internal, and embryos develop in the body of the female. Shelled larvae (acanthors) are shed into the intestine of the host, pass out with the fecal material, are eaten by a crustacean, insect, mollusk or fish intermediate host, and develop into an acanthella then to an encysted cystacanth larval stage in the second intermediate host. When the final host consumes an infected intermediate host, the cystacanth develops into an adult in the intestine. Big game fishes are final hosts for a few spiny-headed worms and are sometimes infected by larval stages of marine mammal spiny-headed worms. Adults absorb nutrients from the gut contents of their hosts. Proboscis spines (or hooks) cause some mechanical damage, but this is only serious in a heavy infection. Treatments seldom are necessary. Fortunately, natural infections in big game fishes usually consist of only a few worms per host. Some inshore, northern fishes are routinely infected with hundreds to thousands of spiny-headed worms. These worms rarely harm humans since they are usually discarded with the intestine and other internal organs when fish are cleaned, but contamination is possible. Thorough cooking kills these parasites. Tuna and other big game fishes are prized ingredients of Japanese raw-fish

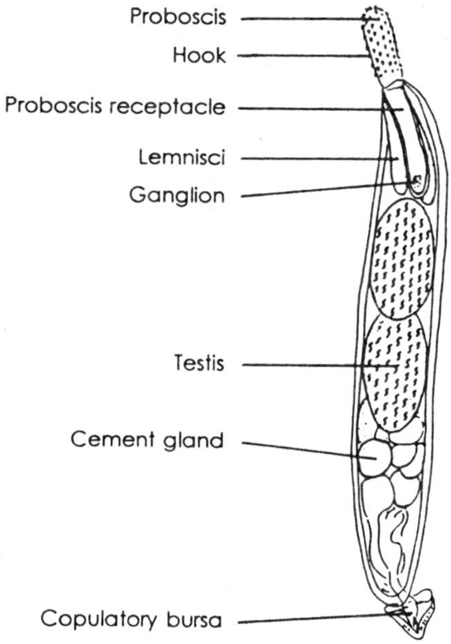
Proboscis
Hook
Proboscis receptacle
Lemnisci
Ganglion
Testis
Cement gland
Copulatory bursa

dishes, but most of these products are frozen long enough to kill parasites before they are served "fresh" in Japan.

A necropsy is necessary to find these worms in the intestine. Spiny-headed worms in big game fishes can be identified in wet mounts for routine examinations. For more detailed study, the proboscis must be fully everted before preserving. Worms must be refrigerated in distilled or fresh water for 12-24 hours before preserving in 5% formalin. The thick cuticle of these worms does not allow alcohol solutions or stains to readily penetrate. The cuticle must be pierced before dehydrating in alcohol solutions and staining.

Classification and Contents

*Adult and larval forms in big game fishes.

Gorgorhynchoides elongatus Cable and Linderoth

This parasite is a rare "taxonomic ghost" with virtually nothing known of its biology or affect on big game fishes.

Name - Linton found this worm during his extensive collections at Woods Hole, recognized it as a new species and new genus, deposited type specimens (USNPC 8044, 8045), but died before he could publish his results. Cable and Linderoth (1963) described the genus *Gorgorhynchoides* based on the material deposited by Linton. Three similar species, *G. elongatus*, *G. bullocki* Cable and Mafarachisi, and *G. lintoni* Cable and Mafarachisi are recognized in western Atlantic jacks. These forms are similar in shape, size, hosts and locality. Their descriptions were based on few specimens (*G. elongatus* = 1♀, *G. bullocki* = 1♂, 1♀, 4 immature ♀ and *G. lintoni* = 2♂, 3♀) including only 3 males which are taxonomically more important than females in distinguishing spiny-headed worm species. These parasites are known to be highly variable in their characteristics. Examination of additional specimens may establish these forms as valid species, but we prefer to treat them as variants of a single, poorly known, species.

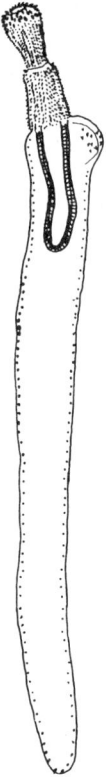

Diagnostic Characters - The proboscis is short, broad and bulbously expanded on the anterior end, and has numerous hooks. Proboscis hooks are larger anteriorly and smaller posteriorly (24-28 longitudinal rows of 16-22 hooks each). The neck has numerous spines followed by a hump-like dorsal swelling of the anterior trunk. The forms *G. bullocki*, *G. elongatus*, and *G. lintoni* largely differ by having no spines on the trunk swelling, few spines, or many spines, respectively. The constancy and separations in this gradation need to be substantiated with many worms to be considered diagnostic.

Records - Four females and 2 males occurred in 2 of 7 bar jacks from Mona Island (Puerto Rico) (USNPC); 1 female in a blue runner from Curaçao (USNPC 60345); 1 female, 1 male and 4 immature females in crevalle jack from the Gulf Coast of Florida (USNPC 62970); and 3 females and 2 males in almaco jack and greater amberjack from Woods Hole, Massachusetts, USA (USNPC 36619, 38644 and 38645) (forms *G. elongatus*, Curaçao; *G. bullocki*, Florida; *G. lintoni*, Woods Hole).

Geographic Range - Western Atlantic. Our collections are the first in the insular Caribbean.

Location in Host - Intestine.

Length - Female 31.3-76.0 mm, male 40.0-68.0 mm (forms *G. elongatus* ♀ 31.3; *G. bullocki* ♀ 53.0, ♂ 40.0; *G. lintoni* ♀ 49.5-76.0, ♂ 66.0-68.0).

Host Specificity - It is family specific to jacks, but apparently occurs too sporadically to be a characteristic parasite of any species. The 3 forms of this worm have been attributed to different species of jacks, but those records are based on few collections. Bar jack is a new host.

Cable and Mafarachisi (1970) redefined the genus and suggested that the species were "rigidly" host specific to jacks, and that parallel evolution had occurred among these fishes and parasites. Their suggestions are intriguing but seem a bit bold considering the low number of available collections with so few specimens. They further noted "widely separate localities" as the "isolating mechanism" for these parasites to speciate. Actually the localities are not very widely separated when the wide ranging abilities of these hosts is considered.

Rhadinorhynchus pristis (Rudolphi)

These large, orange worms are obvious in the gut of many big game fishes around the world.

Name - *Rhadinorhynchus selkirki* Van Cleave is a synonym; and *R. katsuwonis* Harada, *R. ornatus* Van Cleave, and *R. seriolae* Yamaguti could be synonyms. Any of these species noted from the Atlantic were probably *R. pristis*. Some of these species were placed in the genus *Nipporhynchus* which is a synonym of *Rhadinorhynchus* (the Japanese must be relieved at the demise of this genus which apparently means "Japanese nose"). The "*R. trachuri* Harada" of Chen and Yang, 1973 in Pacific skipjack tuna and yellowfin tuna, were probably *R. pristis*.

Diagnostic Characters -The proboscis is elongate, slender and cylindrical. Proboscis hooks are large and uniform in size (14-16 rows of 26 hooks each or 22-25 longitudinal rows of 36-40 hooks each) with a row of longer hooks at the base. A few hooks are present on one side of the anterior body. Females are large and orange in color, males smaller and cream-colored.

Records - We found 1 female in an albacore off La Parguera; 2-3 females in 2 of 3, and 1 female in 1 of 8 Atlantic blue marlin off western Puerto Rico (USNPC 84705); 1-16 females and 0-1 males in 5 of 14 (USNPC 84707-9) and 1-5 females in 3 of 6 dolphin, 1 female in 1 of 5 king mackerel and 2 males in a little tunny off La Parguera; numerous females and males in 2 skipjack tunas from Arecibo and 2 from south of Patillas and 9-12 females and 8-9 males in 2 off Ponce (USNPC); and 1 female in a white marlin off western Puerto Rico (USNPC 84704). One male and 2 females occurred in a dolphin off Curaçao (USNPC 60341); and 18 females and 2 males in 5 of 9 little tunny and 151 females and 85 males in a skipjack tuna off Bermuda. It has also been found in Atlantic mackerel, chub mackerel, and frigate tuna in the western Atlantic; sailfish in the Gulf of Mexico; 1-2 females in 4 of 303 swordfish from the northwest Atlantic (ARC 2413); albacore from Europe, and chub mackerel and skipjack tuna from Japan. The *Rhadinorhynchus* sp. reported from bullet tuna in the Pacific and the *Rhadinorhynchus tenuicornis* of Rego, Carvalho-V., Mendonca and Alfonso-R., 1985 in 24 of 80 Atlantic mackerel from Portugal could also be this worm.

Geographic Range - Worldwide.

Ecology - Occurs in many offshore, but also in some inshore, fishes. We only found it in big game fishes in the Caribbean.

Location in Host - Stomach, intestine. Throughout gut of skipjack tuna.

Length - Female 20.0-76.0 mm, male 12.0-20.0 mm.

Host Specificity - The incidence and sex ratios in skipjack tuna suggests that this worm is a characteristic parasite. It may also be a characteristic parasite of Atlantic mackerel. It is a secondary parasite in dolphin, at least in the Caribbean. Incidences in most other big game fishes are less certain. The occasional occurrence of low numbers of this worm in Atlantic blue marlin, king mackerel, little tunny and swordfish suggest that these are false hosts. This parasite may prefer big game fishes, but occurs in many other fishes. Atlantic blue marlin and king mackerel are new hosts.

Damage to Host - No damage was found in the fishes examined in this study, but the heavy infections in skipjack tuna may cause problems in this host.

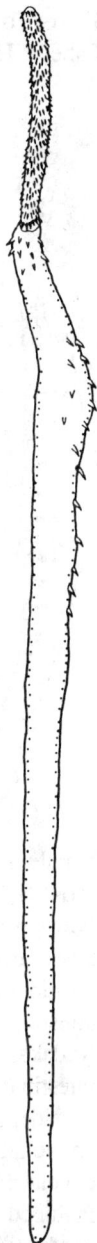

Detection - The large, orange-colored females are quite obvious in the gut of fishes. Unlike many parasites, they do not disintegrate in frozen hosts.

Serrasentis sagittifer (Linton)

This parasite is found in cobia and immature forms are encysted in a variety of marine fishes including dolphin.

Name - *Serrasentis chauhani* Datta, *S. giganticus* Bilqees, *S. longa* Tripathi, *S. longiformis* Bilqees, *S. scomberomori* Wang, and *S. socialis* (Leidy) are synonyms.

Diagnostic Characters - This parasite has distinctive rows of spines (combs) on the ventral surface of its body in adult and encysted stages. The proboscis is short, bulbous and expanded on the anterior end, and covered with numerous, uniform spines (16-24 longitudinal rows of 14-18 hooks each).

Records - Adults occur in cobia along the USA Atlantic and Gulf coasts, off Europe and West Africa. Immature stages occur in a variety of fish host including dolphin. An unidentified spiny-headed worm encysted on the stomach wall of 1 dolphin off North Carolina (Rose 1966) was probably this parasite. Adult worms have also been reported in permit, *Trachinotus falcatus* (Linnaeus), from Miami, Florida, USA.

Geographic Range - Worldwide.

Location in Host - Intestine and pyloric ceca; body cavity, mesenteries and external surfaces of internal organs (encysted forms).

Length - Female 6.0-130.0 mm, male 8.6-75.0 mm, juvenile female 4.0-6.4 mm, juvenile male 2.6-4.2 mm.

Host Specificity - This worm may be a characteristic parasite of cobia.

Damage to Host - Heavy infections of this rather large worm could injure the host. Encysted forms damage the tissues of their intermediate fish hosts and should produce significant injury if they occur in heavy infections. Severe intestinal damage was caused in cobia by adult *Serrasentis nadakali* George and Nadakal from India. Although this parasite did not deeply penetrate the intestinal tissues enough to even cause discontinuity of the mucosa, it caused considerable histopathological alterations including connective tissue hyperplasia, epithelial metaplasia, muscle hypertrophy, mucus epithelium necrosis and degeneration and extensive destruction of intestinal villi. Host responses included mobilization of lymphocytes and macrophages, and excessive production of mucus in the sight of infection.

Detection - The large, slender females are as long as your finger and are thus quite obvious in the gut of fishes.

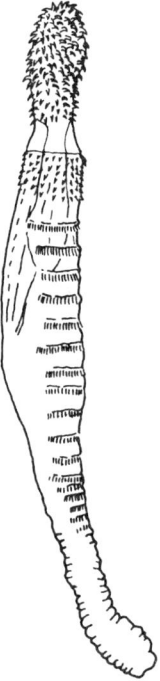

Bolbosoma vasculosum Rudolphi

Immatures of this marine mammal parasite are occasionally found in big game fishes.

Name - *Bolbosoma thunni* Harada is a synonym.

Diagnostic Characters - The body has a distinct bulge near the proboscis covered with 1 broad band of small hooks. A second band occurs on the body between the bulge and the proboscis. The proboscis is short, club-shaped and has numerous large, uniform hooks (16-20, usually 18, longitudinal (spiral) rows of 8-9 hooks each). Lemnisci (in adults) are elongate. The form *B. thunni* was distinguished because it had short lemnisci (0.8 mm long).

Records - We found 1 adult worm in 1 of 6 king mackerel off La Parguera, Puerto Rico. Immature forms have been found in the body cavity of albacore and jacks in the eastern Atlantic and yellowfin tuna off west Africa, and in the intestine of Atlantic mackerel off Russia and bluefin tuna in Japan. Adults occur in common or saddleback dolphin, *Delphinus delphis* Linnaeus, and North Sea beaked whale, *Mesoplodon bidens* (Sowerby) in the Atlantic, Mediterranean and Pacific.

Bolbosoma spp. were reported from bullet tuna, chub mackerel and yellowfin tuna in the Pacific. These forms could have been *B. vasculosum*.

Geographic Range - Worldwide (at least in the northern hemisphere). More commonly reported from the northern Atlantic and North Pacific and Mediterranean. Our collections are the first in the Caribbean.

Life History - Crustaceans are the first intermediate hosts, fishes the second intermediate hosts for the encysted cystacanth larvae, but also serve as intermediary hosts for immature and young worms. Fish-eating marine mammals are the final hosts.

Location in Host - Encysted forms occur in various fish tissues, immature forms are found in the intestine of fishes, and adult worms occur in intestine of marine mammals.

Length - Immature females in fishes 8.0-13.5 mm, adult females in mammals 12.0-15.0 mm.

Host Specificity - Big game fishes with immature worms are probably false hosts (see *Gorgorhynchus xiphias*). Adults only occur in common dolphin and North Sea beaked whale, while cystacanths and immatures seem rather unselective occurring in almost any fish. The worldwide distribution suggests that the choice for a first intermediate host crustacean can also be diverse. King mackerel is a new host.

We found *Bolbosoma capitatum* (Linstow) and *Bolbosoma* sp. in a shortfin pilot whale, *Globicephalus macrorhynchus* Gray, from Puerto Rico. Our collection is the first in the Caribbean and shortfin pilot whale is a new host.

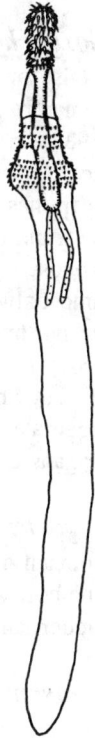

Miscellaneous Spiny-headed Worms

Gorgorhynchus xiphias **Hogans and Brattey** - Swordfish is probably a false or accidental host for these worms as they occur in low numbers as immature females. This new species was described by Hogans and Brattey (1982) in an unpublished report. It appears to be similar to *Bolbosoma vasculosum* which also occurs as immature females in big game fishes. This worm has a rather small, slender trunk which is expanded on the anterior end. the trunk is armed with 2 distinct bands of circular spine rows anteriorly. The proboscis has 14-18 longitudinal rows of recurved hooks. Light infections, almost always (98%) 1 per host, occurred in 295 swordfish from 4 localities in the northwest Atlantic (1-4 in 20 of 73 from Cape Hatteras, North Carolina, USA; 1 each in 6 of 89 from the Georges Bank; 1-3 in 12 of 70 from the Scotian Shelf; and 1 each in 9 of 63 from the Grand Banks). It occurs in moderate-sized hosts (115-174 cm FL). All the information above is from Hogans and Brattey (1982)

Tegorhynchus pectinarium **Van Cleave** - This worm was reported in the stomach of a "Medialuna" or *Seriola* sp. from the Pacific coast of Costa Rica. The host was probably a half moon, *Medialuna californiensis* (Steindachner), a rudderfish (Kyphosidae), not a big game fish.

Telosentis tenuicornis **(Linton)** - Cable and Linderoth (1963) listed Atlantic mackerel as a host for this worm, as *Rhadinorhynchus tenuicornis*, but these parasites were probably *R. pristis*.

CRUSTACEA (CRUSTACEANS)

Crustaceans are one of the phyla of animals with hard, segmented shells (exoskeletons) something like Medieval knights in armor. They are largely aquatic, while the insects and spiders and their allies (arachnids) are mostly terrestrial. All these groups are sometimes lumped together as Phylum Arthropoda, but we prefer to consider Arthropoda a subkingdom. Crustaceans generally have 2 pairs of antennae; respire through gills or the body surface; and anteriorly or throughout have paired, segmented, usually biramous appendages. More than 40,000 living species and many fossil species have been described including copepods, ostracods, fish lice, barnacles and isopods. A series of books defines crustaceans (Bliss 1982-85).

Classification and Contents

OSTRACODA (SEED SHRIMP)

Seed shrimp, ostracodes or ostracods are a rather large subclass of small crustaceans. The name "ostraco" means shell, an appropriate descriptor. They are macho, with the longest sperm known, and have one of the best and longest continuous fossil records in the animal Kingdom (since the early Cambrian 550 million years ago). Ostracodes are of value chiefly because their abundance, ubiquity, and exacting ecological requirements make them excellent environmental indicators today and for the distant fossil past. These qualities have been most utilized to locate petroleum deposits, but they might be used also to answer some fundamental questions about global changes. More than 10,000 living and 40,000 fossil species are known and 1/4 of these (about 1/2 of the living) have been described in the overwhelming literature of the last 30 years or so. The spurt of interest, when most other taxonomies were in decline, was caused by financial support, due to their use in petroleum exploration, and the arrival of a new tool to define their tiny structures, the scanning electron microscope. Also, the general availability of computers and more advanced computer programs aided their study since the fossil record of ostracodes has been described as exceeding the comprehension of any one human. Some effort has been made to combine the fossil (paleontological) and living (biological) classifications into a single system. A "taxonomic inflation" joke among ostracodologoists is that if you can tell 2 ostracodes apart they are different genera; if you cannot, they are different species! Living adults range from 0.1 to over 33 mm, with almost all tending toward the lower end of this scale; fossil forms can be over 80 mm long (leperditicopids), but most are in the range 0.3-3.0 mm. Almost all ostracodes are characterized by having a body which is completely enclosed in a clam-like (bivalve) shell (specialized head shield) which is usually calcareous and is hinged dorsally. The body is either unsegmented or the segments are obscure. Most ostracodes swim using their antennules and antennae. Their trunk regions are greatly reduced and have none to 2 appendages, but the tail projections (caudal rami) often are well developed. The larval stages are encased in bivalve shells; except punciids which have a single headshield. All ostracodes, except punciids, brood their eggs between the upper (dorsal) part of the body and the shell. In some groups 1-2 larval molts occur before the larvae are shed. Most species lay eggs freely or attach them to something. One nauplius stage is followed by 5-8 metanaupliar molts (periodic shedding of the exoskeleton to allow enlargement and growth). Most adults do not molt. Sexes are separate. Most ostracodes are free living. Some are commensal on sea stars and their allies (echinoderms), sponges and other crustaceans, but only a very few occur on the gills and nares of sharks and rays or rarely bony fishes. Males and females occur together on hosts. Most ostracodes are detritus or filter feeders, a few scavengers, others parasitic. They are not known to transmit diseases; but some freshwater species prey on the juveniles of schistosoma-transmitting snails.

Classification and Contents

Vargula parasitica Wilson

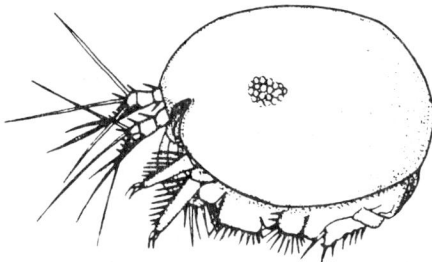

This unusual parasite of sharks has also been found on blue runner. It is only known from Jamaica.

Name - The name "parasitica" is derived from it being the first parasitic ostracod described in fishes, although normally free-living, *Vargula mediterranea* (Costa), had previously been found in a fish from near Elba in the Mediterranean. Both ostracodes were originally placed in the genus *Cypridina*. Harding (1966) redescribed *V. parasitica*. Another cypridinid species, *Sheina orri* Harding, was found in the gills and nares of sharks and rays from Heron Island, Australia.

Diagnostic Characters - It has an oval shell with a notch near anterior end and relatively large eyes. The first antennae has 4 segments and 3 long setae.

Records - Three males occurred in a blue runner from Jamaica (USNM 43604). Also 50, 50 and 12 males and females were found in 3 smooth hammerhead (USNM 43581, 43586, 43603) and 1 in a rock hind, *Epinephelus adscensionis* (Osbeck), (USNM 43599).

Geographic Range - Unknown.

Life History - Most female ostracodes do not swim and reside in the bottom sand or mud, but fish-parasitic females occur on the hosts with the males. Males and females scraped off fish gills into sea water were able to swim.

Location in Host - Most specimens were attached to the gill filaments, but 12 males in 1 smooth hammerhead were in the nares (USNM 43603). Oddly the 2 sharks with 50 ostracodes each in their gills had none in their nares. All those in the gills were attached between the bases of the filaments in contact and at right angles to the axis of the gill arch. Only 1 ostracod was found between each set of filaments. The exact positioning, attachment, tissue reaction of the host, and sheer numbers in a host indicate that these ostracodes were parasitic.

Length - Female 2.0-2.1 mm, male 1.7-1.9 mm.

Host Specificity - This parasite is probably subclass specific to sharks and rays. Those in blue runner and rock hind may have been accidental.

Damage to Host - The gill tissue appeared to surround each ostracod. This could have caused by erosion into the filament by the ostracod, minor cell proliferation around the attachment site, or both. Fifty ostracodes could impair a considerable area of gill tissue.

Detection - The raised areas on the gill filaments should make these small animal a bit easier to find. More carefully-documented collections would be of considerable use in understanding this unusual association.

COPEPODA (COPEPODS)

Copepods form a class in the crustaceans. The common name copepod means "oar-foot." They are found in marine and fresh water, most are free-living and are very important food items for a variety of aquatic life. Approximately 10,000 species have been described and about 2000 of these parasitize fishes. Many fish-parasitic species remain to be named. Copepods range in length from 0.5-25 cm, but most are less than 1 cm long. Egg strings of some species may exceed 60 cm. Body shapes vary tremendously from a generally cylindrical shape to a flattened or saucer shape. The body is theoretically divided into 16 segments or somites (head or cephalic=5, thoracic=7, and abdominal=4), but most of these are fused together, combined or overlapped so they cannot be seen. The first 6-9 somites are fused into a expanded "head", cephalothorax or cephalosome; and the remainder are variously fused or separated into thorax and abdomen units. Appendages are modified into mouthparts and other structures in the cephalosome, legs and other appendages in the thorax, and the abdomen has no appendages, and usually terminates in a bifurcate tail with projections (caudal rami). We illustrate females, use their morphological characters, and seldom mention males, because females are usually larger, more available, and have more distinct characters.

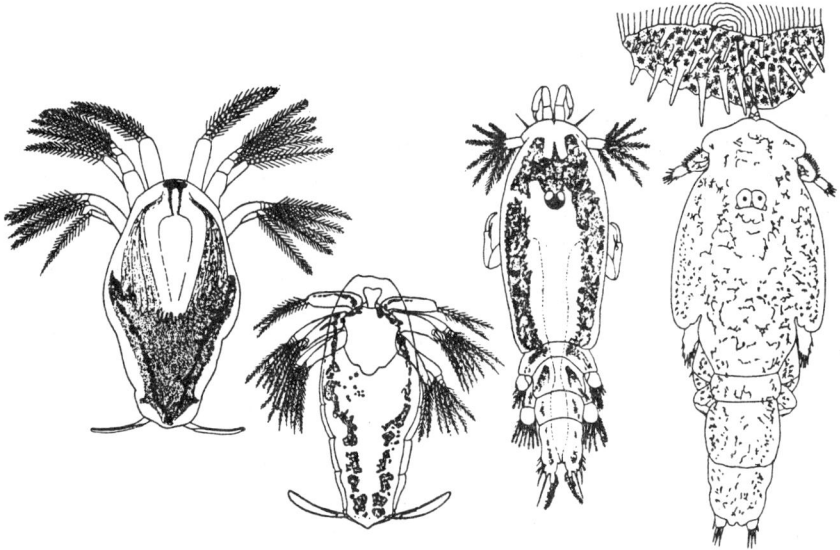

In most parasitic forms, the life cycle is direct, but typically involves a series of free swimming, planktonic stages. Some have intermediary hosts, such as *Pennella* spp. on squids, and shark copepods embedded in coral reef fishes. Finding a final host a serious problem for parasites, especially those that parasitize offshore, big game fishes. The hatching nauplii can often be observed by merely holding egg strings in bowls of sea water until they hatch. Nauplii of many species have never been described or drawn. Raising the other planktonic stages of parasitic copepods is more complicated, but can be accomplished. (A newly hatched nauplius of *Caligus elongatus*; an early nauplius, later nauplius, and metanauplius of *C. bonito*; and chalimus of *C. elongatus* attached to a host scale, are illustrated above.) Sexes are separate with males often much smaller than females. The life cycle stage that first attaches to fishes (copepodid, sometimes chalimus) can be very damaging to young fishes. Copepods frequently occur on the gills or skin of fishes, but highly specialized species burrow into the flesh or head sinuses, or crawl into the nose (nares or nasal fossae or lamellae) or eyes (orbits). They also associate with or parasitize a variety of invertebrates. We found one damaging a basket sea star in Puerto Rico (Williams and Wolfe-Walters 1990). Large fish-parasitic copepods are capable of biting humans, but such injury has seldom been reported. Most fishermen would not admit being attacked by a mere copepod! They can be of value to humans. Eskimos eat a giant parasitic copepod from the gills of Atlantic cod, *Gadus morhua* Linnaeus. Those on fishes are usually permanent parasites, feeding on mucus, sloughed epithelial cells and tissue fluids. Copepods can directly transmit microbial diseases.

Copepods are the most diverse and among the most abundant parasites of big game fishes. Collected specimens can be preserved and stored in 70% ethanol. They can be examined in alcohol or in a mixture of alcohol and glycerine to clear some structures. Smaller specimens or parts can be mounted in glycerine jelly for convenience in handling.

Popular Reference - Kabata (1970) "Crustacea as enemies of fishes."

Classification and Contents

Order Poecilostomatoida

Most of these copepods in big game fishes are modern discoveries. Their small size, ability to move rapidly on the body of the host and their attachment positions in the orbits and nares of fishes probably contributed to their being overlooked. Thus, we know very little about these parasites. Many have been described and never seen again, not from rarity but neglect. In this group, a prime opportunity exists for anyone to collect new and interesting information.

Many of these parasites look like free-living copepods. The bomolochids are among the least modified, most generalized and smallest of the fish-parasitic copepods, yet others in this order are modified, *Shiinoa inauris*, or highly modified, *Philichthys xiphiae*, from the free-living form. Von Nordmann must not have been very impressed with these copepods as he named them "bomolochos" which means toady, beggar or buffoon. The Family Bomolochidae was established by Claus in 1875 [Not Sumpf in 1871 as noted in Yamaguti (1963)], but was generally ignored until the 1930's. Many of the genera, much less species, of bomolochids appear remarkably similar, and these similarities have resulted in great difficulties in the taxonomy and incorrect (synonymous) genera (*Bomolochoides* Vervoort, *Parabomolochus* Vervoort, *Pseudobomolochus* Wilson). None of these tiny bomolochids are easily distinguished. Body shapes and even proportions vary with swelling due to the state of maturity. The only reliable characters are the structure and appendages of the first antennae, mouthparts, and legs of the female. These minute parts must often be miraculously detached and mounted on microscope slides, and examined with a compound microscope. Attempting this process gives one a much greater admiration of "copepod-ologists" (carcinologists). In most groups of parasites, we have been able to suggest methods for separating species without resorting to intricate dissections. For bomolochids, we suggest some identification tricks, but reluctantly provide the more detailed and technical characters necessary for absolutely confirming species. If all else fails, send these tiny copepods to us.

None of these lively creatures is known to harm their hosts to any noticeable extent, much less to hurt humans, or have any obvious effect on the sport fishing for their hosts. Just because these copepods are minuscule in size and occur in light infections does not necessarily mean they are unimportant. They occur in the highly sensitive nares and nasal passages of their hosts. These copepods can cause extreme irritation and can probably affect the health of the host. They may also be valuable as biological tags to distinguish stock, indicate migration, or distinguish host species. These eye and nose parasites are host specific. This is unusual among the copepod parasites of big game fishes, but is not surprising. Anything this minuscule in such a great ocean is either closely tied to the specific habits of its host or is lost. Bomolochids can only be detected with a careful host dissection. They appear only as tiny specks of discoloration in the mucus to the unaided eye. Just looking into, opening or scraping materials from the nares may not be sufficient. Tissues and mucus from the nasal areas and sinus or mucus canals of the head should be removed, placed in a small dish of sea water and examined with a dissection microscope.

A few other fish-parasitic families and numerous genera and species, that do not reside in the sinuses of fishes, are found in this order, but none of them have infiltrated the open ocean world of big game fishes. This suggests that the sinuses of fishes is a pioneer niche that is being used by this order to invade a new habitat - the open ocean. Such an invasion should begin at the margin and spread out with the near-shore pelagic hosts having the most species of these copepods. Four out of the 10 species parasitize inshore pelagics, 4 parasitize both inshore and offshore pelagics, and 2 species only parasitize offshore pelagics. Interestingly, 4 of these species occur on little tunny. This inshore pelagic appears to be a real "stepping stone" to the offshore hosts. Two of these copepods occur on all 3 species of near shore Spanish mackerels, but not on the offshore king mackerel. This also indicates some degree of habitat differentiation between inshore and offshore pelagics. The one species that does occur on the king mackerel is not found on the other 3 species of hosts. These 2 species of *Holobomolochus* on inshore and offshore Spanish mackerels are very similar and probably enjoyed a common ancestor. A perfect example of the inshore to offshore transfer.

Ceratacolax euthynni Vervoort

This nasal copepod occurs across the entire Atlantic in the Atlantic bonito, but in a more restricted distribution in the little tunny.

Name - It is named for the genus of one of its hosts.

Diagnostic Characters - The thorax has 2 distinct saddle-shaped segments. Microscopically, the first antennae of the female has a long, heavily sclerotized hook between the first and second segments.

Records - One to 10 females (average 3) and 0-5 males (average 2) occurred in little tunny from the Atlantic and Gulf coasts of the USA and Atlantic bonito throughout the Atlantic. Both nares were found infected in each of 226 little tunny from west Africa. It has also been recorded from Venezuela, Brazil, Spain and South Africa.

Geographic Range - Atlantic.

Ecology - This copepod parasitizes hosts in near-shore pelagic to offshore pelagic areas.

Associations - *Ceratacolax euthynni* and *Unicolax anonymous* occur together in the nares of little tunny. *Unicolax collateralis* often occurs with *U. mycterobius* in little tuna in the same geographic regions known for *C. euthynni*, but neither has been found with *C. euthynni*.

Location in Host - Nares (nasal lamellae).

Length - Female 3.7-4.2 mm, male 1.3-1.6 mm

Host Specificity - This parasite only occurs in the Atlantic bonito and little tunny. These hosts are both scombrids, but are not otherwise related.

Significance to Sportfishing - If the distribution of this copepod on little tunny is limited to the northern Gulf of Mexico and Atlantic coasts of the USA, it may be of value as a biological tag. We expect this odd distribution is an artifact of limited collecting instead of a restricted host range, particularly since it has also been reported from west Africa.

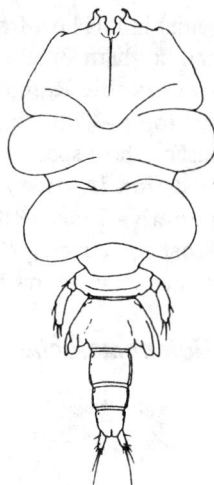

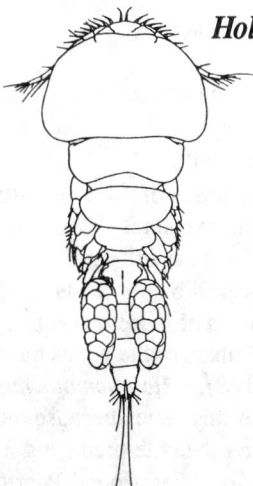

Holobomolochus asperatus Cressey and Cressey

Light infections occur on king mackerel throughout the southern half of the western North Atlantic.

Name - The name "asperatus" refers to the patches of hairs on the abdomen and caudal rami.

Diagnostic Characters - This copepod is most easily distinguished by its host, and location in the host. Microscopically, females of this genus have first antennae with unmodified (not hooked) setae. Homobomolochus asperatus can be distinguished from other members of this genus because of the patches of hairs on the caudal rami.

Records - One to 2 females occurred in king mackerel off Cuba (USNM 172242-3). It has also been found in this host from Georgia, Florida, and Texas in the USA, and Trinidad and northern Brazil.

Geographic Range - Western Atlantic.

Ecology - This copepod occurs on the offshore king mackerel, but not on 3 inshore host species in the same genus and in the same regions.

Location in Host - Nares (nasal lamellae).

Length - Female 1.8 mm, male unknown.

Host Specificity - This parasite only occurs on king mackerel. It is probably a characteristic, or at least, a primary parasite of this host.

Holobomolochus crevalleus Cressey

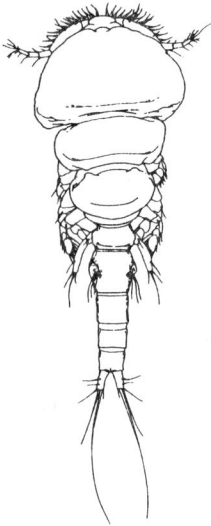

This small nasal and gill chamber copepod occurs in light infections on crevalle jacks.

Name - "Crevalleus" refers to the common name of the host, crevalle jack.

Diagnostic Characters - It is most easily distinguished by its host. Microscopically, female members of the genus have the setae of the first antennae unmodified (not hooked). *Holobomolochus crevalleus* differs from *H. asperatus* by having large patches of spinules on the endopod segments of the second and third legs; and from *H. divaricatus* by having ornamentation on the ventral surface of the caudal rami. Egg strings are not shown in the accompanying figure because they have not been observed or described.

Records - One to 2 females in each of 4 crevalle jacks, and 14 other females from an undetermined number of this host, from the west central Gulf coast of Florida.

Geographic Range - Unknown.

Location in Host - Gill chambers and nares (nasal lamellae).

Length - Female 1.5 mm; male unknown.

Host Specificity - This copepod is only known from the crevalle jack.

Holobomolochus divaricatus Cressey and Cressey

Light infections of this small copepod occur in the noses of all 3 inshore western Atlantic mackerels, but not on the offshore king mackerel.

Name - Named for the "spread-legged" appearance of the caudal rami.

Diagnostic Characters - It is most easily distinguished by its hosts, and location in the host. Only *Shiinoa inauris* shares the nares of these mackerels, and its body is cylindrical. Microscopically, female members of the genus have the setae of the first antennae unmodified (not hooked). *Holobomolochus divaricatus* can be distinguished from other members of this genus because the distal-most spine of the exopod on the third leg is shorter than the preceding 2.

Records - We found 3-4 each in 35 cero from various localities around Puerto Rico; and in 10 Spanish mackerel from Dauphin Island, Alabama, USA. It is apparently found in cero, Spanish mackerel and serra Spanish mackerel throughout the western Atlantic.

Geographic Range - Western Atlantic.

Ecology - This parasite occurs on 3 species of inshore Spanish mackerels, but not on the offshore king mackerel in the same regions. Only a few copepods occur on each host. Females are usually more numerous (approximately 3:1), but are sometimes equal in numbers with the males.

Associations - Another copepod, *Shiinoa inauris*, occurs in the nares of these Spanish mackerels, but these 2 parasites have not been reported from the same host specimen.

Location in Host - Nares (nasal lamellae).

Length - Female 2.4-2.8 mm; male 1.1-1.3 mm.

Host Specificity - This copepod is a characteristic parasite of these 3 species of Spanish mackerels. It is also genus specific (*Scomberomorus*).

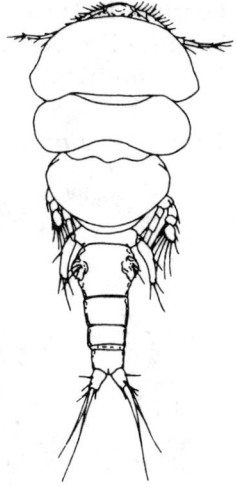

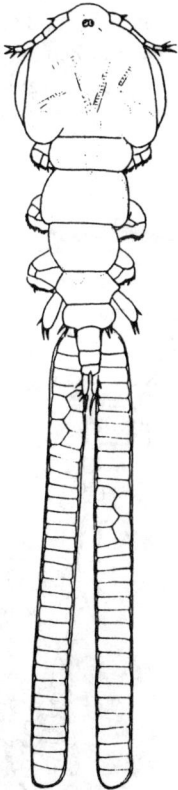

Pseudoeucanthus uniseriatus Wilson

This is a small and little known parasite of the blue runner in Jamaica.

Name - "Uniseriate" refers to the eggs that occur in single rows in the egg strings (although some multiserate do occur, see figure). The genus was named "*Pseudoeucanthus*" because it was similar to the genus *Eucanthus*, but this name had already been used for a genus of beetles. Thus the copepod genus *Eucanthus* was changed to *Anchistrotos* (but *Pseudoeucanthus* was not changed), and now we are left with a copepod genus name that means "false some kind of beetle!"

Diagnostic Characters - The cephalosome is round. Body segments 2-6 are more narrow than the cephalosome and are all of equal width. The pair fifth legs are rudimentary and sixth legs merely small setae. The abdomen is divided into 3 segments and is about 1/3 the width of the genital complex. The caudal rami are longer than the last abdominal segment. Eggs occur in a single row (uniseriate) in the egg strings except for short segments with 2 rows. The egg strings are longer than the body. The body is dark gray.

Records - Three females with egg strings occurred in a blue runner from Jamaica (USNM 43510, 42256).

Geographic Range - Unknown.

Life History - Eggs strings contain 30-35 eggs each.

Location in Host - Mouth.
Length - Female 1.2-1.3 mm, male unknown.
Host Specificity - Only known from the blue runner.

Unicolax anonymous (Vervoort)

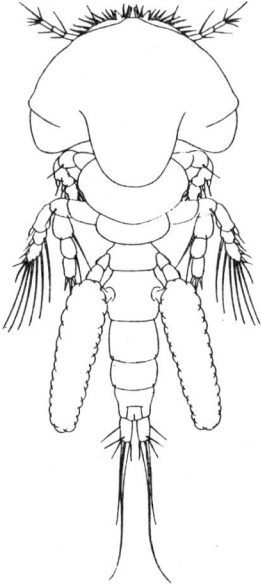

This rather small, enigmatic nasal copepod has only been collected in little tunny from 2 localities on either side of the Atlantic.

Name - This copepod was originally described in the genus *Parabomolochus*.

Diagnostic Characters - These are minuscule nasal copepods. Females have 3 pairs of exposed legs in the mid-section of the body with an oblong shield over each pair. Microscopically, this copepod differs from *U. mycterobius* by having exopod spines of legs 2-4 serrated instead of edged with fine hairs.

Records - Fifteen females and a male were found in a little tunny off Alabama, USA. Previously, it was reported from an undisclosed locality in the Gulf of Mexico and off Ghana, West Africa. This small copepod can easily be overlooked and probably occurs over a broader geographic range than the collections indicate.

Geographic Range - Atlantic.
Life History - Males are rarely found.
Associations - See *Ceratacolax euthynni*.
Location in Host - Nares (nasal lamellae).
Length - Female 0.9-1.0 mm, male 0.8 mm.
Host Specificity - This parasite only occurs on little tunny. It is probably a characteristic parasite, or at least, a primary parasite of this host.

Unicolax collateralis Cressey and Cressey

This nasal parasite occurs in a variety of small tunas, bonitos and mackerels in both inshore and off-shore pelagic habitats.

Name - "Collateralis" means standing side-by-side, and refers to its occurrence with *U. mycterobius*.

Diagnostic Characters - The thorax has 2 distinct saddle-shaped segments. Microscopically, the first antennae of the female has a long, heavily sclerotized hook between the first and second segments.

Records - One to 12 females (average 2) and 0-5 males (average 2) occurred in little tunny from the

Caribbean between Colombia and Panama; and Brazil. It was also found in bullet tuna and frigate tuna from Massachusetts, USA, and in these hosts in the Mediterranean. This copepod occurs on other species of bonitos and little tunas around the world.

Geographic Range - Worldwide.

Ecology - It parasitizes hosts in near-shore pelagic and in offshore pelagic habitats.

Associations - This copepod often occurs with *Unicolax mycterobius* in little tunny, bullet tuna and frigate tuna, but their interactions have not been studied. *Ceratacolax euthynni* and *U. anonymous* occur in the nares of little tunny in the same geographic regions, but have not been found with *U. collateralis*.

Location in Host - Nares (nasal lamellae).

Length - Female 1.5 mm, male 1.1 mm.

Host Specificity - This parasite occurs in little tunas of the genera *Euthynnus* (all 3 species), *Auxis* (both species), and bonitos. This pattern of hosts suggest that little tunas (Katsuwonini) and bonitos (Sardini) might be more closely related than other scombrids. Why this copepod parasitizes bonitos in the Pacific, but not Atlantic bonito, might be a question worthy of further investigation.

Unicolax mycterobius (Vervoort)

This copepod occurs in little tunas worldwide.

Name - This copepod was originally described in the genus *Parabomolochus*.

Diagnostic Characters - These minuscule nasal copepods have 3 pairs of exposed legs in the mid-section of body with an oblong shield over each pair. Microscopically, it differs from *U. anonymous* by having exopod spines of legs 2-4 edged with fine hairs instead of being serrated.

Records - One female and 2 males occurred in a frigate tuna from Massachusetts, USA; and 1 female in a little tunny from Pensacola, Florida, USA. Off west Africa, 63 of 72 frigate tuna were infected, usually in both nostrils. The examiner suggested that all host specimens were probably infected, but the smaller copepods were overlooked. It was also found in little tunas from the Mediterranean, Hawaii, Japan and the Philippines.

Geographic Range - Worldwide.

Ecology - Males are found on the host as often as females.

Associations - *Ceratacolax euthynni* and *U. anonymous* also occur in the nares of little tunny, but they have not been found in the same host specimen with *N. mycterobius*.

Location in Host - Nares (nasal lamellae).

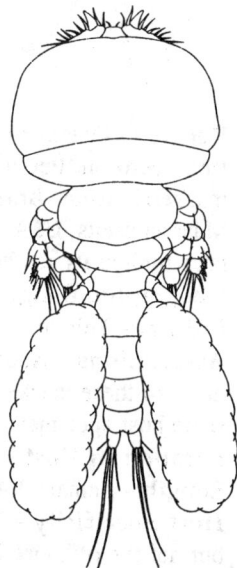

Length - Female 1.7-2.6 mm, male 0.7-1.4 mm.
Host Specificity - This parasite is tribe specific to little tunas (Katsuwonini).
It is probably a characteristic parasite of frigate tuna.

Shiinoa inauris Cressey

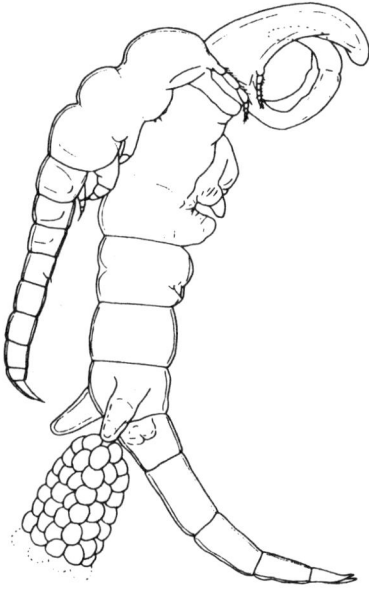

This tiny, cylindrical copepod occurs in very light infections in the nares of all 3 inshore Spanish mackerels, but not offshore king mackerel. The piggy-back attachment of the male is unusual among copepods.

Diagnostic Characters - It has a cylindrical body and a long curved "nose" (rostrum). The male is often attached on the dorsal surface posterior of the rostrum of the female (as illustrated). The rostrum and second antennae form a loop which anchors the copepod through a hole in the nasal lamella. This highly modified copepod is distinct from any other copepods found in the nares of western Atlantic big game fishes. A broken egg string is figured because an intact one has never been found.

Records - One to 3 (usually 1) females, often with attached males, were found from cero in Puerto Rico, Cuba, Surinam and Venezuela; serra Spanish mackerel from Brazil; and Spanish mackerel from Florida, Texas and Massachusetts, USA. Cressey (1975) reported this copepod from Argentina, but later limited its southern range to Brazil (Cressey and Cressey 1980).

Geographic Range - Western Atlantic.

Ecology - This copepod is found on inshore but not offshore Spanish mackerels.

Associations - Another copepod, *Holobomolochus divaricatus*, occurs in the nares of these mackerels, but these 2 parasites have not been reported from the same host specimen.

Location in Host - Nares (nasal lamellae).

Length - Female 3.4-3.7 mm; attached male 1.9 mm.

Host Specificity - The 3 inshore species of Spanish mackerels were infected but not the offshore king mackerel.

Detection - The nares must be carefully opened to search for these small copepods. Egg sacs may be more easy to see than the body, they are usually broken during the examination and may not remain attached to the copepod.

Philichthys xiphiae Steenstrup

This most unusually shaped copepod is hidden in the head sinuses canals of swordfish around the world. **Name** - The genus name means a friend of fish ("phil"=friend, "ichthys"=fish), a slight misnomer. The specific name refers to swordfish. Yamaguti (1963) placed this copepod in its own order (Philichthyidea), and this copepod and bomolochids have traditionally been placed in separate orders at extremes of the copepod phylogenetic scheme. Modern classification unites these seemingly different forms through similarities in less modified structures. This scheme does unite all the nasal copepods of big game fishes into a single order which seems appropriate.

Diagnostic Characters - This copepod is considerably larger than any other sinus copepod and the only one noted from swordfish. The highly modified body of the female resembles a twisted mass of PVC plastic tubing. The swimming legs, obvious in most other copepods, are absent. The body is white and eggs olivaceous.

Records - Reported in swordfish from the New England coast of the USA. There are also a few other widely dispersed records but none have been reported from the tropical and subtropical regions. It has also been reported from striped marlin, *Tetrapterus audax* (Philippi), from the eastern Pacific.

Geographic Range - Worldwide.

Life History - Younger females are smaller and also have less elaborate and convoluted projections.

Ecology - It is only found in the offshore and pelagic habitat.

Location in Host - This parasite occurs in the mucus canals in the head of swordfish and, oddly, embedded in the opercle bone of striped marlin.

Length - Female 14.3-27.8 mm, male 4.0-6.0 mm.

Host Specificity - This parasite has only been found in swordfish and striped marlin. It may be a characteristic parasite of swordfish. The location of this copepod in striped marlin was unusual, and may have been an accidental host.

Damage to Host - The possibility of heavy infections was suggested but not confirmed by Wilson (1932). High numbers of this large copepod in the mucus canal would probably injure swordfish. It produces swelling in the host tissues.

Detection - Unlike most tiny sinus copepods, this large copepod is easy to find. Opening and examining the mucus canals requires more dissection than just looking in the nares.

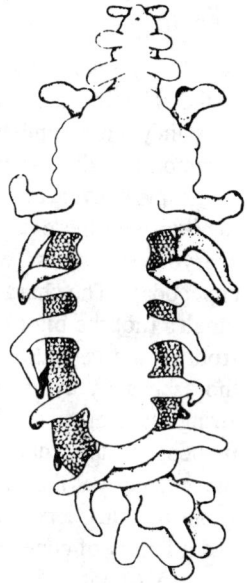

Genus *Caligus* Müller

A *Caligus* was the second species of fish-parasitic copepods ever mentioned in the scientific literature and the genus was established in 1785. Chronologically they were number 2, but in big game fishes, they are number 1 - the most common and diverse genus of parasites.

Almost everyone who has ever seen a freshly caught big game fish is familiar with these copepods. This genus is the stereotypical fish copepod that everyone envisions (what the Shell Oil sign is to mollusks, this genus is to copepods). The characters that are so distinctive for this genus include: having lunules (not the big headlights that they appear, but attachment devices) on the front of the cephalosome; H-shaped grooves on top of the cephalosome; the thorax usually cylindrical; the male usually smaller than the female; and egg strings that are usually longer than the body. They attach to the host with prehensile appendages and are capable of sometimes surprisingly rapid movement over the surface of a host. This large (200+ species) and important genus of skin-scurrying copepods has been the basis for various ill-fated orders, and a family of copepods that still survives. It has more species (at least 20) on western Atlantic big game fishes than any other genus of parasites.

There are a lot of these creatures on offshore big game fishes, sometimes multiple species on a single host (although this is seldom reported), and some are a little tricky to tell apart. These parasites are some of the larger copepods on fish, but you may need a good dissection and possibly a compound microscope to tell all of them apart. Much of the confusion in identifying these copepods has come from the use of variable or undependable characters such as hosts, size, body width, etc. We try to use dependable but more easily seen characters, such as the separation of lunules on the front of the cephalosome. We define 3 categories of separation: (1) widely = separated by 3 or more diameters of the lunules, (2) moderately = 2 diameters more or less, (3) narrowly = 1 diameter or less. All of our characters sound good on paper, but may fall apart on a pitching deck, when all you have is a hand full of copepods and a hand lens. Let us know which characters fail field tests. Some species are so similar that they can only be separated by using microscopic structures. We have tried to avoid using these "third hair on the fifth toe" characters, but sometimes have to resort to the technical and tiny.

These relatively large copepods are not known to bite or otherwise harm humans. They move around quickly, thus a host must be examined immediately after capture to determine the correct positions and numbers of these parasites. These copepods may leave or be knocked or washed off the host and attach to anything available, even your fingers. Many erroneous host records have been established by mixing sport fishes on the decks of vessels.

Hundreds of these copepods can occur on a single fish. They often congregate in small areas that provide protection or easy feeding and produce open sores or lesions. The feeding of some species penetrates into muscle tissue of the host and leaves obvious scars. Wilson (1932) perceived caligoids as threats to food fishes because of their ability to move about on the host and swim to and congregate on weakened hosts. Most copepods are permanent parasites that do not change hosts in the wild, but some in this genus apparently swim between hosts. His vision adequately describes some of the copepod problems in modern cage culture of marine fishes, particularly salmon, yellowtail, amberjack and possibly dolphin.

All of these copepods on big game fishes are sufficiently large to cause damage, but seldom occur in numbers higher than a few on a host. Most do not attach in one place and erode a site, but move around on the host. We know of no cases of obvious damage to big game fishes, although all parasites cause minor damage. They could be of more significance to sport fishes by their use as biological tags. Unfortunately, the early literature is so confused, and examinations by modern copepod people are so limited, that sufficient information is lacking to properly understand these "biological tags." We expect that few are strictly host, genus, family or region specific, but some may be close enough to use as biological tags.

Margolis, Kabata and Parker (1975) provided a synopsis of the world literature on this genus and Cressey (1991) surveyed those in the Gulf of Mexico.

Caligus balistae Steenstrup and Lütken

This copepod is rarely transmitted to dolphins as a false host from sargassum triggerfish that they eat. Beyond this curious example of prey-to-predator transfer, it has no significance to big game fishes.

Name - The species name would more logically represent the family of the principle hosts (Balistidae), but it was actually named for the genus of the unknown original host (*Balistes* sp.). *Caligus alatus* Heegaard, *C. canthidermis* Yamaguti and Yamasu, *C. polycanthi* Gnanamuthu, and *C. sensilis* Kabata and Guzev are synonyms.

Diagnostic Characters - It has a series of wrinkles in the dorsal cephalosome between the lunules. The cephalosome is about 1/2 of the body length, the lunules are moderately separated. The genital complex is rectangular, about 1/2 to 2/3 as wide as the cephalosome. The 1-segmented abdomen is short, less than 1/2 the length of the genital complex. The orange egg strings are longer than the body.

Records - One female occurred on 1 of 20 dolphin off La Parguera, Puerto Rico. Cressey (1991) also found a female on a dolphin from either the southern USA or the northeast coast of South America. It was also reported once from bluefin tuna (as *C. calistae*, a misspelling).

Geographic Range - Worldwide. Puerto Rico is a new locality and Williams, Bunkley-Williams and Rand (1994) noted this copepod for the first time off Bermuda.

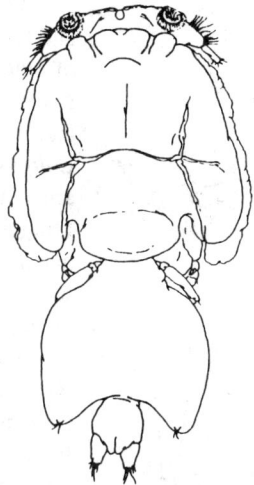

Life History - A few chalimus stages were found attached by frontal filaments to the bodies of West Indian filefishes (Wilson 1905).
Ecology: - This copepod occurs on hosts in both inshore benthic and offshore pelagic habitats.
Associations - This copepod is very likely transmitted to the dolphin from prey items. Sargassum triggerfish, *Xanthichthys rigens* (Linnaeus), are an important food item for dolphin. We find them in almost every dolphin stomach we examine.
Location in Host - Fins and body.
Length - Female 4.0-4.5 mm, egg strings 4.6 mm; male 3.5-4.0 mm.
Host Specificity - This parasite is family specific to triggerfish and filefishes (Balistidae). It is a characteristic parasite of some triggerfishes, but dolphin is probably a false host.
Significance to Sport Fishes - This rare parasite has little effect on dolphin. Other big game fishes that consume sargassum triggerfish may also become infected. This transfer of a normally family-specific copepod could be a pathway for eventually forming new species on the predator species. Big game fishes may have more open niches for parasites than coastal hosts.

Caligus bonito Wilson

⁀ This ubiquitous copepod is a common parasite of bonitos and tunas around the world, but also occurs on a great variety of other fishes. Heavy infections probably injure bonitos.
Name - It is aptly named for bonitos, its most common host, and was redescribed by Lewis (1967) and Pillai (1971). *Caligus auxisi* Pillai, *C. kuroshio* Shiino and *C. sarda* Pearse are synonyms.
Diagnostic Characters - It has an oval cephalosome and narrowly separated lunules. The abdomen is elongate and 1-segmented. It is similar to *C. productus* but can be distinguished for having 7 instead of 4 setae of the last segment (exopod) of leg 1.
Records - One to 6 females occurred on horse-eye jack and coral reef fishes from La Parguera, Puerto Rico. It was also found on Atlantic bonito, bluefin tuna, cero, dolphin, little tunny and skipjack tuna in the Atlantic, and a variety of bonitos and tunas in the Indo-Pacific. It was reported on king mackerel and Spanish mackerel in the Atlantic, but these records need to be re-confirmed. Wilson (1905) found as many as 100 of these copepods on a single Atlantic bonito. Silas and Ummerkutty (1962) found 2-10 copepods on all 50 adult to juvenile striped bonito, *Sarda orientalis* (Temminck and Schlegel), they examined off India.
Geographic Range - Worldwide (except polar oceans).
Life History - Silas and Ummerkutty (1962) found chalimus stages and immatures on bonitos, but did not describe them.

Ecology - This copepod is more common offshore, but occurs in a variety of inshore habitats.

Associations - Males and females of this parasite are in turn hyperparasitized by the copepod worm, *Udonella caligorum*, and covered with the attached eggs of this worm. We have only seen this worm and copepod combination on a large inshore fish, dog snapper, *Lutjanus jocu* (Schneider), but the association may occur on offshore fishes as well.

Location in Host - Most attach to the roof of the mouth and the bases of the branchial arches. A few occur on the gill filaments and inside the operculum.

Length - Females 4.9-8.5 mm, egg strings 8.0 mm, males 4.0-6.5 mm. The smallest occurred in the warmest waters and the largest in the coldest waters.

Host Specificity - Both the number of hosts infected and the number per host indicate that bonitos are the preferred hosts of this parasite. It occurs commonly, but less often on tunas, rarely on Spanish mackerels and jacks, and also occurs on a wide variety of hosts. It may be a characteristic parasite of Atlantic bonito. We found it in 5 new hosts including horse-eye jack.

Damage to Hosts - One hundred of these large copepods, as noted by Wilson (1905), could stunt or kill hosts as large as Atlantic bonito.

Caligus chorinemi Krøyer

This is a much misunderstood parasite of jacks in the western Atlantic.

Name - This copepod was named for the genus of the original host, *Chorinemus saliens* (=leatherjacket), in 1863. *Caligus germoi* Pearse, *C. rectus* Pearse and *C. tenax* Heller are synonyms.

Diagnostic characters - It has widely spaced lunules. The 1-segmented abdomen is about as long as the genital complex. The caudal rami are small (less than 1/10 the length of the abdomen). It is similar to *C. isonyx* and *Caligus* spp. (some called *C. tenax*) from Indo-Pacific jacks. It differs from *C. isonyx* by hosts and, microscopically, by having the terminal-most seta of leg 4 in the female twice as long as the other 2 terminal seta, instead of being similar in length; and the spiniform process of the first maxilla bearing an accessory process.

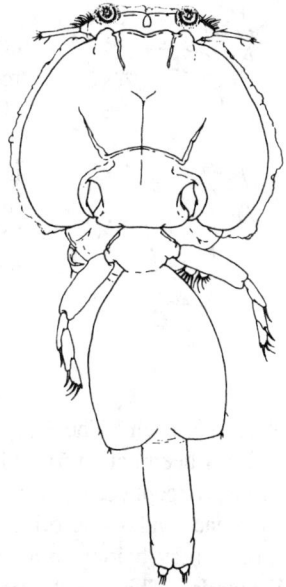

Records - One female occurred in an albacore from Bimini, Bahamas (USNM 88569); and in blue runner and yellow jack from Belize (USNM). Eleven females were found in 7 crevalle jack from Port Aransas, Texas (USNM 92665); and in crevalle jack from Florida, USA, and Brazil.

Geographic Range - Western Atlantic. Margolis, Kabata and Parker (1975) suggested that it occurs in the New World tropics in the western Atlantic and eastern Pacific. Despite a confused history under many names with various

Indo-Pacific records, Cressey (1991) found this copepod only in the Western Atlantic.

Life History - The egg strings contain 105 eggs.

Location in Host - Gills.

Length - Female 2.6-5.1 mm, egg strings about 3/4 body length 3.4 mm; male 2.9 mm.

Host Specificity - This parasite is genus specific to jacks (*Caranx* spp.). The single record from an albacore may have been a false or accidental host or just contamination.

Caligus coryphaenae Steenstrup and Lütken

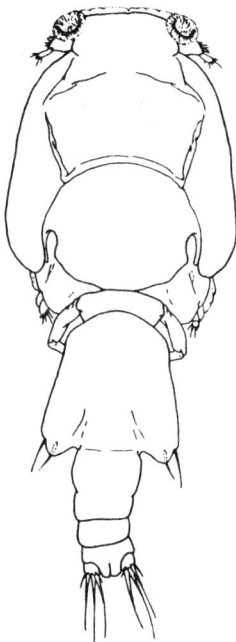

This is a ubiquitous parasite of tunas, little tunas and dolphins everywhere but polar seas. It is probably important but is virtually unstudied.

Name - Despite being named for dolphins, this copepod is as often found on tunas. *Caligus aliuncus* Wilson, *C. elongatus* Heegaard, *C. tesserifer* Shiino and *C. thymni* Dana (sometimes spelled *C. thynni*) are synonyms.

A record of this copepod on cobia by Causey (1953b) was actually *Tuxophorus caligodes*. A similar record on crevalle jack in Texas, USA, by Causey (1953b) could have been *C. bonito* or *T. caligodes* as this specimen was not available for examination, and many of Causey's copepod identifications were incorrect (Cressey and Nutter 1987).

Diagnostic characters - All species in this genus have an H-shaped series of grooves on top of cephalosome, but it is easily distinguished by an additional groove across the top of the H. It has moderately separated lunules. The cephalosome is about 1/2 the body length; the genital complex and abdomen are about 1/4 each. The 3-segmented abdomen (sometimes looks like 2 segments, and has been called 5). Microscopically, it differs from other members of the genus, except *Caligus regalis* Leigh-Sharpe, by having a spine below the antennae, and a sclerotized process near the base of the sternal furca. These 2 species may belong in a new genus (Cressey 1991).

Records - Three to 20 males and females occurred on blackfin tuna, dolphin, little tunny, pompano dolphin and skipjack tuna from various localities off Puerto Rico. Females were found in little tunny off the Dry Tortugas, Florida, USA (USNM 64044); 25 females on 1 and 1-24 on 22 of 30 bluefin tuna off Prince Edward Island, Canada (ARC 2488-83); and 2 females in a swordfish from off Massachusetts, USA (USNM 54103). It has also been noted on albacore, bigeye tuna, bluefin tuna, skipjack tuna and yellowfin tuna from the western Atlantic; and bullet tuna, frigate tuna and wahoo from the Pacific.

Geographic Range - Worldwide (except in polar oceans).
Life History - Male copepods occur on the host almost as commonly as females. Egg strings contain about 40 eggs each.
Location in Host - Body surface and sometimes gills.
Length - Females 4.5-8.0 mm; male 3.5-5.6 mm. The egg strings are longer than the body. Atlantic specimens on scombrids tend to be a bit larger (5.8-6.5 mm) than those from the Indo-Pacific (4.5-6.0 mm)(Cressey and Cressey 1980).
Host Specificity - Little tunas (Katsuwonini), dolphin (Coryphaenidae) and tunas (Thunnini) are the preferred hosts of this parasite. Its preference for this family and tribes and avoidance of similar and numerous species in other scombrid tribes is difficult to explain. The record from a swordfish could have been an accidental or false host.

Caligus elongatus Nordmann

This generalist has the least host specificity of all the fish-parasitic copepods, attacking the world's fishes at random. It may be more important in temperate and colder waters.
Name - This name has been used 3 times (Nordmann, 1832; Edwards, 1840; Heegaard, 1943) for 3 different species of copepods. Nordmann failed to note the host and locality for this parasite and did not publish the plate figuring this copepod, but the species is inexplicably credited to him. It has been confused with *C. rapax* Edwards since 1850 and recorded numerous times around the world under that name. This copepod was redescribed by Parker (1969).
Diagnostic Characters - It has widely separated lunules. The fourth leg-bearing segment, genital complex and abdomen appear to be continuous, without segments. The posterior corners of the abdomen have or do not have gently rounded posterior lobes. The abdomen is 1-segmented. Microscopically, the terminal-most seta on the end of the fourth leg is twice as long as the other 2 terminal setae. Extreme variation in parts, appendages and color have been noted.
Records - This copepod occurred in Atlantic mackerel (USNM 12620-2), blue runner, crevalle jack, inshore remora, shark remora and swordfish off the northern USA Atlantic coast. Reports from crevalle jack, king mackerel and Spanish mackerel off Texas (Causey 1953b) are in doubt because Cressey and Nutter (1987) identified the copepod collected by Causey from the Spanish mackerel as a new species of *Caligus* [although this was not mentioned in a subsequent summary Gulf of Mexico *Caligus* spp. (Cressey 1991)].
Geographic Range - Worldwide. Possibly not as common in the tropics.
Life History - The first larval stage to hatch out of eggs (nauplius) and the stage that develops after settling onto the host (chalimus) were described and figured by Wilson (1905).

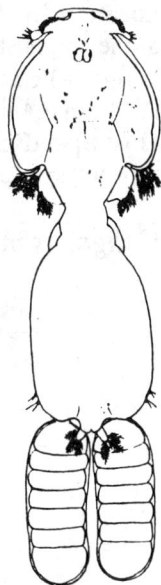

Ecology - This copepod appears to parasitize largely inshore fishes (shark remoras and ocean sunfish are exceptions), even the big game fishes infected are largely coastal and none of the oceanic tunas are parasitized. Wilson (1905) stated that this copepod was the most abundant one on the northeast Atlantic coast of the USA, and Kabata (1979) said much the same about Britain. Even hosts which bury themselves in the sand or mud cannot dislodge this parasite. Both sexes occur on the host and sometimes swim off the host and are caught in plankton tows. They are more likely to be off the host at night. This may help to explain their great range of hosts. Wilson (1905) suggested that many hosts were only temporary resting places (intermediary hosts) between preferred hosts. They appear to be more active than other caligoids. Because of color variations observed in this parasite, it is reputed to be able to change color to agree with the color of the host. Attachments to remoras and ocean sunfish probably transmit these copepods out to the open ocean.

Location in Host - This copepod attaches anywhere on the external surfaces of the fish host, but may prefer the dorsal fin.

Length - Female 5.0-7.0 mm, egg strings 2.6-3.0 mm; male 4.0-5.2 mm; nauplius larva 0.4 mm, chalimus stage 2.0 mm increasing gradually to 3.5-4.0 mm.

Host Specificity - This parasite has no specificity, being recorded from more than 100 species of bony fishes and elasmobranchs in 17 orders and 45 families.

Caligus isonyx Steenstrup and Lütken

These copepods are so obvious scurrying around on the body of great barracuda that you can see them while snorkeling. It is a characteristic parasite of this host.

Name - This copepod was described from a single female taken from a great barracuda at an unknown locality in the West Indies in 1861. Wilson (1905) translated the original description and refigured this copepod. Cressey and Cressey (1980) synonymized it with *C. diaphanus* Nordmann, but Cressey (1991) redescribed and re-established this species.

Diagnostic Characters - It has widely separated lunules. The genital complex is wide (approximately 80% of cephalosome width) and broadly triangular. The abdomen is approximately equal in length to the genital complex.

Records - We found 3-15 females on 28 of 47 great barracuda from various localities around Puerto Rico; and 9 on this host from off Matthew Town, Great Inagua, Bahamas (USNM). It also occurred in Belize (USNM); Biscayne Bay, Florida, USA; and Jamaica.

As in other commercially handled fishes, these parasites may be knocked off.

Geographic Range - West Indies. Margolis, Kabata and Parker (1975) suggested that it occurs in the New World tropics in the western Atlantic and eastern Pacific.

Associations - Isopods, *Excorallana tricornis* and *Gnathia* sp. often occur with this copepod. We collected a small inshore remora from a great barracuda infected with all 3 of these crustacean parasites. The remora had consumed gnathid isopods from the host, but had ignored numerous *Caligus isonyx* and *Excorallana tricornis*.

Location in Host - Body, rarely in the gill chambers or mouth. When approaching this fish underwater, you can see these parasites scurrying around on the outside of a hovering barracuda.

Length - Female 4.5-5.4 mm; male unknown.

Host Specificity - This copepod is only known from the great barracuda, and it is a primary parasite of this host. A single record from a flyingfish in the Galapagos Islands seems unlikely to be the same copepod.

Significance to Sport Fishing - Back in our young-and-foolish days, we speared and ate barracuda. Despite what Anonymous (1992) may say, this is a delicious fish. Unfortunately, it is also a dangerous fish to eat because it is a well known carrier of ciguatera toxins. The absence of isopods has been suggested as a possible indicator of ciguatera fish poisoning. Copepods might also serve in this role.

Caligus lobodes (Wilson)

Its lobes are so distinctive that it was once placed in its own genus based on this character. It occasionally occurs at injurious levels on great barracuda.

Name - It is aptly named for the abdominal lobes characteristic of this species. It was placed in a new genus *Midias* (for the golden-touch King Midas?) by Wilson (1911), but removed to *Caligus* by Kabata (1979). Lewis (1967) erected type specimens from Wilson's materials. This copepod should not be confused with *C. lobatus* (=*C. productus*) named by Wilson (1935a) from a pilotfish off the north coast of Puerto Rico.

Diagnostic Characters - This copepod is unique in this genus by having small lobes on the first abdominal segment. It has small, widely spaced lunules. The abdomen (with the lobes) is as wide as the genital complex.

Records - Over 100 females and males occurred under the jaw of a great barracuda off Salinas, Puerto Rico; and 2-20 females on 19 of 47 of the same host from various localities around Puerto Rico. Forty were found on a great barracuda from off Montego Bay, Jamaica (USNM 39613, 112846-7). It

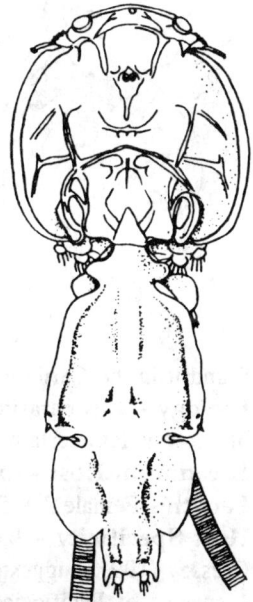

occurred on this host from Florida and Texas, USA; Hawaii (USNM 112888; and from the Indian Ocean.

Geographic Range - Worldwide.

Associations - Two *Excorallana tricornis* occurred in the mouth of a host which was infected with 2 males of this copepod on the body.

Location in Host - Body.

Length - Female 12.0 mm, male 6.3-7.1 mm.

Host Specificity - This copepod is only known from great barracuda, but is only a secondary parasite of this host. The record from the Indian Ocean was on an unidentified species of barracuda.

Damage to Host - The hundred copepods we found on a single host could probably cause problems. The fish appeared otherwise healthy and the congregation of large copepods had produced no obvious lesions.

Significance to Sport Fishing - see *Caligus isonyx.*

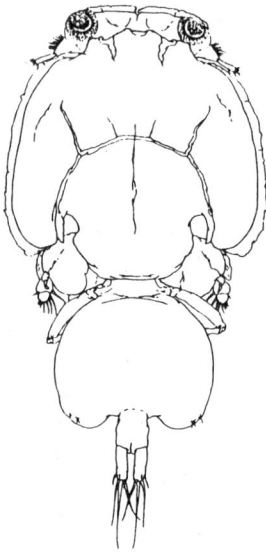

Caligus longipedis Bassett-Smith

This little known, external copepod parasitizes jacks around the world.

Name - *Caligus amplifurcus* Pearse is a synonym.

Diagnostic Characters - It has moderately separated lunules. The cephalosome is more than 1/2 of the total body length. The genital complex is wider than long and much longer (more than 4 times) than the abdomen. The caudal rami are as long as the abdomen. Microscopically, it differs from all other members of the genus except *C. rubustus* by having crescent-shaped sclerotized areas on the last segment of the inside branch (endopod) of leg 2.

Records - One to 26 females and 1-3 males occurred on blue runner from Florida, USA, and Belize, and on crevalle jack from Florida. It was found on a number of Indo-Pacific jacks.

Geographic Range - Worldwide. We have not found it in the Caribbean.

Ecology - This parasite occurs on a number of inshore fishes. Its abundance offshore is less certain.

Location in Host - External surface.

Length - Female 3.8-5.5 mm; male 2.4-5.5 mm.

Host Specificity - Jacks appear to be the dominant hosts for this parasite. Cressey (1991) suggested that this copepod had only previously been found on 1 species of Pacific jack, but it had been noted on several species of jacks including a blue runner from the Gulf of Mexico (Lewis 1967). Cressey (1991) found it on 9 species of coral reef fishes in Florida and Belize, but it appears to occur most abundantly on jacks.

Detection - This copepod moves about very actively on the host and may be lost from fishes that are not examined soon after capture.

Caligus mutabilis Wilson

This unusual parasite uses Spanish mackerels as intermediary hosts. It prefers inshore big game fishes.

Name - "Mutabilis" means changeable and refers to the shape of the genital complex.

Diagnostic Characters - It has an oval cephalosome, less than 1/2 the total body length, and with closely spaced lunules. The genital complex is longer than wide. The abdomen is about twice as long as wide and incompletely divided into 2 segments. The egg strings are about 1/2 as long as the body. Some variation in ornamentation occurred on copepods collected in the Atlantic versus those collected in the Gulf of Mexico and further south.

Records - One to 6 immature females occurred on king mackerel from Surinam; serra Spanish mackerel from Brazil and Costa Rica; and Spanish mackerel from the west coast of Florida, USA; and 1 female on a chub mackerel from Campeche, Mexico. Cressey and Cressey (1980) found immature copepods in 3% of the western Atlantic Spanish mackerels they examined. Adults were found on Atlantic bonito and skipjack tuna off the Atlantic coast of the USA. Records of this copepod in the Eastern Pacific were probably *C. omissus* Cressey and Cressey.

Geographic Range - Western Atlantic.

Life History - Egg strings have about 50 eggs each. Cressey and Cressey (1980) suggested that this copepod utilizes Spanish mackerels (*Scomberomorus* spp.) for its immature forms (intermediary hosts) and other hosts for its adults. They found a similar situation with *C. biseviodentatus* Shen which uses Indo-Pacific Spanish mackerels as intermediary hosts and bullet tuna and frigate tuna for final hosts. This is a very interesting idea, but the limited data on *C. mutabilis* could as easily suggest that Spanish mackerels are such poor or accidental hosts that this copepod cannot develop into adults. Young Spanish mackerels might serve as decoy hosts.

Ecology - This parasite only occurs inshore.

Location in Host - Gill filaments, gill chamber and mouth.

Length - Female 5.0-5.8 mm, egg strings 2.0-2.5 mm; male 3.0-3.5 mm. Cressey and Cressey (1980) found females 2.8 mm long.

Host Specificity - This parasite is almost habitat specific to tunas and jacks found inshore and on similar, fast-swimming inshore fishes (Cressey 1991) but also occasionally occurs on a variety of other fishes.

Caligus pelamydis Krøyer

This is an important parasite of bonitos worldwide, it also occurs on other scombrids.

Name - This copepod was appropriately named for one of its preferred hosts, Atlantic bonito (formerly called *Pelamys sarda*), and not for skipjack tuna (formerly *Gymnosarda pelamis*) as Wilson (1905) stated. Cressey and Cressey (1980) redescribed it. *Parapetalus* sp. of Silas and Ummerkutty (1967) is a synonym.

Diagnostic Characters - The cephalosome has widely spaced lunules and is 40-45% of the body length. The 1-segmented abdomen is 23-25% of the body length. The genital complex is roughly triangular.

Records - One to 11 females with a male occasionally associated were found on Atlantic bonito, Atlantic mackerel, chub mackerel, and little tunny in the Atlantic; and bullet tuna and frigate tuna in the Pacific. Causey (1953a,b, 1960) reported this copepod from a wide variety of fishes in the Gulf of Mexico, but Cressey and Nutter (1987) re-examined his copepods and found all he identified as *C. pelamydis* were other species.

Geographic Range - Worldwide. Cressey and Cressey (1980) suggested that it does not occur in the Indian Ocean, but they also noted that *Parapetalus* sp. from India was the same as this copepod(?), and later Cressey (1991) noted that it occurred in all major oceans. It has not been reported from the Caribbean possibly because many of its preferred hosts do not occur in this region. This may be another copepod that is limited to temperate and cooler waters.

Life History - The egg strings contain 30-50 eggs each.

Ecology - Males are seldom found on the host. Scott and Scott (1913) found 1 male on 1 of 1500 Atlantic mackerel, but Cressey and Cressey (1980) found males about 4% as often as females on bonitos and other scombrids. Males were always associated with females.

Associations - Sumner et al. (1913) found that this copepod usually associated with *C. bonito* off the Atlantic coast of the USA.

Location in Host - Gill filaments, arches or on inner wall of operculum.

Length - Female 3.0-4.6 mm, egg string 2.0 mm, juvenile female 1.9 mm; male 1.9-2.9. Differences in sizes are correlated with water temperature and not with the species of host. Larger specimens of this copepod are found in the coldest waters, and smaller ones in the warmer waters.

Host Specificity - This copepod is almost genus specific to bonitos (*Sarda*), a secondary parasite of bonitos, and occurs approximately 13% of the time in bonitos around the world. It occurs in lower numbers on other scombrids and occasionally on many non-scombrid fishes. Most records from other hosts may be erroneous or accidental, but it may occasionally occur on non-scombrids. Silas and Ummerkutty (1962) found it was "relatively rare" even on scombrids.

Caligus productus Dana

This common and important parasite of scombrids around the world is remarkably consistent in size.

Name - Much confusion exists over this name because another species of copepod from sharks was accidentally given the same name (*C. productus* Müller). This naming error creates what is called a "homonym." Fortunately the shark parasite was transferred to another genus and is now called *Dinematura producta*, but these copepods have often been confused in the scientific literature. *Caligus qalalongae* Krøyer, *C. katuwo* Yamaguti, *C. lobatus* Wilson named from Puerto Rico (Wilson 1935a), *C. microdontis* Heegaard, and *C. mirabilis* Leigh-Sharpe are synonyms.

Diagnostic Characters - The round cephalosome, with moderately separated lunules, is about as wide as long and is less than 1/2 of the body length. The posterior projections of the genital complex are rounded and extend well beyond the beginning (insertion) of the abdomen. The abdomen has 1 segment.

Records - We found 1-20 females and 1-7 males in cero, dolphin, skipjack tuna, wahoo, longbill spearfish and white marlin from various localities around Puerto Rico (USNM); and 1 female in 1 of 5 dolphin, and 2 females in 1 of 2 yellowfin tuna off Dauphin Island, Alabama, USA. Twelve females and 2 males occurred in a pilotfish off the north coast of Puerto Rico (USNM 64059-60); in blackfin tuna from several localities in the West Indies and Nicaragua; cero from the Dominican Republic and the U. S. Virgin Islands; little tunny from the Anagada Passage and Bermuda; skipjack tuna from the Dominican Republic, Venezuela and Brazil; and in yellowfin tuna from the Dominican Republic, Bermuda and Brazil. It was found in albacore from North Carolina, USA; skipjack tuna from Alabama and New Jersey, USA; bluefin tuna from the Gulf of Mexico; and bluefin tuna, dolphin, king mackerel and yellowfin tuna from several localities on the east coast of USA. This copepod occurred in bigeye tuna, bullet tuna, frigate tuna, other scombrids and great barracuda from the Indo-Pacific.

Cressey and Cressey (1980) found this copepod on 14 species of scombrids, but only commonly on blackfin tuna (92%), skipjack tuna (52%), yellowfin tuna (45%), and bluefin tuna (28%). They did not find it on 40 bigeye tuna.

The records of this copepod from Atlantic bonito are errors and those from Spanish mackerel are questionable. Many of the records of this copepod in the literature were based on misidentifications.

Geographic Range - Worldwide.

Life History - The egg strings contain 30 eggs each. Chalimus stages were described by Shiino (1959).

Ecology - Adults have occasionally been found free swimming. Females are 3-4 times more abundant than males on the host.

Location in Host - Mouth, occasionally gills, rarely body.

Length - Female 3.8-6.0 mm, egg string 2.2 mm; male 3.8-4.7 mm. Numerous specimens from the Atlantic, Pacific and Indian Ocean were remarkably consistent in size.

Host Specificity - It is almost family specific (Scombridae). This copepod infects most western Atlantic species of scombrids except mackerels (*Scomber* spp.). Most records from non-scombrid hosts may be errors, but it may occasionally occur on these fishes. This copepod is a characteristic parasite of blackfin tuna, a primary parasite of skipjack and yellowfin tunas, and a secondary parasite of bluefin tuna. Longbill spearfish and white marlin are new hosts.

Caligus quadratus Shiino

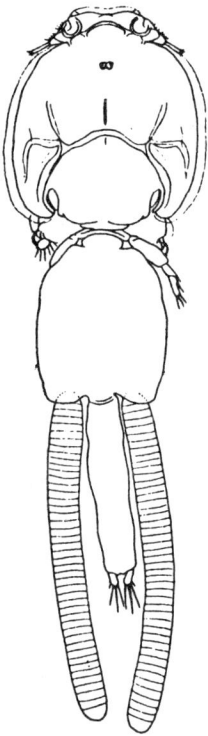

This worldwide parasite on all sizes of dolphin is occasionally found in other big game fishes.

Name - It is named for its quadrate genital complex. It has been confused with *C. coryphaenae*, *C. productus* and other species in this genus.

Diagnostic Characters - It has a round to oval (as wide as long to longer) cephalosome with moderately separated lunules. The square genital complex has parallel sides. The 1-segmented, elongate abdomen is longer than the genital complex and about 1/3 as wide.

Records - Two females occurred in 1 of 5 dolphin from off Dauphin Island, Alabama, USA; 3-5 females and 1-2 males on dolphin off south Florida and off the Atlantic coast of the USA; and in 126 of 145 dolphin from the Straits of Florida. It also occurred in dolphin, Indo-Pacific sailfish, skipjack tuna and yellowfin tuna in the Indo-Pacific.

Geographic Range - Worldwide.

Life History - The egg strings contain 30 eggs each.

Ecology - This parasite seems to infect all sizes of dolphin from 3.2 mm juveniles to 1.4 m adults (SL). Mean numbers of copepods per host increased gradually from 0.2 in the smallest to 38.0 in the largest fish. It parasitized the broadest range of sizes with the highest numbers of any of the copepods of dolphins.

Location in Host - This copepod is usually found inside the operculum, but occasionally in the mouth, on the body, out side the gill chamber or in the gills.

Length - Female 3.9-6.2 mm, egg strings 1.2-3.1 mm; male 3.2-4.5 mm.

Host Specificity - Dolphin is the dominant host of this copepod. It is a primary parasite of dolphin, at least along the Atlantic coast of the USA.

Damage to Host - The ability of this copepod to parasitize all sizes of dolphin and to maintain relatively high numbers may allow it to cause disease problems in dolphin aquaculture.

Caligus robustus Bassett-Smith

This is a common parasite of jacks and tunas worldwide.

Diagnostic Characters - It has a round cephalosome that is about as long as wide and less than 1/2 the length of body. The lunules are moderately separated. The fourth leg is robust (the width of the first leg segment is more than 1/2 the length). The genital complex is roughly triangular and about as long as the abdomen. The caudal rami are almost square and almost touching.

Records - Two females and a male were found on a bar jack off La Parguera, Puerto Rico (USNM); 2 females on a blue runner from Jamaica (USNM 42268); on bar jack, blue runner and yellow jack from Belize (USNM); crevalle jack from Florida and Texas, USA; and jacks, yellowfin tuna and other scombrids in the Indo-Pacific.

Geographic Range - Worldwide.

Location in Host - Body and gill chamber.

Length - Female 4.2-10.0 mm, egg strings 2.0-3.3 mm; male 2.6-5.0 mm.

Host Specificity - Jacks are the preferred hosts for this copepod, but it also parasitizes scombrids. A few records from fishes other than jacks and tunas have been reported. It was oddly ignored in the Silas and Ummerkutty (1962) summary of scombrid parasites. Many parasites tend to favor tunas or jacks, but this is an unusual host combination.

Caligus spinosus Yamaguti

This distinctive copepod is a rare parasite of Atlantic jacks, but occurs commonly enough to damage Pacific amberjacks.

Name - Both *Caligus spinosurculus* Pearse and *C. spinosus* were named for the unusual spiny structures on either side of the base of the cephalosome. Shiino (1960) suggested that *C. spinosurculus* was a synonym of *C. spinosus*, but did not formally synonymous them. The unique and distinctive spiny structures on the cephalosome and third leg of *C. spinosus* and *C. spino-surculus* strongly suggest that they are the same species. Most of the other structures of these 2 forms are similar, with the exception of slightly closer spaced lunules of *C. spinosus* and other minor differences. Pearse (1951) was aware of Yamaguti's description because he quoted his paper. Why he did not compare these 2 forms is inexplicable. *Caligus spinosurculus* is a synonym of *C. spinosus*.

Diagnostic Characters - The round cephalosome (as wide as long) is about 1/2 as long as the whole body, has moderately separated lunules and distinctive spiny structures at the base. The genital complex is vase-shaped and about 1/3 of the body length. The 1-segmented abdomen is short (about 1/3 of the genital complex length). Caudal rami are as wide as long and small (1/5 or less of the abdomen length).

Records - One female each occurred in a crevalle jack and a yellow jack from Bimini, Bahamas (USNM 88566). A mutilated copepod, of questionable identity, from a rock hind was also reported as this copepod by Pearse (1951). It occurs on the commercially important yellowtail and other amberjacks in Japan. There is a questionable record in a barracuda from India.

Geographic Range - Worldwide.

Location in Host - Gills.

Length - Female 2.5-5.2 mm, egg strings 2.9 mm; male 2.1-3.8 mm.

Host Specificity - The only reliable records of this copepod have been from jacks. It could be family specific to jacks.

Damage to Host - Heavy infections develop in greater amberjack and yellowtail held in confinement and culture. This copepod injures and occasionally kills these aquaculture fishes.

Treatment - Masoten has been use to effectively control heavy infections of this copepod on cultured yellowtails.

Significance to Sportfishing - Greater amberjack and yellowtail aquaculture is practiced in Japan and Hawaii and may eventually be conducted in other areas. This copepod is supposed to be worldwide in distribution, but the forms in Japan appear to be particularly damaging. Great care should be taken to avoid the dispersion of this copepod to regions where it may not occur. A gillworm, causing devastating diseases in cultured fishes, has similarly been exported from the USA west coast to Hawaii, Japan and China in greater amberjack.

Caligus wilsoni Delamare-Deboutteville and Nunes-Ruivo

This practically unknown copepod rarely parasitizes dolphins off the Atlantic coast of the USA.

Name - Wilson (1905) redescribed and refigured copepods from pompano dolphin as *C. belones* Krøyer, and later noted it from dolphin (Wilson 1932). Delamare-Deboutteville and Nunes-Ruivo (1958) distinguished the original needlefish copepod (*C. belones*) from the dolphin copepod and named the latter for Wilson (*C. wilsoni*). Yamaguti (1963) re-clouded the issue by noncommittally retaining Wilson's pompano dolphin host for both *C. belones* and *C. wilsoni*. This treatment perpetuated the use of *C. belones* and neglect of *C. wilsoni* for this copepod of dolphins in the modern literature, to the extent that Burnett-Herkes (1974) called dolphin a new host for *C. belones*, and Palko et al. (1982) noted dolphin and pompano dolphin as hosts for *C. belones* and not

C. wilsoni in a checklist that quoted Delamare-Deboutteville and Nunes-Ruivo (1958) as a source. Cressey and Collette (1970) did not find any *C. wilsoni* in their survey of copepods of needlefishes, although they mention this species. Later, in a paper concerning *Caligus* spp. from the Gulf of Mexico, Cressey (1991) decided he did find *C. wilsoni* in needlefish in the north Atlantic. This name has been treated in a most confusing and unsatisfactory manner. We call the form in dolphins *C. wilsoni* out of respect for the opinions of Dr. Cressey, but we suspect that it is a synonym of *C. belones*.

Diagnostic Characters - The round cephalosome (as wide as long) is about 1/2 as long as the whole body, and has moderately separated lunules. The genital complex is longer than wide, and longer than the abdomen. The 1-segmented abdomen is about 3 times as wide as the constricted attachment to the genital complex. The caudal rami are short and as long as wide. It only differs microscopically from *C. belones* by lacking lateral setae on the last exopod segment (end of outer branch) of leg 4.

Records - Two females occurred on a pompano dolphin from the North Atlantic (USNM) and 2 females from a "small" dolphin near Woods Hole, Massachusetts, USA; 1 female each in 2 of 145 dolphin from the Straits of Florida; on gray snapper, *Lutjanus griseus* (Linnaeus), from Florida and needlefish, *Belone* sp. in the north Atlantic (the host and original locality for *C. belones*).

Only females of this copepod have been collected, but Wilson (1932) described the male. He tended to blend old and new information without explanation. The description of the male may have been from a previously published description of *C. belones*. Only 9 specimens of this apparently rare copepod have ever been recorded.

Geographic Range - Western Atlantic.

Life History - The egg strings contain 30-40 eggs each.

Location in Host - Body.

Length - Female 4.8-5.0 mm, egg strings 3.0 mm; male unknown, but erroneously listed as 4.0-5.0 mm by Wilson (1932).

Host Specificity - This copepod was known only from dolphins until Cressey (1991) reported it from snappers and needlefish.

Lepeophtheirus bermudensis (Heegaard)

This rare, odd-shaped copepod on skipjack tuna near Bermuda is virtually unstudied.

Name - This copepod has been placed in 2 other genera (*Homoiotes* and *Dentigryps*). It is named for the locality in which it was found.

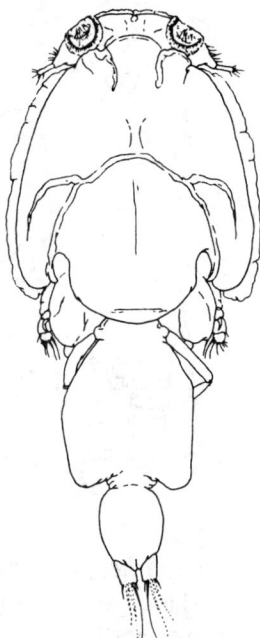

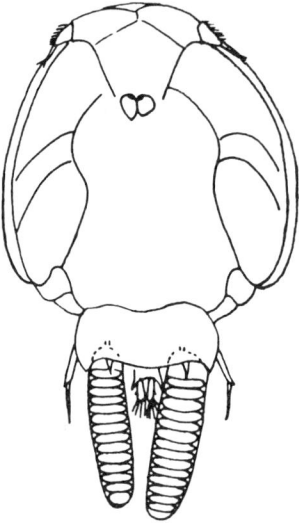

Diagnostic Characters - It has a caligoid cephalosome without lunules that is about 3/4 the total length. The other segments of the body are reduced. The fourth segment is fused with the genital complex and covered by the same plate. The genital complex is about twice as wide as long. The tiny abdomen is shorter than the caudal rami.
Records - This copepod occurred on skipjack tuna from Bermuda.
Geographic Range - Unknown.
Location in Host - Body.
Length - Female 3.0 mm, egg strings 1.2 mm; male 3.7 mm.
Host Specificity - This parasite is only known from skipjack tuna.

Lepeophtheirus dissimulatus Wilson

This copepod is largely a parasite of groupers, but is sometimes found on other hosts. It probably only accidentally occurs on skipjack tuna and chub mackerel.
Name - The genus name means scale louse. The name is from "dissimulo" meaning to conceal what exists, and refers to the hidden abdomen.
Diagnostic Characters - It has a caligoid body without lunules, and an oval cephalosome which is more than 1/2 of the total length of the body. The oval genital complex is wider than long and has a series of short projections along its posterior margin. The short abdomen is almost entirely concealed by the genital complex. The egg strings are not as long as the body. The female and male are dark yellow and lack pigment spots.
Records - This copepod occurred on skipjack tuna off Bermuda and chub mackerel in the eastern Pacific. It has been found on a number of species of groupers and other fishes around the world.
Geographic Range - Worldwide.
Life History - The egg strings contain 15-30 eggs each.
Ecology - This copepod is most often found on benthic groupers.
Location in Host - Gill cavity or body.
Length - Female 2.5-3.5 mm, egg strings 1.0-2.0 mm; male 2.0-2.5 mm.

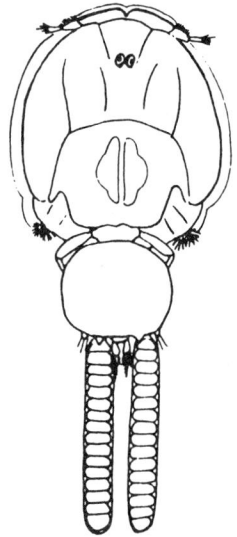

Host Specificity - Groupers (Serranidae) may be the preferred hosts, but this copepod has been found on a variety of other bony fishes. Chub mackerel and skipjack tuna may be accidental hosts.

Detection - The color of this copepod blends with that of the host, thus careful examination is necessary.

Lepeophtheirus edwardsi Wilson

Edward's scale louse has a most peculiar geographic distribution and a wide range of hosts. It probably only accidentally occurs on crevalle jack.

Name - This copepod was first found on flounders from Woods Hole in 1875, but was not described until 1905. The genus name means scale louse, thus the name "Edward's scale louse" is intended to bestow honor. It is not named for the famous Milne-Edwards, as one would suspect, but for the collector of the copepods.

Diagnostic Characters - It has a caligoid body without lunules, and an oval cephalosome which is more than 1/2 the total length. The oval genital complex is longer than wide and has no projections along the posterior margin. The abdomen is short and not concealed by the genital complex. Egg strings are not as long as the body. The female is pinkish yellow in life, and not speckled with pigment spots like the male.

Records - One copepod occurred on a crevalle jack off Woods Hole, Massachusetts, USA. It has also been found on various hosts from the northern Atlantic coast of the USA from Massachusetts, USA, to Charles Island, Northwest Territories, Canada; off Bermuda; and China.

Geographic Range - Worldwide.

Life History - The egg strings contain 75-80 eggs each. Typical nauplius and chalimus stages were described and illustrated by Wilson (1905) and figured by Yamaguti (1963).

Ecology - It is largely a parasite of benthic, inshore flounders, and also occurs on groupers, skates and goosefish. When disturbed, males scuttle about over the body of the host, while females remain motionless. When placed in an aquarium both sexes swim about, but males are more energetic and usually live longer. They live for greater periods of time off the host than most other fish copepods. Egg strings are not dislodged from females even during rough handling, and do not darken when ripe because there is little pigment in the larvae. The nauplii are easily hatched in aquaria.

Location in Host - Dorsal side of the body.

Length - Female 6.5-7.5 mm, egg strings 5.5-5.7 mm; male 3.0-3.8 mm; chalimus stage 2.6-2.8 mm, nauplius stage 0.5 mm.

Host Specificity - Flounders (Bothidae) are the dominant host of this parasite (Wilson 1932), but it is occasionally found on crevalle jack and a variety of other bony fishes and rays.

Detection - The color of this copepod blends with that of the host, thus careful examination is necessary.

Parapetalus occidentalis Wilson

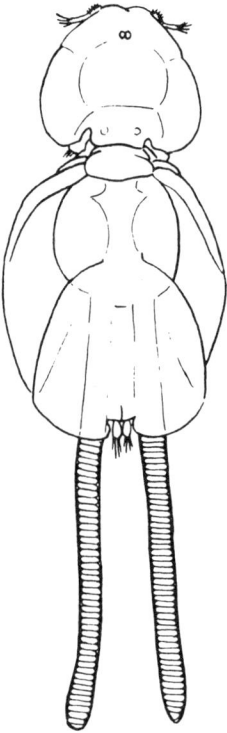

This menacing, caped creature hides in the gill chambers in cobia and injures the gill cover.

Name - "Occidentalis" refers to the western hemisphere to contrast with *P. orientalis* Steenstrup and Lütken from the east. *Parapetalus gunteri* Pearse is a synonym. Many of the Indo-Pacific species in this genus appear rather similar to this copepod and could be synonyms. None of these questionable species have been reported from our big game fishes, but the genus is in need of revision.

Diagnostic Characters - The caligoid cephalosome with moderately separated lunules is wider than long and 25-33% of the length of the body. The genital complex is circular and almost as wide as the cephalosome and has broad membranous wings extending back almost to the end of abdomen. The 1-segmented abdomen is shaped like an inverted heart with membranous wings, similar to those of the genital complex, extending posteriorly as far as the caudal rami or further. The body is milky white and the egg strings develop reddish purple spots when mature.

Pearse (1952a) used the length of the egg strings as a character to separate his species although he showed more than 100% variation in this character in his few specimens.

Records - Numerous females occurred in a cobia from North Carolina, USA; and 11 females in 8 cobia from Texas, USA.

Geographic Range - Atlantic coasts of the USA.

Life History - The egg strings hold 60-100 eggs each. The first larval stage (nauplius) that emerges from the egg was described and figured by Wilson (1908).

Ecology - The females swim actively when removed from the host, but not as rapidly as *Caligus* spp. or *Lepeophtheirus* spp. They swim to the surface and float with the aid of a little air under the membranous wings, possibly waiting for another host. The wings become easily wrinkled or snarled while swimming and floating.

Location in Host - Gill chamber, particularly inside the gill cover in the dorsal corner where 4-5 may congregate close together.

Length - Female 6.0-8.2 mm, egg strings 6.0-13.0 mm; male 4.2 mm; nauplius 0.4 mm. Wilson (1908) reported that the egg strings were shorter than the body, but in his figure they are obviously longer than the body.

Host Specificity - This copepod is only known on cobia and it is a characteristic parasite of this host.

Damage to Host - This copepod congregates in the upper corner inside the gill cover and may produce wounds.

Tuxophorus caligodes Wilson

This little collected, external copepod of cobia may be spread by intermediate hosts, prey-predator and fish-associate transfers.

Name - Wilson (1908) created a new genus for this species. Many of the species subsequently placed in this genus have been from big game fishes: *T. cybii* Nunes-Ruivo and *T. solandri* Kurian (=*T. cybii*) from Indian Ocean wahoo, *T. cervicornis* Heegaard from Indo-Pacific scombrids, and *T. collettei*. The genus name means to bear a plate and refers to the 2 plates over the fourth thoracic segment. *Caligus aliuncus* reported from cobia by Causey (1953b) was actually *T. caligodes* (Cressey and Nutter 1987), and the *C. aliuncus* he reported from a crevalle jack was probably also this copepod. *Caligus remorae* Brian from an unidentified remora in the Red Sea (not Mediterranean as stated in Yamaguti, 1963) is a synonym of this copepod.

Diagnostic Characters - It has a caligoid body. The cephalosome has moderately spaced lunules, is wider than long, and about 1/2 the body length. The dumbbell-shaped plates on the fourth thoracic segment cover the bases of the fourth legs and extend posteriorly over part of the genital complex. The genital complex is almost square but has broadly rounded projections of the posterior corners. The abdomen is 2-segmented and shorter than the genital complex. The body is pale brownish gray with brown or purple spots.

Records - Females and males occurred on cobia (USNM 32805), females on inshore remora (USNM 32806), young females on a pilotfish and chalimus stages on a needlefish from North Carolina, USA; both sexes on cobia and probably a crevalle jack from Texas, USA. It was also found on jacks and other fishes and the Red Sea.

Geographic Range - Worldwide.

Life History - The occurrence of chalimus stages on the fins of a needlefish could suggest that this copepod settles out of the plankton, attaches and develops on an intermediary host, and then moves to a final host. This could be a decoy host. Both inshore remoras and pilotfish associate with a variety of big game fishes and might transfer this parasite. Each egg string contains about 50 eggs.

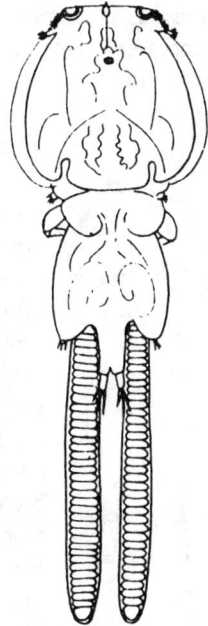

Ecology - Females removed from the host swim little and usually remain inactive near the bottom of the aquarium or floating at the surface (a possible host-seeking behavior). Males are active and constantly swim.

Location in Host - Body. Five chalimus stage copepods were attached by frontal filaments to the anal fin and 1 each to the caudal, dorsal and pectoral fins.

Length - Female 5.7, egg strings 4.3; male 3.6; chalimus 0.8 mm.

Host Specificity - Cobia is the preferred host, but inshore remoras and pilotfish are also hosts for this copepod and associate with cobia. These possible transfers from intermediary and decoy hosts suggest some fascinating biological processes. This intriguing mystery could be solved with additional collections and study.

Tuxophorus collettei Cressey and Cressey

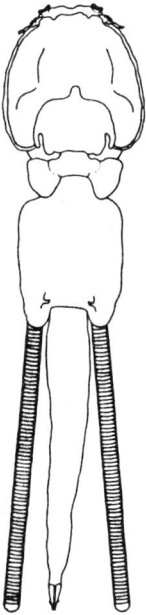

Little is known about this long-tailed, external copepod of cero.

Name - Named for Dr. Bruce B. Collette, who made many of the collections used in the Cressey and Cressey (1980) study.

Diagnostic Characters - It has a caligoid body. The cephalosome has moderately spaced lunules, is about as wide as long, and about as long as the genital complex. The wing-shaped plates on the fourth thoracic segment cover the bases of the fourth legs and extend posteriorly over part of the genital complex. The genital complex is longer than wide and has broadly rounded posterior projections. The abdomen is almost twice as long as the genital complex.

Records - Thirteen to 14 females and a male occurred in each of 2 cero caught off the U.S. Virgin Islands (USNM 172250-2).

Geographic Range - Unknown.

Location in Host - Body.

Length - Female 9.0 mm, male 6.1 mm.

Detection - This parasite is probably easily lost from the body of its host. This may explain why it has been so rarely seen.

Host Specificity - This copepod is only known from cero.

Euryphorus brachypterus (Gerstaecker)

Light to moderate infections of this copepod are commonly found in the gills of larger tuna species worldwide. Very heavy infections cause bleeding wounds.

Name - This copepod was previously placed in genus *Elytrophora*, and juveniles placed in *Dysgamus*, but both are synonyms of *Euryphorus*. *Arnaeus thynni* Krøyer, *D. longifurcus* Wilson, *D. sagamiensis* Shiino, *Elytrophora atlantica* Wilson, *E. hemiptera* Wilson, *E. indica* Shiino; various subspecies ending in *atlantica*, *brachyptera*, or *indica*; and possibly *Caligeria bella* Dana are synonyms.

Diagnostic Characters - It has a caligoid body. The cephalosome lacks lunules and is slightly wider than long. Two small sets of shields cover the fourth thoracic segment and genital complex. The abdomen is shorter than the genital complex. Egg strings vary in length from much shorter than the body (as shown) to 1/3 longer. The body is yellowish brown, the egg strings yellow.

In colder waters of both the northern and southern hemispheres, this copepod has the armature on the fourth leg with inner setae more strongly developed. This variation seems to be caused by temperature rather than being an indication of a different species, since it occurs on opposite ends of the world. Temperature-related size differences have also been noted in other fish-parasitic copepods.

Records - Six to 15 females and 0-6 males occurred in blackfin tuna from St. Thomas; on all large tunas (albacore, bigeye tuna, blackfin tuna, bluefin tuna, yellowfin tuna) throughout the Atlantic; and on many of these and other tunas in the Indo-Pacific. It appears to be more abundant in the Atlantic than the Indo-Pacific.

Geographic Range - Worldwide.

Life History - Males occur on the gills with the females, but in lower numbers (40% as often). Juvenile stages of this copepod have been found on jacks and other non-scombrid fishes in the Indo-Pacific.

Ecology - Offshore, pelagic.

Associations - In very heavy infections, females often had males attached to the ventral surface of their genital complexes.

Location in Host - They are reported from the inside surface of the gill cover, on gill filaments, etc. Very heavy infections seem to target the pseudobranchs. The exact location in the gill area is unclear since tunas are not examined immediately after capture and these copepods may move or be dislodged before they can be collected.

Length - Female 6.1-12.1 mm, egg strings 6.0-15.5 mm; male 5.0-9.0 mm; juvenile 3.9-4.8 mm.

Host Specificity - This parasite is almost genus specific to the larger tunas (*Thunnus*), but has also been reported from a bonito in the Pacific.

Damage to Host - Very heavy infections of this copepod have been noted in bluefin tuna off Europe. The pseudobranch was completely covered with a solid "carpet" of overlapping female copepods, open and bleeding wounds were produced in the skin, but the hosts appeared to be otherwise healthy. Densely packed copepods covering several square centimeters of gill filaments have also been reported in tunas.

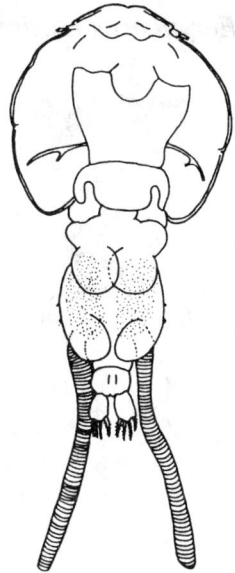

Euryphorus nordmanni Milne-Edwards

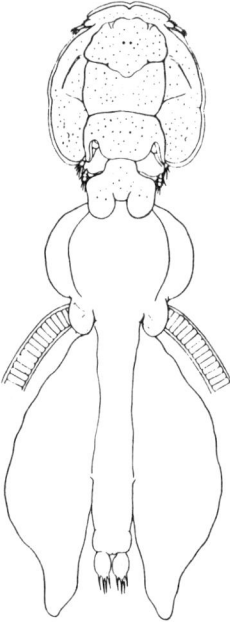

This copepod occurs in low numbers on dolphin around the world. Although widespread, it is poorly known.

Name - Two copepods, *Euryphorus coryphaenae* Krøyer and *E. nympha* Steenstrup and Lütken, have been considered the tropical cousins of this copepod, but they are actually synonyms of *E. nordmanni*.

"*Electrophora coryphaenae*" [a misspelling of *Elytrophora coryphaenae*] was described by Pearse (1952a) from a single "female" 5.6 mm long without egg strings. The copepod he described and figured is actually a male of *Euryphorus nordmanni*. This synonymy has possibly been overlooked because Pearse drew his copepods inverted (ventral instead of dorsal side up) making them more difficult to compare.

Silas and Ummerkutty (1962) incorrectly call "*E. nordmanni* Kirtising, 1937" (=*E. nordmanni* Milne-Edwards, 1840), a synonym of *E. nympha* Steenstrup and Lütken, 1861.

Diagnostic Characters - It has a caligoid cephalosome that is freckled with pigment spots, but lacks lunules. A butterfly-shaped plate lies over the fourth thoracic segment. The round genital complex is as wide or wider than the cephalosome. The elongate abdomen has large, wing-shaped expansions.

Records - One female occurred on 1 of 20 dolphin examined off La Parguera, Puerto Rico, and it has been collected numerous times in this host around the world. One was found in a cobia from Port Aransas, Texas, and 1 in 1 of 18 dolphin from Texas, USA (USNM 92673). It also occurred in albacore, bigeye tuna, pompano dolphin, yellowfin tuna in the Pacific.

Geographic Range - Worldwide between 40°S and 40°N. Our collections are the first in the Caribbean.

Life History - Each female often has a male attached to its genital complex with the ventral surfaces in contact and body axes aligned.

Ecology - Offshore, pelagic.

Location in Host - Inner surface of operculum, gill chamber or mouth.

Length - Female 7.8-10.5 mm, egg strings 9.2 mm; male 5.3-6.4 mm.

Host Specificity - This parasite prefers dolphin. It is a secondary parasite of this host based on the collection records, but may occur more abundantly and be lost from the host before it is examined. The single reports from cobia, tunas and 1 other fish may be accidental infections or false hosts.

Genus *Gloiopotes* Steenstrup and Lütken

These are relatively large, caligoid-shaped copepods distinguished by their ornamentation and colorfulness (blue bodies and red egg strings) and the absence of lunules. Species in the genus only occur on billfishes (Istiophoridae), swordfish (Xiphidae) and wahoo (Scombridae) but not other scombrids.

These copepods are more host specific than most of the other copepods that attach externally to big game fishes. Their presence and abundance has been used to suggest relationships among their hosts (see Discussion). Records from odd hosts, such as bigeye tuna, were probably based on misidentifications.

Williams (1978) reported the first record of striped goose barnacle attached to a fish-parasitic copepod that was not permanently embedded in its host. Causey (1960) reported a similar instance of what was possibly this barnacle, *Conchoderma* sp., on *Gloiopotes costatus* Wilson [=*G. huttoni* (Tomson)] on sailfish off Mazatlan, Mexico.

These copepods do not appear to damage the host even when they occur in large numbers, although the thousands per sailfish reported by Williams (1967) off east Africa, would certainly have injured these hosts. The life history is unknown. It may be more complicated than the normal copepod life cycle. Simply dispersing the few larvae into the vast ocean would seemingly quickly extinct these parasites. They are not known to bite or otherwise harm humans.

Records of the number of copepods (geographic position caught, species and size of host) from fishermen would help us understand the number of hosts parasitized and the number of copepods per host. These external copepods are so easily lost that our examinations hours after the hosts are caught may have little relation to the original infection.

References - Cressey (1967) revised the genus. Yamaguti (1963) incorrectly noted that these copepods also occurred on elasmobranchs (sharks and rays), but listed none. He also described the first leg of these copepods as uniramous (with 1 terminal projection) when they are biramous (2 projections).

Gloiopotes americanus Cressey

These large and brightly colored copepods are found on the skin of sailfish and may be useful as biological tags.

Name - This parasite was confused with *Gloiopotes ornatus* until it was separated and described by Cressey (1967).

Diagnostic Characters - Live copepods have a bluish-purple body and red egg strings. It is rather similar in appearance to *G. ornatus*, but differs by occurring on different hosts, by having a shorter fifth leg (does not extend to or beyond abdomen), and by

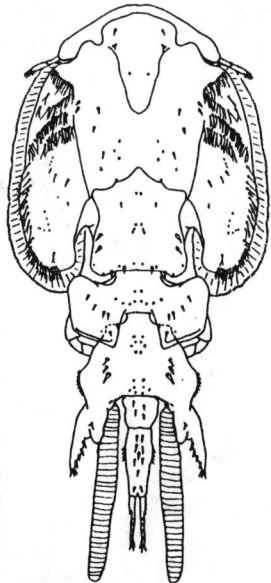

other technical characters (see *G. ornatus*). It differs considerably from *G. hygomianus* by having conspicuous ornamentation and in body shape. The egg strings curl back over the posterior of this copepod in a U-shape (We show them flattened to avoid obscuring details of the body). Oddly, Cressey (1967) did not mention this characteristic.

Records - We found a female and male on 1 of 2 Atlantic sailfish caught off Arecibo, Puerto Rico (USNM); and 1 female on each of 2 Atlantic sailfish off Dauphin Island, Alabama, USA. This parasite probably always occurs on sailfish, but rinsing, drying and rough handling may knock most of them off before fish are examined. It is also known from the Atlantic coast of Florida.

Geographic Range - Tropical and subtropical Atlantic. Our collection is the first in the Caribbean.

Ecology - Pelagic and offshore.

Location in Host - Body. We found it on the gills of 1 sailfish, but all previous records were external, and our few specimens may have been washed onto the gills when fishermen rinsed the sailfish.

Length - Female 10.0-11.7; male 8.8-10.0 mm.

Host Specificity - This parasite only occurs on Atlantic sailfish and is probably a characteristic parasite of this host.

Significance to Sportfishing - The apparently restricted geographic range might make it a useful biological tag to distinguish stocks or movements of sailfish.

Gloiopotes hygomianus Steenstrup and Lütken

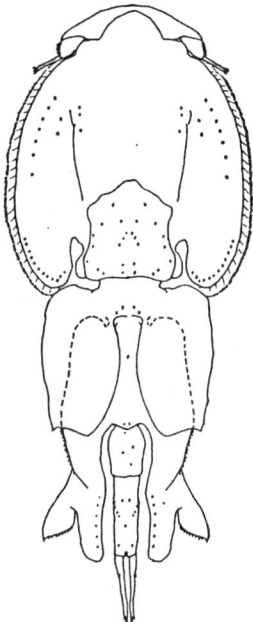

This moderate-sized copepod occurs on wahoo around the world. It is less ornamented than others in the genus, but is still quite colorful.

Diagnostic Characters - Live copepods have a bluish-purple body and red egg strings. This copepod appears naked compared to the other 2 conspicuously ornamented species of *Gloiopotes* from Atlantic billfishes.

Records - We found 6-20 females and 1-2 males on 6 of 15 wahoo from various localities around Puerto Rico; and 2-5 females on 4 wahoo off Dauphin Island, Alabama, USA. Cressey (1967) also noted this copepod from Puerto Rico (USNM). Iversen and Yoshida (1957) found this copepod in 52 of 96 (54.2%) wahoo off the Line Islands in the Pacific. A record from albacore in the Pacific is probably an error.

Geographic Range - Worldwide.

Ecology - Pelagic and offshore.

Location in Host - Body.

Length - Female 13.6-17.7 mm, egg strings 10.9-13.9 mm; male 9.4-12.5 mm. Copepods from Hawaii are smaller than those from other localities worldwide.
Host Specificity - It only occurs on wahoo and is a characteristic parasite.

Gloiopotes ornatus Wilson

These large and brightly colored parasites scamper around on the skin of all Atlantic blue marlin.

Name - One of our former graduate students called this the "red, white and blue" copepod for all its bright colors. It is a spectacularly beautiful animal and large enough for sport fishermen to enjoy its color. The name "ornatus" describes the elaborate ornamentation on this copepod.

Diagnostic Characters - Live copepods have a bluish purple body and red egg strings. The rather similar *Gloiopotes americanus* only occurs on Atlantic sailfish. Microscopically, adult females of *G. ornatus* differ from *G. americanus* by having a distinct bulbous lateral expansion of the second abdominal segment, and more pronounced swollen lateral areas of the genital complex. It differs considerably from *G. hygomianus* by having conspicuous ornamentation and in body shape.

Records - We found 25-150 on 40 Atlantic blue marlin; and 2-10 on 3 white marlin from various localities around Puerto Rico (USNM). They also occurred on these hosts off Havana, Cuba; Brazil; and Woods Hole, Massachusetts, USA. Previous records from "swordfish" (USNM 6209) and "spearfish" appear to refer to blue marlin and white marlin, respectively.

Geographic Range - Western Atlantic.

Ecology - Strictly an offshore pelagic parasite.

Location in Host - Body. This copepod is sometimes found in the mouth or gill cavities, but this may represent movement after host death, or handling contamination.

Length - Female 10.0-12.9 mm; male 8.0-11.1 mm.

Host Specificity - This copepod is only known from blue marlin and white marlin. It is family specific to billfishes (Istiophoridae) and a characteristic parasite of blue marlin and possibly white marlin.

Hatschekia amplicapa Pearse

This small copepod infects the gills of great barracuda.

Diagnostic Characters - The round cephalosome is attached directly to the elongate trunk region. The caudal rami are relatively tiny.

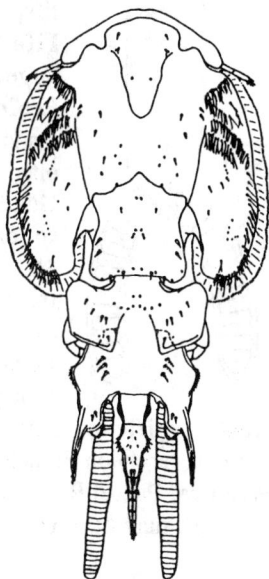

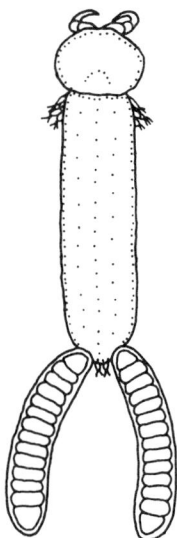

Records - Two to 10 females occurred in 6 of 47 great barracuda from various localities around Puerto Rico (USNM); and 8 females in a great barracuda from Bimini, Bahamas (USNM 88602).

Geographic Range - West Indies. Our records are the first from the Caribbean.

Life History - The egg strings contained 16 relatively large eggs each.

Ecology - This genus of copepods is usually limited to inshore and coral reef fishes, but *H. oblongata* Wilson was once reported from a Pacific crevalle jack, *Caranx caninus* Günther, in the eastern Pacific; and we found a *Hatschekia* sp. once in a little tuna off La Parguera, Puerto Rico. The "*H. mulli*" reported by Causey (1955) on king mackerel from Louisiana, USA, was actually *Pseudocycnoides buccata*.

Location in Host - Gill filaments.

Length - Females 1.0-1.3 mm, male unknown.

Host Specificity - This parasite only occurs on great barracuda. We found this copepod rarely on French grunt, *Haemulon flavolineatum* (Desmarest), from La Parguera, Puerto Rico (USNM). French grunt is a new host for this copepod, but these may have been only accidental infections.

Pseudocycnus appendiculatus Heller

This elongate copepod is found on the gills of tunas, and a few other big game fishes worldwide. It grows larger in colder waters.

Name - *Pseudocycnus spinosus* Pearse and *P. thynnus* Brandes are synonyms.

Diagnostic Characters - It has a distinctively long genital complex that is as wide as the cephalosome. The caudal rami are long, 1/2 of the length of the genital complex. The body is bright red on the dorsal surface and yellow-brown on the rest of the body. The egg strings are brown.

Records - We found 1 female and 1 male in 1 of 2 blackfin tuna, and 2 females in 1 of 40 dolphin from various localities around Puerto Rico; 2 females in a bluefin tuna, and 2 females in 1 of 2 yellowfin tuna off Dauphin Island, Alabama, USA. One to 5 females (usually 2) often, and 1-2 males (average 0.3) rarely, occur on all large tunas (albacore, bigeye tuna, blackfin tuna, bluefin tuna, yellowfin tuna), little tunny and skipjack tuna; and occasionally on Atlantic bonito and dolphin from the Atlantic, and some of these hosts and other tunas, little tunas and bonitos from the Indo-Pacific.

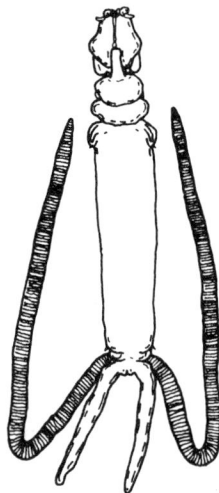

Geographic Range - Worldwide.
Location in Host - Gill filaments.
Length - Female 7.3-24.0 mm, usually 13.0-17.0; male 2.7-5.0 mm. The longer specimens of females (18-24 mm) occurred in regions of colder waters. The very smallest (7.3 mm) were described from Atlantic bonito.
Host Specificity - This parasite is almost family specific to scombrids, but rarely, and possibly accidentally, occurs in dolphin. Tunas (Thunnini), little tunas (Katsuwonini) (little tunny and skipjack tuna in the Atlantic) are the preferred hosts, with an infection rate of approximately 10%; but 2% of the bonitos (Sardini) examined by Cressey and Cressey (1980) worldwide were also infected. This copepod is a secondary parasite of tunas and little tunas.

Pseudocycnoides buccata (Wilson)

This parasite occurs in all species and on most specimens of Spanish mackerels throughout the Americas. The cumulative loss of these valuable sport fishes due to this parasite must be substantial.
Name - *Cybicola elongata* Pearse, *Hatschekia mulli* of Causey, 1953 and *Pseudocycnus elongatus* (Pearse) are synonyms. The genus *Pseudocycnopsis* Yamaguti, once used for this parasite, is a synonym of *Pseudocycnoides* Yamaguti.
Diagnostic Characters - It has a distinctively long genital complex that is as wide as the cephalosome. The caudal rami are short, about 1/10 the length of the genital complex. The first 3 pairs of legs are rudimentary. The first pair is located between the bases of maxillipeds and not easily seen. The body is red and the egg strings brown.
Records - We found 1-5 females in 18 of 35 cero and 8 of 14 king mackerel from various localities around Puerto Rico (USNM); and 1-2 in 1 of 2 king mackerel and 1 each in 2 of 4 Spanish mackerel from off Dauphin Island, Alabama. Cressey and Cressey (1980) suggested that this copepod occurred commonly in light to moderate infections on all its hosts (cero, king mackerel, serra Spanish mackerel, Spanish mackerel, and Eastern Pacific Spanish mackerels) (USNM 88538).
Geographic Range - Western Atlantic and Eastern Pacific.
Life History - Males are seldom seen on the host (6-7% of infected hosts).
Ecology - This copepod is very similar in appearance to the gill filaments of its host, possibly an adaptation to conceal it from cleaner fishes such as remoras.
Location in Host - Gill filaments, sometimes on pseudobranchs.
Length - Female 4.0-5.3 mm; male 1.9 mm. Causey (1960) found those in the Pacific to be slightly smaller than the ones in the Gulf of Mexico.
Host Specificity - This parasite is genus specific *(Scomberomorus)*, and is a primary parasite of these fishes.
Damage to Host - Low to moderate infections do little damage to individual hosts, but the high prevalence on Spanish mackerels means that minor damage occurs throughout the population. Slight growth reduction in hundreds of millions of mackerel translates to the loss of millions of kilos of valuable fishes.

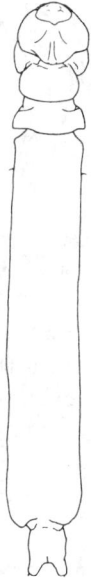

Lernanthropus giganteus Krøyer

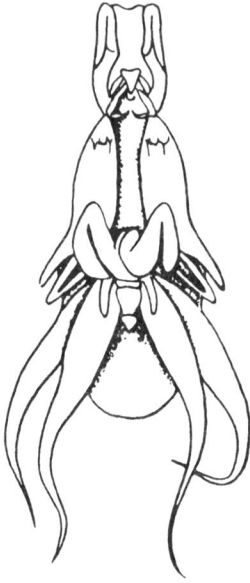

This relatively large, obvious copepod occurs on jacks around the world in the tropics. It damages the gills and heavy infections stunt or kill jacks.

Name - The specific name obviously refers to its large size. *Lernanthropus paenulatus* Wilson only differs from this copepod by having a slightly longer shield or skirt and we consider it a synonym.

Diagnostic Characters - Species in this genus are generally cylindrical in shape and have distinctive elongate projections from the ventral side of the trunk. The ventral side of this species is illustrated so that these projections can be seen. The fourth segment has an expanded plate on the dorsal side that partially covers the projections. The body is beige.

Records - We found 1 female each in 1 of 3 blue runner from Aguadilla, Puerto Rico; 1 of 19 bar jack, in 3 of 20 crevalle jack and in 5 of 28 horse-eye jack from various localities around Puerto Rico; in a yellow jack from St. Lucia; and in 1 of 2 crevalle jack from Gulf Shores, Alabama, USA. Bunkley-Williams and Williams (1995) found about 15% of crevalle jacks and horse-eye jacks in Puerto Rico infected with 1 female copepod each. Both sexes of this copepod occurred in blue runner (USNM 42277) and crevalle jack (USNM 42282) from Jamaica. A male and a female was reported from a crevalle jack from Texas, USA; and both sexes were found on a greater amberjack from Massachusetts and North Carolina, USA. It is also reported in other jacks from the tropical Indo-Pacific.

Geographic Range - Worldwide.

Location in Host - Gill filaments.

Length - Female 8.0-9.5 mm, egg strings 16.8-21.5 mm; male 2.2-4.1 mm.

Host Specificity - This parasite is family specific to jacks. It is a secondary parasite of crevalle jack and horse-eye jack. Bar jack, horse-eye jack and yellow jack are new hosts.

Damage to Host - The gill filaments surrounding this copepod have thickened surfaces (epithelium).

Significance to Sportfishing - This is a large and damaging copepod. It usually occurs as a single female or as a female-male pair on a host. These low levels cause little damage. Heavier infections could stunt or kill jacks.

Lernaeenicus longiventris Wilson

This giant, common, and impressive copepod embeds its head in the flesh and debilitates dolphin and other big game fishes. The body trails across the back of its host like a ribbon.

Name - It is appropriately named for the unusual shape of the abdomen (*longus*=long, *venter*=abdomen).

Diagnostic Characters - This is a very large, elongate copepod with a T-shaped cephalosome embedded in the flesh of the host. The long narrow posterior projection from body is almost as long and is similar in appearance to the egg strings. The "neck" is longer than the body. The body is white, the cephalosome bright pinkish red and the eggs strings are maroon when ripe.

Records - We found 1 female each on 1 of 19 bar jack, 4 of 20 crevalle jack, and 1 of 27 horse-eye jack from various localities around Puerto Rico; in 3 of 7 horse-eye jack from Joyuda Lagoon, Puerto Rico (USNM); in a horse-eye jack from St. Lucia; in 1 of 3 crevalle jack, and in 1 of 5 dolphin from off Dauphin Island, Alabama, USA. It is reported to commonly occur on many dolphin off North Carolina, Louisiana and Texas, USA, and in the northwest Atlantic (USNM 47800, 47806), and off the west coast of Africa; also on greater amberjack, blue runner (USNM 2107, 47804-5), cobia, crevalle jack (USNM 42346), pompano dolphin (USNM 47801), Spanish mackerel (USNM 6192, 47802), off the Atlantic and Gulf coasts of USA; and serra Spanish mackerel off Brazil. Usually 1 female occurs per host, but we found 9 on a liza, *Mugil liza* Valenciennes. Causey (1953) found 25% of crevalle jack off Texas, USA, were infected.

Geographic Range - Atlantic.

Life History - Eggs in the egg string which are beginning to hatch gradually become a dark maroon color. A newly hatched nauplius stage was figured by Wilson (1917).

Behavior - The female contracts its neck when touched (tactilely stimulated), pulling 1/2 to 2/3 of the exposed body (genital complex) into the host. This might be a defensive reaction to make a smaller target for cleaner fishes, or to prevent damage to this long-trailing copepod during violent feeding or swimming bouts by the host.

Associations - The mechanism preventing a second female from infecting a host has not been determined. Simple rarity of infective stages does not appear to be the answer. If the female is excluding others, this highly interesting process should be examined and explained (see Damage to Host). The exposed body of this copepod is often covered with hydroids and algae.

Location in Host - This copepod embeds its head in the host's body usually along the dorsal or anal fin near the tail. It was reported once embedded in the operculum.

Length - Females 40.0-50.0 mm, egg strings 10.0-15.0 mm; nauplius stage 0.25 mm.

Host Specificity - Crevalle jack, dolphin and pompano dolphin are the preferred hosts of this parasite, but it is only a secondary parasite of these hosts. It occurs occasionally to rarely on a variety of fishes including many big game fishes. Bunkley-Williams and Williams (1995) reported horse-eye jack as a new

host, and 2 other new hosts that were not big game fishes. Bar jack and serra Spanish mackerel are additional new hosts.

Damage to Host - A fibrous membrane forms around the embedded portion of the copepod. This large parasite may be detrimental to the host, but the extent of injury has not been studied. The normal infection of 1 female per host could suggest that fishes cannot survive multiple infections.

Detection - This long copepod spectacularly streams off the back of its hosts.

Preparation for Study - The embedded neck and cephalosome must be carefully dissected from the host tissues.

Significance to Sportfishing - This parasite appears to damage many big game fishes. Sport fishes infected with this parasite are said to not put up the same fight on hook and line as unparasitized fish (Causey 1955).

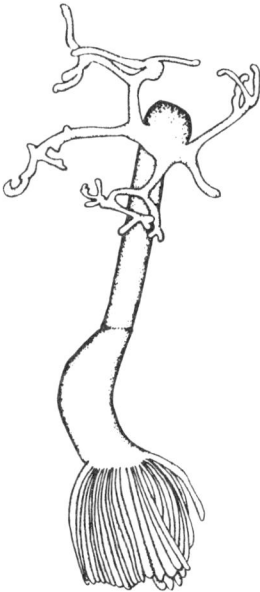

Lernaeolophus striatus Wilson

This large, and long lost, tissue-embedding copepod must cause considerable damage to great barracuda.

Name - "Striatus" means fluted or grooved and refers to the sides of the cephalosome.

Diagnostic Characters - This large copepod has dendritic projections from the fluted cephalosome. The neck and cephalosome are longer than the trunk and are embedded in the tissue of the host.. The anterior body and horns are a pale wine-red, the trunk is white and the appendages pale yellow. A dense mat of thick caudal projections is present on the posterior end of the body.

Records - We found 1-2 females in 4 of 44 great barracuda from various localities around Puerto Rico (USNM). Two females were found in a barracuda from Jamaica (USNM 43320). This copepod was collected in Jamaica in 1910 (described in 1913) and has not been reported again until now (86 years).

Geographic Range - Caribbean.

Location in Host - This copepod attaches in the throat just inside the lower jaw, with their cephalosomes embedded near the aorta and their bodies trailing back along the gill arches.

Length - Female 27.0-31.0 mm, male unknown.

Host Specificity - This parasite is only known from great barracuda. Few tissue embedding copepods are specific to a single host.

Damage to Host - This large, tissue embedding copepod must be harmful to great barracuda. Infections of more than a few copepods per host could be fatal.

Preparation for Study - The cephalosome and neck must be carefully teased from the host tissues. The caudal projections should be examined for algae and other encrusting organisms.

Genus *Pennella* Oken

These large elongate parasites attract a lot of attention with their bodies and egg strings sticking several feet out of hosts. They were noted in classical antiquity, medieval literature, and will probably eventually be recognized in the earliest, prehistoric coastal cave paintings of fishes. Aristotle wrote of these parasites, which were undoubtedly the first fish-parasitic copepods acknowledged by humans. Small ones can be mistaken for scientific fish tags. The name *Pennella* in Latin means "little feather" [penna=feather, -ella=little (diminutive)] and refers to the feather-shaped posterior projections. Many species in this genus vary extremely in shape and have little host specificity. The shape of the cephalosome and horns, and length of neck and trunk, have been used to distinguish species, but are unreliable in most cases. Some structures change with maturity or vary with the firmness of the surrounding host tissue. Older copepods are more elongate. A few specimens of these interesting copepods are often saved out of curiosity, but adequate numbers and assortments for comparison of these offshore and ephemeral copepods have usually eluded taxonomists, resulting in insufficient and repeated descriptions (synonyms). The genus became bloated with so many synonyms, poorly defined and questionable species that individual *Pennella* sp. specimens were quite difficult to identify to species. Recently, Hogans (1988b) reviewed and stabilized this genus and consolidated it into 7 species.

Females of this genus have a long cylindrical body. The cephalosome (armed with 2-3 projections or horns) and neck are embedded through the skin or fins of the host into the muscle or other internal organs. The body extends from the host and terminates in a dense "beard" or feather-like mat of simple or branched lateral projections. Older copepods have larger posterior beards. The egg strings are straight and are often as long as or longer than the body. This length may be related to the necessity of producing many eggs in the pelagic environment where hosts are so sparse and to support a complex two-host life cycle. The eggs hatch and release nauplius larvae, a series of larval stages develop in the plankton, females settle onto hosts, penetrate the body, and develop into adults. Immature females parasitize decoy host squids (*Pennella varians* Steenstrup and Lütken has been found on common cuttlefish, *Sepia officinalis* Linnaeus; elegant cuttlefish, *Sepia elegans* Blainville; and European squid, *Loligo vulgaris* Lamarck, in the eastern Atlantic). This is probably a strategy for finding sparse fish hosts in the open ocean as squid is a prey item for big game fishes. It is also an example of a permanent prey-to-predator parasite transfer. Males are not parasitic on hosts. Other organisms are found attached to the exposed portions of these copepods. Up to 18 striped goose barnacles have been found attached. Filamentous algae, hydroids and possibly other encrusting organisms grow in the beard at the end of the body and sometimes cover it in dense mats.

All 7 known species may occur in Puerto Rico. Two of the 4 species in big game fishes are only known from Puerto Rico (see below). This does not mean that Puerto Rico is a speciation center for copepods, but just indicates our poor state of knowledge. *Pennella exocoeti* (Holten) occurs on flyingfishes (*Exocoetus* spp.) preyed upon by many big game fishes worldwide and will probably be found off Puerto Rico. We collected *P. diodontis* Oken on a local spiny puffer, *Diodon holacanthus* Linnaeus (USNM, new host and locality). The other 2 known species are noted below. Most of these copepods are worldwide or at least circumtropical/temperate in distribution. Life histories are largely unknown. Many species occur quite sporadically and unpredictably on various hosts. These copepods are largely offshore and pelagic. Only *P. diodontis* has inshore, shallow-water hosts. The smallest and most delicate *P. sagitta* (Linnaeus) (2.2 cm long) occurs on sargassumfish, *Histrio histrio* (Linnaeus), or frogfishes. The largest copepod in the world, *P. balaenoptera* Korea and Danielson, occurs on the largest animals on Earth, baleen whales, *Balaenoptera* spp. The body of this copepod is longer than 20 cm and is rumored to exceed 1 foot (30.5 cm) with egg strings many feet long. Both of these copepod species could occur off Puerto Rico, but may be restricted to areas further north because we have not found them on sargassum fish and whales we examined.

The cephalosome of this parasite is often located near vital blood vessels or organs where it has an ample source of blood. This placement and subsequent damage can be disastrous for small or developing hosts. Host reaction can be extreme with enormous cysts occurring around the parasite. Many young big game fishes may be killed or debilitated and perish from predation because of this parasite. Massive infections that have been rumored, but never documented, could kill adult big game fish. The pathological impact of these parasites has never been studied, but many authors have suggested that they weaken hosts, particularly big game fishes. These parasites are harmless to humans.

The adult female protruding from the side of a host is obvious. Settling juveniles, males or developing females must be detected with skin scrapings viewed with a microscope. To correctly identify these copepods, the cephalosome and its complicated and delicate projections must be dissected out of the flesh intact. Simply pulling the copepod out of the host usually breaks the copepod at the neck and the cephalosome and neck remain in the flesh of the host. Even if the cephalosome is successfully pulled out (5-10% success), most of the projections will break and remain in the host. Cutting a large chunk of flesh out of the host around the parasite is the best method of saving these copepods. Save as many samples as possible. More than 1 species may be present on the same host. Many specimens may be needed to identify the copepod. Remember copepods that look different, are different sizes, or are attached in different positions on the host may represent different species. Photographs of unusual groupings of copepods or heavy infections would be useful in understanding these parasites.

Pennella filosa (Linnaeus)

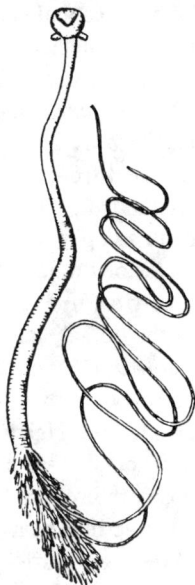

This large, worldwide parasite hangs out of the side of many big game fishes, particularly swordfish.

Name - "Filosus" means thread-like. The only information of use in the original description by Linnaeus was the name of the host. *Pennella costai* Richardi, *P. crassicornis* Steenstrup and Lütken, *P. germonia* Leigh-Sharpe, *P. germonia fagei* Poisson and Razet, *P. histiophori* Thompson, *P. orthagorisci* Wright, *P. pustulosa* Baird, and *P. remorae* Murray are synonyms.

This copepod is morphologically identical to *P. balaenoptera* that occurs on whales. They are essentially separated on the basis of their hosts. Morphologically identical species are rare but can exist if the biological differences maintain isolation. This mystery warrants additional study.

Diagnostic Characters - The female is very large (greater than 50 mm long). The large cephalosome is bulbous to cylindrical and has 3 short (less than the width of the cephalosome) unbranched projections or horns which protrude and extend perpendicular to the neck. The flat or truncated portion of the cephalosome is completely covered with papillae. The cephalosome and neck are yellow and the trunk is dark brown.

Records - We found 1-50 females on 6 of 40 Atlantic blue marlin, 1 female on 1 of 3 swordfish and 5 females on 1 of 3 yellowfin tuna from various localities around Puerto Rico. It has also been found on albacore, Atlantic sailfish, bluefin tuna and white marlin around the Atlantic and the world; on ocean sunfish; and on an unidentified dolphin off Australia.

Hogans, Brattey and Hurlbut (1985) found 182 of 303 swordfish in the northwest Atlantic infected with either this copepod or *Pennella instructa*. A maximum of 15 copepods occurred on a single host. A few protruded from scar tissue, although whether they caused the damage or were attracted to it was not clear. Only 12 copepods were dissected from these hosts and identified, thus the numbers of each species, association or competition between them, size ranges and location preferences was not determined. The *Pennella* sp. of Cressey and Cressey (1980) in 3 of 57 bluefin tuna and in 1 of 61 wahoo were probably *P. filosa*.

Geographic Range - Worldwide. Our collections are the first from the Caribbean.

Life History - Young females have only 2 horns on the cephalosome. The third (dorsal) horn develops last and is always smaller.

Ecology - Ocean sunfish, flyingfishes and pilotfish are probably important in maintaining population levels in big game fishes of this pelagic, open ocean species. Copepods in ocean sunfish with relatively soft muscle tissue develop bulbous cephalosomes, while those in relatively tough-muscled tunas develop more cylindrical cephalosomes.

Associations - This copepod is found in tight groups of 8-25 specimens with 12-50 *P. makaira* on the skin of Atlantic blue marlins off Puerto Rico. *Pennella instructa* is also found on swordfish, but these 2 copepods have not been reported from the same host specimen. This parasite occurs on remoras in the Atlantic and Mediterranean, which in turn attach to many of the big game hosts of this copepod. These associations may allow new hosts to be infected with males or immature females.

Location in Host - Skin, penetrating into muscle (subcutaneous musculature), of the dorsal, lateral and ventral surfaces of the body, but not on the head.

Length - Female 15.0-20.0 cm, egg strings 12.5-35.0 cm and can be twice the body length or more; immature female 9.4 cm; male unknown.

Host Specificity - The early literature is too inconsistent about copepod and host identifications, and modern collections are too limited to determine exact host preferences, but swordfish and ocean sunfish may the preferred hosts. · Atlantic blue marlin is a new host.

Damage to Host - Sumner et al. (1913) found infections of 30-40 copepods per host impaired the vitality of the fish. Hogans, Brattey and Hurlbut (1985) found that this copepod weakened the host by damaging the swimming muscles. "There is 1 species (*Pennella filosa*) in the Mediterranean, 7 or 8 inches long, which penetrates the flesh of the swordfish, the tunny, and the sunfish, and torments them horribly." (Cuvier 1830).

Pennella instructa Wilson

This is a very large parasite found in the side of swordfish in the western North Atlantic. Sport fishermen could help to determine its exact distribution and importance.

Name - "Instructus" means arranged in definite order and refers to the cephalosome papillae. *Pennella zeylandica* Kirtisinghe is a synonym. This species was redescribed by Hogans (1986).

Diagnostic Characters - The female is very large (greater than 50 mm long). The bulbous to cylindrical cephalosome has 2 long (greater than the width of the cephalosome) unbranched projections or horns which protrude and extend posteriorly and parallel to the neck. The flat or truncated portion of the cephalosome is partially covered with papillae. The cephalosome and neck are yellow, the trunk dark brown.

Records - One to 8 females occurred in swordfish from off Massachusetts (USNM 47751) to Maine (USNM 47750), USA, and in the northwest Atlantic. Up to 4 copepods commonly occur in a single host (see "Records" in *Pennella filosa*). It is also found in black marlin and 2 other species of Pacific billfishes.

Geographic Range - Worldwide. However, the records are widely spaced from the northwest Atlantic, Indian Ocean, and Australia.

Ecology - This species is less common than *Pennella filosa*. A cylindrical cephalosome is found in copepods embedded in hard tissues such as the aorta or heart, while a bulbous cephalosome is found in those in soft tissues.

Associations - *Pennella filosa* is also found on swordfish, but these 2 copepods have not been reported from the same host specimen. This copepod is often covered with algae and hydroids but not striped goose barnacles.

Location in Host - Skin, penetrating through muscle (subcutaneous musculature) and attaching in internal organs of the body cavity and major blood vessels of the dorsal, lateral and ventral surfaces of the body, but not on the head.

Length - Female 20.0-25.0 cm, egg strings vary from shorter to longer than the body, 10.0-33.0 cm. Two females described by Hogans (1986) were much smaller, 14.3 and 15.3 cm long.

Host Specificity - This copepod is only known from swordfish and may be a primary parasite.

Damage to Host - A thick fibrous cyst up to 5 cm in diameter often forms around this copepod. One formed a large cyst in a swordfish ovary. The aorta and heart can be injured by this copepod. Hogans, Brattey and Hurlbut (1986) found that this copepod weakened the host by damaging the heart.

Pennella makaira Hogans

This is an uncommon large copepod that sometimes occurs in heavy infections on Atlantic blue marlin near Puerto Rico.

Name - This copepod was described with specimens collected off Puerto Rico.

Diagnostic Characters - The female is the smallest reported on billfishes (less than 50 mm long). All other members of this genus from billfishes are greater than 50 mm long. The bulbous cephalosome has 2 long (greater than the width of the cephalosome) unbranched projections or horns which protrude and extend posteriorly at an oblique angle to the neck. The flat or truncated portion of the cephalosome is completely covered with papillae. The neck is shorter than the trunk. The cephalosome and neck are yellow, the trunk dark brown.

Records - We found 12-50 females on 10 of 40 Atlantic blue marlin from various localities around Puerto Rico.

Geographic Range - Unknown.

Associations - This copepod occurs in tight groups of 12-50 specimens among 8-25 *P. filosa* on the skin of Atlantic blue marlins off Puerto Rico. The gregariousness of this species could be due to preferred sites on the host, attraction to adult individuals, and/or the physics of settling onto an actively swimming host. A striped goose barnacle attached to a *P. makaira* on an Atlantic blue marlin off Arecibo, Puerto Rico.

Location in Host - Skin and muscle.

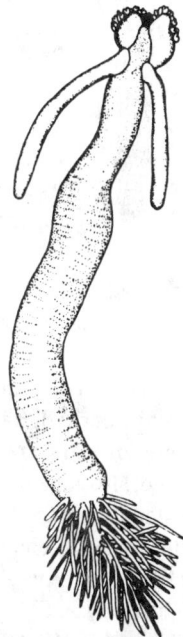

Length - Females 27.0-29.0 mm; male unknown.
Host Specificity - This copepod is only known from the Atlantic blue marlin, but occurs so seldom that it is only a secondary parasite.
Significance to Sport Fishing - Its abundance in Puerto Rico and possibly the Caribbean, apparent absence in the Gulf of Mexico and other parts of the Atlantic, relative long life in the tissue of the host, obvious location externally, host specificity, and ease of identification by field observation, may make it a highly effective biological tag.

Pennella sp.
This is a new species of moderate-sized copepod on dolphin which is only known from Puerto Rico.
Name - We are cooperating with Dr. William Hogans in describing and characterizing this new copepod.
Diagnostic Characters - The female is small (less than 50 mm). It is similar to *Pennella exocoeti* with a cephalosome with 2 pad-like processes on each side.
Records - We found 6-8 females on 13 of 17, and 1 each on 3 of 13 dolphin off Parguera, Puerto Rico; and 5 females and 1 juvenile on a dolphin off Desecheo Island, Puerto Rico.
Geographic Range - Unknown.
Ecology - Offshore, pelagic.
Location in Host - Skin or fins embedded in muscle.
Length - Female 22.5-43.0 mm.
Host Specificity - This parasite only occurs on dolphin, and is a secondary parasite in Puerto Rico.
Significance to Sport Fishing - See *P. makaira*.

Brachiella thynni Cuvier
This large copepod occurs worldwide on scombrids, especially wahoo. It is adapted to hide in the pit behind the pectoral fin base.
Name - It was named for tunas, but may be found more often on wahoos.
Diagnostic Characters - The cephalosome and neck are bent or curved anteriorly and are longer than the remainder of the body (excluding projections). Two attachment processes, approximately 1/2 as long as posterior processes, extend from the base of the neck. There are 2 pairs of unequal projections from the posterior end of the body; 1 pair (ventral processes) are about 2/3 the length of the trunk, the second pair (dorsal processes) are about 2/3 as long as the first. The body is light brownish yellow.
Records - We found 1-4 females in each of 19 wahoo, and 1 female on 1 of 40 dolphin from various localities around Puerto Rico. It has been found in albacore, greater amberjack (USNM 39585) bigeye tuna, bluefin tuna, cero, king mackerel and yellowfin tuna in the western Atlantic, and these and other scombrids around the world. The *Brachiella* sp. Iversen and Yoshido (1957) reported from wahoo in the Pacific was probably this copepod.

Geographic Range - Worldwide. Our collections are
the first from the Caribbean.

Life History - The males are rarely found on fishes.
In females, the right egg string is longer than the left,
370-860 eggs occur in each egg string.

Location in Host - The female seems to be adapted in
body shape and size to the cavity behind the pectoral
fins (axil) of big game fishes. This site specialization
is rather unusual. It rarely occurs on other parts of the
body, mouth or gills. Another species in this genus on
Pacific Spanish mackerels, *Scomberomorus* spp.,
attaches in the gills and nasal lamellae.

Length - Female 12.4-21.7 mm, egg strings 6.2-15.9
mm; male 1.2-2.3 mm.

Host Specificity - This copepod is a characteristic
parasite of wahoo. Wahoo is the preferred host. It also
occurs on a variety of other scombrids and a few non-
scombrids, but it is no more than a secondary parasite
of these hosts. Dolphin is a new host.

Detection - Surprisingly, this large
copepod can be missed in a cursory
external examination. They are often completely hidden in the
cavity behind the base of the pectoral fin (axil).

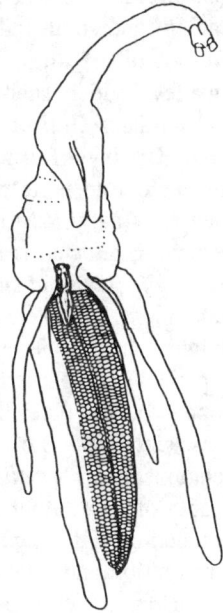

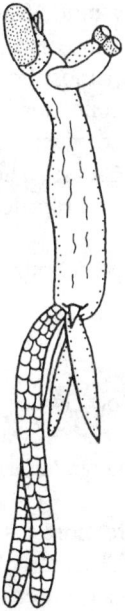

Charopinopsis quaternia (Wilson)

This characteristic parasite of dolphin occurs in light to
moderate infections on the gills.

Name - "Quaternia" means having 4 parts and refers to the
posterior processes. *Brachiella coryphaenae* Pearse is a
synonym. Wilson placed this species in a genus, *Charopinus*,
which contains copepods of chimaeras, rays, sharks and skates,
but Yamaguti (1963) erected a new genus. It has often been
incorrectly spelled "*C. quaternius*".

Diagnostic Characters - It is a tiny to small copepod with a
cylindrical body. The cephalosome and neck are shorter than the
trunk. Two elongate projections (posterior processes) extend off
the posterior end of the trunk. Two attachment processes,
shorter than the posterior processes, extend from the base of the
neck, and terminate in bulbs that look like boxing gloves.

Records - We found 3 females on 1 of 40 dolphin from various
localities around Puerto Rico; and 1-2 females on 2 of 5 dolphin
off Dauphin Island, Alabama, USA. Light infections occurred in dolphin from
the Dry Tortugas, off the Florida Keys, USA (USNM 64009-11) and from the
Straits of Florida, between Florida and the Bahamas; 11 females on 13 dolphin
from Port Aransas, Texas, USA (USNM 92663, 92688); and on Spanish

mackerel from Louisiana, USA. It has also been reported from Hawaii in the Pacific, and south India in the Indian Ocean.

Geographic Range - Worldwide (circumtropical/subtropical). But this is based on a few, widely spaced, records. Our collections are the first in the Caribbean and northern Gulf of Mexico.

Life History - Burnett-Herkes (1974) suggested that this parasite did not re-infect older hosts, if true, this would explain why their numbers are reduced and they are finally lost from larger dolphin. What conditions favor younger fish becoming infected is not known.

Ecology - Dolphin smaller than 38 mm are not parasitized (all SL), but young dolphin 38.1-39.9 cm are the most heavily parasitized (average 12.0 copepods), dolphin 40.0-79.9 cm are parasitized in lower numbers (average 1.7-5.9 copepods), dolphins 80.0-96.5 cm are more lightly parasitized (average 0.5 copepod), and older dolphin above 1 meter long do not have this parasite.

Associations - Burnett-Herkes (1974) found that this copepod had a negative relationship with *Caligus productus* and *Euryphorus nordmanni* in the gills and mouth of 145 dolphin. He suggested that either both of these copepods were competing with *Charopinopsis quaternia* or there was a combination of competition and a lack of re-infestation by *C. quaternia*.

Location in Host - Gill filaments. Reports from the gill chamber and operculum are of copepods dislodged after the death of the host.

Length - Female 6.2-7.3 mm, egg strings 6.5-8.2 mm; male 0.4 mm. The females from the Gulf of Mexico are about 80% as large as those from Hawaii.

Host Specificity - This is a primary parasite of dolphin, and is almost host specific. The single record on Spanish mackerel was probably contamination of these copepods from dolphin on sportfishing boats. This copepod must not occur very often on Spanish mackerel since it was not found by Cressey and Cressey (1980) in their extensive survey of scombrids. The record of 6 females and a male on a slender searobin is more difficult to explain.

Significance to Sportfishing - This distinctive and common copepod might be of use as a biological tag, if its distribution is limited.

Clavellisa scombri (Kutz)

It occurs on mackerels worldwide, but in light infections on few fishes.

Name - The name is appropriate for this genus-specific copepod. It was inadvertently omitted from the monograph by Yamaguti (1963) although he had collected, redescribed and refigured this species (Yamaguti 1939).

Diagnostic Characters - The cephalosome and neck combined are more than twice as long as the trunk. The head has a sclerotized dorsal shield. The trunk is more or less circular and has a noticeable anal tubercle on the posterior end. No genital process is present. The specimen figured has the microscopic male attached on the neck.

Records - One to 3 females occurred in chub mackerel from Alabama, USA; off Campeche, Mexico, tropical west Africa, Peru the Philippines and Japan;

Atlantic mackerel off Europe in the Atlantic and in the
Mediterranean; and in a Pacific mackerel from Australia and Taiwan.

Geographic Range - Worldwide.

Ecology - Offshore and pelagic.

Location in Host - Gill filaments.

Length - Female 5.4-8.5 mm, male 0.3-0.4 mm.

Host Specificity - This copepod is genus specific to
mackerel (*Scomber*, all 3 species). It is widespread
geographically, but occurs in light infections in low
percentages of the available hosts. It was originally
described from Atlantic mackerel in Europe, but in an
extensive survey, examining 97 specimens of this host,
Cressey and Cressey (1980) failed to find the copepod
in this host.

Damage to Host - It is a relatively large copepod
capable of injuring the gills. Apparently few of these
parasites occur on a host, thus damage is limited.

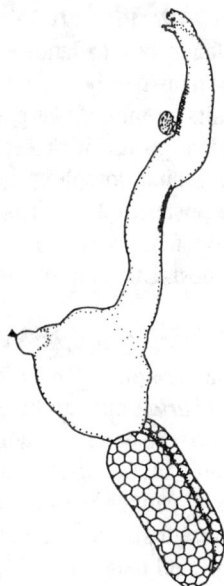

Miscellaneous Copepods

Genus *Alebion* - Alebion was one of the sons of Neptune, God of the seas,
in Roman mythology. These copepods are strictly external parasites of inshore
sharks. The single females reported, once each, on different big game fishes
must have been the result of contamination from sharks landed on the same
deck. The distinctive genus has a caligoid body, a cephalosome about 1/2 the
length of the body without lunules, segment with fourth legs covered with a
separate often ornate plate, fourth leg reduced to 1 segment, genital complex
about 2/3 as wide as cephalosome and usually with posterior projections extending along side and beyond the end of the abdomen, abdomen in 2 segments and
much shorter than genital complex, posterior projections 1/10 to 1/2 as long as
abdomen and with setae as long as or longer than the projections, egg strings
long. We found *Alebion elegans* Capart on great hammerhead, *Sphyrna
mokarran* (Ruppell), in Puerto Rico, which is a new locality for the Caribbean.

Alebion carchariae **Krøyer** - This copepod was found on a pompano
dolphin from the Atlantic. It can be distinguished because the segment with the
fourth legs is about 1/2 as wide as the genital complex and butterfly-shaped, the
genital complex has posterior projections that extend back beyond the end of the
abdomen and end in sharp points, the abdomen is shaped like a trident and has
posterior projections about 1/2 as long as the abdomen and longer than the
caudal rami. This parasite occurs around the world. The female is 7.6-9.0 mm
and male 6.0 mm long.

Alebion glaber Wilson - A female (USNM 32840) was found on an Atlantic bonito landed off Massachusetts, USA. This copepod can be easily distinguished because the segment with the fourth legs is almost as wide as the genital complex, the genital complex is almost square and lacks any trace of the typical posterior projections, the abdomen is about as long but 1/2 as wide as the genital complex, and has a bulbous or round anterior abruptly tapering on the posterior 1/2. It is known only from the north Atlantic coast of the USA. The female is 10.0-12.0 mm, egg strings 15.0 mm, male 7.0-7.8 mm, chalimus on host 2.0 mm, and metanauplius 1.2 mm long.

Alebion gracilis Wilson - A female (USNM 32727) was found on an Atlantic bonito landed off Massachusetts, USA. This copepod is similar to *C. carchariae* but can be distinguished by the lateral projections from the anterior end of the abdomen which are shorter than the caudal rami in this copepod, but longer in *C. carchariae*. It is known from the eastern Atlantic coast of the USA. Other western north Atlantic and the eastern Pacific records were of different species. The female is 9.0-9.6 mm, egg strings 9.0 mm; male 5.3-6.3 mm; and nauplius 0.3 mm long. This copepod may be more rare than noted as it was frequently confused with *C. carchariae* even by Wilson.

Anuretes heckelii (Kollar in Krøyer) - This parasite rarely and possibly accidentally occurs on big game fishes. Dojiri (1983) redescribed, refigured and established types for this species. It was formerly placed in *Lepeophtheirus*. *Eirgos anurus* Bere is a synonym. It has a caligoid body. The cephalosome is more than 1/2 of the total length of the copepod, and lacks lunules. The genital complex is ovoid, wider than long, almost as large as the cephalosome, and has posterior corners that extend beyond the caudal rami. The abdomen is relatively small and much wider than long. The egg strings are about as long as the body to longer. It was reported once in crevalle jack from Tuxpan, Mexico; and 4 females occurred in a Spanish mackerel from Texas, USA. We found females in a spadefish, *Chaetodipterus faber* (Broussonet), from La Parguera, Puerto Rico (USNM) and it has been reported from this host from several localities along the U.S. Gulf and Atlantic coasts, and Brazil. Our collection is the first in the West Indies. This copepod is known from the western Atlantic, and occurs in the gill chamber or mouth of its host. The egg strings contain 22-33 eggs each. The female is 2.1-2.9 mm long, egg strings 2.2-3.1 mm, immature female 2.4 mm long, male 1.2 mm. This copepod prefers spadefish, but has been found (once each) in 4 other hosts from 3 other families of fishes. Crevalle jack and Spanish mackerel may only be accidental hosts.

Brachiella elegans Richiardi - This is either a rare parasite or accidental infection in the gills of greater amberjack. It may be a synonym of *Brachiella thynni*, but differs slightly in shape. Both of these copepods have been found on greater amberjack. This copepod has a cephalosome and neck that are aligned in the same axis as the rest of the body instead of being curved toward the body and are much shorter than the remainder of the body (excluding the projections). Two attachment processes, approximately 1/2 as long as the posterior processes, extend from the base of the neck. There are 2 pairs of unequal projections from the posterior end of the body, 1 pair (ventral processes) are about 2/3 the length of the trunk, the second pair (dorsal processes) are less than 1/2 as long as the first. The body is dark yellowish brown. Five females and 1 male occurred in a greater amberjack from Massachusetts, USA (USNM 39585). It has also found on other fishes in the Mediterranean. The egg strings contain 180-210 eggs each. It occurs in the gill chamber of its hosts. The female is 10.0-12.6 mm, egg strings 5.0-6.0 mm, and male 1.4 mm long.

Caligus chelifer Wilson - The preferred hosts of this copepod are menhadens, but it has been recorded from a variety of hosts (anchovies, cutlassfish, drums, herrings, swordfish). Wilson (1905) described it from swordfish off Massachusetts, USA; Wilson (1932) suggested that this was a characteristic parasite of the swordfish and that this fish was the "primary" host; and Benz (pers. comm.) found 1 on a swordfish from the northwest Atlantic in 1978. The rarity of infections on swordfish suggests that these could be acidental infections. This female of this copepod was redescribed and the male described by Kabata (1972). It has a caligoid body with lunules moderately separated, and an abdomen with 2 segments. This copepod is known from the mid-Atlantic coast of the USA to Texas in the Gulf of Mexico. A record of this copepod in plankton off the west coast of Africa was apparently erroneous. The number of eggs in egg strings is 45-50. The female is 4.9-6.5 mm, and egg string 3.2 mm long.

Caligus confusus Pillai - This copepod is aptly named as it was based on the confused specimens of several authors. That was not the end of the confusion, Yamaguti (1963) listed a record from dolphin in the eastern Pacific which was actually a rainbow runner. Confusion still exists in the *Caligus* spp. of Indo-Pacific jacks.

Caligus curtus Müller - This copepod was reported on dolphin off Brazil, but this parasite is actually confined to the colder regions of the North Atlantic. The identity of the copepod in this report cannot be determined.

Caligus haemulonis Krøyer - Reported on blue runner and cobia from Louisiana, USA, by Causey (1953a, 1955). The reports are in doubt since Cressey and Nutter (1987) found he misidentified most of these copepods; this copepod has not been found on big game fishes before or since; and grunts (*Haemulon* spp.) are, appropriately, the preferred hosts for this copepod with other fishes only serving as inadvertent or accidental hosts (Cressey 1991). At least one of these copepods has been found on a big game fish. Pearse (1952) also described a female copepod from the gills of a blue runner in Texas (USNM 92670) as a new species, *C. validus*, but it is a synonym. It has a caligoid body with narrowly separated lunules, cephalosome less than 1/2 of the body length, roughly circular genital complex which is longer than the abdomen, abdomen in 1 segment with short caudal rami which are as wide as long. It is only known from the West Indies and Gulf of Mexico. The average length of the female is 3.6 mm.

Caligus patulus Wilson - Two females were found on 2 of 145 dolphin in the Straits of Florida (Burnett-Herkes 1974). It was previously known from milkfish, *Chanos sp.*, in Panama Bay, Panama, in the eastern Pacific. Dolphin may be an accidental host for this copepod. It has a caligoid body with widely separated lunules, a genital complex that is wider than long, an abdomen that is as wide as long, much shorter than the genital complex and is almost surrounded by posterior projections of the genital complex. The female is 6.1 mm long.

Caligus praetextus Bere - It was reported on crevalle jack from Louisiana, USA, by Causey (1953a). However, Cressey and Nutter (1987) found he misidentified most of these copepods; and Bere (1936) and Cressey (1991) did not find this copepod on crevalle jack. It has a caligoid body with widely separated lunules, cephalosome about 1/2 of the body length, roughly rectangular genital complex which is longer than the abdomen, abdomen 1-segmented with inwardly directed caudal rami. Microscopically the sternal furca (wish-bone shaped structure in the middle of the underside of the cephalosome) is square. It is only known from the northern Gulf of Mexico from the middle of the west coast of Florida to Texas. The limited distribution and distinctive appearance would make this copepod a useful biological tag, if it parasitized any wide-ranging big game fishes. The female is 2.2 mm long. It demonstrates no host specificity in abundance or frequency of occurrence on any host species.

Cecrops latreillii Leach - A female was reported only once from a tuna, *Thunnus* sp., in the Atlantic and the collector suggested that this might have been a mistake in labeling or an accidental transference to this host. The body is rectangular and more than twice as long as wide with all segments about the same width. The cephalosome is almost rectangular (longer than wide) with broad posterior lobes, a notch in each side and no lunules. An oval plate (wider than long) covers the fourth thoracic segment and overlaps the genital complex. Long posterior plates of the genital complex cover the abdomen and look like the back of a beetle. Egg strings are irregularly coiled and hidden under dorsal plates of genital complex. It occurs worldwide in temperate and cooler waters. This copepod breeds from May to October. The ocean sunfish host provides the opportunity for this parasite to infect or be transferred to offshore big game fishes. It occurs on the gills of the host. Female is 25-30 mm and male 10-17 mm long. Ocean sunfish is the preferred host, but it occurs on other fishes.

Lernaeolophus hemiramphi (Krøyer) - A single female of this parasite of Caribbean halfbeaks was recorded once from cobia in the Gulf of Mexico. This apparently accidental infection could have been caused by a prey-predator transfer of immature copepods. We examined numerous specimens of halfbeaks off Puerto Rico and named a new species of isopod from these hosts, but did not find this copepod. It is a large copepod with the anterior portions embedded in the tissues and the posterior portion with projections shaped like peacock feathers (abdominal process branched terminally). It has a bulbous trunk with spiral-shaped egg strings. The female is 16.0 mm long.

Lernaeolophus sultanus (Nordmann) - One female occurred on a cobia from Mississippi, USA; a 13.0 mm female on a swordfish off Ceylon; 1 each on a wahoo in the Pacific and on a black jack from an unknown locality. Despite these rare records in big game fishes, this copepod almost always occurs on inshore, benthic fishes. It is a large tissue-embedded copepod with dendritic projections from cephalosome and dense mat of thick, 10 or more branched caudal projections along each side of a projection from the posterior end of the body. The neck and cephalosome are shorter than the body. We only found this copepod on coral reef fishes in Puerto Rico. The copepods we collected attached in the roof of the mouth of their hosts and often penetrated through the head to caused a large open lesion on the top of the head. The single female in a swordfish attached in the body near the anus of the host; and the female in a cobia was embedded in the body just posterior to the last dorsal fin ray. These are unusual positions for this copepod, and may indicate that the infections were accidental. The female is 12.0-15.0 mm long. The caudal projections of this copepod are often covered with algae and protozoans, the one from a cobia had a striped goose barnacle attached. One we collected was densely covered in algae. The projections become more branched in older and larger copepods. The head wound and the parts of the copepod that projects into the wound are often covered with dense tufts of algae. During an underwater monitoring project, we observed a coral reef fish with a large bump on top of its head. Three days later this lesion erupted into an open, crater-shaped wound caused by this copepod. Whether this copepod always produces a head lesion, and if hosts survive this severe injury, is not known.

Lernanthropus hiatus Pearse - One male 1.7 mm long occurred on the gill filaments of an albacore from Bimini, Bahamas (USNM 88560) (Pearse 1951). This species was based on a single male specimen and is thus questionable. It differs from the known males in the genus by having a wide space between the antennae and the mouth tube. Cressey and Cressey (1980) did not find any members of this genus of copepods on tunas.

Lernanthropus micropterygis Richiardi - This copepod was described from greater amberjack in the Mediterranean and later found on another jack in the Red Sea; and 1 female each on a greater amberjack in the Pacific off Mexico and an unidentified jack, *Seriola* sp., possibly alamaco jack, off Costa Rica. We are skeptical of the eastern Pacific identification as this copepod has not been found in the Atlantic. As it stands, this parasite is genus specific to 3 species of jacks (*Seriola* spp.) and has a peculiarly disjunct geographic distribution. It was named for the host, but unfortunately greater amberjack was called *Micropteryx dumerili* in 1885 when it was named.

Pandarus sinuatus Say - Causey (1953b) possibly found as few as 1 (number unstated) females on the body of a crevalle jack from Port Aransas, Texas. He complained in his paper about sport fishermen "abusing" fishes (gaffing, dragging across docks, weighing, hanging, posing and photographing) and knocking off or contaminating copepods from other hosts before he was permitted to examine them, and also about dislodged copepods clinging to improper hosts including human fingers. We believe this characteristic parasite of sharks stuck to this jack through such contamination. Causey was impressed that these dark brown (almost black) females with long brown egg strings could be identified 20 feet away. The average length of the female is 6.5 mm. This copepod only parasitizes inshore sharks. *Pandarus satyrus* Dana was probably similarly contaminated once onto a Pacific marlin. Eldridge and Wares (1974) found large numbers of caligoid copepods irritating the skin and causing redness in eastern Pacific billfishes. Some of these were identified as *Pandarus* sp. Possibly some accidental infections do occur on big game fishes.

Thysanote longimana Wilson - This shaggy looking copepod is an external parasite of larger snappers and probably only accidentally occurred in a bar jack. The name means long arms and refers to the second maxillae. The cephalothorax is round and attached to a vase-shaped body which lacks obvious segments. A pair of attachment arms and 4 dendritic branches extend from the neck, the arms joining at their terminal ends. Four more branches extend from the trunk just anterior of the posterior end, 2 are simple projections and extend posteriorly from between the egg strings. It is yellowish white in color. Two females occurred on a bar jack off Carabiñero Beach, Mona Island, Puerto Rico (USNM). Our collections appear to be the first reported since this parasite was collected more than 85 years ago. It was originally described in a misidentified snapper from Jamaica, and we found it in 3 species of snappers from Puerto Rico. This copepod is only known from the Caribbean. It occurs in inshore, benthic habitats. This parasite attaches on the outside of the throat of its hosts. The female is 8.0-9.0 mm, egg strings 4.0 mm; and male 1.3-1.4 mm long. It is family specific to snappers (Lutjanidae). The 1 record in a jack could be accidental. Bar jack is a new host record for this copepod. This copepod is easy to see. We speared a bar jack at Mona Island because we noticed these copepods on its throat. We have seen many thousands of bar jacks before and since this collection and have not noticed this copepod.

Thysanote ramosa (Richardi) - This copepod was described, as *Brachiella ramosa*, from Mediterranean swordfish. Silas and Ummerkutty (1962) and a few uncritical checklists suggest it also occurred off Massachusetts, USA, but this appears to be an error.

BRANCHIURA (FISH LICE)

Fish lice, argulids or branchiurans form a small subclass of crustaceans. They can be very harmful to fishes, especially those in hatchery or culture facilities. Fish lice can infect the eyes of humans and bite careless handlers of live fishes. Approximately 150 species have been described in 5 genera, more than 120 in the genus *Argulus*. They are relatively large parasites varying from a few to 20 mm long.

The body is flattened (strongly depressed) and has a large, expanded head (carapace), thorax and an abdomen. The thorax has 4 ill-defined segments and the abdomen is completely fused. The appendages of the carapace are modified into mouthparts and suckers, and those of the thorax are 4 pairs of unmodified legs. Most have large suckers on the under side (dorsal surface) of the front of the carapace, something like the caligoid lunules only relatively much larger, in a different position and origin. Many have a long and vicious sting (stylet) in front of the mouth and between the antennae. The abdomen has no appendages, and terminates in a bifurcate tail.

They mate while free swimming off the host. Eggs are held in the body of the female. Females leave the host to deposit eggs in clusters attached to the substrate. *Argulus* spp. hatch as nauplius larvae, but members of the other genera hatch as juveniles from eggs in 15-55 days and develop directly into adults. Swimming juveniles must find a host in 2-3 days and once attached develop into adults in 30-35 days. Sexes are separate.

They attach on the body, fins, gills and mouth of fishes and sometimes on frogs and tadpoles. They are obligate parasites, feeding on blood, but adults are capable of changing hosts and spending prolonged periods off any host. They may prefer some fishes, but are usually not host specific. Heavy infections can kill fishes. A combination of moderate infections, *Anilocra acuta*, a bacterial infection and polluted conditions have caused mortalities in wild inshore fishes in the Gulf of Mexico. Fish lice directly transmit viral and bacteria diseases. They have introduced microbial diseases into culture facilities and caused epizootics.

They are the only crustacean fish-parasites known to infect humans. Others may bite or attack humans, but only *Argulus* spp. penetrate, survive in, and cause diseases in humans. Hargis (1958) reported the first case of human argulosis in a child infected by *Argulus laticauda* Smith while swimming in salt water off the Atlantic coast of the USA. We recently interviewed an aquaculture specialist from South America who became infected with *Argulus* sp. during her attempt to control losses of cultured tilapia caused by very heavy infections of this parasite in fresh water. One of these argulids was splashed into her face and lodged between her eye and the orbit. It caused severe irritation and minor tissue damage for 24 hours before it was discovered and removed. She was able to sleep with this horrid little beast in her eye. All fish lice should be treated with caution.

These parasites are more important in fresh, brackish and inshore marine waters. None occur in the open ocean realm of big game fishes probably because this habitat does not provide substrates for their eggs.

Classification and Contents

Argulus bicolor Bere

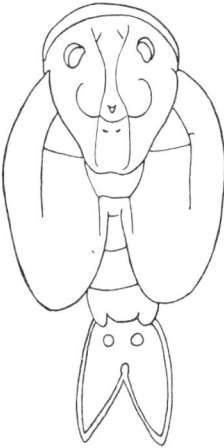

This is a rare and possibly accidental parasite of great barracuda in inshore waters.

Name - The name refers to the predominant green and rust colors of the body.

Diagnostic Characters - The carapace is elongate and longer than wide, and 2 suckers occupy almost its entire width of the ventral surface (not shown in the illustration of the dorsal surface). Lobes of the carapace do not extend to the abdomen. The posterior corners of the last thoracic segment form rounded lobes. The abdomen is relatively large (about 1/3 of the total length).

Records - This louse occurred on a great barracuda and another fish from Biscayne Bay, Miami, Florida, USA; and on other fishes from the west coast of Florida (USNM 69863).

Geographic Range - Unknown.

Location in Host - Body.

Length - Female 4.0 mm; male 3.2 mm.

Host Specificity - Needlefish (Belonidae) appear to be the preferred hosts of this parasite. The occurrence on great barracuda may have been accidental.

CIRRIPEDIA (BARNACLES)

Barnacles form a subclass in the crustaceans. The common name "barnacle" is from the Middle English "bernak" (a goose); and/or the French "bernicle." Apparently for the shape of "goose" barnacles. The barnacle goose in Europe was reputed by the ancient Greeks to spawn spontaneously from goose barnacles. They are famous for incrusting the bottom of your boat and other marine structures. Cleaning barnacles from structures, antifouling methods and the transport of exotic organisms involve serious economic and environmental problems. Barnacles also associate with or parasitize a variety of commercially important marine organisms. A great variety of organisms eat these animals, including "barnacle eaters" (filefishes, *Alutera* spp.). Barnacles were eaten by native Americans, are a delicacy in Europe, and the world's largest barnacle supports an important fishery in Chile.

More than 1000 living species have been described, and most are free living. Barnacles vary in size from the minute acrothoracicans, which burrow into the calcareous skeletons of corals and sea shells, to parasitic rhizocephalans anastomosing throughout the body of large crabs. The crustacean body form is greatly modified in all barnacles, but is drastically altered in some parasitic species. Most barnacles have a heavy calcarious shell, which is unique among crustaceans, composed of several to many parts imbedded in a soft mantle which surrounds the animal. Free-living forms are either attached by long stalks (goose) or directly to the base (dorsum) of their shells (acorn or volcano). Free-living barnacles filter feed by sweeping slender, jointed appendages (cirri) through the water. Parasitic forms live on or in various marine crabs and other crustaceans, echinoderms (sea stars, etc.) and soft corals; and most have lost the shell, appendages and body segmentation of free-living barnacles. Some barnacles are specialized associates of particular crabs, sea shells, other invertebrates, turtles and whales; while others attach to a variety of substrates or organisms.

The larvae are planktonic. Most barnacles have both female and male sexual organs (hermaphroditic), but some groups, particularly parasitic ones, have separate sexes. They attach externally, burrow inside skeleton or endoparasitically in a variety of hosts. Barnacles vary from free-living through various levels of association to permanent parasites. Parasitic barnacles feed on the tissues of their host. The shells of barnacles fossilize well and have left a good fossil record which shows a comparatively recent radiation (expansion in number of species and importance) in the middle of the Carboniferous Period (approximately 230 million years ago). Barnacles may have evolved from wholly parasitic ancestors as suggested by the many parasitic and host-associated species remaining today and the primitive parasitic ascothoracicans. However, closely related subclasses have free-living ancestors, which tends to argue against a parasitic origin of barnacles. Fertilization occurs in the mantle cavity or at the base of the oviduct; eggs (ova) generally develop to the first-stage nauplius within the mantle cavity, and are expelled by pumping movements of the body. The triangularly-shaped nauplius larva has corners tipped with prominent spines. It molts through 6 stages in the plankton, and then seeks a host or substrate. The thin, transparent bivalve-shelled, ostracod-like cyprid larvae rapidly swims and crawls around the substrate, selects a site for attachment, cements itself in place, and metamorphoses into a barnacle. One free-living species has been reported associated with big game fishes, and another may be confirmed.

References - Anderson (1993).

Classification and Contents

Conchoderma auritum (Linnaeus) - rabbit-ear barnacle

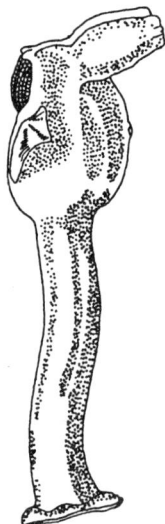

This large pelagic, rabbit-ear barnacle attaches to whales or ship hulls, occasionally sharks, and may be found on big game fishes.

Name - It is called "rabbit-ear" barnacle, or "rabbit-ear whale" barnacle, for the projecting "ears" and frequent association with whales. We expect that it occurs on big game fishes, but has been confused with striped goose barnacles. Great variations in the shape of this barnacle have inspired the unfortunate description of many unjustified species (synonyms).

Diagnostic Characters - This is a moderate-size to large goose barnacle with 2 elongate, ear-shaped projections on the anterior end, and usually a base stem (peduncle) that is distinct from the body (capitulum). The ears are the only consistent characteristic to distinguish this barnacle from striped goose barnacles. The ears only occur in adults. Immatures often cannot be physically identified.

Records - This barnacle has been rarely reported from sharks and whales in the Gulf of Mexico; whales, sharks and bony fishes in the Atlantic, Indo-Pacific and Arctic. It occasionally attaches on ship hulls and buoys.

Geographic Range - Worldwide.

Ecology - Oceanic, pelagic.

Location in Host - It attaches to barnacles on the skin of whales, but does not attach directly on whale skin. This barnacle can attach to baleen, palate, penis and teeth of whales; or any external, exposed hard parts such as bone or shell of marine mammals, sea turtles or fishes.

Length - 10.0-30.0 mm.

Host Specificity - It is usually found on acorn barnacles, *Coronula diadema* (Linnaeus), attached to whales, but sometimes on striped goose barnacles on sea turtles and whales. This barnacle has been reported to only occur on slow-moving fishes. This may explain its absence on big game fishes, but its great variety of incidental hosts, suggests it may infect almost any fish. It appears to prefer living hosts more than inanimate floating objects.

Preparation for Study - Records on big game fishes should be confirmed by preserving specimens of these barnacles in alcohol (151 proof rum, or rubbing alcohol) or 10% formalin. If these chemicals are not immediately available, specimens may be sealed in a plastic bag and held on ice or in a refrigerator for no more than 2-4 days before preservation.

Conchoderma virgatum (Spengler) - striped goose barnacle

This goose barnacle spectacularly attaches to crustacean parasites on fishes, including big game fishes.

Name - It is called "striped goose barnacle" for its markings. The great variations in the shape of this barnacle have inspired the description of many unwarranted species (synonyms).

Diagnostic Characters - This small to large goose barnacle lacks the elongate ears of *C. auritum*. The base stem (peduncle) and body (capitulum) are blended together without forming a distinct separation.

Records - We found 1 on 1 of 6 partially embedded copepods, *Pennella makaira*, attached on an Atlantic blue marlin off Arecibo, Puerto Rico. It occurred on a partially embedded copepod, *Lernaeolophus sultanus*, on a cobia off Mississippi, USA; and on *Pennella filosa* on swordfish off the Atlantic coast of the USA. This barnacle was reported on *Pennella instructa* on Indo-Pacific sailfish, swordfish, and other billfishes from the Indian Ocean, but other studies suggest that it does not occur on this copepod. It has also been reported from a variety of hosts and substrates including floating objects, boat hulls, sea turtles, sea snakes, whales and fishes.

Geographic Range - Worldwide.

Ecology - This barnacle is odd because it only grows at shallow, mid-water depths. Most other barnacles are quite happy to grow at the surface of the ocean. Offshore, big game fishes make excellent platforms for these associates, but they require some solid surface unhindered by scales and fish mucus to attach. We have found these barnacles attached to parasitic copepods and isopods on host fishes, exposed bone from host wounds, and on fish tags.

This barnacle may attach to offshore sport fishes while they are near shore. Leatherback turtles, *Dermochelys coriacea* (Linnaeus), moving from the Atlantic to Caribbean islands to spawn, arrive without any striped goose barnacles, but soon become a substrate for this associate. It is also very common on *Pennella* spp. partially embedded in ocean sunfishes and flyingfishes that never venture inshore.

Williams (1978) reported the first record of striped goose barnacle attached to a fish-parasitic copepod not permanently embedded in the host and Benz (1984) reported 4 more cases. Causey (1960) found a similar instance of what was possibly this barnacle (*Conchoderma* sp.) on *Gloiopotes huttoni* on the Indo-Pacific sailfish off Mazatlan, Mexico.

Associations - This barnacle attaches to parasitic copepods and isopods on fishes. It competes for space with other barnacles on the shells of sea turtles.

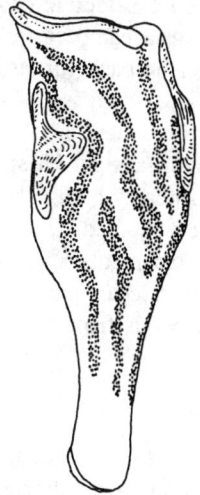

Location in Host - It usually attaches on the external surfaces or crustacean parasites on hosts, but we found 1 attached to a copepod in the mouth of a fish (Williams and Williams 1986).
Length - 7.2 to 25.0 mm.
Host Specificity - This barnacle has no host specificity, but occurs on any crustacean parasite or exposed hard part on a host. It is sometimes common on leatherback turtles; copepods, *Pennella* spp., partially embedded in offshore fishes; and isopods, *Nerocila* sp., on inshore fishes.   *Pennella makaira* is a new copepod host, and Atlantic blue marlin a new fish host.
Damage to Host - Direct attachment to exposed bone or shell of the host is probably benign and may even help to cover or close wounds. These barnacles are reputed to increase the water resistance of copepods or isopods by their attachments.   This force should increase the tissue damage of embedded crustacean parasites, but may pull non-permanently attached copepods and isopods from their host.

ISOPODA (ISOPODS)

Isopods are an order in the crustaceans. The name refers to all legs (pods) being approximately similar in size and shape (iso). Isopods kill, stunt and damage commercially important fishes. Approximately 9.4% of the chub mackerel along the Peruvian coast are parasitized by *Meinertia gaudichaudii* (Milne-Edwards) causing a 15% loss in body weight and costing Peruvian fishermen approximately 1.3 billion kilograms of fish annually. This is unfortunately not an isolated case. A few fish-parasitic isopods actively swim after and bite humans, sometimes alarmingly in mass attacks, but bites are more likely to occur when handling infected fishes. Free living isopods are reported to clean *Saprolegnia* spp. (fungus) from fishes. Locally, *Anilocra* spp. are dried and used to make a tea to treat colds. New England fishermen use "salve bugs" (*Aega* spp.) for medicinal purposes. Isopods are eaten by a variety of animals. Giant isopods, *Bathynomus* spp., are fished commercially for human food in Japan and Mexico and Hawaiians eat a smaller species. The presence of parasitic isopods on marine tropical fishes allegedly indicates that they do not contain high amounts of ciguatera (fish poisoning) toxins. This is not proven, but highly interesting, particularly since large barracuda and jacks are commonly implicated in ciguatera poisoning, and often have attached isopods.

Approximately 4000 species of isopods have been described, and more than 450 species are known to associate with fishes. They vary from 0.5-440 mm in length. The world's largest species, *Bathynomus giganteus* Milne-Edwards, is found off Puerto Rico and beyond. The head is fused with first thoracic segment (cephalothorax), and they have a 7-segmented thorax and 6-segmented abdomen (often fused into 2-5). One pair of thoracic appendages is modified into mouthparts, and 7 pairs are unmodified. The abdomen has 6 pairs of appendages, and ends in a terminal, often shield-shaped segment called the pleotelson. Eggs, larval forms and juveniles develop either in a brood pouch beneath, or in pouches in the abdomen of the female. Most isopods possess free swimming juveniles that develop into adults, but gnathiid juveniles parasitize the gills and skin of fishes and are free living as adults. Sexes are separate in most isopods, while others begin life as males and later become females (protandrous hermaphrodites). They are common in most environments, including dry land. They parasitize fishes, crabs, shrimp and other isopods. Fish-associated isopods vary from accidental (cirolanids), temporary or casual (corallanids and aegids) to permanent (cymothoids) parasites. They attach in a variety of locations including the skin, gills,

Head (Cephalothorax)
Leg (Pereopod)
Thorax (Pereon)
Broodpouch
Abdomen (Pleon)
Pleopods
Pleotelson
Uropods

inside the mouth, on the fins and some even burrow under the skin to form a cyst in the flanks of fish. A broad range of food habits occur. The fish-associated forms feed on blood or ooze from wounds. The wounds isopods cause may provide entry points for microbial diseases. Isopods can be preserved and stored in 70% ethanol (151 proof rum will do) or 40% isopropanol (rubbing alcohol).

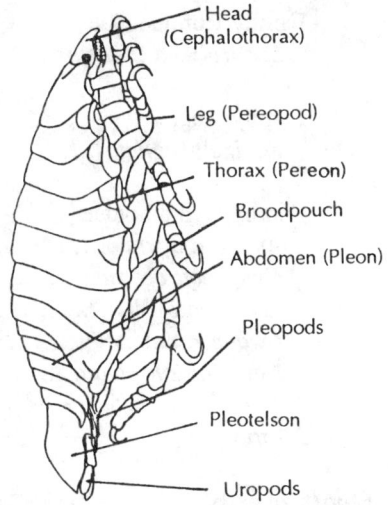

Most isopods associated with fishes occur inshore, except those on flying-fishes and pelagic needlefishes. The majority of our records from big game fishes were accidental infections while these hosts were inshore, or transfers from flyingfishes or other prey fishes. Only *Cymothoa oestrum* on jacks and great barracuda and *Livoneca redmanii* on Spanish mackerels occur commonly on big game fishes. Even these isopods first attach when their hosts are inshore.

Free living isopods are found in the stomachs of big game fishes often enough to be listed in some food item studies. Large parasitic cymothoids [*Glossobius auritus* Bovallius, *Glossobius impressus* (Say), *Nerocila excisa* (Richardson)] have been reported from the stomachs of dolphin in the Pacific, and *Glossobius impressus* has been reported from the stomachs of yellowfin tuna in the Caribbean and Pacific. These isopods parasitized flyingfishes that were eaten by these big game fishes. At least 2 species of isopods have been transferred from prey species to big game fishes (see Discussion).

Popular references - "Isopods" (Williams and Bunkley-Williams 1997), "Marine isopod crustaceans of the Caribbean" (Kensley and Schotte 1989).

Classification and Contents

*Larval form

Gnathia spp.

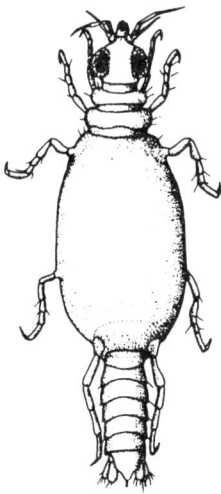

These tiny crustaceans swarm over Caribbean reef fishes at night and keep the cleaner fishes and shrimp busy picking them off during the day. They are rarely reported from big game fishes.

Name - Benz (1994) called them "sea gnats". The juveniles and immature females that occur on fishes are extremely difficult to identify to species since most species characters are based on the adult, free-living male.

Diagnostic Characters - These minuscule to tiny isopods have only 5 pairs of legs (small juveniles of other isopods have 6-7 pairs of legs). The head has a constricted "neck" instead of being fused into the remainder of the body.

Records - One each occurred in 3 of 45 great barracuda and 2 on 1 bar jack from various localities around Puerto Rico. It was also reported from a blue runner and a yellow jack from Jamaica.

Geographic Range - Members of this genus occur around the world.

Life History - Eggs develop into juveniles in cavities in the body of the female brood pouch. Juveniles attach, probably at night, to the gill filaments, body or fins of fishes and suck blood, their flexible bodies swelling as they fill. They eventually drop off the fish and mature into free-living males or females. Males develop large heads, some with massive mandibles (jaws), occupy benthic habitats (commonly coral reefs) and have harems of many females.

These isopods were not thought to change hosts or to take more than 1 blood meal from a host. However, *Haemogregarina bigemina* (a protozoan parasite of fish blood cells) has been shown to complete its life cycle in the body of a *Gnathia* sp., which then transmits the protozoan between fish hosts. For this to occur, a gnathiid must take a blood meal from a protozoan-infected host, drop off long enough for the protozoan to develop, and then contaminate a second host by taking another blood meal. Thus, the host relationships of gnathiids may be more complex and long lived than once thought.

Ecology - This is not a parasite of the open ocean. *Gnathia* spp. are largely restricted to inshore or deep sea fishes more closely associated with substrates where the adult gnathiids can develop.

Associations - One *Gnathia* sp. was found attached to an *Excorallana tricornis* in the mouth of a great barracuda from Puerto Rico.

Location in Host - Gill filaments and skin.

Length - Up to 5.0 mm.

Host Specificity - These isopods are assumed to have no host specificity, but the biology of most species is unknown.

Damage to Host - Usually a few isopods do little damage. Heavy infections cause tissue damage and kill hosts in confined or culture situations.

Detection - These small isopods can barely be seen on fishes, and look like tiny red spots. They are more easily seen and identified with the use of a dissection microscope.

Significance to Sport Fishing - They appear to be too rare to cause problems in big game fishes, but transmission of *H. bigmina* may injure young big game fishes.

Excorallana tricornis (Hansen)

These small isopod have horn-like processes on the male's head. They casually associate with many species of fishes, but will readily "abandon ship".

Name - The name "*tricornis*" refers to the 3 horns on the head of the male. Delaney (1984) revised this genus and designated *E. tricornis* as the type species.

Diagnostic Characters - There are 3 large horns on the head of the male (more obvious in profile, than when viewed from above, as in our figure). The body is elongate. There are small spines on all legs rather than large hooks.

Records - We found 2-20 in 6 of 45 great barracuda from various localities around Puerto Rico. It has been found in blue runner, crevalle jack and great barracuda from Jamaica. This isopod is also known from the northern coast of Yucatan (Mexico), the Gulf of Mexico, Panama and we recently reported it from Colombia (Williams, Bunkley-Williams and Sanner 1994) The eastern Pacific "sister species" occurs in fishes including a jack.

Geographic Range - Caribbean and Gulf of Mexico.

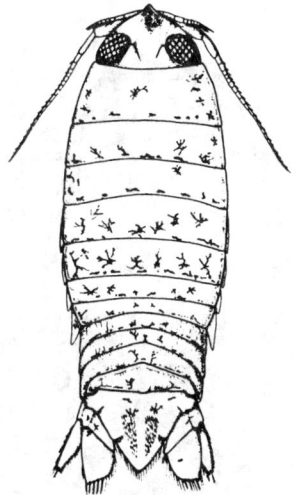

Life History - These isopods probably breed throughout the year, but increased numbers of planktonic juveniles occur in the spring and fall. Gravid females are seldom captured. They probably do not feed and brood eggs through juveniles in seclusion in the substrate in shallow waters. Juveniles leave the female and live in the plankton for an unknown period of time, then settle onto the substrate and develop into adults.

Ecology - It is an inshore species that only occasionally infects big game fishes when they are near shore.

Location in Host - Gill chamber, nares or external folds in the throat (gular) and gill cover. Occasionally in the mouth, skin or fins.

Length - Females 4.0-9.6, males 3.9-9.9, juveniles 1.0-3.0 mm.

Host Specificity - None.

Damage to Host - Few isopods occur on a host. Blood feeding might be significant on small hosts, but no tissue damage has been reported.

Detection - These isopods are easily seen. They readily detach from the host and fall onto the deck, so fishes should be immediately examined after capture. Also, look for loose isopods on the deck and under the catch.

Preparation for Study - Quickly seal gills, heads, etc. in plastic bags. Later, the sediment from these bags can be decanted and examined for the presence of this isopod.

Rocinela signata Schioedte and Meinert

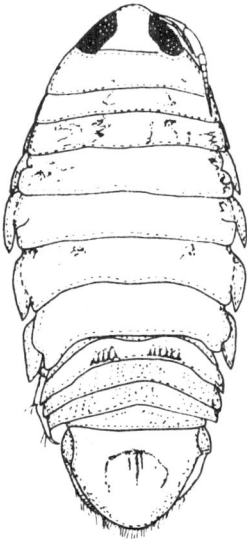

The monogram isopod is the most common and ubiquitous medium- to large-sized isopod found in the gill chambers of Caribbean fishes. It is known to severely bite swimmers and divers, sometimes in mass attacks (Garzon-Ferreira 1990).

Name - Called the "monogram isopod" for the mark on the tail (pleotelson).

Diagnostic Characters - It has an M- or W-shaped mark on the tail and is a moderate-sized, flattened isopod with an oval body outline. Large hooks occur on the first 3 pairs of legs, but only straight segments on last 4 pairs.

Records - We found 1 in 1 of 35 cero, 2 in 1 of 45 great barracuda, 1 in 1 of 15 king mackerel from various localities around Puerto Rico; and 1 in a cero from Jamaica. It has also been reported from albacore from the Atlantic and in other fishes from Florida, USA and Brazil.

Geographic Range - Tropical western Atlantic.

Life History - Gravid females do not occur on fishes. They probably consume a large blood meal before dropping off a host and do not feed again until the offspring emerge as juveniles. Then the female molts and loses the flaps forming the brood pouch and feeds again and continues to repeat the reproductive process. Juveniles have a planktonic stage, and then are found free living in or around the substrate or temporarily parasitic on fishes. Isopods of all sizes have been collected from fishes. They remain good swimmers throughout their lives, except for gravid females.

Ecology - This is an inshore species. The few isopod reported on offshore fishes may have been carried from the shallows to pelagic areas on these hosts. They have been collected from depths of 55 m in the Gulf of Mexico, 60-93 m off Mexico, and we have seen it on fishes caught in deep water traps off Colombia (Williams and Bunkley-Williams 1994).

Location in Host - Gill chamber, rarely externally.

Length - Up to 15.0 mm.

Host Specificity - No fish host preference is apparent and since it feeds off humans, we suspect that it also attacks sea turtles and mammals, as well.

Damage to Host - This isopod does not associate for sufficient periods of time on the host to cause tissue damage. Usually they occur in too low of numbers to cause much injury.

Detection - The adults are easily seen, but juveniles must be found with a dissection microscope.

Harm to Humans - These isopods are known to bite swimmers and scuba divers with mass attacks driving divers out of the water off Colombia (Garzon-Ferreira 1990). The bites are painful and can be bloody. One of our aquanauts in a saturation NOAA Habitat mission made an emergency stop inside an underwater talking bubble to remove a monogram isopod from under his ear. When he did so, blood streamed down his neck. This is the only isopod known to treat humans as routine prey!

Anilocra acuta Richardson

This external rider of gars and other fresh- and brackish water fishes, can kill its host. It has been reported from big game fishes only once, but in spectacular fashion.

Name - *Acuta* (=acute) for its pointed head.

Diagnostic Characters - The head is distinctly pointed. It is a moderate-sized flattened isopod, with the body roughly triangular in outline.

Records - We found this isopod far offshore in the throat of a king mackerel off North Carolina. This indicated accidental transfer of an adult isopod from a prey to predator host and survival of an external isopod in the throat of an new host (Williams and Bunkley-Williams 1994).

Geographic Range - Atlantic through Gulf coast of the USA from New York to Texas, and possibly into the Gulf coast of Mexico (Williams and Bunkley-Williams in press).

Ecology - Limited to coastal freshwater and brackish water areas, although it survived in full-strength seawater in the king mackerel. Members of the genus

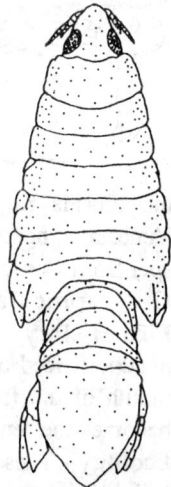

Anilocra are essentially tropical and marine. This is the only exclusively temperate member and freshwater species.

Associations - A combination of this isopod, bacteria, *Aeromonas hydrophila*-complex, and fish lice, *Argulus lepidostei* Kellicott, have caused disease and mortalities in coastal gars (Lepisosteidae) in the Gulf of Mexico.

Location in Host - Skin or fins. The occurrence in the throat was highly unusual and an example of site transfer.

Length - Female 24.5-34.2 mm, male 20.4 mm.

Host Specificity - Usually occurs on gars, but occasionally on other coastal fresh and brackish water fishes. The preference for gars appears to imply limited host specificity.

Damage to Host - Although known to cause lethal diseases (see Associations above), it more often simply stunts fishes as do all fish-parasitic isopods.

Cymothoa oestrum (Linnaeus)

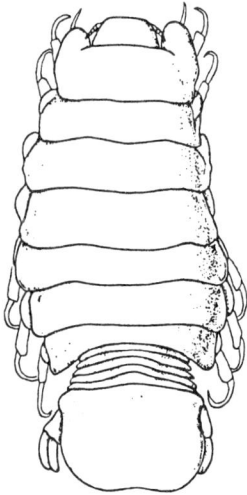

This "jack-choking" isopod stunts wild adults and kills aquarium fishes. Caribbean folklore suggests that jacks and barracuda with this isopod do not have ciguatera fish poison. This fable requires testing.

Name - They are also called "tongue-biters" for its habit of occupying most of the oral cavity of jacks.

Diagnostic Characters - It is a large, white or cream-colored isopod with a rectangular body outline and has "shoulder-pad" projections beside the head.

Records - We found a female-male pair in each of 2 of 19 bar jack, 1 of 2 blue runner, 7 of 20 crevalle jack, 4 of 14 great barracuda, and 9 of 27 horse-eye jack from various localities around Puerto Rico; 1 blue runner each from Bermuda and West Palm Beach, Florida, USA; 1 horse-eye jack each from Curaçao and St. Lucia; and a crevalle jack from Trinidad. It has also been reported in bar jack from the Florida Keys, USA, and Carrie Bow Cay Belize; crevalle jack from Venezuela; horse-eye jack from the Bahamas and Barbados; and jacks (*Caranx* sp.) from Curaçao and Jamaica.

Geographic Range - Western Atlantic.

Life History - Juveniles are released from the brood pouch, swim in the plankton, feed off a variety of small fishes as transfer hosts, finally enter the mouth of the final host and mature into adults. The first juvenile to arrive becomes the female, and a subsequent juvenile the male.

Ecology - These parasites range from inshore brackish waters to offshore high salinity waters and jacks even carry these isopods into fresh water in Puerto Rico (Bunkley-Williams and Williams 1995). They appear to be more common on big game fishes living inshore, but are also found in hosts offshore.

Location in Host - The adult female attaches on the top of the tongue, facing out. The male is behind and beneath her and lying across the gill rakers.

Length - Female 23.0-38.0 mm, juveniles 6.5-9.7 mm, first 4 juvenile stages 6.5, 7.2, 8.1 and 9.0 mm (Williams and Bunkley-Williams 1994).

Host Specificity - It commonly occurs on crevalle jack and horse-eye jack, and occasionally occurs on other jacks and great barracuda. Records from "scombroid fishes" appear to have been in error. In marine aquaria it will infect almost any fish exposed to juvenile isopods.

Damage to Host - Little physical damage to the host is apparent. There is probably some general stunting. Jacks with isopods eat different food items, presumably because the isopod takes up so much room in the mouth of the host. Large numbers of juveniles kill fishes. Juvenile jacks can be killed by a few isopods. We have landed crevalle jack by hooking them only through the isopod in their mouths, demonstrating the strength of the isopod's grip on the host.

Detection - The light-colored female quite obviously fills the mouth of the host.

Harm to Humans - Larger jacks and barracuda in Puerto Rico are notorious for carrying harmful amounts of ciguatera fish poisoning toxins. The sale of these fishes is banned in Puerto Rico. Caribbean folklore suggests that fishes with isopods are free from ciguatera. In some fish markets in the Lesser Antilles, isopods are illicitly added to fishes to make them sell. This legend has not been proven and should not be taken as fact. Research is needed to confirm or deny this intriguing idea.

Significance to Sport Fishing - This parasite may kill a few jacks, so slightly fewer are available for sport fishing. Infected jacks are smaller than uninfected ones of the same age. Jacks with isopods do not fight as well or as long on hook-and-line. Large isopods in the mouth may alarm some sport fishermen, but they have no effect on the quality of the fish as food.

Aquaculture - Thousands of planktonic juveniles of this isopod superinfected an adult crevalle jack held in a shallow water trap near Magueyes Island, La Parguera, Puerto Rico (Williams and Bunkley-Williams 1994). These isopods occur abundantly in the plankton and may cause severe problems for any big game fishes cultured in the Caribbean.

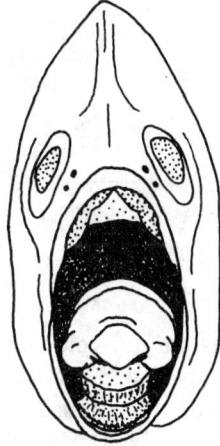

Livoneca ovalis (Say)

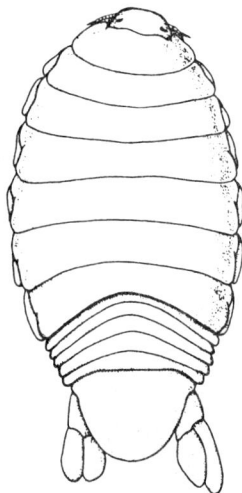

This ubiquitous gill-dwelling isopod of the U.S. Atlantic coasts is very damaging and important to inshore fishes, but relatively rare on big game fishes. **Name** - This isopod is morphologically similar to *L. redmanii* (the next parasite in this book) and several authors consider that they are the same. *Livoneca redmanii* is genus specific to Spanish mackerels and always occurs in female-male pairs, while *L. ovalis* has no host specificity and occurs singly. We believe that these are distinct species.

"*Aegathoa oculata*" has been reported from Spanish mackerel. This genus was used in the past before it was recognized that these isopods were juveniles of cymothoid isopods. The genus is now considered invalid and is not in use. The isopod was probably a juvenile of *L. ovalis*.

Diagnostic Characters - This isopod is large, cream- or grey-colored, with an oval body shape. It occurs singly (females not accompanied by males).

Records - We found a single immature specimen in a Spanish mackerel from Dauphin Island, Alabama, USA. It was also reported once from crevalle jack off New York and a juvenile occurred in a Spanish mackerel off Florida, USA.

Geographic Range - Atlantic and Gulf Coasts of the USA.

Ecology - Occurs from coastal fresh waters to open ocean, but more commonly in inshore marine and brackish water areas.

Location in Host - Usually in the gill chamber, but occasionally in the mouth. It has been reported from the stomachs of several dolphin from off North Carolina, as a result of host predation.

Length - Up to 21.0 mm.

Host Specificity - None.

Damage to Host - It frequently erodes up to 1/3 of the gill filaments of a host. This isopod has been accused of directly transmitting lymphocystis disease, but this is unlikely since they permanently associate with a single fish.

Detection - Easily seen. It sometimes causes an obvious bulge the gill flap and often its tail or hind-body is exposed out from under the gill flap of the host.

Harm to Humans - A court case alleged that this isopod caused injury to someone eating an infected Spanish mackerel in August 1994 on the Atlantic coast of the USA. We provided testimony in this case and in a similar court case in Puerto Rico in 1992 involving an isopod in imported eastern Pacific snapper (Isopod Newsletter 1992; 81:1). Fish parasitic isopods in fishes do not harm humans that eat these fishes. (If isopods were that dangerous, our isopod research would be better funded!)

Livoneca redmanii Leach

This isopod, found in pairs in the gill-chamber, is extremely damaging to mackerels and can kill them, causing significant loss of these valuable sport fishes. **Diagnostic Characters** - It is a large, tan, oval-shaped isopod that always occurs in female-male pairs in the gill chambers of Spanish mackerel.

Records - We found 2-4 in 26 of 35 cero from various localities around Puerto Rico, 2-4 in 2 cero from Barbados, 2 in a serra Spanish mackerel from Colombia, 2-4 in 2 cero from Jamaica and 2 each in 3 serra Spanish mackerel from Trinidad. These levels may be biased by spearing the hosts. Fishes parasitized with this isopod may be more easily collected than non-parasitized ones. Records from king mackerel and Spanish mackerel are questionable and require confirmation. Caribbean records of this isopod on the Spanish mackerel probably refer to the serra Spanish mackerel as the 2 fish were previously confused and the geographic range of this isopod apparently does not overlap that of Spanish mackerel.

Geographic Range - Caribbean and South American coast to Rio de Janeiro, Brazil. It was absent from extensive surveys of Spanish mackerels in Mexico.

Ecology - Like their Spanish mackerel hosts, they are found around coral reefs and in pelagic and offshore habitats.

Location in Host - The female is located in the ventral portion of the gill chamber, facing forward with the dorsal surface against gill flap. The male is beneath and partly behind the female.

Length - Female 19.5-26.0 mm.

Host Specificity - Only found on cero and serra Spanish mackerel.

Damage to Host - A female-male pair occupies the gill chamber and destroys 1/3-2/3 of the gill filaments, thus stunting the growth of the host. Eight of 26 infections in Puerto Rico and 1 each in Barbados and Jamaica had a pair of adult isopods in both gill chambers. These "doubly infected" hosts have very poor length-to-body-weight ratios, are generally in poor physical condition, and often suffer from other parasite and bacterial diseases. Double infections appear to kill the host. A proliferation of gill chamber epithelial tissue (granuloma) was found in the identical position of the isopod attachment site of a cero that had a pair of isopods in the opposite gill chamber. The productivity of these important sport and commercial fishes is drastically reduced by this isopod.

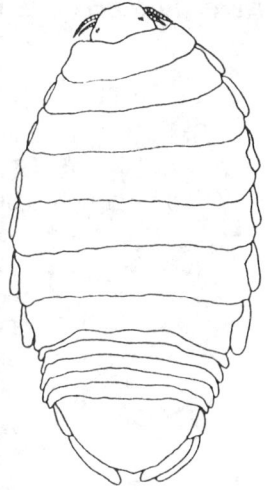

Nerocila lanceolata (Say)

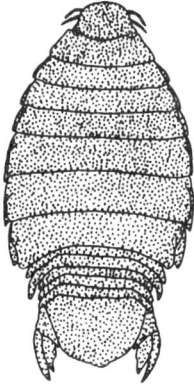

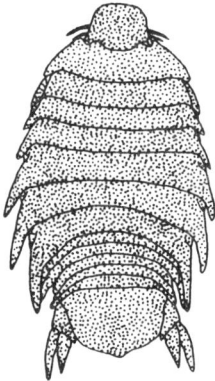

This dark, external isopod is a "shape shifter" of varied body forms that digs large holes in the host flesh. Fortunately for big game fishes, it occurs largely on inshore fishes.

Name - The great variety of body forms demonstrated by this parasite (see figures) has caused it to be repeatedly named as different, unwarranted species. *Nerocila acuminata* Schioedte and Meinert is the most popular of these synonyms.

Diagnostic Characters - It is a large black to black and white striped, external isopod. The posterior margin of the head is distinctly trilobed.

Records - Williams, Bunkley-Williams and Rand (1994) reported this isopod on a new host, blue runner, and new locality in Bermuda.

Geographic Range - Atlantic and Gulf Coasts of the USA and Central America, Bermuda and Cuba.

Life History - Juvenile or immature isopods occur on small fishes, but it is unclear if these are temporary or permanent hosts.

Ecology - This isopod occurs largely on inshore fishes but rarely infects big game fishes.

Associations - It is often infected with external hydroids and algae. Striped goose barnacle has been reported attached to this isopod and to *Nerocila californica* Schioedte and Meinert. This isopod is sometimes found with missing or damaged pleopods, pleotelson or legs (pereopods). These injuries are probably due to attacks by cleaner fishes.

Location in Host - Skin and fins.

Length - Female 14.0-25.0 mm, male 10.0-20.0 mm.

Host Specificity - This isopod occurs more commonly on certain inshore, bottom (benthic) fishes, but a great variety of fishes are parasitized. *Nerocila californica* occurs on Indo-Pacific sailfish and other billfishes in the eastern Pacific, while *N. lancéolata* does not occur on billfishes in the Atlantic. All *Nerocila* spp. on big game fishes may be a result of prey to predator transfer.

Damage to Host - This parasite causes considerable tissue damage. External lesions often cover more surface area of the host than the isopod. Secondary bacterial infections sometimes occur.

PISCES (FISHES)

Big game fish associates are found in all classes of living fishes (Subphylum Pisces). It was spelled "fisch", "fissh" or "fisc" in Middle English, and "fisc" or "fish" in Anglo-Saxon. "Fish" is both the singular and plural form for 1 or more specimens of a single species of these animals, but the plural "fishes" is used for more than 1 fish species. Remoras sometimes harass or bite human swimmers and cookiecutter sharks have severely injured fishermen. Fishes are our most important source of protein, and have enormous economic value.

More than 25,000 recently living species of fishes exist, but 4-5 times that many names occur. Adult fishes vary in length from the 8 mm central Indian Ocean dwarf goby, *Trimmaton nannus* Winterbottom and Emery, to the 12.6 meter whale shark. Length of fishes is measured 3 ways: (1) total length (TL) - chin to end of tail, (2) fork length (FL) - chin to the middle of the fork of the tail, and (3) standard length (SL) - chin to the crease at the base of the tail (hypural plate) caused by folding the tail over. TL will be used when available. SL is used by scientists to avoid variations caused by worn or damaged fin tips. FL replaces SL for big game fishes, sharks etc. whose tails do not fold. See Host Summaries for a labeled illustration of lengths and external structures.

Sailfish may be the fastest fish (clocked at 68 miles-per-hour [122 KPH]); and sturgeons, the longest lived (at least 150 years). Fishes live only in water (aquatic), respire with permanent gills, have fins, a 2-chambered heart, a skin usually covered with scales, an internal skeleton of bone or gristle (cartilaginous) and are usually cold blooded (some tunas and offshore sharks are notable exceptions to the "cold-blooded" criteria).

Associates occur in all 3 classes of fishes: (1) Lampreys are primitive, eel-like and lack jaws, scales, paired fins and bone. Only 1 of the 38 known species found in marine and fresh waters in North America and Eurasia associates with western Atlantic big game fishes. (2) Sharks have jaws, an internal skeleton of cartilage and 5-7 gill slits on each side. Two of the approximately 2000 known living species associate with our big game fishes. (3) Bony fishes have jaws, an internal skeleton of bone and a single gill opening on each side. Eight of the 20,000 known living species associate with big game fishes.

The sexes of fishes are separate, although some species change sexes during their lives. Fertilization is external or internal. Development is direct whether in the plankton or in the body of the female. Reproduction must be a problem for those fish associates isolated on big game fishes.

Fishes are not permanent (obligate) parasites of big game fishes and can move freely from host to host. Lampreys and cookiecutter sharks usually just attach to the host for feeding. Lampreys slowly feed on blood and dissolving flesh, while cookiecutter sharks are assumed to more quickly twist out plugs of muscle and skin. This can be called "micro-predation" or "casual parasitism". It is not so different from that found in leeches and aegiid isopods, which are traditionally lumped with obligate parasites. Remoras attach, but most are loosely, and pilotfish do not attach, to big game fishes. They only eat abandoned scraps of food, voided fecal material and obligate parasites they pick from these hosts. Remoras and pilotfish are traditionally called "commensals" of big game fishes. Although some young remoras live in the host gill chambers, spend more time with their hosts and may feed directly on host materials. Family groups are sometimes reared on a single big game host without leaving the fish. These relationships could be more intimate than those of the other host associates and could eventually develop into parasitism for at least part of their life cycles. Williams and Bunkley-Williams (1994) have suggested possible paths that free-living organisms take toward parasitism. In addition, these associates may transmit or disseminate parasites and diseases to their large hosts although this has not previously received any attention (see Discussion).

These associates or parasites should be examined for their own parasites before they are preserved. To preserve these fishes, the right side of the body should be slit into the body cavity, and the whole fish placed in 10% formalin that is at least 10 times the volume of the fish.

Classification and Contents

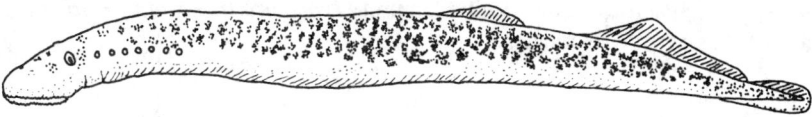

Petromyzon marinus Linnaeus - sea lamprey

This lamprey kills or mutilates big game fishes.

Diagnostic Characters - Sea lampreys are elongate fish with a dorsal fin separated into 2 parts by a deep notch. The mouth is a sucking disk lined with teeth (horny cusps). The wound this fish produces is circular with the scales and skin (epidermis) of the host completely abraded by the teeth of the sucking disk, and a hole rasped through the skin in the center of the wound.

Records - It occurs on Atlantic mackerel and swordfish off Atlantic coast of the USA; and on a variety of fishes on both sides of the North Atlantic from Labrador (possibly Greenland) to Florida and the northern Gulf of Mexico, and from northern Norway through much of the Mediterranean.

Geographic Range - North Atlantic and Mediterranean.

Life History - The larvae (ammocoetes) live in the mud of streams 5-13 years, before they metamorphose, at a length of 10-20 cm, into adults, and move down to the ocean or lakes where they begin to attack fishes. Adults spend about 2 years parasitizing a wide variety of fish hosts, then return to freshwater streams to breed (anadromous) in April to July. They build nests in streams with rapidly moving water and gravel stream beds, and die after spawning. They produce 124,000-305,000 eggs, which is the highest for any lamprey species. Spawned out lampreys may be parasitized by fungi *Saprolegnia* spp. before they die.

Ecology - Sea lampreys tolerate a wide range of temperatures and salinities (0-35 ppt). They are eaten by other fishes in fresh water and by swordfish and striped bass at sea. Sea lampreys appear to be more common in inshore and even brackish waters, but are found offshore to a depth of 200 m and occasionally down to depths of at least 1100 m. They are not caught on hook-and-line, and seldom in nets, thus little is known of their habits at sea.

Parasites and Diseases - Sea lampreys from the ocean have rarely been examined for parasites and diseases. A roundworm, *Truttaedacnitii stelmioides* (Vessichelli), occurs in this lamprey from the Mediterranean and North Sea. In fresh waters, they have a typical freshwater parasite fauna.

The liquefying and slurping of host tissue seems to transfer larval parasites from the host to the lamprey in fresh waters. The same mechanism probably occurs in the ocean. This results in the ironic situation that the final hosts of the sea lamprey are the intermediate and intermediary hosts for its parasites.

Location in Host - Sides.

Length - 13.5-86.0 cm TL, occasionally up to 120.0 cm. Sea lampreys are the largest species of lampreys.

Host Specificity - Sea lampreys parasitize almost any large fish, but usually not whales. They have rarely been reported from a variety of porpoises and whales. Their Pacific cousin, Pacific lamprey, *Lampetra tridentata* (Gairdner), attacks fishes as well as whales.

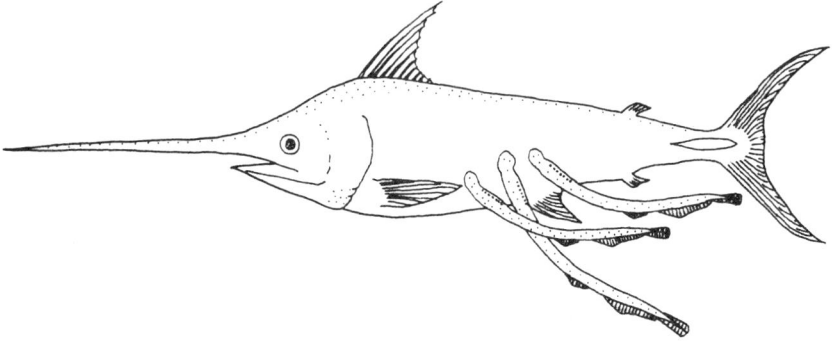

Damage to Host - This parasite rasps a hole in the side of the host's body, and sucks blood and body fluids, and slowly dissolves and consumes other tissues. More than 1, sometimes 3-4 lampreys, may attack the same host and cause severe injury. Weakened hosts with open wounds are more susceptible to other parasites and microbial diseases.

Significance to Sport Fishing - This parasite kills and severely injures freshwater sport fishes. The damage to offshore big game fishes must be considerable, but is more difficult to determine. Young sea lampreys are used as bait for freshwater sport fishes. Sea lampreys are food items for swordfish, and in turn sea lampreys attack and feed on swordfish. This is a most circular, and peculiar, predator-prey relationship.

Land-locked populations occur in freshwater lakes. Sea lampreys do terrific damage to freshwater sport fishes. After the Welland Canal was opened around the barrier of Niagara Falls, this parasite was transferred into most of the Great Lakes of North America, and at least 3 species of locally important sport and commercial fishes were destroyed. The ecologically and economically disastrous transfer of this exotic disease organism into much of the Great Lakes is a classic case study of unintended results often incurred during ecological modifications.

Comments - Sea lamprey was considered a delicacy in Europe during the Middle Ages, and was a commercial fish in New England until about 1850. The flesh is reputed to be delicious, if you can avoid considering how they earn a living. They are usually caught when breeding or ascending streams to breed (spring run). Sea lampreys are frequently used as preserved specimens in biology classes, and live ones can be used in classroom experiments (Cochran 1989). They may be one of the best studied of all parasites, yet little is known of their behavior and habits in the open ocean.

Isistius brasiliensis (Quoy and Gaimard) - cookiecutter shark

This small, but violent shark tears fist-sized chunks of flesh out of some of our most important offshore game fishes. Wounds and scars from these attacks are unfortunately quite common.

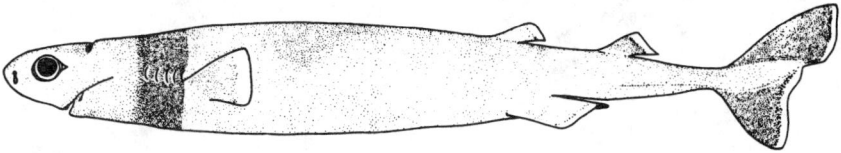

Name - It was called "cigar shark" by Robins et al. (1991), but "cookiecutter shark" has been used in most publications.

Diagnostic Characters - It is a relatively small, cigar-shaped shark with a darkly pigmented collar behind the head. The caudal fin is high. There are 25-31 rows of teeth in the lower jaw. It produces large, cone-shaped wounds, sometimes called "crater wounds", on the outside of big game fishes.

Records - Occasionally 1-3 (usually 1) wounds were seen on albacore, Atlantic blue marlin, blackfin tuna, dolphin and yellowfin tuna from various localities off Puerto Rico. These wounds are seen on big game fishes off Cuba; are common on dolphin off Florida; 1-3 (usually 1) on swordfish from the Gulf of Mexico; and albacore, Atlantic blue marlin, bigeye tuna, blackfin tuna, bluefin tuna, dolphin, pompano dolphin, wahoo, white marlin and yellowfin tuna throughout the oceanic western Atlantic. We saw 1 wound each on albacore, bluefin tuna and yellowfin tuna off Okinawa and off the Ryukyu islands east of Taiwan. It also occurs on black marlin, Indo-Pacific blue marlin, Indo-Pacific sailfish, rainbow runner and other jacks and scombrids from Hawaii; and on albacore, dolphin, skipjack tuna and wahoo in the central Pacific. These wounds are also found on a variety of marine mammals.

Geographic Range - Worldwide. Fresh wounds are seen on hosts in warm-water areas, while only old wounds and scars are seen in temperate and colder areas. This indicates that cookiecutter sharks occur in tropical and subtropical areas, and that wounded hosts may move further north or south after attacks.

Life History - This fish presumably holds eggs in the body and releases hatched young (ovoviviparous). Ovaries contain 6-7 large eggs, but embryos and litter size is not known. Young are about 14 cm long at birth. Males mature at a length of 31-37 cm, females at 38-44 cm.

Ecology - Besides chunks of host flesh, this shark also eats squids almost as large as itself, deep water lightfishes (Gonostomatidae) and crustaceans. It probably attacks fishes and mammals basking near the surface. Fast swimming tunas and porpoises probably seek out the cookiecutter shark as potential prey, and are attacked before they realize their mistake. This has not been observed, but circumstantial evidence supports this scenario: (a) cookiecutter shark luminescence appears to be a predator attracting device, (b) many wounds are near the head, often made from in front of the host, of these large predators, suggesting a head-to-head encounter with the cookiecutter shark, (c) wounds only appear on some predators after they achieve a body size associated with predation on fishes, (d) a cookiecutter shark was found in the stomach of a large Spanish mackerel, *Scomberomorus* sp., caught in the tropical eastern Pacific, although they have not been noted in the stomach contents of other big game fishes.

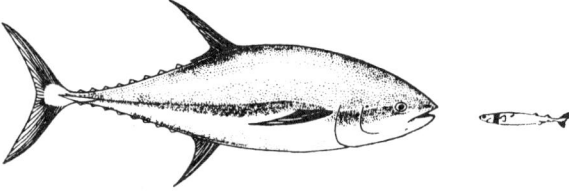

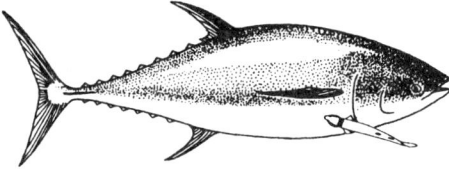

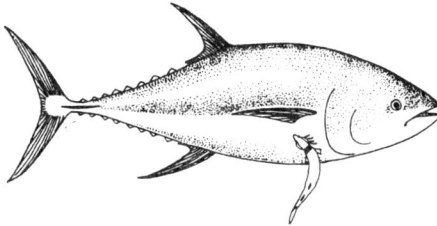

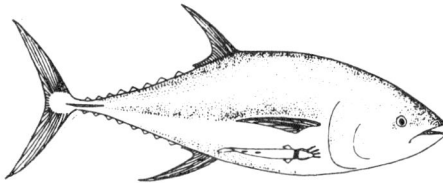

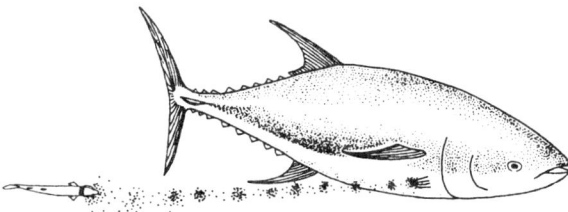

This fish is collected from the surface at night, but usually at depths from 85-3500 m (epipelagic to bathypelagic). Its preferred and maximum depths are not known. This shark seems to migrate vertically from great depths to at or near the surface at night (vertical migrator, diel cycle). It is more commonly found near islands, whether this is caused by using an inshore pupping ground, or the attraction of more hosts, is not known. This shark may be able to tolerate areas of low oxygen. The relatively large and oily liver and body cavity may be a buoyancy adaptation to its deep habitat or its heavy skeleton necessary to support violent attacks. The entire belly and particularly the neck is covered with luminous organs (photophores) which bathes the shark in a bright, ghostly green light at night. This luminescence may lure in large predators (such as the cyalume lights used on longlines). Luminescence fades when the fish dies.

This shark does not appear to be very abundant in most areas, but is so common in the eastern Atlantic that it is bottom trawled for fish meal production. Studies have reported multiple wounds on every swordfish observed in some areas of the eastern Atlantic. The large, offshore game fishes in this region must take a beating from these parasites.

Parasites and Disease - Unknown.

Location in Host - Body. The wound is often near the head of the host, but may be on the flank or any part of the body.

Length - 14.0-50.0 cm TL; female up to 50.0 cm; male 39.0 cm; wounds 2.0-7.0 cm (1.2-5.0 cm wide).

Host Specificity - This fish has no specificity. It may prefer larger hosts. Cookiecutter sharks even bite the rubber sonar domes off nuclear submarines. Marine mammals including most dolphins and whales are attacked. It does not even spare fellow sharks, such as megamouth shark, *Megachasma pelagios* Taylor, Compagno and Struhsaker.

Damage to Host - This shark attaches to the body of a host with highly specialized sucking lips and a strongly modified pharynx. It can grab hosts with the sharp teeth of its upper jaw. This parasite drives the razor-sharp, triangular teeth of the lower jaw into the host, and swings its body in a circle, cutting out a cone-shaped piece of flesh.

Compagno (1984) suggests that the mortality rate of offshore game fishes might be increased by the attack of this shark. The wounds encourage infection by microbial and parasitic diseases. However, the abundance of these scars suggest that many hosts survive.

In an ancient Samoan legend, atu [=skipjack tuna] entering Palauli Bay left small round pieces of their flesh near the beach as sacrifices to Chief Tautunu. This was evidenced by people catching atu, who found fresh, round wounds on the fish sides.

Harm to Humans - No reports of attacks on free-swimming humans are known, possibly because few people swim or dive in oceanic waters at night. If you are contemplating a midnight swim off your boat, you should consider that this shark seems willing to attack any large animal. As you would expect in a small fish attacking giant predators, this shark has remarkably quick reactions.

Preparation for Study - This fish should be examined for parasites. The stomach and intestine should also be examined for fish flesh and scales which may be used to identify its recent hosts.

Significance to Sport Fishing - Some fishes may die after cookiecutter shark attacks, and others may suffer reduced growth. These obvious wounds, or scars from the wounds, are distressing in your trophy game fish. Commercially, the wounds may reduce the price paid for "perfect" tuna.

Many whales receive multiple wounds when they migrate into warm waters each year. These scars are permanent, but change in color and appearance over time. The series of wounds received each year can be recognized and used to determine how many migrations have occurred. These wounds might be used similarly as biological tags to identify migrating big game fishes.

Comments - These wounds were once thought to be caused by small, internal parasites, bacterial diseases or even the isopods sometimes found in these wounds. Thus scientific thought about this phenomenon, until recently, was little better than the Samoan legend. Solving this mystery was a neat bit of oceanography pieced together from the indirect evidence of chunks of flesh resembling the wounds and the odd teeth of the cookiecutter shark, and scientists twisting holes in pieces of fruit and big game fishes on the deck with dead cookiecutter sharks.

Popular Reference - Klemm (1984).

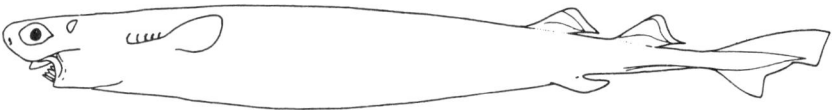

Isistius plutodus Garrick and Springer - largetooth cookiecutter shark

This shark has proportionately the largest teeth of any living shark. Fortunately it is rare, as it bites off larger chunks of flesh and bone from big game fishes than the cookiecutter shark.

Diagnostic Characters - This small, cigar-shaped shark lacks a darkly pigmented collar behind the head. The tail (caudal fin) is low. There are 19 rows of teeth in the lower jaw. It gouges out characteristically elongate plugs of tissue from its hosts, but it may also produce round wounds which are similar to those made by the cookiecutter shark.

Records - We found 1-2 oval, elongate wounds in 2 of many Atlantic blue marlin and in 3 yellowfin tuna caught from various localities off Puerto Rico. Wounds have been found on albacore, bluefin tuna and yellowfin tuna in the Pacific, but only 2 specimens of largetooth cookiecutter shark have been collected (one 100 miles south of Dauphin Island, Alabama, USA; and another off Okinawa, Japan).

Geographic Range - Worldwide. Our observations of the wounds of this shark are the first from the Caribbean.

Ecology - This fish was collected from the surface at night over depths from 814-997 m. Its preferred and maximum depths are not known. This shark probably migrates vertically from great depths to at or near the surface at night (vertical migrator, diel cycle). The relatively large and oily liver and body cavity may be a buoyancy adaptation to its deep habitat or its heavy skeleton necessary to support violent attacks. Its smaller fins suggest it is a weaker, less active swimmer than the cookiecutter shark, yet it has a larger mouth, more powerful jaw, and larger teeth. It has fewer luminous organs (photophores) and is therefore not as brightly lit as the cookiecutter shark. The rarity of this shark may be due to it possibly occurring at greater depths than the cookiecutter shark. This shark also has a more binocular-type vision than the cookiecutter shark. This kind of vision, more similar to our own, is well suited to a parasite seeking highly mobile hosts.

Length - at least 42.0 cm TL.

Host Specificity - Unknown. Atlantic blue marlin is a new host.

Damage to Host - The wounds caused by this shark are larger than those of cookiecutter sharks, and involve bone as well as tissue. They may be more harmful.

Comments - Life History, Location in Host, Parasites and Disease, Detection, Harm to Humans, Preparation for Study, and **Significance to Sport Fishing** are the same as for cookiecutter shark above.

Family Echeneidae (Remoras or Suckerfishes)

The 8 species of remoras form a family of bony fishes. The Greek "echeneis" and Roman "remora" refer to the belief that these fishes could attach to ships and hold them back. Various mystical properties have been assigned to suckerfishes. Remoras are blamed for the ill fates of Emperor Caligula and Mark Antony. Shamans in Madagascar still attach part of the suction disks of remoras to the necks of wives to ensure faithfulness to absent husbands.

Remoras are easily recognized by the sucking disk (a modification of the first dorsal fin) on top of their heads. This organ consists of numerous pairs of cross ridges or laminae. The movable disk ridges work much like a Venetian blind. When the rear edges are raised, a suction for holding on to a host is created. Pulling a remora backward only increases the suction, while pushing it forward releases the hold. The size of the sucking disk in adults can be correlated to the activity of their hosts (those on the most active or fastest hosts have the largest) and to their body width (the widest or bulkiest have the largest).

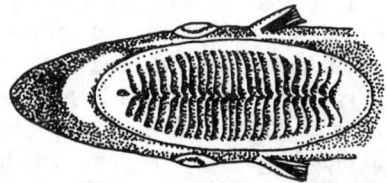

Most can swim swiftly, but probably not great distances. Their coloration can be quite beautiful, particularly in young, and it is unfortunately, quite variable at any age. Identification of young remoras is difficult, and the adults of 2 species are very similar in appearance. Many previous host records are highly suspect. Development is direct, but some species have a long filament on the tail in larval and postlarval stages. Early stages are planktonic. Some develop multiple fangs of mysterious function in their jaws. They begin attaching to hosts when they reach a length of 4-8 cm, and still have the tail filament. Wahoo and a variety of other smaller fishes have been called "trial hosts" (intermediary hosts) because only small or young remoras are found on them. Larger remoras are more specific. Two species almost always attach to billfishes, and 1 each prefer great barracuda, sharks, or manta rays, while whale remoras, *Remora australis* (Bennett), are only found on marine mammals. Two species attach to a variety of inshore fishes, sea turtles, mammals and even ships and buoys. Some spend considerable time free swimming away from any host. Remoras usually attach on the bodies of their hosts, but some can be found in the gill cavities or mouths.

Remoras receive transportation, some degree of protection, and food from their hosts. In return, they pick parasites and damaged or diseased tissues from the bodies, gills and mouths of their hosts. Host cooperation in this supposed "partnership" is less certain. Some hosts appear to try to avoid or shake off remoras, and they have been found in the stomach contents of their hosts.

Much argument but less data occurs in the literature concerning the food habits of remoras. They seem to be opportunists taking host ("scraps" or debris of food from their large host's meals, ectoparasites, and possibly wastes [feces]) and non-host materials (plankton and possibly small fishes from the water column). The food of most remoras is pieces of fishes, plankton is less important, and parasites occur in token amounts. Besides the standard preparations mentioned above, their stomach contents should be quickly examined or preserved for parasites (before they are digested) that they may have cleaned from their host. The reason that only copepods and isopods have been found in the stomachs of remoras may be that the "shells" (exoskeleton) of these parasites do not quickly digest or decompose. Stomachs of remoras must be immediately removed, opened, and placed in 10% formalin. Only then can we find capsalid and other gill worms, tissue flukes and other fragile parasites that they may pick off their hosts.

Remoras are easily seen on the body of hosts, but are less obvious in the gill cavity or mouth. Just how important their parasite removal may be to large offshore game fishes is unclear. They appear to cause little damage or irritation to their large hosts. Remoras attached to lines have been used by fishermen to snag large fish and turtles. The most famous report was reputedly by Christopher Columbus of suckerfish "living fish hooks" by the Arawak Indians in Cuba. The technique is actually worldwide and ancient.

One fossil remora resembles a pilotfish, suggesting free-swimming associated fishes may have evolved into remoras. A Tertiary (1-70 million years ago) fossil remora had fewer (7-8) and more widely spaced sucker laminae, while another specimen had a disk similar to inshore remora. The number of laminae may have increased and the spacing decreased during remora evolution. Aristotle (384-322 B.C.) observed "dolphin's louse" on dolphin in the Mediterranean. The former common names of remoras were established before much of their biology and habits were understood, and thus some are inappropriate, and they employ a hodgepodge of 4 synonymous terms (diskfish, remora, -sucker, suckerfish).

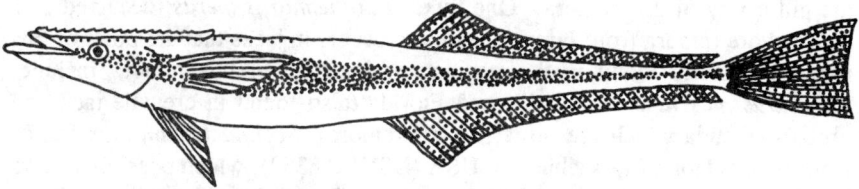

Echeneis naucrates Linnaeus - inshore remora

This most common and largest remora is found mostly inshore and on almost any kind of host. It often harasses humans.

Name - The accepted common name of this fish is "sharksucker", and it is also called "shark remora". These names are inappropriate as *Echeneis naucrates* is a generalist occurring on a variety of inshore hosts, not just sharks.

Diagnostic Characters - The body is slender. The sucking disk is relatively long, extending backward slightly beyond the middle of the pectoral fin, and has 21-28 (usually 23-24) pairs of laminae, with 3-4 rows of spinules along the posterior margin. The caudal fin is truncated in the adult, but has a long central filament in young 10 cm or smaller. As the remora grows, the filament gradually decreases in relative length, until at 18 cm, it is reduced to a short lobe. The body is usually striped with brown or black. Normally the belly is white, but when it attaches with its body upside down, it reverses its color pattern.

Records - We found 1-3 (usually 1) on 3 of 47 great barracuda, 2 of 20 crevalle jack and 1 of 27 horse-eye jack from various localities around Puerto Rico. It has also been found on great barracuda from St. Thomas, U.S. Virgin Islands, and Florida, USA. We have also seen it on small coral reef fishes, and 8-12 on 6 of 25 West Indian manatees, *Trichechus manatus* Linnaeus, from various localities around Puerto Rico. This remora attaches to sharks (up to 12 per host), large bony fishes, rays, whales, boats, floating timbers and other objects around the world.

Geographic Range - Worldwide, except in the eastern Pacific.

Life History - This remora is often found swimming away from a host. It may not have the problem of locating a mate, unlike more host-dependant remoras.

Ecology - It occurs on both inshore and offshore hosts. An unusual development of the respiratory muscles allows this fish to pass a considerable amount of water over the gills, thus allowing it to thrive in still waters and on hosts with a variety of activity patterns. This remora is not a rapid swimmer. It is the most common, inshore remora found in the western Atlantic. Inshore remoras can easily be caught with hook and line. This remora appears to be rather loosely associated with hosts and to change fish hosts frequently. They often abandon hosts when hosts are removed from the water.

Parasites and Disease - Two gillworms occur in the gills of inshore remora, *Dioncus agassizi* from the Indian Ocean and *Dioncus remorae* from West Indies and the New York Aquarium. *Dioncus agassizi* is also found in cobia, shark remora and spearfish remora, and *D. remorae* occurs in crevalle jack, which is a host for inshore remora. Larval tissue flukes, *Didymozoides* sp., occurred in the gill cavity of this remora. One fluke, *Parahemiurus merus*, occurred in 1 of 2 inshore remora from Jamaica, and also occurs in jacks that are hosts of this remora. Flukes found in the stomach or intestine of this remora include: *Sterrhurus musculus* off Mexico and Florida (also found in crevalle jack and great barracuda which are hosts for this remora); *Lecithochirium monticellii*, from Woods Hole, Massachusetts, USA (USNPC 8352), which possibly occurs in blue runner and little tunny from the same locality; *Echeneidocoelium indicum* Simha and Pershad from the Indian Ocean; *Stephanostomum imparispine* (Linton) (which also occurs in western Atlantic cobia) and *Tubulovesicula lindbergi* (Layman) from the South China Sea; and *Tormopsolus echenei* Parukihin from the Gulf of Tonkin. Two larval tapeworms, *Nybelinia robusta* in the stomach and *Tentacularia coryphaenae* encysted postlarvae in the stomach and intestine of inshore remora, from Woods Hole, Massachusetts, USA. The later species also occurs in a variety of big game fishes. Five roundworms occurred in the intestine of this remora, *Spirocamallanus olseni* Campana and Razarihelissoa, from the Sea of Nossi-Bé; *Ascarophis* sp. of Parukhin, *Capillaria echenei* Parukhin, *Raphidascaris* sp. of Parukhin, and *Spinitectus echenei* Parukhin from the South China Sea. Three spiny-headed worms, *Telosentis tenuicornis* (Linton), from Massachusetts, USA; *Gorgorhynchus medius* (Linton) from the South Atlantic; *Serrasentis sagittifer* were found in the intestine of inshore remora from the South China Sea. The following copepods occur on this host, *Tuxophorus caligodes*, and on cobia from the Western Atlantic; *Caligus praetextus* from the Gulf of Mexico off Florida; and *Lepeophtheirus longipes* Wilson in the mouth from west Africa. *Caligus coryphaenae* was reported externally on an *Echeneis* sp.(?) in the eastern Pacific. This could have been an inshore remora, but this fish is not supposed to occur in the eastern Pacific. This copepod occurs on a variety of big game fishes. A fish louse, *Argulus varians* Bere, was reported on this fish from the Gulf of Mexico off Florida, USA. Striped goose barnacles occurred on inshore remoras from west Africa.

Cleaning Behavior - Inshore remoras clean parasites from their host, but parasitic copepods and isopods were not a major food item (16% of 87 stomachs containing food). Smaller remoras (57-85 mm) occasionally picked parasites, medium-sized (86-311 mm) often cleaned, while larger fish (311-630 mm) had no parasites in their stomachs.

It is frequently seen free swimming and may often move from host-to-host. Five free-swimming fish had parasitic crustacea in their stomachs, and 1 remora on a lemon shark, *Negaprion brevirostris* (Poey), had a *Caligus* sp. in its stomach, a copepod that does not occur on sharks. In 7 other cases, the copepods in the stomach of the inshore remora apparently originated from the species of host on which it was associated, suggesting that it does remain on one host in some cases. We found *Caligus lobodes* in the stomach of an inshore remora from a barracuda, the host of this copepod; and it has previously been reported from this association.

Predation - It occurred in stomachs of Indo-Pacific sailfish and striped marlin in the Pacific.

Associations - Two attached to a white marlin with a white remora; and it shares West Indian manatees with whitefin remoras.

Location in Host - Body, never in the gill cavity or mouth.

Length - 5.7-100.0 cm (rarely 1.22 m), but usually less than 60.0 cm. Reputed observations of 1.3 m inshore remoras have not been confirmed by measurements. The largest individuals have been found associated with the largest fish, whale sharks.

Host Specificity - This remora will attach to almost any large to medium-sized fish, sea turtle, marine mammal or boat. Oddly, We have seen them attached to coral reef fishes that were smaller than the remora, such as sand divers, trunkfishes and parrotfishes. Schwartz (1977) found some fishes in 125,000 liter tanks could out swim or otherwise avoid attachment of this remora.

Damage to Host - We have observed many fishes attempting to scrape off or knock off inshore remoras. The remora is generally faster than the host, and simply dodges the impacts, until the host tires. This would suggest that many species of fishes are irritated by the presence of this remora. Schwartz (1977) found some species of captive fishes were severely damaged or killed by prolonged or repeated disk attachment of inshore remoras, but those most injured were not naturally used as hosts in the wild.

Harm to Humans - Inshore remoras frequently harass bathers and divers. We are not certain if most of these "attacks" are attempts to attach or to pick imagined parasites off of humans. Few people are sufficiently calm under the attention of this remora to learn their intentions. A "crazed" specimen harassed human swimmers, including our ichthyology professor, in the "swimming area" off the Magueyes Island Marine Laboratories Medusa Dock for days.

A friend, who was scuba diving in the northern Gulf of Mexico, was severely bitten on the breast nipple by an inshore remora. The fish apparently mistook this tissue for a dark, juicy copepod or isopod.

Echeneis neucratoides Zuieuw - whitefin remora

This less common cousin of inshore remora is poorly understood. These 2 remoras are very similar in appearance and have often been confused.

Diagnostic Characters - It is similar to inshore remora, but the body is usually striped, stouter, and fins have more white areas (unfortunately, these characters are comparative and almost useless, unless fresh specimens of both species are available). The sucking disk is long, extending backward slightly beyond the

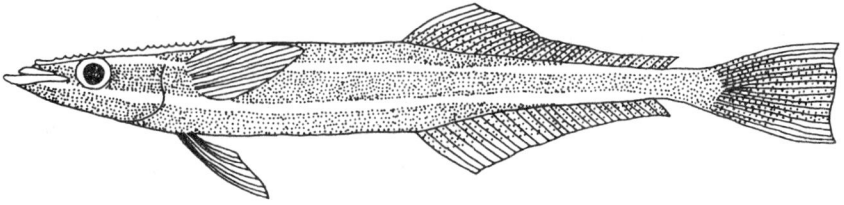

middle of the pectoral fin, and has 18-23 pairs of laminae. The caudal fin is truncated in the adult, and has a long central filament in small young. The body is usually striped

Records - This remora probably occurs on big game fishes inshore, but has been confused with inshore remora. We found it on West Indian manatees in Puerto Rico, and it has been reported from sharks and other inshore fishes.

Geographic Range - Western Atlantic. It is the only remora that does not occur worldwide.

Ecology - This remora is an inshore species. It is much less common than inshore remoras, but is often mistaken for this species. It can be taken with hook and line.

Parasites and Disease - Unknown.

Food Habits and Parasites - Strasburg (1959) discounted the reports of remoras feeding on their hosts' wastes (feces) in Smith (1950). He further suggested that materials in the stomach contents of remoras could have been from their hosts' scraps or feces, and the 2 sources could not be distinguished. The principal item in the stomach contents of a whitefin remora we collected from manatees was fecal material from the host. Manatees do not eat fish, thus fish scraps are not available for associated remoras. Manatee fecal material is largely of plant origin, and can be more certainly identified than feces from piscivorous hosts. Our records suggest that fecal material is an important component in the diet of remoras. The consumption of fecal material may directly transmit alimentary tract parasites between fish hosts and remoras.

Associations - See inshore remora.

Location in Host - Body.

Length - 6.0-81.0 cm, but usually less than 60.0 cm.

Host Specificity - Unknown.

Phtheirichthys lineatus (Menzies) - slender remora

This rare remora has only been consistently found in the gills of great barracuda.

Name - The accepted common name of this fish is "slender suckerfish". It is also called "slender remora", "striped louse-fish" and "Pega de las Picudas" (sucker of barracudas in Spanish).

Diagnostic Characters - The body is elongate, and the head and sucking disk are relatively small. The sucking disk has 9-11 (usually 10) pairs of laminae. The caudal fin is rounded in the adult, but has a long central filament in young smaller than 9 cm. The body is usually striped.

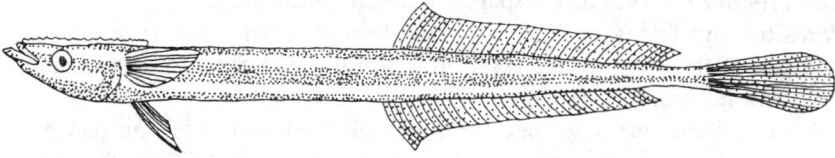

Records - It occurred often in many great barracuda from Cuba; 1 in a great barracuda from Hog Sty Island, Bahamas; and 1 in 1 of many great barracuda from Dry Tortugas, Florida, USA. It was also found attached to Pacific sea turtles, long-line buoys, bait, or free swimming.

Geographic Range - Worldwide.

Life History - Planktonic larva 14 mm or shorter do not have sucking disks. The developing disk just touches the back of the head in remoras 21.2 mm long. In 32 mm long fish, the disk is 2/3 on the head, and progresses further onto the head in larger fish. It is fully formed in 50 mm fish.

Parasites and Disease - Unknown.

Cleaning Behavior - Parasitic copepods have been found in its stomach.

Predation - This remora is not immune from predation by its larger hosts. It has been found in the stomachs of Atlantic mackerel, in unidentified Pacific tuna, and yellowfin tuna.

Location in Host - Gills, mouth, rarely body.

Length - 4.4-71.0 cm, but usually less than 50.0 cm.

Host Specificity - It has been most frequently reported from great barracuda.

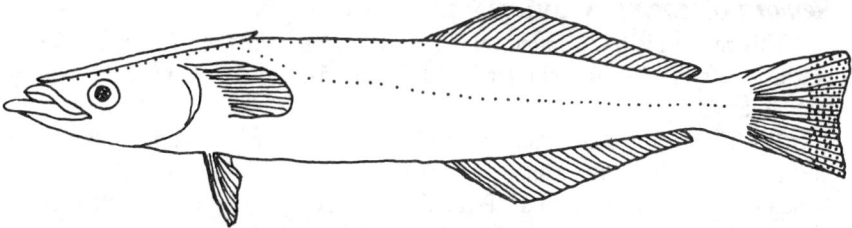

Remora brachyptera (Lowe) - spearfish remora

It is often found on the body or in the gills of billfishes and swordfishes. Its habits are similar to the marlin remora, but it is easily distinguished.

Name - It is sometimes placed in the genus *Remoropsis*.

Diagnostic Characters - The body is short and robust. The sucking disk extends posteriorly to slightly beyond the front edge of the base of the pectoral fin, and has 14-19 pairs of laminae (15-19 in the Gulf of Mexico, 14-17 in the Pacific). The caudal fin is truncated.

Records - It occurs on Atlantic blue marlin, Atlantic sailfish, longbill spearfish, swordfish, white marlin in the Atlantic; black marlin and other billfishes in the Pacific; rarely in barracuda and other fishes; and occasionally free swimming. Two or more spearfish remoras may occur on a host.

Geographic Range - Worldwide.

Life History - Larvae and postlarvae have no caudal filament.

Parasites and Disease - The gillworm, *Dioncus agassizi*, occurs in the gills from the Atlantic coast of the USA. It is also found in cobia, inshore remora and shark remora.

Cleaning Behavior - It does not appear to feed very often on parasitic copepods, but only 38 stomachs have been examined (17% with food). Immature caligid copepods occurred in the stomach of a spearfish remora from an Atlantic sailfish, *Gloiopotes watsoni* Kirtisinghe from black marlin, and *Gloiopotes huttoni* from striped marlin.

Predation - This remora has been found in the stomachs of yellowfin tuna and unidentified tunas. The stomach contents of this remora contained an unidentified remora off Hawaii.

Location in Host - Body or gill chamber.

Length - 2.7-30.0 cm, but usually less than 20.0 cm.

Host Specificity - It is almost always found on billfishes and swordfishes.

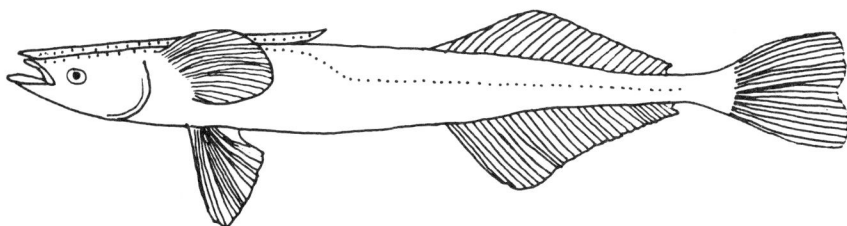

Remora osteochir (Cuvier) - marlin remora

This remora is often found on the body or in the gills of sailfish and white marlin. Its habits are similar to the spearfish remora, but it is easily distinguished.

Name - The accepted common name of this fish is "marlinsucker". This name means essentially the same as "marlin remora", and we prefer this standardization. Also called "Pega de los Agujas" (sucker of billfishes in Spanish). Sometimes placed in the genus *Rhombochirus*.

Diagnostic Characters - The body is slender and has a deep longitudinal groove along the midline of the lower (ventral) surface. The sucking disk is spectacularly large, extending backward well beyond the tip of the pectoral fin, and has 17-20 (usually 18) pairs of laminae. The caudal fin is truncated.

Records - We found 1-2 (usually 2) in 5 of 40 Atlantic blue marlin and 1 in 1 of 5 Atlantic sailfish from various localities around Puerto Rico. Gudger (1926) repeated sportfishermen reports that it occurred in almost every sailfish caught off the Florida Keys. Cressey and Lachner (1970) found it on 82 white marlin, 55 sailfish, but less often on Atlantic blue marlin, swordfish, longbill spearfish, and dolphin. It also occurred in great barracuda from the New York Aquarium and the Florida Keys; on wahoo, Pacific billfishes, Pacific sharks, ocean sunfish from the Pacific; and occasionally free swimming.

Geographic Range - Worldwide.

Life History - Multiple specimens of this remora occur on many hosts and almost always include both sexes. Thus marlin remoras are not dependant on the congregation of many hosts to ensure reproduction. Larval and postlarval remoras do not have a caudal filament. Small marlin remoras occur on smaller fishes, such as wahoo, while small to large ones are found on billfishes.

Ecology - This small remora seems to be more dependent on the host for transport and protection than other species of remoras. It may also feed on mucus and materials from the gills of the host. Other remoras are associates of fishes, but marlin remoras show some characteristics found in parasites. Cressey and Lachner (1970) suggested that these remoras were intimately associated with their hosts, probably breed on the host, and form "families" on a single host consisting of a gravid female, a ripe male, 1-2 large juveniles and several smaller juveniles. This association could be evolving toward parasitism.

Parasites and Disease - The copepod, *Lepeophtheirus crassus* (Wilson), occurred on the body of this remora from the Gulf of Mexico, on shark remora and white remora from the Indian Ocean, and whale remora from the Pacific.

Cleaning Behavior - Unlike inshore remoras and shark remoras, larger (166-230 mm SL) marlin remoras appear to utilize parasites as a source of food more often than the smaller (26-125 mm SL) ones. However, this distinction was only based on 8 stomachs with copepods. Parasitic copepods *Gloiopotes americanus* were found in the stomachs of marlin remoras on the Atlantic sailfish; *Gloiopotes ornatus*, caligoid, and *Pennella* sp. from white marlin; and *Pennella* sp. and *Caligus* sp. from Atlantic blue marlin. These copepods match the hosts in which the remoras were found as would be expected in this associate that is not thought to often change hosts.

Predation - This remora has been found in the stomach of a swordfish.

Location in Host - Gill cavity, sometimes mouth.

Length - 2.6-38.6 cm, but usually less than 30.0 cm. Those found in Atlantic blue marlin are usually larger than those in white marlin, and those on Atlantic sailfish are smaller still. Small marlin remoras (24-26 mm SL) have been found on small sailfish (24 mm SL) (Cressey and Lachner 1970).

Host Specificity - This remora is almost always found on sailfish and white marlin, but has occasionally been reported from other big game fishes. Cressey and Lachner (1970) suggested that marlin remoras only occur on billfishes, and records from sharks and other fishes are the result of contaminating other fishes with remoras from billfishes in mixed long-line catches on ship decks.

Remora remora (Linnaeus) - shark remora

This is the most common remora associating with offshore sharks, and occasionally big game fishes. It does not occur inshore.

Name - The accepted common name of this fish is "remora". This is inappropriate and sometimes confusing because the name is also used as a general term for any species in the remora family. A better name is "shark remora" because it is almost always is found on sharks.

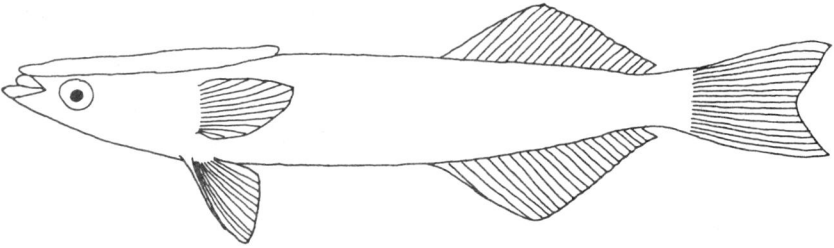

Diagnostic Characters - The body is short and rather robust. The sucking disk is comparatively large, extending to the middle of the pectoral fin, and has 16-20 pairs of laminae. The caudal fin is deeply forked.

Records - This remora almost always occurs on large sharks; rarely on Atlantic sailfish, white marlin, yellowfin tuna, sea turtles, boats, or free swimming in the western Atlantic and around the world. Up to 16 remoras may occur on the body or in the gills of a host. Whole "families" of various sizes may associate on 1 host.

Geographic Range - Worldwide.

Life History - Planktonic larva shorter than 8 mm do not have sucking disks. The developing disk is behind the head in remoras 9.8 mm long. In 12 mm long fish, the disk is 1/2 on the head, and progresses further onto the head in larger fish. Larval and postlarval remoras do not have a caudal filament.

Ecology - It is the most common offshore remora. This associate is limited to pelagic hosts, because it requires a swift passage of water over the gills and cannot survive in still waters or on inactive hosts.

Parasites and Disease - The gillworm, *Dioncus agassizi*, occurs in the gills of cobia and shark remora from Woods Hole, Massachusetts, USA; and is also found in inshore remora and spearfish remora. The flukes *Brachyphallus crenatus*, *Hemiurus montcellii* (Linton), and *Lecithochirium monticellii* occurred in the intestine or stomach, and the tissue fluke, *Torticaecum fenestratum* (Linton) (USNPC 8352), encysted in the stomach wall of shark remoras, from Woods Hole, Massachusetts, USA. *Echeneidocoelium indicum* Simha and Pershad also occurred in the intestine of this host from the Indian Ocean. The larval tapeworms, *Bothriocephalus* sp., *Callitetrarhynchus gracilis*, *Nybelinia bisculcata*, *Nybelinia robustum* and tetraphyllid larvae were found in this remora from the western Atlantic; and *N. robustum* from Europe. The following copepods occur on shark remoras: *Caligus elongatus* from the northeast coast of the USA; *Pennella filosa* on this remora and its hosts worldwide; *Perissopus oblongus* (Wilson) (=*Achtheinus dentatus* Wilson), a parasite of sharks, with which the shark remora associates, that may have only accidentally occurred in this remora, from the south Atlantic; *Lepeophtheirus crassus* from the Indian Ocean, and on marlin remora from the Gulf of Mexico, white remora from the Indian Ocean, and whale remora from the Pacific. Striped goose barnacles occurred on a shark remora in the western Atlantic.

Cleaning Behavior - Smaller (45-165 mm SL) young remoras eat more parasitic copepods than larger (166-210 mm SL) old individuals. Parasitic copepods from sharks form an important part of their diet, but this has not been studied on remoras from big game fishes. Those on sharks feed on copepods from the body and gill chambers of their hosts, but usually avoid the fins of hosts, possibly due to fin movements. This may be why many copepods are isolated on the fins.

Predation - This remora is sometimes eaten by tunas.

Location in Host - Adults usually occur on the body, rarely in the gills. Smaller remoras are often found in the gill cavity.

Length - 4.9-91.0 cm, but usually less than 38.0 cm.

Host Specificity - It usually attaches to large offshore sharks, but can occur on a variety of offshore hosts. The relationships of this remora on sharks appear to be rather stable and long term, because copepods from their stomach match with those found on their host.

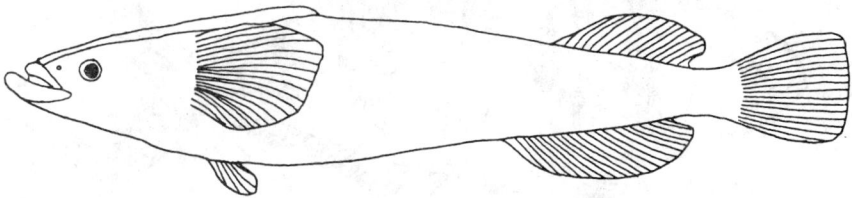

Remorina albescens (Temminck and Schlegel) - white remora

This small remora is usually found in the gills of manta rays, but can rarely be found in the gills of billfishes.

Name - The accepted common name of this fish is "white suckerfish", but it is also called "white remora".

Diagnostic Characters - The body is rather short, and whitish gray to brownish in color. The sucking disk is broad, as wide as 3/4 of the length of the disk, and has 12-14, usually 13-14, pairs of laminae. The caudal fin is truncated.

Records - One occurred in a white marlin off the U.S. Atlantic coast (Goldstein pers. comm.). It is seldom seen swimming off a host. We have heard rumors of this remora being seen on sailfish and longbill spearfish, but these records could not be confirmed.

Geographic Range - Worldwide.

Life History - Larval and postlarval remoras do not have a caudal filament. Females become gravid at a length of 20.6 cm SL.

Ecology - Rarely seen near shore.

Parasites and Disease - The copepod, *Lepeophtheirus crassus*, occurred on the body of this remora and shark remora from the Indian Ocean, on marlin remora from the Gulf of Mexico, and whale remora from the Pacific.

Associations - The specimen we recorded shared the host with an inshore remora that was attached to the head of the fish. This is one of the few records of different species of remoras occurring on the same host.

Parasites and Disease - Unknown.

Location in Host - Gill cavity and mouth, occasionally body. The white marlin specimen was in the gill chamber with the tail extending out of the chamber.

Length - 4.7-30.0 cm, but usually less than 30.0 cm. The white remora we noted from a white marlin was approximately 30 cm long.

Host Specificity - This remora prefers manta rays (Family Mobulidae), but is also found on sharks and bony fishes. White marlin is a new host.

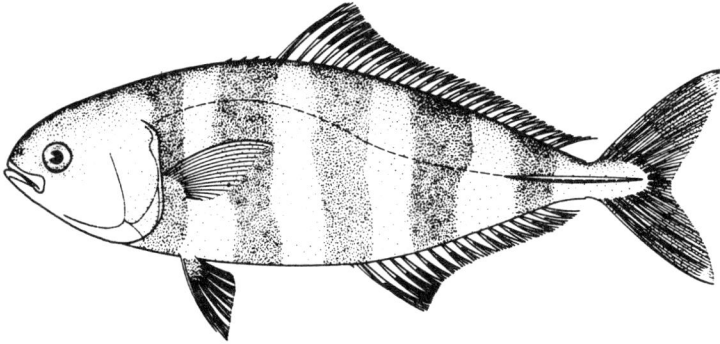

Naucrates ductor (Linnaeus) - pilotfish

Pilotfish do not attach to the fishes they follow, and are the most loosely associated fish that we consider. They do pick parasites off their large hosts.

Name - They are called "pilotfish" because them are so coordinated in copying the turns and movements of their larger hosts that they appeared to be guiding these fishes.

Diagnostic Characters - The normal body coloration is 6-7 black bars against a light silvery background, but it temporarily turns silvery with blue blotches when disturbed. The lobes of the caudal fin have prominent white tips. The caudal peduncle has fleshy keels, and dorsal and ventral notches (peduncle grooves).

Records - Pilotfish are always found associated with large sharks, rays, bony fishes including offshore big game fishes, sea turtles, ship hulls or driftwood.

Geographic Range - Worldwide.

Life History - The larval forms are widespread in oceanic waters between the surface and 100 meters depth (epipelagic). Juveniles associate with seaweeds and jellyfish. They mature at a length of approximately 23 cm.

Ecology - They are completely offshore and pelagic organisms. They feed on scraps (debris) from their host's meals, small fishes and invertebrates in the water column, and their host's external parasites. Pilotfish can be caught on hook and line.

Parasites and Disease - The gillworms, *Ancyrocotyle bartschi* Price, occurred on this fish from Puerto Rico; and *Ancyrocotyle vallei* (Parona and Perugia) from the Mediterranean. *Neobenedenia melleni*, a highly dangerous capsalid gillworm, was found on pilotfish from the New York Aquarium, but this was probably an accidental infection. The giant stomach fluke, *Hirudinella ventricosa*, occurred in this host from the Canary Islands and is found in many of the big game fishes with which pilotfish associate; *Stephanostomum naucrotis* Nagaty, from the Red Sea; and encysted metacercaria from the Mediterranean. Two larval tapeworms were found in pilotfish, *Lacistorhynchus bulbifer*, from the western Atlantic, which also occurs in a variety of big game fishes; and *Nybelinia lingualis* from Europe, which also occurs in skipjack tuna and swordfish. A spiny-headed worm, *Serrasentis lamelliger* (Diesing), from the Atlantic only occurs in this host. The copepod, *Caligus productus*, from Puerto Rico and the Indian Ocean; and the tissue-embedded copepod, *Pennella filosa* occurred on pilotfish, and both copepods also occur on a variety of big game fishes.

Predation - Mediterranean spearfish, *Tetrapturus belone* Rafinesque, routinely eats pilotfish, and they have been found in the stomachs of striped marlin, Indo-Pacific sailfish and yellowfin tuna in the Pacific. Three pilotfish were found in the stomach of 1 of 1097 yellowfin tuna in a Pacific food-item study.

Location in Host - Pilotfish swim ahead, or ahead and beside their hosts.

Length - up to 70.0 cm, but usually less than 35.0 cm FL.

Host Specificity - Pilotfish usually accompany large offshore sharks, but occasionally associate with other fishes, including big game fishes.

Damage to Host - They eat scraps (debris) from their host's meals, but these materials might have been lost by the host even if the pilotfish was not present. They may nip or bite damaged or infected tissues of the host while "cleaning off" external parasites, but the tissue removal is probably beneficial to the host.

Preparation for Study - Besides the standard preparations noted for fishes, their stomach contents should be quickly examined for parasites (before they are digested), or opened and quickly preserved in 10% formalin. The suggestion that they clean parasites from their hosts requires documentation from stomach contents.

OTHER DISEASES AND CONDITIONS

Viruses

Viral nervous necrosis (VNN) caused by striped jack nervous necrosis virus (SJNNV), in Family Nodaviridae, and yellowtail ascites virus (YAV), a birnavirus, cause serious losses in seed production of striped jack, *Caranx vinctus* (Jordan and Gilbert), in pen mariculture in Japan (Muroga, Nakai and Nishizawa 1994). Similar viruses may exist in western Atlantic jacks, but have either not been expressed or not yet noted. Fishes held in confined culture conditions are observed closely and die-offs due to viral causes are more likely to be detected than in fishes in the wild. Viruses may have more opportunities in culture conditions for transmission than are possible in the wild. Future efforts at culture of big game fishes may create conditions favorable for virus expression and discovery.

Bacteria

A variety of pathogenic bacteria have killed and injured yellowtail and greater amberjack in intensive culture in Japan, including *Nocardia seriolae* Kudo, Hatai and Seino (commonly called *N. kampachi* Kariya et al.), *Pasturella pisicida* (Bein), *Streptococcus* sp. and *Vibrio anguillarum* (Bergman) (Kawahara et al. 1986). Descriptions of these bacteria, their known geographic range, epizootiology, diagnosis and pathological manifestations, are given by Plumb (1994). Dolphin are also being cultured in Hawaii, Japan and possibly in Puerto Rico in the future. As western Atlantic big game fishes are held, and particularly reared in captivity, primary pathogenic and opportunistic bacteria may attack these fishes. The possibility that these bacteria attack wild fishes remains unexplored. Bashirullah et al. (1995) reported that 6 of 17 sailfish examined for parasites had sloughing, bloody intestinal mucosa and hypothesized that it was caused by a bacterial infection. Bacterial isolation or histological confirmation was not made.

Atlantic mackerel are often infected with "fish tuberculosis", *Mycobacterium* spp. *Mycobacterium* sp. was associated with visceral granulomas in an Atlantic mackerel collected off England (RTLA 4634) (Anonymous 1975b), and France (RTLA 4689, 4699) (Anonymous 1989), and other big game fishes may be affected. Plumb (1994) suggested that "all teleosts should be considered as possible hosts" for *Mycobacterium* spp. Skin granulomas in humans have been caused by mycobacteria, especially *Mycobacterium marinum* Aronson. Human infections are usually contracted in freshwater or saltwater swimming pools, tropical fish aquaria, or estuaries, but could be acquired from infected fishes. Human infections can be extremely resistant to treatment, and have even required surgery or amputation.

Multiple nodular or ulcerated lesions occurred in the skin and muscle of 4 crevalle jacks from north Biscayne Bay off Miami, Florida, USA, (RTLA 2102-2105, 3105, 3375, 3403-5, 4133-4, 4148). The lesions were associated with inflammation due to infection by unidentified bacteria (Harshbarger 1979).

Although catch-and-release fishing is unlikely to transmit bacteria from one fish to another, the transmission is possible, especially through cross contamination by fresh blood or material from active lesions. Cleaning gear between catches would be a prudent precaution to prevent possible cross infections.

Tumors (neoplasms)

Tumors in fishes can be enormous. The largest tumor reported was a 20 kg lipoma described below. One tumor in a blackfin tuna was 1/9 of its body weight. Tumors, more technically called "neoplasms", are masses of new tissue which grow independently of their surrounding tissues. Tumors either rarely occur in big game fishes, or at least have been rarely reported. Two were found in one of the best studied big game fishes, Atlantic mackerel, an iridophoroma (neoplastic iridophores in the dermis of the skin) from France (RTLA 4691) (Anonymous 1989), and a pineal chondroma (tumor of the pineal organ with cartilage formation). Two lipomas (fatty tumors) partly bordered by skeletal muscle occurred in a little tunny caught off Miami Beach, Florida, USA (RTLA 1922) (Harshbarger 1978); and 1 in the body wall of an Atlantic bonito from off Miami, Florida, USA, (RTLA 2359) (Harshbarger 1980). In bluefin tuna, there are records of a melanoma (RTLA 3919) an osteoma (RTLA 2745), a fibroma (RTLA 2744) and 2 lipomas (RTLA 2743 and 1518) (Harshbarger pers. comm.) The second lipoma (RTLA 1518) was a 20 kg growth on an 180 kg bluefin tuna off Massachusetts. An oval, 21x16 cm lipoma plus adjacent lobules occurred in a southern bluefin tuna (RTLA 2456) from Australia. A schwannoma (invasive malignant peripheral nerve sheath tumor) protruded from the flank of a blackfin tuna off Pensacola, Florida, USA (RTLA 5391); and an osteoma (10 cm ossified growth) was attached to the vertebral column of an albacore of the Pacific coast of the USA (RTLA 1384).

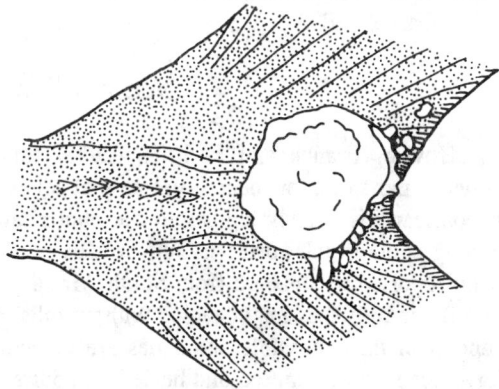

Caudal fin growths on a crevalle jack.

Pseudotumors

Non-neoplastic pseudotumors have also been rarely noted. Three crevalle jacks were collected with (1) skeletal muscle granulomas (scar tissue) that protruded into the visceral cavity (RTLA 1894), (2) multiple growths in the skeletal muscle (RTLA 1900), and (3) growths on the caudal fin (RTLA 1895) (see illustration on the previous page) (Harshbarger 1978). Each lesion was associated with unidentified protozoans. An abscess occurred in the ovary of one dolphin (RTLA 2360), and a nodular growth (muscle atrophy, necrosis and chronic inflammation due to traumatic injury) occurred in the muscle of a second dolphin (RTLA 2221) (Harshbarger 1980). A mass of granuloma tissue in the liver; enteritis of the gut and pyloric ceca with mucosal sloughing; and cecal, intestinal and vascular smooth muscle hyperplasia in response to unidentified trematodes occurred in an Atlantic sailfish (RTLA 2467) (Harshbarger 1989). These 5 non-neoplastic pseudotumors and 2 of the tumors above, came from off Miami Beach, Florida, USA, not because the conditions are particularly conducive to tumor formation in that region, but through the efforts of one interested observer. This is a good example of what can be accomplished by any motivated amateur scientist. Additionally, an Atlantic mackerel with hemosiderosis (numerous pigment granules in macrophage aggregates of the kidney and spleen) was found off Maryland, USA, (RTLA 4421) (Anonymous 1981). An Atlantic mackerel with nodules in the gill lamellae (branchial nodules with epithelial hyperplasia and fibrosis) was found in the northwest Atlantic (RTLA 4472) (Anonymous 1989). A granuloma was found in an Atlantic mackerel from Europe; and hyperplasia (great increase in the number of normal cells arranged normally in a tissue) was reported from a captive chub mackerel in Japan. An inflammatory fibrosis was noted in dermis, hypodermis and adjacent skeletal muscle in a wild chub mackerel from Japan (RTLA 2038) (Harshbarger 1978).

Anomalies

Howse, Franks and Welford (1975) found unusual tissue connections between parts of cobia hearts (pericardial adhesions) that were probably caused by pericarditis. They suggested the abnormal condition occurred frequently among cobia in the northern Gulf of Mexico. Mesentery adhesions have also been reported in albacore from South Africa.

Some billfishes may develop without bills or with malformed bills, but the reports of these possible anomalies are difficult to distinguish from bills that have been simply injured and healed. Reports suggest that fish with partial or missing bills appear to adequately feed and survive. A dolphin with a healed "broken back" (fracture of centrum of 2 vertebrae with exuberant callus formation) was noted off Miami Beach, Florida, USA (RTLA 2167) (Harshbarger 1979).

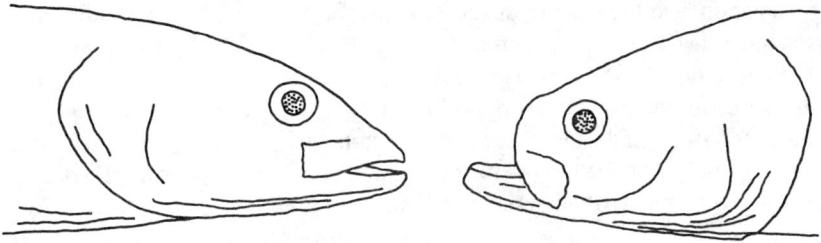

Pugheaded (right) and normal (left) cobia.

Franks (1995) reported the first cobia with a blunt shortened upper jaw and forehead, a condition often called "pugheaded", caught in the northern Gulf of Mexico in 1991. Feeding, growth and sexual maturity was not altered by this condition. One great barracuda with fused vertebrae has been reported on the Atlantic coast of the USA, and one bluefin tuna with vertebral anomalies was noted in the eastern Atlantic.

Hermaphroditism

Three skipjack tuna have been reported with both male and female sexual organs occurring in the same fish: one fish from India and 2 from Japan. We have received a report of a fourth fish, 51.3 mm and 2.7 km, from the Federated States of Micronesia (Itano pers. comm.).

Stomach ulcers

Evans and Wares (1972) found gastric ulcers in 73 of 563 striped marlin and in 33 of 151 Indo-Pacific sailfish off southern California and Mexico. Iversen and Kelley (1974) found gastric ulcers in the stomachs of 10 of 114 Indo-Pacific blue marlin and 2 of 3 black marlin examined from 1967 to 1969 at the Hawaiian International Billfish Tournament. Up to 6 ulcers that were wider than 10 mm and 50 smaller ulcers occurred in a stomach, ranged in width from 3-13 mm, had slightly raised edges, sharply demarcated margins, bases covered with brown shaggy material, and had an indurated texture. In tissue sections, the lesions could be seen to extend through the wall of the stomach obliterating the usual muscular layers. Jolley (1977) occasionally found stomach and intestinal ulcers in Atlantic sailfish. Bashirullah et al. (1995) reported small "petechiae and/or ulcers" in the empty stomachs and intestines of white marlin, Atlantic sailfish and swordfish. We rarely found stomach ulcers in Atlantic blue marlin, albacore (RTLA 6329) and in one longbill spearfish from Puerto Rico. All are new host records for this condition. Histological examination of the longbill spearfish revealed that the submucosa of the stomach was severely inflamed. Unidentified tissue fluke fragments and eggs 15-20 μm long were present in the outer layer of the muscularis or serosa but there was little inflammation near the worms, suggesting that they may not have been the cause of the gastritis (Grizzle pers. comm.). Iversen and Kelley (1974) suggested that the spines of prey fishes caused the wounds, but thought nematodes, *Maricostula histiophori*, might also play some role as they occurred in many ulcers. The number and shape of the ulcers supports the spine-wounds theory, but the lesions appear to be complicated by bacterial infection. Fresh ulcers should be evaluated with standard bacterial isolation procedures.

Pollution effects

Most effects occur inshore in highly polluted areas thus only those big game fishes entering these regions are involved. "Examination of samples of developing embryos of Atlantic mackerel from the New York Bight plankton disclosed cytological abnormalities (in the form of disruption of the mitotic apparatus) and cytological abnormalities (ranging from stickiness and chromosome bridges to complete pulverization). Statistical correlations of high prevalences of chromosomal anomalies with degree of environmental contamination provided evidence for possible impacts on estuarine/coastal populations." (summarized from the literature by Sindermann 1993). As the general pollution of the world's oceans progresses, other big game fishes may be affected. The example of deteriorating coral reefs may be pertinent to this discussion. Coral reefs live in low nutrient environments and can be destroyed by what would be considered insignificant pollutants in other environments. Coral reefs, unfortunately, form close to shore and therefore are subject to human effects. Big game fish also rule a low nutrient realm, which is more isolated. Only minor, although global, pollution may cause anomalies in big game fishes. The health of big game fishes may prove to be a useful monitor of global change.

Toxins

Ciguatera fish poisoning

Ciguatera fish poisoning of humans is caused when fishes contaminated by ciguatoxins are eaten. These toxins are found in the flesh but are actually more concentrated in the internal organs of affected fishes. Symptoms include nausea, headache, reversal of the sensation of hot and cold, tingling of the hands and face. Symptoms vary between cases possibly because different combinations of a variety of different toxins are involved. This is a seriously debilitating disease that is sometimes fatal. Recovery usually takes months and symptoms may recur months or years after the initial attack. The severity of the symptoms may depend on the levels of toxins in the consumed fish and the prior exposure of the victim. No satisfactory treatment is known and there are no tests to identify contaminated flesh. Cooking does not break down the toxin. Ciguatera occurs in tropical fish worldwide. In Puerto Rico, it is so common in great barracuda and many large jacks, including crevalle jacks and horse-eye jacks, that their sale for human food is forbidden by law. The original sources of the toxins are substrate-dwelling dinoflagellates or algae. These toxins appear to accumulate up the food chain and particularly concentrate in piscivorous fishes associated with coral reefs. Offshore, big game fishes have seldom been implicated in ciguatera poisoning of humans, although greater amberjack have poisoned people in the Pacific. Ciguatera occurs so commonly in particular food fishes in different areas that these resources are not utilized. The disease is under-reported because medical treatment is seldom sought. Many of our friends and colleagues have suffered ciguatera poisoning and research attempting to solve this problem has been conducted in our Department of Marine Sciences.

Scombroid poisoning

Scombroid poisoning is also called histamine poisoning because it is caused by high levels of histamine that are ingested from poorly processed or handled fish flesh, particularly in Scombridae and Scomberesocidae. Histamine is produced by the bacterial breakdown of histidine which is abundant in the muscle of these fishes. Bacteria convert the histidine to histamine in a chemical process that can take place even after the bacteria have been killed. Several species of bacteria can cause this reaction and are naturally found either on the gills or in the intestine of fishes and are transferred to the flesh during processing. Human symptoms include rash, flushing of the face, diarrhea, sweating and headache. Some victims report a metallic or peppery taste. The onset of symptoms is very soon after consuming contaminated fish. These symptoms help distinguish this intoxication from ciguatoxin. Prevention is accomplished by immediate freezing of the fish and keeping it very cold throughout processing. Proper handling during food preparation is also essential to prevent the growth of the bacteria on fish flesh. The disease is relatively mild and self-limiting and is usually responsive to antihistamine therapy. This intoxication occurs worldwide. Several countries keep records of the incidence and in the 1980's hundreds of cases were reported in the USA and England. Fewer cases are reported in Canada and other more northern regions possibly because processed fish stay colder in cold climates. This relatively mild disease is thought to occur far more often than it is reported. Fishes in Puerto Rico and the western north Atlantic likely to cause this disease are noted in the Host-Disease Checklists.

Burnt Tuna

Burnt tuna (yake niku=cooked meat in Japanese) was thought to be a breakdown of muscle tissue due to the struggle during capture. Actually, it is caused by enzyme action after death (calcium-activated proteases and their enhancement by high blood catecholamine levels). This condition causes bigeye tuna, yellowfin tuna and possibly other species to have flesh that is soft, exuding a clear fluid, and slightly sour in taste, instead of red, translucent and firm with a delicate flavor. In the Hawaiian sportfish and small-boat long-line fisheries, half of the tuna trolled and 1/4 taken on long-lines were affected. The condition ranges from mild to severe and is found in 5-100% of the flesh of each fish. It prevents the use of tuna in raw-fish dishes by sport fishermen and keeps the small-boat fishermen from selling tuna in the Japanese market. Burnt fish may deteriorate more rapidly, but are otherwise safe to eat. The quality of cooked or canned meat is little affected by this condition.

Mass Mortalities

A mass mortality killed more than 20,000 tons of mackerel in the Arabian Sea during the second week of June 1957 (Jones 1962). This tonnage was nearly equal to the world catch of mackerel at that time. The event was never studied or explained.

Strasburg (1959) found a mass mortality of larval frigate tuna south of Lanai in the Hawaiian Islands. The cause of death could not be determined, and there were no obvious signs of predation, disease or parasitism. It was probably caused by the passage of the larvae through an area with marked discontinuities in water temperatures. Larvae measured 2.2-8.2 mm TL. The rate of mortality increased with size, and larvae about 5 mm were the most affected. Jones (1963) suggested that bullet tuna must have also been killed in this mass mortality. A similar, sudden mass mortality of shrimps has been observed from a submersible.

Health (1992) suggested that parasites may show developmental stage specificity for larval or young fishes and may cause short duration mass mortalities in a population. We are not aware of any practical evidence supporting this interesting suggestion.

DISCUSSION

Parasites are a normal part of the biology of their hosts. Usually, parasites and hosts have reached an evolutionary point where the host can support the parasite without the frequent or premature death of the host. The nature of the host-parasite relationship can also tell us much about the host, often including its recent and long-term diet and behavior and, occasionally, its evolutionary history. For example, parasites tell us that humans were originally tropical creatures, because our parasite fauna in this region is more diverse and rich.

HARM CAUSED BY PARASITES

The first question everyone asks about parasites is "Can they hurt me?" and the second is "Do they hurt the fish?" That is why this information was provided for every parasite in the text when it was available, and is discussed below.

Fish Diseases in Humans

Some big game fish roundworms can infect people [see Nematoda (Roundworms)]; fish tuberculosis, ciguatera poisoning and scombroid poisoning occasionally injure or kill humans (see Other Diseases and Conditions). A few, large tropical big game fishes (jacks and great barracuda) should never be eaten, but, in general, properly prepared big game fishes are safe, wholesome and delicious.

Damage to Hosts

Parasite damage to big game fishes is probably much greater than noted in our parasite summaries. Much of the damage occurs in the open ocean where it is not recorded. The hosts that can be examined are largely caught by hook and line, and this technique selects healthy fishes. Injured or damaged fishes are quickly eaten by other fishes or sink out of sight. Scientists were recently surprised to learn that the surface waters of the world's oceans are filled with viruses. No one had bothered to look before. We know nothing about the ecologically important disease processes at work in the open ocean.

All parasites can damage their host if they are present in sufficient numbers. We believe that this situation does not occur often, but we cannot be certain. All parasites are like tax collectors, they are always irritatingly present, and they always take their cut. Every fish is smaller, takes longer to grow, or is sometimes a little slower and gets eaten, because of parasites. This may seem minor, but it adds up to trillions of kilos of fishes and potentially billions of dollars worth of game and commercial fish value lost each year due to routine parasites.

TRANSMISSION OF PARASITES

Offshore game fishes are usually widely dispersed, as any frustrated fishermen can attest! This big sea, few fishes, and little contact between hosts, is an enormous problem for tiny parasites and pathological microbes. All parasites have complex strategies to get from one host to another, the odds against the parasite in the open ocean are even higher than in almost any other environment. The tricks big game fish parasites use are incredible. Unfortunately, we have discovered very few of them. Some of the more simple tricks include releasing offspring when the hosts breed or congregate and dropping eggs when the adult host breeds in the inshore nursery area, with the eggs timed to hatch when the new generation of host is maturing.

Parasite Transfer From Associated Fishes

Pilotfish and remoras pick parasites off their large, big game fish associates, but they are also parasitized by some of the same gillworms and copepods as their hosts. Thus they also serve as "parasite taxis" carrying parasites between hosts, among host species, or from inshore to offshore localities.

These associates also share many of the internal parasites of their hosts. Some of these can be transmitted to big game fishes when they occasionally eat their fish associates. These parasites can be easily transmitted to associates that consume fecal material of big game fishes.

These fish associates also greatly benefit the shared parasites by "expanding the playing field". One big game fish carrying 5 remoras and surrounded by 4 pilotfish provides 10 times the potential hosts for a parasite. Just by providing many more hosts in the open ocean, and thus more infective units, these associates may make parasitism of the sport fish much more likely.

Prey to Predator Transfer

Several of the isopod species reported on big game fishes have obviously escaped from their normal prey hosts as they were eaten, and reattached to their false host predators. The little we know about the life cycles of a few gillworms, copepods and possibly flukes suggests that they may occur on inshore or prey hosts as immatures, transfer to predators that consume their intermediary or decoy host, and mature as adults in the predator. This system could be widespread among big game fish parasites. Apparently it is employed by many of the tissue flukes. It allows the parasite to use more common, slower, or available prey fish and squid hosts as a stepping stone to the appropriate, but less available, final host.

International Transfer of Exotic Parasites

International commerce of big game fishes is largely confined to frozen carcasses or cooked and canned flesh. Cooking or adequate freezing kills parasites and minimizes the risk of their transmission. However, 2 new trends threaten the isolation of big game fish parasites: (1) air shipping of fresh tunas and other fishes, (2) aquaculture and subsequent shipping of live brood stock or young fish.

The protozoan, *Hexacapsula neothunni* Arai and Matsumoto, was described from the Tokyo Fish Market, it causes a disease called "jelly-meat" that dissolves muscle of albacore, bigeye tuna and yellowfin tuna. This parasite has only been found in the Banda Sea (between New Guinea and Borneo) and in the Solomon Sea (east of New Guinea). It occurs most frequently in fish 30-45 kg and from June to August. One of every 200 fish is affected and jelly-meat is found in both red and white meat. This is only one among many examples of devastatingly dangerous parasites with limited geographic range that could easily be introduced with air shipped fresh big game fishes. All that is necessary is the careless disposal of contaminated flesh into the environment. Something as simple as washing off a cleaning table and allowing the waste water to run into the ocean could start this pest.

Greater amberjack fry were taken from the west coast of the USA, shipped to Hawaii, Hong Kong, Okinawa, and the main islands of Japan. A dangerous capsalid gillworm, *Neobenedenia girellae* (Hargis), was introduced with this host. It has not only caused disease problems in these cultured fishes, but has also injured wild fishes in these localities. Importing exotic amberjacks (resulting in the establishment of this exotic parasite) was unnecessary because all of these localities have their own local stocks of greater amberjack.

Two species of blood flukes, *Paradeontacylix* spp., cause mass mortalities of cultured greater amberjack and yellowtail in Japan. These parasites were introduced in the 1980s from China and Hong Kong along with greater amberjack fry and quickly became a major problem. Our own Atlantic blood fluke in this genus from greater amberjack could also be a problem in its mariculture.

Many other dangerous parasites and microbial agents could be just as easily be spread. See Bunkley-Williams and Williams (1995) for methods to avoid introducing parasites.

Catch-and-Release Transfer

Catch-and-release of big game fish is an honorable and ecologically friendly concept. However, it may also be a way to spread "the plague" among our favorite fishes, if we are not careful. The poor fish has been punctured in the mouth with a hook, abraded against the side of the boat, possibly gaffed and tangled in lines. If any or all of this equipment is contaminated with disease organisms from a previous catch, then it is practically inoculated into these wounds. Parasites knocked off one fish and laying on the deck are perfectly happy to jump on the next host they encounter.

A caught-and-released fish is about as "stressed out" as it is will ever be and still stay alive. Any weakened host is a bonus for a parasite or microbial disease. Whatever resistance or immunity the host may have possessed is lost or greatly reduced during the recovery period following release. The "incubation period" of diseases may be shorter than the recovery period of the host. Thus a contaminated fish may contract a fatal disease before it can recover from being caught. Most immediate losses of freshwater game fish following catch-and-release tournaments are caused by improper handling, but most longer-term losses are due to disease complications. The fate of released big game fishes has not been explored, but probably is similar to what occurs in freshwater game fishes.

We are not suggesting that catch-and-release program do not work. We are merely pointing out that some of these fishes perish. At this point no studies have been conducted to determine how many die. What you can do to increase the likelihood that your caught-and-released fish will survive is to handle it as gently and briefly as possible, and to clean your handling gear and deck between catches to prevent any possible cross contamination of diseases between fishes.

USEFULNESS OF PARASITES

Environmental Indicators

Parasites of big game fishes may be good indicators of changing environmental conditions. Many parasites have an enormous reproductive capacity or amazing techniques to find enough hosts to survive. Minor changes in the environment may either favor survival or death of parasite reproduction and/or disrupt the methods of host finding. These effects would be magnified by the system and expressed by either many more parasites per host or many fewer (see cero in Host Summaries). Minor environmental changes may cause major changes in the abundances of many parasites. Parasite levels may be a highly sensitive barometer of changes in the environment of big game fishes.

Biological Tags

Parasites have been used as biological tags to distinguish populations of fishes including some big game fishes. Those parasites with potential as biological tags are discussed in the individual parasite summaries in the text. Greater basic knowledge about big game fish parasites and their life cycles may provide more tools for fishery biologists to elucidate population movements and other population parameters of big game fishes. We are cooperating in an international effort to establish and characterize parasite biological tags for big game fish.

Parasites as indicators of host relationships

Cobia and remoras are assumed to be closely related because of similarities in shapes and colors of developmental stages and adults. Johnson (1984) suggested that cobia were more closely related to dolphins than remoras on the basis of their bone structure. The parasites of these species suggest that cobia are most similar to remoras, and have little similarities to dolphin. Gillworms are the most host specific of any parasites. Thus, the occurrence of *Dioncus agassizi* on cobia and 3 species of remoras seems indicative of a close relationship. The adult of *Serrasentis sagittifer* is host specific to cobia, thus an accidental record from inshore remora is interesting. Flukes are not usually host specific, thus are less useful in comparisons. However, cobia share their western Atlantic flukes with no other big game fishes, but one also occurs in inshore remora. *Tuxophorus caligodes* also occurs on inshore remora, possibly other remoras, and jacks. *Lernaeenicus longiventris* rarely occurs on cobia, but it is more typical of dolphin and jacks. Thus, the parasites shared by cobia and remoras suggest that they belong in a common family. However, only one species of parasite, *Dioncus agassizi*, would be family specific to a joined family, and a high percentage of cobia parasites are unique to this host. The isolation suggested by its parasites makes the cobia better suited to remain in its own family. On the basis of its parasites, cobia seems to be a remnant of an old family that has lost all of its species but one.

Parasites of members of the fish genus *Caranx* are all but identical and interchangeable. There is some interchange or alternation among a few species but the host lists are essentially the same. This may explain some of the problems in separating species in the genus *Caranx*. The parasites suggest that none of the host species are very well separated. Some ichthyologists divide this genus of fishes into several genera, but the parasites of these fishes argues against such action.

The parasites of jacks in genus *Caranx* are inshore denizens. The few parasites they share with scombrids have little specificity and are only found in those scombrids that spend considerable time nearshore. This parasite pattern may be due to habitat specificity more than host preference. Only *Caligus robustus* infects both jacks and offshore scombrids. Those with low host specificity include *Caligus bonito* which occurs on inshore and offshore scombrids and we found it on horse-eye jack. *Lernaeenicus longiventrus* prefers crevalle jack and dolphins, but is also found on inshore scombrids and cobia. It is one of the few parasites sharing Spanish mackerels and jacks.

Amberjacks have more parasites in common with scombrids than with other jacks. *Brachiella thynni* prefers scombrids, but is also found on greater amberjack and we found it on dolphin. *Koellikeria bipartita* only occurs on greater amberjack and large tunas, another species of tissue fluke occurs on tunas and Pacific amberjacks, and 3 more occur on tunas, Pacific amberjacks and skipjack tuna. The copepod may be relatively non-host specific, but tissue flukes select specific hosts. Amberjacks seem to have some odd relationship to tunas. Amberjacks are obviously not related to scombrids, thus similarities in habitat and behavior must be responsible for their shared parasite fauna.

Dolphin share 7 non-specific parasites with scombrids, jacks and billfishes. Otherwise they have no parasites in common with these or any other big game fishes.

Caligus productus rarely, and possibly accidentally, occurs on great barracuda. It prefers scombrids, but also occurs on billfishes. This tenuous, almost non-existent, overlap with other big game fishes and 2 non-host specific protozoans are all that connect great barracuda with fishes other than barracudas. Great barracuda parasites suggest that this host is almost completely isolated from other fishes.

Chub and Atlantic mackerel are in the same genus and should be rather similar. They have 3 genus-specific parasites in common, but of 90 species of parasites found on these 2 hosts, only 14 occur on both.

The scombrid family has 8 family-specific parasites, while their separate tribes have 25 (tunas), 7 (Spanish mackerels), 7 (little tunas), 5 (mackerels), and 1 (bonitos) tribe-specific parasites. This suggests that tunas form a strong tribe but the other tribes are less cohesive.

King mackerel occur a bit further offshore than the 3 other western Atlantic Spanish mackerels. Their parasites differ a bit from the other 3 which have almost identical parasites. King mackerel have a similar, but different species of nasal copepod, and lack a second species of nasal copepod that is found in all the others. King mackerel have a spiny-headed worm, and a pit-dwelling copepod that are more typical of offshore hosts. They lack the genus-specific isopod and tissue fluke that is shared by the 3 more inshore Spanish mackerels.

The parasites of the western Atlantic Spanish mackerels are otherwise all but identical differing only by interchanges of similar species, missing genus-specific species that would probably be found with more examinations, or slightly different non-host-specific parasites. They share 11 genus-specific parasites and 2 almost genus-specific ones, but have only 1 species-specific parasite. They have no family-specific parasites, the only group in the scombrids to be so isolated. In contrast, the similarly isolated inshore jacks (genus *Caranx*) have 6 family-specific parasites. This suggests that Spanish mackerels are the most isolated, and possibly youngest, scombrids. They are more separated from each other in nearshore habitats, yet their parasites are more uniform than their more wide-ranging relatives, just the opposite of what would be predicted.

The arrangements of parasites in these Spanish mackerels is very similar to what is found in the *Caranx* spp. of the jacks. Possibly the nearshore habitat was the last habitat occupied by both jacks and scombrids. The nearshore jacks and scombrids would be expected to be the youngest of their families. Each time the continents joined and separated this habitat was disrupted, contracted or expanded. The more geologically recent ice ages lowered sea level and similarly disrupted the nearshore, but not the offshore and oceanic habitats. In comparison, the offshore and oceanic jacks have enjoyed relatively stable habitats.

The inshore jacks (*Caranx* spp.) and inshore scombrids (*Scomberomorus* spp.) have shared identical habitats, foods, conditions and histories. If environmental conditions determined parasite faunas, then their faunas would be identical. Under the same conditions, inshore jacks and scombrids developed parallel, but completely different parasite faunas. This is a powerful argument for the use of parasite faunas in analyzing host relationships (phylogeny).

Wahoo is an unusual fish that is difficult to place within the scombrid tribes. It shares parasites with most other scombrids. Morphologically, wahoo resemble Spanish mackerels, and that is where they are usually placed. They share 8 parasites, including one almost host-specific gillworm, with little tunas, but only have 3 parasite species in common with Spanish mackerels.

There are 5 species of copepods in the genus *Gloiopotes*, 1 is found on Atlantic sailfish, 1 on wahoo, 1 on other Atlantic billfishes and 2 species on Indo-Pacific billfishes. The cosmopolitan distribution of the wahoo and its *Gloiopotes* copepod contrasts with the other 2 *Gloiopotes* species that are isolated in the Atlantic, and the 2 species restricted to the Indo-Pacific. This could indicate that (1) the wahoo association is older, (2) wahoo migrate more frequently between the Atlantic and Indo-Pacific, or (3) the various billfish species in the Atlantic and Pacific are isolated in each realm and migrate so little that separate species of copepods (and host fishes) arose. In Indo-Pacific collections identified by Cressey (1967), 16 Indo-Pacific sailfish were parasitized by 4 *G. huttoni* and 12 *G. watsoni* (1:3 preference); and 22 striped marlin by 14 *G. huttoni* and 8 *G. watsoni* (about a 2:1 preference). The preferred host is probably the one on which each parasite originally speciated. The mix of hosts and copepods in the Indo-Pacific also suggests that these parasites are older than the more host-conservative, and probably more recent, Atlantic species.

Bonitos have physical features that share characteristics with at least 2 other tribes of scombrids. This group of fishes has provided one of the major arguments for not splitting up the scombrids, since bonitos are intermediate between 2 of the proposed tribes. The parasites of the Atlantic bonito provide little definitive evidence for this question. This fish shares its parasites with many of the other scombrid tribes. It has no distinct, unique parasite fauna. Only one of its parasites could be considered almost tribe specific. Thus there is no strong parasitological evidence to join bonitos with any particular scombrid tribe, and little to suggest that bonitos form their own cohesive tribe. The best, if weak, evidence suggests similarities between bonitos (Sardini) and little tunas (Katsuwonini). Atlantic bonito and little tunny only share 1 copepod, *Ceratacolax euthynni*, but it is found nowhere else. One nasal copepod, *Unicolax collateralis*, has been found in most bonitos and little tunas around the world. Oddly, it has not been found in the Atlantic bonito.

Frigate tuna and skipjack tuna are in the little tuna tribe, but have rather few parasites in common. Their roundworms are interestingly quite similar. Two genera of these worms, *Ctenascarophis* and *Prospinitectus*, have only 2 species each. Frigate tuna harbor *C. gastricus* and *P. mollis*; and skipjack tuna the "sister" species, *C. lesteri* and *P.exiguus*.

None of the parasites of skipjack tuna are tribe specific to little tunas. The other western Atlantic little tunas have 1-5 tribe-specific parasites each. If skipjack tuna was placed in the tuna tribe, it would have 9 "tribe-specific" parasites. Gillworms often show more specificity than other parasites. Skipjack tuna and bluefin tuna are both infected by a gillworm, *Hexostoma grossum*; but skipjack tuna does not share any gillworms with the other little tunas. Tissue flukes are host selective since they only develop in specific fishes. Four species of tissue flukes occur only in skipjack tuna and bluefin tuna (another 5 species occur only in skipjack tuna, and 2-3 other tunas). Nasal copepods are almost as specific as gillworms. The 3 other species of western Atlantic little tunas are all infected by 2 species, *Unicolax collateralis* and *U. mycterobius*; but these do not occur in skipjack tuna. The fluke, *Syncoelium filiferum*, has little specificity, but occurs in skipjack tuna and albacore. Parasitologically, skipjack tuna is more closely related to tunas (Tribe Thunnini), than to little tunas (Tribe Katsuwonini).

We found 25 parasite species which were tribe specific to tunas. Bigeye tuna had 48 species of parasites but almost half (22) were tribe specific. This is almost all of the tribe-specific parasites. Yellowfin tuna had the next highest with 17 specific, out of 80 total; while the others had many fewer (bluefin 6/70, albacore 6/39, blackfin tuna 3/9). The preponderance of shared parasites on 1 host species might indicate that this fish is evolutionarily older giving these parasites more time to colonize it, and to develop into tribe-specific parasites.

The description of the host-specific gillworms, *Tristoma adcoccineum* and *T. adintegrum*, from Pacific swordfish by Yamaguti (1968) is the only strong parasite evidence suggesting that Atlantic and Indo-Pacific swordfish might represent different species. We suspect that the swordfish are the same, and that these Pacific gillworms may be found to be synonyms of the Atlantic, *Tristoma coccineum* and *T. integrum*.

The western Atlantic billfishes have relatively few parasites and very few host specific ones. This could mean that they are relatively young evolutionarily compared to other big game fishes, and especially swordfish.

HOST SUMMARIES AND HOST-DISEASE CHECKLISTS

We present a short summary of basic biological information of each host and include a "Name" category where we attempt to list other scientific names that have been used for the host when parasites were mentioned. Some of these are real synonyms of the fish host (those with authors), but many are mistaken names, wrong names or even made-up names that exist no where else. Most of the improper names appeared in the fish-parasite literature without authors. Some of the improper names are the correct scientific names of existing fishes that were only applied erroneously to a parasite host. Older synonyms, or synonyms that have never been used to refer to parasites, are not included; thus we are not providing complete synonym lists for each host species. We also include a short synthesis of the parasites found on each host with comments on the phylogenetic relationships among the hosts as indicated by their parasites. Parasites may only be an indirect indicator of their host's phylogeny and taxonomic relationships, but they are a part of the puzzle and provide additional biological evidence of relationships.

In the disease lists, the parasites, diseases and conditions listed in the **left column** are those normally and routinely found in the western Atlantic. They are discussed individually in the text on the pages indicated in bold face in the Index. Parasites found on these hosts in geographic regions outside of the western Atlantic are noted in the **right column** and are identified with abbreviations that are noted in the box at right. Trivial parasites are similarly identified. The "right-column" parasites are included because some may eventually be found in our area, and for comparison with the western Atlantic fauna. They are not included in the Index.

For this book, we chose bill-fishes, bonito, cobia, dolphins, little tunas, mackerels, Spanish mackerels, swordfish and tunas without exception. Only the larger barracuda and jacks, that are found offshore, were selected. Bluefish is a voracious sport fish, but a bit too

Checklist Abbreviations

[acc] - accidental or contamination parasites
[BSea] - Black Sea
[EAlt] - Eastern Atlantic
    including Europe and Africa
[Eur] - Eastern Atlantic around Europe
[fal] - false hosts
[Ind] - Indian ocean
[IPac] - Indo-Pacific
    (Indian and Pacific Oceans)
[MBS] - Mediterranean and Black Seas
[Med] - Mediterranean Sea only
[Pac] - Pacific Ocean
[RSea] - Red Sea
[SAfr] - South Africa
[SWAfr] - South Africa and Atlantic off Africa
[unc] - uncertain status
    (more study is necessary)
[WAfr] - West Africa (Atlantic off Africa)
[?] - questionable records
  * - larval parasites
  ** - immature adult parasites

small for "big game", oddly does not visit Puerto Rico, and its parasites have already been well defined. Salmon (Salmonidae) are definitely big game fishes, but occur a bit too far north to be included and their parasites are well known. One or 2 sharks (Squaliformes) certainly qualify as big game fish, but their parasites are so different, that they would be better considered in a later, separate volume on sharks and rays.

The name "Spanish mackerel" is confusing because it has been used as the name of a tribe of mackerels, as a western Atlantic species (Robins et al. 1991), and as a name for chub mackerel in the eastern Atlantic. We use the "Spanish mackerel" species name in the text because it is well established in the western Atlantic (particularly in the USA). The more appropriate common name would be "Atlantic Spanish mackerel" as we note in the Checklist. When we use the plural "Spanish mackerels" in the text, it refers to the tribe.

Blue marlin and sailfish of Robins et al. (1991) are separated into Atlantic blue marlin and Indo-Pacific blue marlin, and Atlantic sailfish and Indo-Pacific sailfish. We use the Atlantic and Indo-Pacific names, but list the parasites of the Pacific cohorts as if they were worldwide species. Whether these fishes are separate species or not, their parasites are, interestingly, very similar.

For the purpose of this discussion, we divided the little tunas and tunas into separate tribes to conveniently compare their parasites. This division is presented for expediency, and is not an attempt to revise their taxonomy (historically, proper host taxonomy has been utterly disregarded by fish parasitologists).

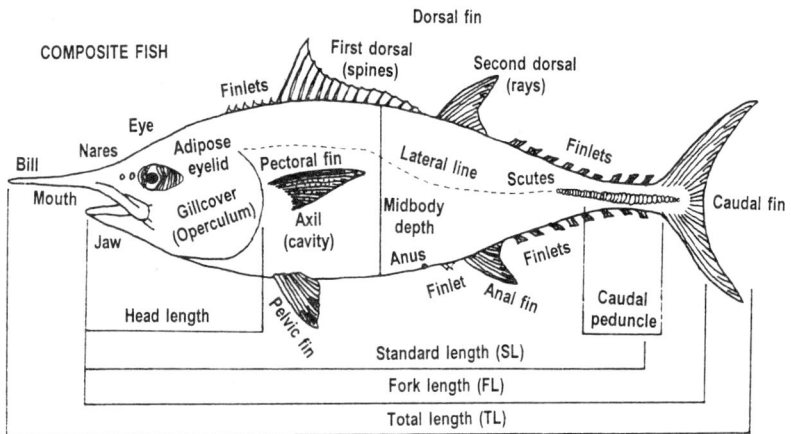

COMPOSITE FISH — Dorsal fin — First dorsal (spines) — Second dorsal (rays) — Finlets — Eye — Nares — Adipose eyelid — Pectoral fin — Lateral line — Finlets — Scutes — Bill — Mouth — Gillcover (Operculum) — Axil (cavity) — Midbody depth — Caudal fin — Jaw — Anus — Finlets — Head length — Pelvic fin — Finlet — Anal fin — Caudal peduncle — Standard length (SL) — Fork length (FL) — Total length (TL)

General biological aspects of fishes are discussed under Pisces (Fishes). In this section we provide an illustration and a descriptive diagnosis of each host. The composite drawing, above, of a mythological fish illustrates the external anatomical features discussed in the diagnoses and "Location on Host" sections of the parasite descriptions. In a few hosts it was necessary to use characters of the gill rakers (finger-like projections on the side of the gill arches opposite the gill filaments) and liver to separate physically similar hosts. A morphological feature not easily illustrated is the lateral line which is a system of pressure or motion sensory organs on the side of the fish. It is usually obvious with a long row of pores through scales. "Muscle" refers to the large skeletal or body muscles. The "nose" or nares of both big game fishes and their bony fish associates consists of an incurrent pore (nare), a canal and olfactory rosette (nasal lamellae) and an excurrent nare. Pseudobranchs are patches of gill-filament-like lamellae found in the upper (dorsal) inner surface of the gill cover (operculum). "Gills" include the gill filaments, arches and rakers. "Gill chamber" includes all inner surfaces except gills and gill cover. "Body" includes skin and fins.

Popular References - Anonymous (1994a), Goldstein (1988), Hammond and Cupka (1975), McClane (1974a,b).

Reference - Fischer (1978).

Order Perciformes, Family Rachycentridae - cobias

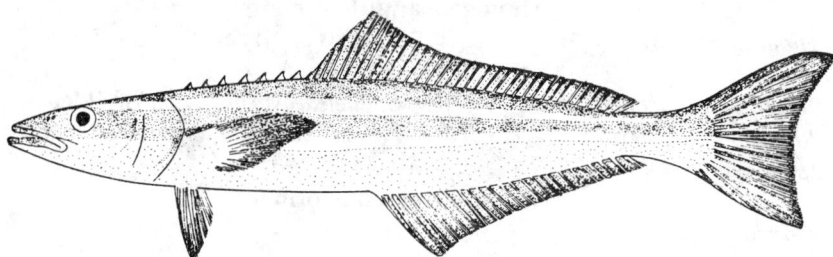

Rachycentron canadum (Linnaeus) - cobia

Name - Other common names include ling, lemonfish, black salmon, black kingfish, sergeant fish, crab-eater, runner and cabio.

Diagnostic Characters - The spines of the first dorsal fin are isolated into individual finlets. The sides of body are marked with 2 sharply defined, narrow, horizontal, silvery bands.

Geographic Range - Worldwide in tropical and warm-temperate waters.

Food Habits - It eats crabs, squids and fishes.

Ecology - Inshore and offshore

Length - Maximum 200.0 cm, common to 110.0 cm.

Weight - Maximum 61.5 kg, common 5.0-28.0 kg.

Parasites - This fish has surprisingly few parasites (31) for such a widespread, abundant and relatively well examined host. However, more than 1/2 (17) are not reported from the western Atlantic, suggesting that fish from our region could be better examined. Further evidence is seen in its copepods, which have been well examined and are all reported from the western Atlantic. Most of the parasites known from cobia are either host specific (10), or possibly host specific (8) suggesting that cobia are not very closely related to any other fishes.

Digenea (flukes)

Mabiarama prevesiculata   *Laruea straightum* [Ind]

Stephanostomum imparispine
Stephanostomum imparispine*
Tormopsolus filiformis

Lecithochirium canadus [Ind]
Lecithochirium monticellii [?]
Lecithocladium jagannathi [Ind]
Lepidapedon megalaspi [Pac]
Paracryptogonimus morosovi [Pac]
Phyllodistomum parukhini [RSea]
Plerurus digitatus [Ind]
Pseudolepidapedon pudens [acc]
Sclerodistomum rachycentri [Ind]
Stephanostomum cloacum [Ind]
Stephanostomum dentatum** [fal]
Stephanostomum microsomum [Ind]
Stephanostomum pseudoditrematis [Ind]
Tormopsolus spatulum [Ind]

Didymozoidea (tissue flukes)

Neometanematobothrioides rachycentri [Pac]

Monogenea (gillworms)

Dioncus agassizi

Dioncus sp. [Pac]

Cestoda (tapeworms)

Nybelinia bisulcata*
Rhinebothrium flexile*
tetraphyllid*

Callitetrarhynchus gracilis* [Med]
Rhynchobothrium longispine* [unc]

Nematoda (roundworms)

Goezia pelagia
Iheringascaris inquies

Acanthocephala (spiny-headed worms)

Serrasentis sagittifer

Serrasentis nadakali [Ind]

Copepoda (copepods)

Lernaeenicus longiventris
Parapetalus occidentalis
Tuxophorus caligodes

Caligus coryphaenae [Pac?]
Caligus haemulonis [?]
Euryphorus nordmanni [Pac]
Lepeophtheirus plectropomi [Pac]
Lernaeolophus hemirhamphi [acc]
Lernaeolophus sultanus [acc]

Cirripedia (barnacles)

Conchoderma virgatum

Condition

heart connections (pericardial adhesions)

Anomalies

pugheaded

Family Carangidae - jacks

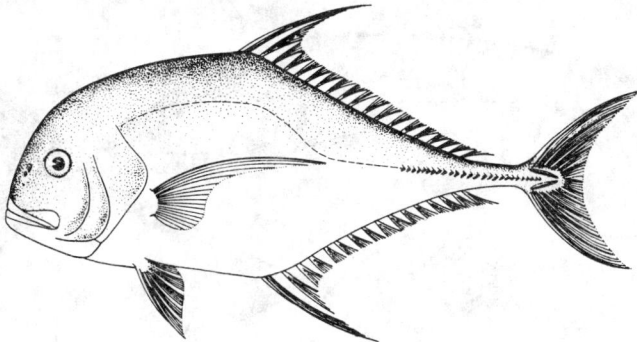

Alectis ciliaris (Bloch) - African pompano

Name - It has also been called "Atlantic threadfin", "Cuban jack", "pennant-fish", *Alectis crinitus* (Mitchill), *Blepharis crinitus*, *Carangoides ajax* Snyder, and *Hynnis cubensis* Poey.

Diagnostic Characters - The first dorsal fin is lacking in fish 17 cm FL and larger. The second dorsal and anal fins have relatively long bases. A row of large scutes on the caudal peduncle makes the tail rigid. Tips of the second dorsal and anal fins are falcate and long (extremely so in young).

Geographic Range - Worldwide in tropical and temperate waters.

Food Habits - It eats fishes and squids.

Ecology - Inshore to oceanic.

Length - Maximum possibly 150.0 cm, common to 90.0 cm FL.

Weight - Maximum 23.0 kg, common to 8.0 kg.

Parasites - Only 4 parasites have been reported from this host. The flukes and tapeworm have no host specificity, and the copepod is almost family specific to a variety of Indo-Pacific jacks. This host requires further examination.

Digenea (flukes)
Lechithochirium sp. [Ind]
Plerurus digitatus [Ind]

Cestoda (tapeworms)

tetraphyllid*

Copepoda (copepods)
Caligus constrictus [Ind]

Caranx bartholomaei Cuvier - yellow jack

Name - It is sometimes placed in genus *Carangoides*.

Diagnostic Characters - The first dorsal fin has a relatively short base, and the second dorsal and anal fins have relatively long bases. A row of large scutes on the caudal peduncle makes the tail rigid. The back of the jaw extends to the front margin of the eye.

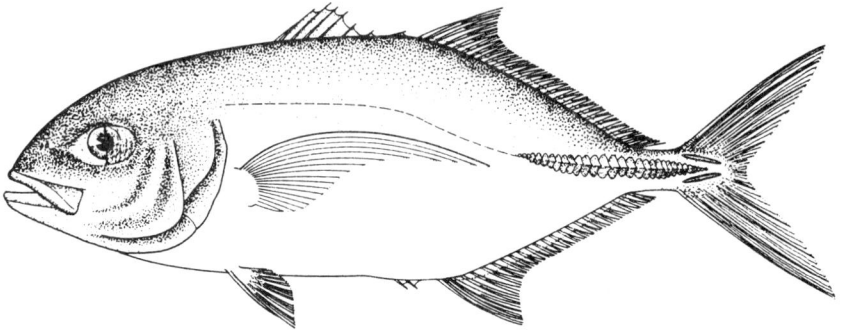

Geographic Range - Western Atlantic.
Food Habits - It eats primarily bottom-dwelling fishes.
Ecology - Inshore to oceanic.
Length - Maximum possibly 100.0 cm (90.0 cm FL), common to 45.0 cm FL. One fish from Puerto Rico was 89.5 cm.
Weight - Maximum 24.0 kg, common to 2.0 kg.
Parasites - With only 15 species of parasites known, this host has obviously not been adequately examined.   All its parasites are found in other species of *Caranx*.   Seven are genus or family specific, 1 only found in jacks and scombrids, and 7 generalists with little host specificity (1 prefers jacks).

Protozoa (protozoans)
Haemogregarina bigemina

Digenea (flukes)
Alcicornis carangis   *Genolopa brevicaecum* [fal]
Brachyphallus parvus   *Podocotyle chloroscombri* [fal]
Bucephalus varicus
Ectenurus lepidus
Pseudopecoeloides carangis
Stephanostomum ditrematis
Stephanostomum megacephalum
Tergestia laticollis

Cestoda (tapeworms)
tetraphyllid*

Copepoda (copepods)
Caligus chorinemi
Caligus robustus
Caligus spinosus
Lernanthropus giganteus

Isopoda (isopods)
Gnathia sp.*

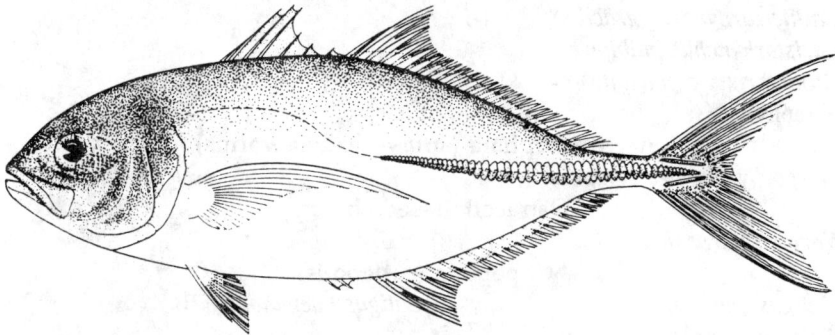

Caranx crysos (Mitchill) - blue runner

Name - It has also been called *Caranx caballus* and *Paratractus caballus*. It is replaced by the similar eastern Atlantic blue runner, *Caranx fusus* Geoffroy, in the eastern Atlantic; and green jack, *Caranx caballus* Günther, in the eastern Pacific. Some parasite records for this fish actually refer to these other species.

Diagnostic Characters - The first dorsal fin has a relatively short base, and the second dorsal and anal fins have relatively long bases. A row of large scutes on the caudal peduncle makes the tail rigid. The back of the jaw extends to the middle of the eye. The tip of the pectoral fins extend back onto the line of tail scutes.

Geographic Range - Western Atlantic.

Food Habits - It eats primarily fishes, but also shrimps, crabs, and other invertebrates.

Ecology - Inshore to oceanic.

Length - Maximum possibly 68.0 cm (62.0 cm FL), common to 35.0 cm FL.

Weight - Maximum 4.0 kg, common to 1.5 kg.

Parasites - One is possibly host specific, 4 genus specific, 3 almost genus specific, 4 family specific, 1 only found in jacks and scombrids and 15 generalists with little host specificity (1 prefers jacks).

Protozoa (protozoans)

Haemogregarina bigemina

Digenea (flukes)

Alcicornis carangis   *Lecithochirium monticellii* [?]
Brachyphallus parvus
Bucephalus varicus
Ectenurus lepidus
Parahemiurus merus
Pseudopecoeloides carangis
Stephanostomum ditrematis
Tergestia laticollis

Monogenea (gillworms)

Allopyragraphorus incomparabilis   *Grubea cochlear* [fal]
Cemocotyle carangis

Cestoda (tapeworms)
*Callitetrarhynchus gracilis**
*Lacistorhynchus bulbifer**
*Otobothrium crenacolle**
tetraphyllid*

Acanthocephala (spiny-headed worms)
Gorgorhynchoides elongatus

Ostracoda (seed shrimp)
Vargula parasitica

Copepoda (copepods)

Caligus chorinemi   *Caligus haemulonis* [?]
Caligus elongatus
Caligus longipedis
Caligus robustus
Lernaeenicus longiventris
Lernanthropus giganteus
Pseudoeucanthus uniseriatus

Isopoda (isopods)
Cymothoa oestrum
Excorollana tricornis
Gnathia sp.*
Nerocila lanceolata

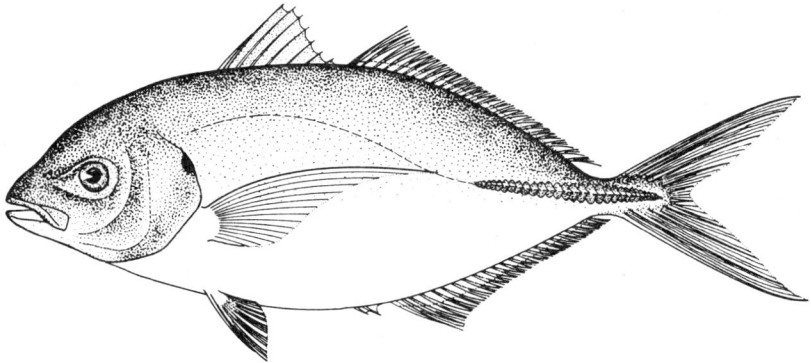

Caranx dentex (Bloch and Schneider) - white trevally
Name - It is also called "guelly jack". This species is sometimes placed in genus *Pseudocaranx*. Records of this fish in the Indo-Pacific refer to guelly jack, *Caranx guara* (Bonnaterre).
Diagnostic Characters - The first dorsal fin has a relatively short base, and the second dorsal and anal fins have relatively long bases. A row of large scutes on the caudal peduncle makes the tail rigid. The first dorsal fin is higher than the second dorsal fin.
Geographic Range - Bermuda, southern Brazil and the eastern Atlantic.

Food Habits - It eats bottom fishes and invertebrates.
Ecology - Inshore and offshore.
Length - Maximum 80.0 cm (68.0 cm FL), common to 40.0 cm FL.
Weight - Maximum 4.5 kg, common 1.4-2.0 kg.
Parasites - With 2 parasite records, this host has obviously not been adequately examined. *Hysterothylacium aduncum* will probably be found in additional jacks.

Cestoda (tapeworms)

tetraphyllid*

Nematoda (roundworms)

Hysterothylacium aduncum

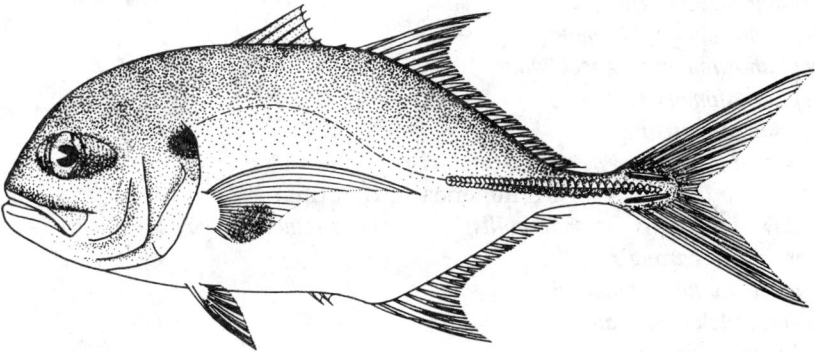

Caranx hippos (Linnaeus) - crevalle jack

Name - It is also called "common jack" and "horse crevalle". This fish replaced by the similar eastern Atlantic crevalle jack, *Caranx* sp., in the eastern Atlantic; and Pacific crevalle jack, *Caranx caninus* Günther, in the eastern Pacific. Parasite records for "crevalle jack" have been noted around the world, but this fish only occurs in the western Atlantic.

Diagnostic Characters - The first dorsal fin has a relatively short base, and the second dorsal and anal fins have relatively long bases. A row of large scutes on the caudal peduncle makes the tail rigid. The back of the jaw extends to the back margin of the eye. The chest has only 1 small patch of scales. There is a black spot on the pectoral fins.

Geographic Range - Western Atlantic.

Food Habits - It eats mostly fishes, but some shrimps and other invertebrates.

Ecology - Inshore and offshore.

Length - Maximum 101.0 cm, common to 60.0 cm FL. Old unconfirmed records of jacks 150.0 cm could have been this species.

Weight - Maximum 26.0 kg, common 2.5-6.8 kg. Old, unconfirmed records of jacks 32.0 kg could have been this species.

Parasites - This host has the most parasite species of any of the *Caranx* (36), probably because it has been examined more often. Nine are genus specific, 2 almost genus specific, 5 family specific, 1 only found in jacks and scombrids, and 19 generalists with little host specificity (2 prefer jacks).

Bacteria
bacterial infection

Protozoa (protozoans)
Haemogregarina bigemina
Trypanosoma sp.

Digenea (flukes)
Brachyphallus parvus   *Bucephalopsis gracilescens*** [acc]
Bucephalopsis arcuata
Bucephalus varicus
Ectenurus lepidus
Parahemiurus merus
Stephanostomum ditrematis
Stephanostomum megacephalum
Stephanostomum sentum
Sterrhurus musculus
Tergestia laticollis

Monogenea (gillworms)
Allopyragraphorus incomperabilis   *Dioncus remorae* [acc]
Cemocotyle carangis
Cemocotyle noveboracensis
Cemocotylella elongata
Helixaxine winteri
Protomicrocotyle mirabilis

Cestoda (tapeworms)
*Callitetrarhynchus gracilis**
*Dasyrhynchus giganteus**
*Eutetrarhynchus lineatus**
*Nybelinia bisulcata**
tetraphyllid*

Nematoda (roundworms)
                    Cucullanus carangis [unc]

Acanthocephala (spiny-headed worms)
Gorgorhynchoides elongatus

Copepoda (copepods)
Caligus chorinemi   *Caligus praetextus* [?]
Caligus elongatus   *Anuretes heckelii* [acc]
Caligus longipedis   *Pandarus sinuatus* [acc]
Caligus robustus   *Tuxophorus caligodes* [?]
Caligus spinosus
Holobomolochus crevalleus
Lepeophtheirus edwardsi
Lernaeenicus longiventris
Lernanthropus giganteus

Isopoda (isopods)

Cymothoa oestrum
Excorollana tricornis
Livoneca ovalis

Pisces (fishes)

Echeneis naucrates

Neoplasms (tumors)

granulomas
nodular lesions

Condition

ciguatera

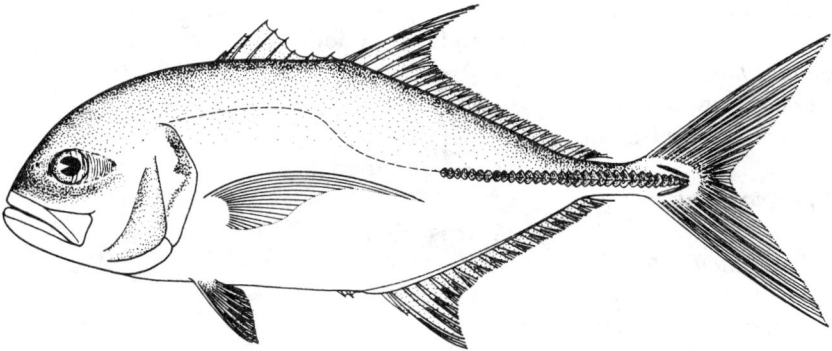

Caranx latus Agassiz - horse-eye jack

Name - It is also called "goggle-eye". A similar species, dusky jack, *Caranx sexfasciatus* Quoy and Gaimard, occurs in the Indo-Pacific and is responsible for earlier parasite records of horse-eye jack in those regions.

Diagnostic Characters - The first dorsal fin has a relatively short base, and the second dorsal and anal fins have relatively long bases. A row of large scutes on the caudal peduncle makes the tail rigid. The back of the jaw extends to the back margin of the eye. The chest is completely covered with scales.

Geographic Range - Atlantic ocean.

Food Habits - It eats fishes primarily but some shrimps and other invertebrates, including sea butterflies (pteropod mollusks).

Ecology - Inshore to oceanic.

Length - Maximum 80.0 cm, common to 50.0 cm FL.

Weight - Maximum 16.0 kg, common to 7.0 kg.

Parasites - Six are genus specific, 2 almost genus specific, 3 family specific, and 8 generalists with little host specificity (1 prefers jacks).

Digenea (flukes)

Alcicornis carangis
Brachyphallus parvus
Bucephalus varicus

Pseudopecoelus elongatus [fal]

Ectenurus lepidus
Parahemiurus merus
Stephanostomum ditrematis
Stephanostomum megacephalum
Stephanostomum sentum
Tergestia laticollis

Monogenea (gillworms)

Allopyragraphorus incomperabilis
Cemocotyle carangis
Cemocotyle noveboracensis
Helixaxine winteri
Protomicrocotyle mirabilis

Cestoda (tapeworms)

tetraphyllid*

Copepoda (copepods)

Caligus bonito
Lernaeenicus longiventus
Lernanthropus giganteus

Isopoda (isopods)

Cymothoa oestrum

Pisces (fishes)

Echeneis naucrates

Condition

ciguatera

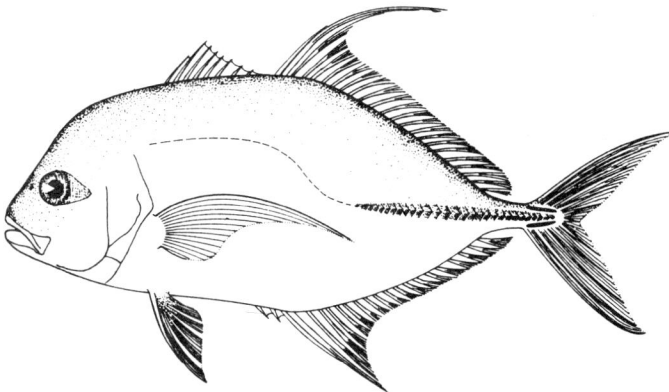

Caranx lugubris Poey - black jack

Diagnostic Characters - The first dorsal fin has a relatively short base, and the second dorsal and anal fins have relatively long bases. A row of large scutes on the caudal peduncle makes the tail rigid. The second dorsal and pectoral fins have long falcate tips.

Geographic Range - Worldwide in tropical, offshore waters. Around the West Indian islands and Bermuda, but well offshore in Florida, the Gulf of Mexico and Central and South America in the western Atlantic.
Food Habits - It eats fishes primarily.
Ecology - Inshore and offshore.
Length - Maximum 99.1 cm (89.0 cm FL), common to 70.0 cm FL.
Weight - Maximum 13.0 kg, common to 4.0 kg.
Parasites - We examined 4 specimens of this host and only found a fluke and a larval cestode. This fish may simply harbor few parasites, but it has obviously not been examined sufficiently to be certain.

Digenea (flukes)

Lecithochirium sp.

Bucephalus carangis [Pac]
Deretrema carangis [Pac]
Elytrophallus mexicanus [Pac]
Lecithochirium priacanthi [Pac]

Cestoda (tapeworms)

tetraphyllid*

Nematoda (roundworms)

Cucullanus pulcherrimus [unc]

Copepoda (copepods)

Caligus longipedis [Pac]
Lernaeolophus sultanus [acc]

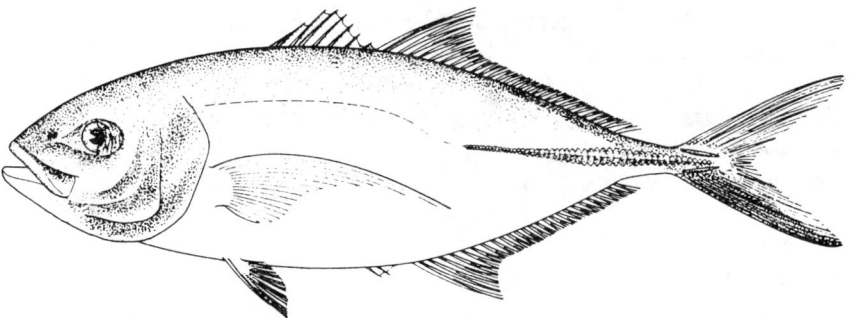

Caranx ruber (Bloch) - bar jack

Name - It is sometimes placed in genus *Carangoides*.
Diagnostic Characters - The first dorsal fin has a relatively short base, and the second dorsal and anal fins have relatively long bases. A row of large scutes on the caudal peduncle makes the tail rigid. A dark bar extends along the back and down the lower lobe of the caudal fin.
Geographic Range - Western Atlantic from New Jersey, USA, to Venezuela including the West Indies and Bermuda, not in the northern Gulf of Mexico. It is the most abundant jack of this genus in the West Indies.
Food Habits - It eats fishes primarily but some shrimps and other invertebrates.
Ecology - Inshore to oceanic.

Length - Maximum 50.0 cm, common to 40.0 cm FL. Larger fish have been reported in the Bahamas and Florida Keys, USA, but not confirmed.
Weight - Maximum 8.2 kg, common to 2.5 kg.
Parasites - Five are genus specific, 2 almost genus specific, 4 family specific, 1 only found in jacks and scombrids, and 7 generalists with little host specificity (1 prefers jacks).

Protozoa (protozoans)

Haemogregarina bigemina

Digenea (flukes)

Alcicornis carangis	*Lasiotocus truncatus* [fal]
Bucephalus varicus	*Opecoeloides brachyteleus* [fal]
Cetiotrema carangis	*Pinguitrema lerneri* [fal]
Ectenurus lepidus	*Prosorhynchus pacificus* [fal]
Pseudopecoeloides carangis	
Stephanostomum ditrematis	
Tergestia laticollis	

Monogenea (gillworms)

Allopyragraphorus incomperabilis
Cemocotyle carangis
Protomicrocotyle mirabilis

Cestoda (tapeworms)

*Callitetrarhynchus gracilis**
tetraphyllid*

Acanthocephala (spiny-headed worms)

Gorgorhynchus elongatus

Copepoda (copepods)

Caligus robustus	*Thysanote longimana* [acc]
Lernaeenicus longiventris	
Lernanthropus giganteus	

Isopoda (isopods)

Cymothoa oestrum
Gnathia sp.*

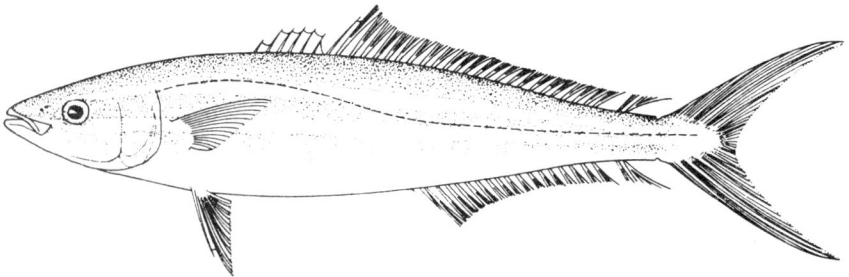

Elagatis bipinnulatus (Quoy and Gaimard) - rainbow runner
Name - It is also called "runner", "rainbow yellowtail" or *Seriola bipinnulata*.

Diagnostic Characters - The first dorsal fin has a relatively short base, and the second dorsal and anal fins have relatively long bases. A finlet with 2 rays follows both the second dorsal fin and the anal fin. It is a colorful fish. The sides are marked with 2 narrow, light blue or bluish-white stripes, with a broader, olive or yellowish stripe in between.

Geographic Range - Worldwide in tropical and subtropical waters.

Food Habits - It eats invertebrates and small fishes.

Ecology - Inshore to oceanic.

Length - Maximum 107.0 cm FL (possibly 120.0 cm), common to 80.0 cm FL.

Weight - Maximum 17.1 kg, common to 6.0 kg.

Parasites - This fish has surprisingly few parasites (12) for such a widespread and abundant host. It has probably not been adequately examined, especially in the Atlantic with only 3 species of parasites known.

Digenea (flukes)

Ectenurus lepidus

Stephanostomum ditrematis

Deretrema hawaiiense [Pac]

Stephanostomum hispidum [Pac]

Tergestia laticollis [Pac]

Monogenea (gillworms)

Pseudomicrocotyle elagatis [Pac]

Pseudomicrocotyle meservei [Ind]

Cestoda (tapeworms)

tetraphyllid*

Nematoda (roundworms)

Terranova sp. [Pac]

Copepoda (copepods)

Caligus confusus [IPac]

Caligus productus [Ind]

Shiinoa elagatus [IPac]

Pisces (fishes)

Isistius brasiliensis [Pac]

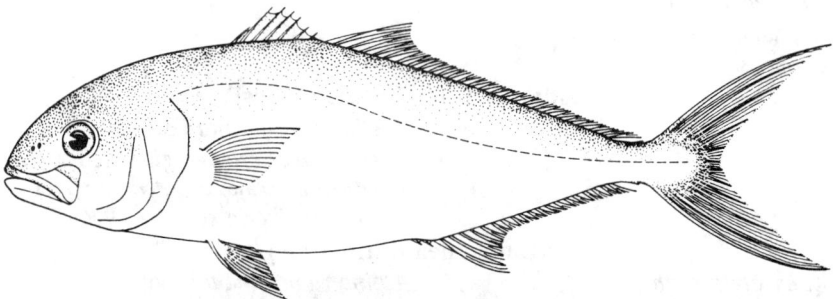

Seriola dumerili (Risso) - greater amberjack

Name - It has also been called *S. lalandi(i)*, *S. rhombica* Smith, *S. purpurescens* Temminck and Schlegel, *S. simplex* Ramsey and Ogilby, and *S. tapeinometapon* Bleeker.

Diagnostic Characters - The first dorsal fin has a relatively short base, and the second dorsal and anal fins have relatively long bases. The caudal peduncle has distinct grooves on the upper and lower surfaces. There are 11-19 gill rakers in fish longer than 20 cm FL.

Geographic Range - Worldwide.

Food Habits - It eats fishes and invertebrates.

Ecology - Inshore to oceanic.

Length - Maximum 183.0 cm (150.0 cm FL), common 70.0-110.0 cm FL.

Weight - Maximum 80.3 kg, common 9.0-36.0 kg.

Parasites - Twenty of the 36 reported occurred in the western Atlantic. Ten of these 20 were also found in western Atlantic *Caranx* spp. Greater amberjack had more host specific parasites (5), but fewer genus specific (2) and family specific (4) ones, than were found in *Caranx* spp. Three were possibly host specific, 1 almost genus specific, 1 only found in jacks and scombrids, and 20 generalists with little host specificity (2 prefer jacks). Amberjacks share more parasites with scombrids than with other genera of jacks, possibly due to their similar habitat and behavior (see Discussion).

Bacteria
Nocardia seriolae [Pac]
Pasturella pisicida [Pac]
Streptococcus sp. [Pac]
Vibrio anguillarum [Pac]

Protozoa (protozoans)
Haemogregarina bigemina

Digenea (flukes)
Brachyphallus parvus   *Paradeontacylix grandispinus* [Pac]
Bucephalus gorgon   *Paradeontacylix kampachi* [Pac]
Bucephalus varicus   *Prosorhynchus kahala* [Pac]
Ectenurus lepidus   *Stephanostomum hispidum* [Pac]
Lecithochirium microstomum   *Stephanostomum seriolae* [Pac]
Paradeontacylix sanguinicoloides
Parahemiurus merus
Stephanostomum ditrematis
Tormopsolus orientalis

Didymozoidea (tissue flukes)
Koellikeria bipartita [EAtl,Med]
Koellikeria micropterygis [Med]
Neomtanematobothrioides periorbitalis [Pac]
Patellokoellikeria seriolae [Pac]

Monogenea (gillworms)
Allencotyla mcintoshi   *Aspinatrium kahala* [Pac]
Neobenedenia girellae [Pac]

Cestoda (tapeworms)
Bothriocephalus sp.*   *Nybelinia puntatissima** [WAfr]
*Dasyrhynchus giganteus**

Pseudogrillotia zerbiae*
tetraphyllid*

Nematoda (roundworms)

Hysterothylacium sp.*   *Hysterothylacium seriolae* [Pac?]

Acanthocephala (spiny-headed worms)

Gorgorhynchus elongatus

Copepoda (copepods)

Brachiella thynni   *Brachiella elegans* [acc]
Lernaeenicus longiventris   *Caligus lalandei* [WAfr]
Lernanthropus giganteus   *Colobomatus lichiae* [Med]

Lernanthropus micropterygis [Med,RSea,Pac]
Nesippus costatus* [Pac,acc]

Condition

scombroid poisoning (rare)   ciguatera [Pac]

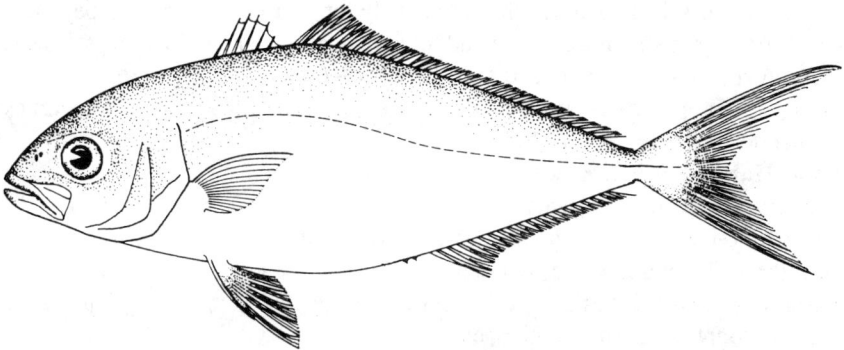

Seriola fasciata (Bloch) - lesser amberjack

Diagnostic Characters - The first dorsal fin has a relatively short base, and the second dorsal and anal fins have relatively long bases. The caudal peduncle has distinct grooves on the upper and lower surfaces. There are 23-26 gill rakers in fish longer than 20 cm FL.

Geographic Range - This fish has a peculiarly disjunct distribution in Puerto Rico to Antigua, Aruba to Curacao, Cuba, and the Atlantic Gulf coasts of the USA and Mexico, and Bermuda. It rarely occurs in the eastern Atlantic.

Food Habits - It eats squids and fishes.

Ecology - Inshore to offshore.

Length - Maximum 67.5 cm FL, common to 39.0 cm FL.

Weight - Maximum 4.6 kg, common to 2.0 kg.

Parasites - Its 2 parasites are also found in greater amberjack.

Digenea (flukes)

Tormopsolus orientalis

Cestoda (tapeworms)

tetraphyllid*

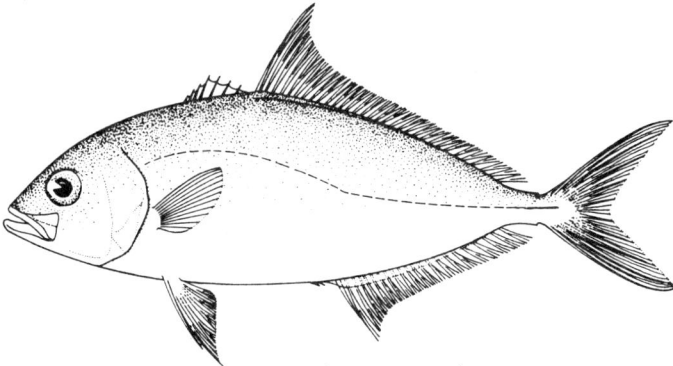

Seriola rivoliana Cuvier - almaco jack

Name - It is also called *S. bovinoculata* Smith, *S. colburni* Evermann and Clark, *S. falcata* Cuvier, and *S. songora* Smith.

Diagnostic Characters - The first dorsal fin has a relatively short base, and the second dorsal and anal fins have relatively long bases. The caudal peduncle has distinct grooves on the upper and lower surfaces. The second dorsal fin is more than 3 times the height of the first dorsal fin.

Geographic Range - Worldwide in tropical, subtropical and sometimes temperate waters.

Food Habits - It eats fishes.

Ecology - Inshore to oceanic.

Length - Maximum 97 cm FL; common to 55-80 cm FL.

Weight - Maximum 60 kg, common 2.5-3.4 kg.

Parasites - This fish has obviously not been adequately sampled. Its 3 parasites are also found in greater amberjack.

Cestoda (tapeworms)
tetraphyllid*

Acanthocephala (spiny-headed worms)
Gorgorhynchus elongatus

Copepoda (copepods)
Lernanthropus micropterygis [Pac]

Family Coryphaenidae - dolphins
Coryphaena equiselis Linnaeus - pompano dolphin

Name - *Coryphaena equisetis* Linnaeus is often used as a correction of the spelling of the original name.

Diagnostic Characters - This fish has a single dorsal fin that extends from behind the eye almost to the caudal fin. The convex anal fin extends from the anus to almost the caudal fin. The pectoral fin is 1/2 of the length of the head.

Geographic Range - Worldwide in tropical and subtropical offshore waters.

Food Habits - It eats a variety of planktonic and sargassum invertebrates and small fishes.

Ecology - Oceanic.

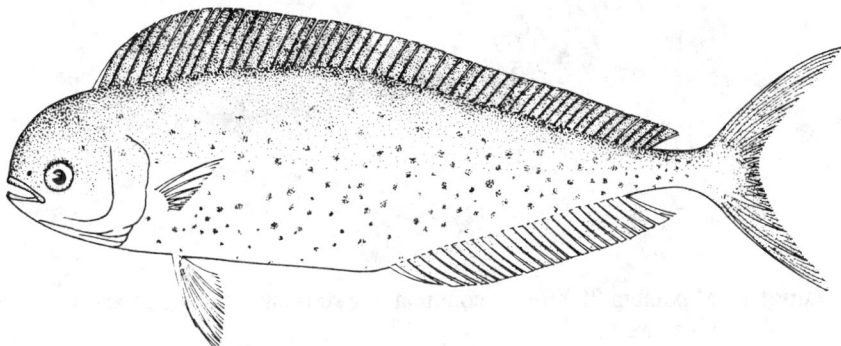

Length - Maximum 76.0 cm, common to 50.0 cm TL.
Weight - Maximum 10.0 kg, common to 7.0 kg.
Significance to Sport Fishing - This fish is usually too small to be taken on most gear used by big game fishermen.
Parasites - Almost all of the few parasites known from this host occur on dolphin.

Digenea (flukes)

Lecithochirium microstomum   Stephanostomum dentatum** [fal]
Dinurus tornatus

Cestoda (tapeworms)

Callitetrarhynchus gracilis*   Nybelinia alloiotica* [WAfr]
Tentacularia coryphaenae*   trypanorhyncha* [EAtl]
tetraphyllid*

Nematoda (roundworms)

Hysterothylacium pelagicum   Anisakis sp.* [Pac]
                                     Parascarophis galeata [unc]

Copepoda (copepods)

Caligus coryphaenae   Alebion carchariae [acc]
Lernaeenicus longiventris   Euryphorus nordmanni [Pac]
                                     Lernaeenicus hemiramphi [Pac?]

Pisces (fishes)

Isistius brasiliensis

Coryphaena hippurus Linnaeus - dolphin

Name - It is also called "common dolphin", "dolphinfish" (to distinguish marine mammals), "mahi mahi" (Hawaiian) and "dorado" (Spanish).
Diagnostic Characters - This fish has a single dorsal fin that extends from above the eye almost to the caudal fin. The concave anal fin extends from the anus to almost the caudal fin. The pectoral fin is more than 1/2 of the length of the head.
Geographic Range - Worldwide in tropical and warm-temperate waters.
Food Habits - It eats fishes predominantly, but some crustaceans and squids.
Ecology - Offshore and oceanic.

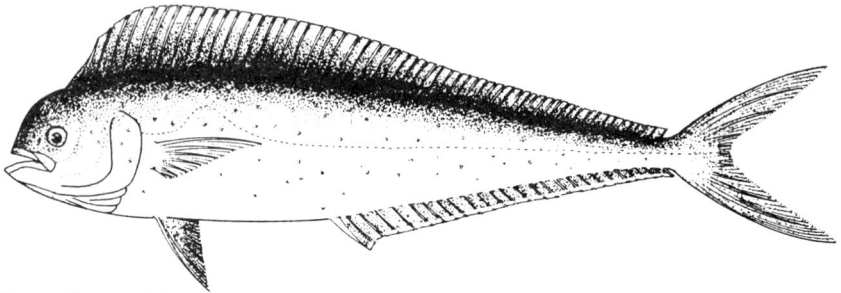

Length - Maximum 200.0 cm, common to 100.0 cm. Most fish are 1 year old, the largest are 4.
Weight - Maximum 39.5 kg, common to 10.0 kg.
Significance to Sport Fishing - This is the most commonly caught offshore big game fish in the western Atlantic and possibly worldwide.
Parasites - Thirty of the 44 parasites reported for this host have been found in the western Atlantic. Seven are host specific, and 37 generalists with little host specificity (3 prefer dolphin). Dolphin share a few parasites with scombrids, billfishes and jacks, but appear to be largely isolated from other families of big game fishes. Seventeen species of larval tapeworms must indicate this fish has a diverse diet of tapeworm intermediate hosts, because the average number among big game fishes is less than 5. Some of its host-specific parasites are only found in the Caribbean or parts of the Pacific, suggesting that this worldwide host may be separated into populations which have little communication.

Protozoa (protozoans)

Haemogregarina bigemina

Kudoa thyrsites [Pac]
Kudoa sp. [Pac]

Digenea (flukes)

Bathycotyle coryphaenae
Dinurus tornatus
Hirudinella ventricosa
Stephanostomum coryphaenae
Tetrochetus coryphaenae

Dinurus hippuri [Ind]
Helicometrina nimia [Pac,acc]

Didymozoidea (tissue flukes)

tissue fluke* [Ind]

Monogenea (gillworms)

Benedenia hendorffi [Pac]
Neothroacocotyle coryphaenae [Pac]
Tristomella laevis [acc]

Cestoda (tapeworms)

Callitetrarhynchus gracilis*
Hepatoxylon trichiuri*
Nybelinia bisulcata*
Otobothrium crenacolle*
Otobothrium dipsacum*

Bothriocephalus janikii* [Pac,unc]
Hepatoxylon stenocephala* [EAtl]
Plerocercoides lonchophorus* [EAlt,unc]
Pterobothrium acanthotruncatum* [Pac]
Tetrarhynchus papillosus* [unc]

*Pelichnibothrium speciosum**
*Pterobothrium heteracanthum**
*Rhinebothrium flexile**
*Tentacularia coryphaenae**
tetraphyllid*

*Tetrarhynchus** sp. [Pac,unc]

Nematoda (roundworms)

Hysterothylacium pelagicum

Anisakis sp. [Pac]
Ascaris sp.* [Pac,unc]
Contracaecum sp. [Pac,unc]
Hysterothylacium marinum [Pac]

Acanthocephala (spiny-headed worms)

Rhadinorhynchus pristis
*Serrasentis sagittifer**

Copepoda (copepods)

Brachiella thynni
Caligus bonito
Caligus coryphaenae
Caligus productus
Caligus quadratus
Caligus wilsoni
Charopinopsis quaternia
Euryphorus nordmanni
Lernaeenicus longiventris
Pennella sp.
Pseudocycnus appendiculatus

Caligus balistae [fal]
Caligus curtus [?]
Caligus patulus [acc?]
Lernaeenicus hemiramphi [IPac]
Lernaeenicus nodicornis [unc]
Pennella varians [Eur,unc]

Isopoda (isopods)

Anilocra physodes [Med]
Glossobius impressus [Pac?][1]
Glossobius auritus [Pac][1]
Nerocila excisa [Pac][1]

Pisces (fishes)

Isistius brasiliensis
Remora osteochir

Neoplasms (tumors)

muscle nodules
ovarian abscess

Condition

broken back
scombroid poisoning (frequent)

head deformities(aquaria) [Pac]

---

[1]Occurred in the stomach of this host, probably parasitized a flyingfish.

Family Sphyraenidae - barracudas

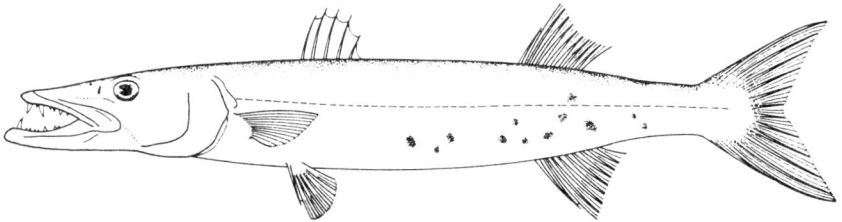

Sphyraena barracuda (Walbaum) - great barracuda

Name - It is also called "giant barracuda" and just "barracuda".

Diagnostic Characters - It is an elongate fish with relatively large, unequal vertical teeth in the upper and lower jaws. The 2 dorsal fins are separated by a distance greater than the combined lengths of their bases. The pelvic fin begins slightly ahead of the first dorsal fin. It usually has several to many inky-black spots of various size on the posterior, lower sides of the body.

Geographic Range - Tropical and subtropical western Atlantic from Massachusetts to southern Brazil. Also eastern Atlantic and western Indo-Pacific.

Food Habits - It eats fishes predominantly, sometimes squids or octopus, occasionally shrimps.

Ecology - Inshore to offshore, but not oceanic.

Length - Maximum 200.0 cm (rumored to over 300.0 cm), common to 130.0 cm. We have seen bigger fish than 2 m TL while snorkeling in the waters around Puerto Rico, but these fish were measuring us! It is rumored to be larger in the Caribbean (Where everything is bigger and better).

Weight - Maximum 38.6 kg, common to 23.0 kg.

Parasites - This is a well known, popular, worldwide fish that has been well examined, but does not have many parasites. Linton (1908) suggested that great barracuda in the Dry Tortugas, Florida, USA, and Bermuda had few parasites. This has been our observation as well. Eighteen of the 31 parasites reported for this host have been found in the western Atlantic. Nine are host specific, 1 possibly host specific, 5 genus specific, 2 possibly genus specific, and 14 generalists with little host specificity. These parasites suggest that this host is almost completely isolated from other fishes. The high numbers of host-specific parasites (9) indicate that this is a relatively old fish evoluntionarily, and well established in its niche. The relatively low number of non-specific parasites (12) suggests that it has unique food habits, behavior and habitats. Some of its host-specific parasites are only found in parts of the West Indies or the Pacific, indicating that this worldwide host may be separated into populations which have little communication. Eight species of tissue fluke occur in 5 other species of barracuda in the Mediterranean, Indian Ocean and Pacific. None of these tissue flukes has been found on great barracuda even though it occurs around the world. More than 600 great barracuda were eviscerated as part of another study in La Parguera, Puerto Rico, but no tissue fluke lesions were observed in any of these fish. The absence of tissue flukes may also suggest that this fish is isolated from other species of barracuda.

Protozoa (protozoans)

Haemogregarina bigemina
Trypanosoma sp.

Digenea (flukes)

Bucephalopsis longicirrus
Bucephalopsis longoviferus
Rhipidocotyle barracudae

Bucephalopsis attenuata [fal]
Bucephalus carangoides [Pac]
Bucephalus kaku [Pac]
Claribulla longula [fal]
Deretrema sphyraena [Pac]
Hirudinella ventricosa [WAfr,acc]
Lecithocladium excisum [fal]
Neolepedapedon belizense [fal]
Opegaster hawaiiensis [Pac]
Plerurus digitatus [Pac]
Plerurus sphyraenae [Pac]
Prosorhynchus longicollis [Pac]
Pseudopecoelus sphyraenae [Pac]
Rhipidocotyle longleyi [fal]
Stephanostomum ditrematis [fal]
Sterrhurus musculus [fal]
Sterrhurus sp. [Pac]
Uterovesticulurus sphyraenae [Pac]

Monogenea (gillworms)

Pseudochauhanea sphyraenae   *Vallisiopsis sphyraenae* [Pac]

Cestoda (tapeworms)

Otobothrium dipsacum*
Tentacularia sp.*
tetraphyllid*

Nematoda (roundworms)

Hysterothylacium marinum [Pac]
Raphidascaris anchoviellae [unc]

Copepoda (copepods)

Caligus isonyx
Caligus lobodes
Hatschekia amplicapa
Lernaeolophus striatus

Caligus productus [IPac]

Branchiura (fish lice)

Argulus bicolor

Isopoda (isopods)

Cymothoa oestrum
Excorollana tricornis
Gnathia sp.*
Rocinela signata

Alcirona krebsii [acc]

Pisces (fishes)

Echeneis naucrates
Naucrates ductor
Phtheirichthys lineatus
Remora brachyptera
Remora osteochir

Condition

ciguatera

Anomalies

vertebral

Family Scombridae, Tribe Scombrini - mackerels

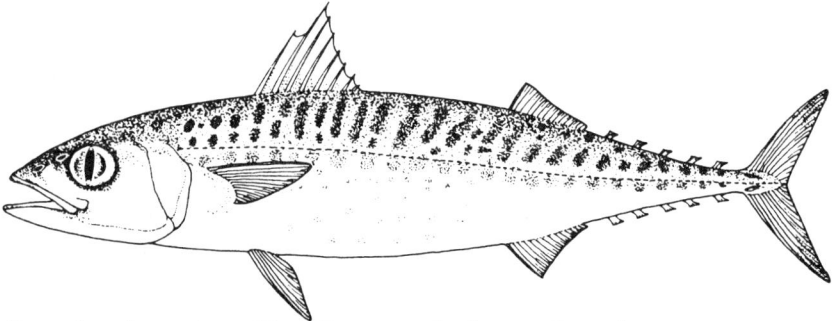

Scomber japonicus Houttuyn - chub mackerel

Name - It is sometimes called *Pneumatophorus colias* (Gmelin), *P. grex*, *P. japonicus*, and *S. colias* Gmelin.

Diagnostic Characters - All scombrids have small finlets behind the dorsal and anal fins. The eye has an adipose eye lid. The space between the 2 dorsal fins is approximately equal to the length of the base of the first dorsal fin. It has dusky blotches on the lower sides and belly. This fish has a gas bladder.

Geographic Range - Worldwide in temperate waters, including the Mediterranean. It is found from Nova Scotia, Canada, to Argentina, but is uncommon in the Gulf of Mexico and Caribbean, except in south Florida and the off the north central coast of South America. The western and eastern Atlantic populations appear to be relatively isolated. Parasites might be useful biological tags to measure the amount of contact.

Food Habits - It eats small pelagic fishes such as anchovies, herrings, and silversides; and pelagic invertebrates.

Ecology - Inshore and offshore.

Length - Maximum 50.0 cm, common to 30.0 cm FL.

Weight - Maximum 2.2 kg, common 0.2-0.3 kg.

Parasites - Only 23 of the 75 parasites reported in this worldwide host have been found from the western Atlantic, suggesting that it has not been adequately examined in our region. Four parasites are host specific, 12 possibly host specific; 7 genus specific, 1 possibly genus specific; 4 family specific; and 47 generalists with little host specificity (1 prefers chub mackerel).

Protozoa (protozoans)

Ceratomyxa inconstans [Pac]
Goussia pneumatophori [Pac]
Pseudoalatospora scombri [Pac]

Digenea (flukes)

Coitocaecum extremum
Hirudinella ventricosa
Lecithocladium excisum
Neolepidapedon retrusum
Opechona orientalis
Tergestia laticollis

Aphallus tubarius [Med]
Aponurus laguncula [acc]
Apocreadium misakiense [Pac]
Cephalolepidapedon saba [Pac]
Dinurus scombri [Pac]
Ectenurus lepidus [Med]
Lecithaster gibbosus [Pac]
Lecithochirium microstomum [Pac]
Lepocreadium ghanense [WAfr]
Lepocreadium scombri [Pac]
Neopechona olssoni [Pac]
Opechona acanthurus [EAtl]
Opechona bacillaris [EAtl,Med,Pac]
Opechona scombri [Pac]
Tergestia acanthocephala [Pac]

Didymozoidea (tissue flukes)

Didyymozoon sp.
Didymozoon longicolle
Nematobothrium scombri

Allonematobothrioides baueri [Pac]
Allonematobothrioides hirosaba [Pac]
Allonematobothrioides scombri [Pac]
Allopseudocolocyntrotrema sp. [SAfr]
Didymocystis wedli [Pac]
Nematobothrioides gomasabae [Pac]
Nematobothrioides pneumatophori [SAfr]
Nematobothrium filliforme [Pac,WAfr]
Nematobothrium robustum [Pac]

Monogenea (gillworms)

Grubea cochlear
Kuhnia scombercolias
Kuhnia scombri

Gastrocotyle japonica [Pac]
Kuhnia sprostonae [Eur,IPac]
Microncotrematoides inversum [Pac]
Pseudokuhnia minor [EAtl,IPac]

Cestoda (tapeworms)

Bothriocephalus sp.*
Callitetrarhynchus gracilis*
Rhinebothrium flexile*
Rhinebothrium sp.*
Tentacularia coryphaenae*
tetraphyllid*

Nybelinia sp.* [WAfr]
Nybelinia surmenicola* [Pac]
pseudophyllid* [Pac]
trypanorhynchid* [Pac,WAfr]

Nematoda (roundworms)

Anisakis sp.*

*Ascaris scombrorum** [Med,unc]
Capillaria sp. [Pac]
Contracaecum sp.* [Pac,WAfr]
Hysterothylacium aduncum [Pac]
Hysterothylacium fabri [Pac]
Hysterothylacium saba [Pac]
Oncophora melanocephala [WAfr]
Phocanema sp.* [Pac,WAfr]
Raphidascaris sp.* [Pac]

Acanthocephala (spiny-headed worms)

Rhadinorhynchus pristis

Bolbosoma sp. [Pac]
Rhadinorhynchus cadenati [WAfr]
Rhadinorhynchus japonicus [Pac]
Rhadinorhynchus lintoni [Eur]
Rhadinorhynchus seriolae [Pac]

Copepoda (copepods)

Caligus mutabilis
Caligus pelamydis
Clavellisa scombri

Advena saba [Pac]
Lepeophtheirus dissimulatus [Pac]
Lernaeocera branchialis [Pac?]
Pumiliopes capitulatus [Pac]
Sarcotretes inflexus [Eur]

Isopoda (isopods)

Meinertia gaudichaudii [Pac]

Pisces (fishes)

Petromyzon marinus

Neoplasms (tumors)

inflammatory fibrosis [Pac]

Condition

scombroid poisoning (frequent)

hermaphroditism [Pac]
hyperplasia (in captivity) [Pac]
malformed jaws (in captivity) [Pac]

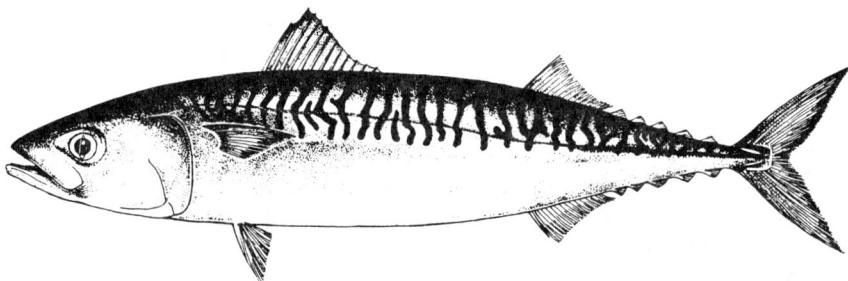

Scomber scombrus Linnaeus - Atlantic mackerel

Name - It is often called "mackerel" and "common mackerel".

Diagnostic Characters - All scombrids have small finlets behind the dorsal and anal fins. The eye has an adipose eye lid. The space between the 2 dorsal fins is greater than the length of the base of either fin. It lacks dusky blotches on the lower sides and belly. This fish does not have a gas bladder.

Geographic Range - Temperate and near-temperate waters of the North Atlantic Ocean, including the Mediterranean and Black Sea. In the western Atlantic, it is found from Cape Hatteras on the USA Atlantic coast into southern Canada. The western and eastern Atlantic populations do not appear to be isolated. Parasites might be useful biological tags to measure the amount of contact.

Food Habits - It eats small, planktonic animals (copepods, *Calanus* sp., other invertebrates including squids, fish eggs and fry).

Ecology - Offshore. This fish swims constantly as it lacks a swim bladder (air bladder) for buoyancy.

Length - Maximum 56.0 cm (50.0 cm FL), common to 30.0 cm FL.

Weight - Maximum 1.8 kg, common to 0.5 kg

Parasites - Forty-six parasites have been reported from this host found throughout the Atlantic, however, only 20 have been found in the western Atlantic. Two parasites are host specific, 4 possibly host specific, 6 genus specific, and 1 family specific; and 33 generalists with little host specificity.

Bacteria

acid-fast bacilli [Eur]
Tuberculosis [Eur]
Mycobacterium sp. [Eur]

Protozoa (protozoans)

Goussia clupearum	*Ceratomyxa parva* [Eur,MBS]
Haematractidium scombri	*Eimeria* sp. [Eur]
Kudoa histolytica	*Haemogregarina bigemina* [?]

Fungi (fungus)

Ichthyophonus hoferi

Digenea (flukes)

*Bucephalopsis arcuata**	*Acanthocolpoides guevarai* [WAfr]
Lecithocladium excisum	*Brachyphallus crenatus* [fal]
	Hemiurus appendiculatus [acc]
	Lecithaster confusus [fal]
	Lecithaster gibbosus [Eur]
	Lecithochirium caudiporum [BSea]
	Opechona bacillaris [Eur,Med]
	Opechona orientalis [Med]
	Opecoeloides vitellosus [?]
	Podocotyle simplex [acc]
	Wardula capitellata [Med]

Didymozoidea (tissue flukes)

Atalastrophion sp.	*Halvorsenius exilis* [Eur]
	Nematobothrium faciale [Eur]

Nematobothrium scombri [Eur,MBS]

Paranematobothrium triplovitellatum [SAfr?]

Monogenea (gillworms)

Grubea cochlear   *Kuhnia sprostonae* [Eur,IPac]

Kuhnia scombri   *Pseudokuhnia minor* [EAtl,Med]

Cestoda (tapeworms)

Bothriocephalus sp.*   *Echeneibothrium* sp.* [Eur]

*Bothriocephalus scorpii**   *Grillotia angeli* [Eur,Med]

*Callitetrarhynchus gracilis**   *Rhynchobothrium longispine** [unc]

*Grillotia erinaceus**   *Tetrabothriorhynchus scombri** [unc]

*Lacistorhynchus bulbifer**   *Tetrarhynchobothrium* sp.* [Eur]

*Nybelinia bisulcata**

tetraphyllid*

Nematoda (roundworms)

Hysterothylacium aduncum   *Anisakis simplex** [Eur}

                                     ascarid sp.* [Eur]

                                     *Ascaris papilligera** [Med,unc]

                                     *Contracaecum pedum** [Eur,unc]

                                     *Contracaecum scombricum** [unc]

                                     Cystoopsis scomber [BSea,unc]

                                     Goezia sp.* [Eur]

                                     *Hysterothylacium aduncum** [Eur]

                                     Oncophora melanocephala [Eur]

Acanthocephala (spiny-headed worms)

Rhadinorhynchus pristis   *Bolbosoma vasculosum* [Eur]

Copepoda (copepods)

Caligus elongatus   *Advena paradoxa* [Eur,Med]

Caligus pelamydis   *Caligus diaphanus* [Eur,Med]

                                     Clavellisa scombri [Eur,Med]

                                     Lepeophtheirus pectoralis [Eur]

Pisces (fishes)

Petromyzon marinus

Neoplasms (tumors)

gill nodules   granuloma [Eur]

hemangioma   iridoporoma [Eur]

hemosiderosis

pineal chondroma

Condition

foreign object embeded   intestinal lesion [Eur]

scombroid poisoning (frequent)

Anomalies

embryo-pollution (cytological)

embryo-pollution (chromosomal)

Tribe Sardini - bonitos

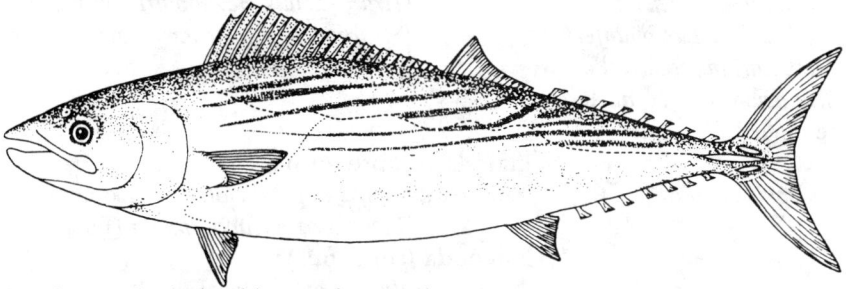

Sarda sarda (Bloch) - Atlantic bonito

Name - This fish can only be canned as "bonito", not "tuna" in the USA ["tuna (bonito)" in Canada]. It has been called "common bonito" and *Pelamys sarda*.

Diagnostic Characters - All scombrids have small finlets behind the dorsal and anal fins. The first dorsal fin is much longer than the second dorsal. It has 5-11 dark, slightly oblique stripes running forward and downward on the back and upper sides.

Geographic Range - Tropical and temperate coasts of the Atlantic Ocean, including the north central coast of South America, north coast of Yucatan, Mexico, northern Gulf of Mexico, southeast coast of South America, Atlantic coast of the USA, the Mediterranean and Black Sea.

Food Habits - It eats small fishes, especially anchovies, herrings, cods, and scombrids.

Ecology - Inshore and offshore.

Length - Maximum 91.4 cm FL, common to 50.0 cm FL.

Weight - Maximum 8.3 kg, common to 2.0 kg.

Parasites - This host has been well examined, but harbors only 27 parasite species, 20 of which have been found from the western Atlantic. Four are host specific, 1 almost tribe specific, 3 family specific, 1 shares this host and little tunny, and 18 generalists with little host specificity (1 prefers this host). These parasites do not suggest that bonitos form a cohesive tribe (see Discussion).

Digenea (flukes)

Bucephalopsis arcuata	*Aponurus tschugunowi* [BSea]
Ectenurus lepidus	*Lecithochirium caudiporum* [BSea]
Hirudinella ventricosa	*Opecoelides vitellosus* [?]
Lecithochirium texanum	
Rhipidocotyle capitata	

Didymozoidea (tissue flukes)

Atalostrophion sardae
Nematobothrium pelamydis

Monogenea (gillworms)

Hexostoma lintoni	*Cabellerocotyla pelamydis* [Med]
	Hexostoma euthynni [acc]
	Hexostoma thynni [Med]

Cestoda (tapeworms)

Bothriocephalus sp.*   Callitetrarhynchus gracilis* [WAfr]
Grillotia erinaceus*   Tetrarhynchus megabothrium* [unc]
Lacistorhynchus bulbifer*   Tetrarhynchus scomber-pelamys* [unc]
Otobothrium crenacolle*
Tentacularia coryphaenae*
tetraphyllid*

Nematoda (roundworms)

Anisakis simplex*   Ascaris appendiculata* [Med,unc]
                                        Oncophora melanocephala [Eur]

Copepoda (copepods)

Caligus bonito   Alebion glaber [acc]
Caligus mutabilis   Alebion gracilis [acc]
Caligus pelamydis
Ceratacolax euthynni
Pseudocycnus appendiculatus

Isopoda (isopods)
Livoneca sp. [WAfr]

Neoplasms (tumors)

lipoma

Condition

scombroid poisoning (rare)

Tribe Katsuwonidae - little tunas

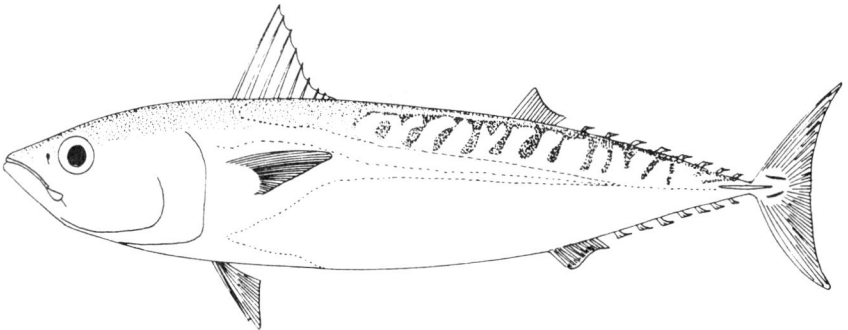

Auxis rochei (Risso) - bullet tuna

Name - Robins et al. (1991) suggested that the name "bullet mackerel" has been used incorrectly too long to change, but the "bullet" part is a recent name [1967]. This fish cannot be legally canned as "tuna" in the USA. It has also been called A. maru Kishinouye, and A. thynnoides Bleeker.

Diagnostic Characters - All scombrids have small finlets behind the dorsal and anal fins. The first and second dorsal fins are separated by a length approximately equal to the base of the first dorsal. There is a complicated pattern of nearly vertical, dark bars on the posterior back that does not extend forward to the posterior end of the first dorsal or pectoral fins.

Geographic Range - Worldwide in the tropics and subtropics, including the Mediterranean.

Food Habits - It eats small fishes, especially anchovies and herrings; crustaceans, especially megalops crab larvae and larval mantis shrimps; and squids.

Ecology - Offshore and oceanic. It comes inshore around Caribbean islands.

Length - Maximum 60.0 cm FL, common to 15.0-35.0 cm FL.

Weight - Maximum 3.6 kg, common 0.5-1.4 kg.

Parasites - Such a widespread host should support more than 17 parasite species, and certainly more than the 7 found in the western Atlantic. The 56 parasites known from the very similar frigate tuna suggest that bullet tuna have not been adequately examined. One parasite is genus specific, 1 tribe specific, 1 almost tribe specific, 1 family specific, 1 shares this host with other little tunas and Atlantic bonito, and 1 this host with other little tunas and tunas, and 11 generalists with little host specificity.

Digenea (flukes)

Rhipidocotyle capitata
Tergestia laticollis

Didymozoidea (tissue flukes)

Didymozoon sp.   *Didymozoon auxis* [Med]

Cestoda (tapeworms)

Callitetrarhynchus gracilis*   *Tetrarhynchus scomber-rocheri** [unc]
tetraphyllid*

Nematoda (roundworms)

Ascaris papilligera* [Med,unc]
Oncophora melanocephala [Eur]

Acanthocephala (spiny-headed worms)

Allorhadinorhynchus sp. [Pac]
Bolbosoma sp. [Pac]
Rhadinorhynchus sp. [Pac]

Copepoda (copepods)

Unicolax collateralis   *Caligus asymmetricus* [IPac]
Unicolax mycterobius   *Caligus coryphaenae* [Pac]
Caligus macarovi [Pac]
Caligus pelamydis [Pac]
Caligus productus [Pac]

Condition

scombroid poisoning (rare)   mass mortality

Auxis thazard (Lacepède) - frigate tuna

Name - The name "frigate mackerel" has been used in the English fisheries literature since 1884, but this change is necessary, if controversial. This fish cannot be canned as "tuna" in the USA. It has also been called *A. hira* Kishinouye, and *A. tapeinosoma* Bleeker.

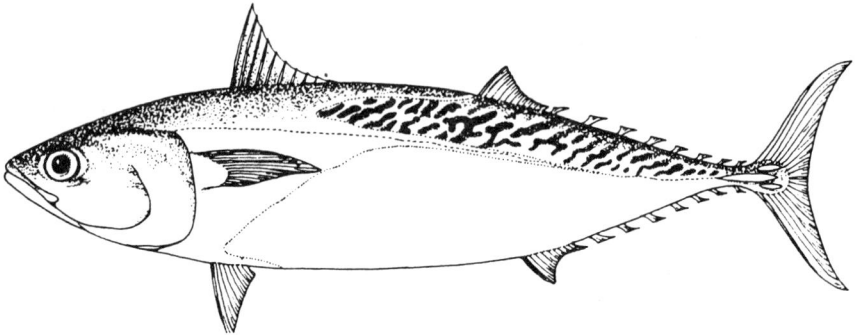

Diagnostic Characters - All scombrids have small finlets behind the dorsal and anal fins. The first and second dorsal fins are separated by a length approximately equal to the base of the first dorsal. There is a complicated pattern of oblique, nearly horizonal, stripes on the posterior back that extends forward to the posterior end of the first dorsal and pectoral fins.

Geographic Range - Possibly worldwide in the tropics and subtropics, but not in the Mediterranean. It occurs in abundance off the northern coast of South America. This fish was confused with bullet tuna in the western Atlantic until recently, thus its distribution has not been determined.

Food Habits - It eats small fishes, especially anchovies and herrings; crustaceans, especially megalops crab larvae and larval mantis shrimps; and squids.

Ecology - Offshore and oceanic.

Length - Maximum 58.0 cm FL, common to 25.0-40.0 cm FL.

Weight - Maximum 4.5 kg, common to 0.5-1.4 kg.

Parasites - With 58 parasite species recorded, this host appears to have been well examined, except in the western Atlantic where only 9 have been found. Six parasites are host specific, 9 possibly host specific, 1 genus specific, 6 tribe specific, 2 almost tribe specific, 3 family specific, 1 occurs on this host and Spanish mackerels, 1 on bonitos and little tunas, and 2 on little tunas and tunas, and 27 generalists with little host specificity.

Protozoa (protozoans)

Haemogregarina bigemina

Digenea (flukes)

Brachyphallus parvus

*Lecithocladium excisum***

Tergestia laticollis

Bucephalopsis gracilescens [Med]

Dinurus euthynni [Pac]

Dinurus scombri [Pac]

Hirudinella ventricosa [Pac]

Lecithochirium texanum [Pac]

Lecithochirium keokea [Pac]

Lecithochirium microstomum [Pac]

Lobatozoum sp. [Pac]

Phyllodistomum lancea [Pac]

Plerurus carangis [Pac]
Plerurus kawakawa [Pac]
Prosorhynchus sp. [Pac]
Rhipidocotyle capitata [Pac]
*Rhipidocotyle capitata** [Pac]
Rhipidocotyle pentagonum [Pac]
Tergestia acanthogobii [Pac]

Didymozoidea (tissue flukes)

Annulocystis auxis [Pac]
Colocyntotrema auxis [Pac]
Didymocystis wedli [Ind]
Didymozoon auxis [Pac]
Didymosphaera mirabilis [Pac]
Lobatozoum multisacculatum [Pac]
Metanematobothrium bivitellatum [Pac]
Oesophagocystis sp. [Pac]
Opepherotrema planum [Pac]
Phacelotrema claviforme [Pac]
Pseudocolocyntotrema yaito [Pac]
Sicuotrema auxia [Pac]

Monogenea (gillworms)

Allopseudaxine macrova [Pac]
Caballerocotyla manteri [Pac]
Hexostoma auxisi [Med]
Hexostoma keokeo [Pac]
Hexostoma thynni [Med]
Metapseudaxine ventrosicula [Pac]
Pseudaxine sp. [Pac]
Pseudaxine triangula [Pac]

Cestoda (tapeworms)

*Callitetrarhynchus gracilis**   *Tetrarhynchus scomber-rocheri** [unc]
tetraphyllid*

Nematoda (roundworms)

Anisakis sp.* [Pac]
Contracaecum sp.* [Pac]
Ctenascarophis gastricus [Pac]
Oncophora melanocephala [Med]
Prospinitectus mollis [Pac]

Acanthocephala (spiny-headed worms)

Rhadinorhynchus pristis   *Filosoma* sp. [RSea]
Neorhadinorhynchus nudus [Pac]
Rhadinorhynchoides sp. [Pac]
Rhadinorhynchus sp. [Pac]

Copepoda (copepods)

Unicolax collateralis   *Caligus asymmetricus* [IPac]
Unicolax mycterobius   *Caligus biseriodentatus* [Ind]

Caligus coryphaenae [Pac]
Caligus macarovi [Pac]
Caligus pelamydis [Pac]
Caligus productus [Pac]
Condition

scombroid poisoning (rare)   mass mortality [Pac]

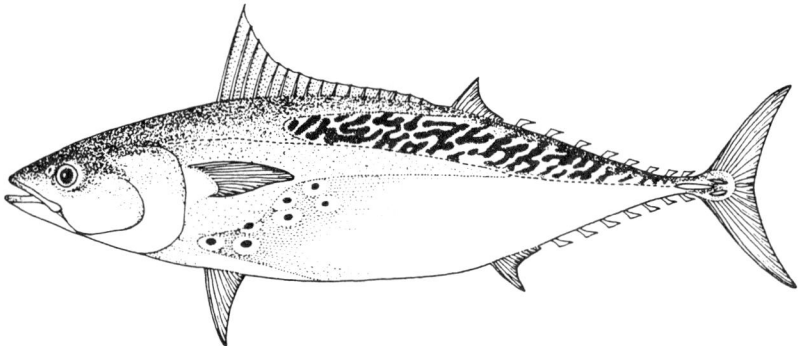

Euthynnus alletteratus (Rafinesque) - little tunny

Name - It is also called "Atlantic little tunny", "little tuna", *Gymnosarda alleterata* and *Thynnus thunnina*.

Diagnostic Characters - All scombrids have small finlets behind the dorsal and anal fins. The first dorsal fin is much longer than the second dorsal. There is a complicated pattern of stripes on the posterior back that does not extend forward beyond the middle of the first dorsal fin. It usually has a few dark spots on the body between the pectoral and pelvic fins.

Geographic Range - Atlantic Ocean from New England, USA, to Brazil; eastern Atlantic and Mediterranean; and sporadically in the Black Sea. All coastal areas in the western Atlantic except the Gulf coast of Mexico.

Food Habits - It eats small pelagic fishes such as anchovies and herrings, fish larvae, squids and crustaceans.

Ecology - Inshore and offshore.

Length - Maximum 100.0 cm FL, common to 75.0 cm FL.

Weight - Maximum 16.0 kg, common to 6.0 kg.

Parasites - This host is abundant and has apparently been rather well examined, but only supports 34 species of parasites, 24 from the western Atlantic. Three are host specific, 2 possibly host specific, 1 genus specific, 2 tribe specific, 1 almost tribe specific, 2 family specific, 1 occurs on this host and Atlantic bonito, 1 on bonitos and little tunas, and 1 on little tunas and tunas, and 20 generalists with little host specificity. This fish has been noted to be the most heavily parasitized tuna in the eastern Atlantic and Mediterranean.

Udonellidea (copepod worms)

Udonella caligorum

Digenea (flukes)

Brachyphallus parvus
Dinurus scombri
Hirudinella ventricosa
Lecithochirium texanum
Rhipidocotyle capitata
Tergestia laticollis

Lecithochirium acutum [Eur]
Lecithochirium monticellii [?]
Sterrhurus sp. [EAlt]
Syncoelium katuwo [WAfr]

Didymozoidea (tissue flukes)

Didymocystis thynni

Allopseudocolocyntotrema alioshkini [Eur]
Oesophagocystis lydiae [Eur]
tissue fluke** [WAfr]

Monogenea (gillworms)

Caballerocotyla manteri
Hexostoma euthynni

Hexostoma thunninae [EAtl]
Tristomella onchidiocotyle [?]

Cestoda (tapeworms)

Lacistorhynchus bulbifer*
Otobothrium crenacolle*
Tentacularia coryphaenae*
tetraphyllid*

Callitetrarhynchus gracilis* [EAlt]
Otobothrium sp.* [EAlt]

Acanthocephala (spiny-headed worms)

Rhadinorhynchus pristis

Copepoda (copepods)

Caligus bonito
Caligus coryphaenae
Caligus pelamydis
Caligus productus
Ceratacolax euthynni
Pseudocycnus appendiculatus
Unicolax anonymous
Unicolax collateralis
Unicolax mycterobius

Isopoda (isopods)

Nerocila orbignyi [EAtl]

Neoplasms (tumors)

lipomas

Condition

scombroid poisoning (rare)

Katsuwonus pelamis (Linnaeus) - skipjack tuna

Name - The Japanese soup-stock product, "dried bonito" flakes or katsuobushi, is boiled, boned, smoke-dried, molded and finally shaven-flaked skipjack tuna. In Japan, what we call "little tunas" are called "bonitos". It has also been called "bonito", "ocean bonito","skipjack", "striped tuna", "watermelon tuna"; also *Euthynnus pelamis* (Linnaeus); *E. pelamys*; *Gymnosarda pelamys*; *K. vagans*; and *Thynnus pelamys*.

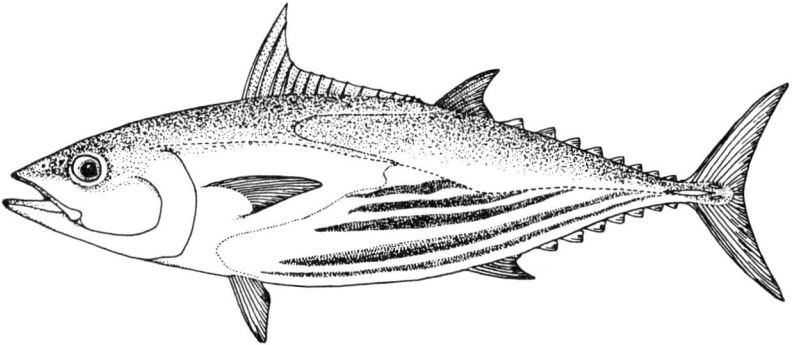

Diagnostic Characters - All scombrids have small finlets behind the dorsal and anal fins. The first dorsal fin is much longer than the second dorsal. It has 4-6 conspicuous longitudinal dark bands on the lower sides and belly.
Geographic Range - Worldwide, cosmopolitan in warm waters, but not in the Black Sea.
Food Habits - It eats fishes, squids, octopus, and crustaceans.
Ecology - Offshore and oceanic.
Length - Maximum 108.0 cm FL, common to 80.0 cm FL.
Weight - Maximum 34.5 kg, common 1.4-3.6 kg.
Commercial Importance - Most "tuna" canned comes from this fish. It is also an important fresh fish over much of the globe.
Parasites - This host appears to have been well examined with 75 parasite species recorded, except in the western Atlantic, where only 19 have been found. Eight parasites are host specific, 18 possibly host specific, 5 family specific, 5 occur on this host and bluefin tuna, 4 on tunas, 2 on bluefin tuna and yellowtail, 1 on a Pacific little tuna and a yellowtail, 1 almost genus specific but to mackerels (*Scomber*) not this host, and 3 on little tunas and tunas, and 29 are generalists with little host specificity. Its parasites suggest that it belongs in the tuna instead of the little tuna tribe (see Discussion).

Digenea (flukes)

Hirudinella ventricosa   *Dinurus euthynni* [Pac]
Tergestia laticollis   *Lecithochirium microstomum* [Pac]
                               Syncoelium filiferum [Pac]
                               Syncoelium katuwo [Pac]

Didymozoidea (tissue flukes)

Adenodidymocystis intestinalis [Pac]
Annulocystis katsuwoni [Pac]
Coeliodidymocystis abdominalis [Pac]
Coeliodidymocystis kamegaii [IPac]
Didymocylindrus filiformis [Pac]
Didymocylindrus simplex [Pac]
Didymocystis abdominalis [Pac]
Didymocystis bilobata [Pac]

Didymocystis ovata [Pac]
Didymocystis philobranchia [Ind]
Didymocystis reniformis [Pac]
Didymocystis rotunditestis [Ind]
Didymocystis soleiformis [Pac]
Didymocystis submentalis [Pac]
Didymocystis thynni [Eur]
Didymocystis wedli [Pac]
Didymocystoides intestinomuscularis [Pac]
Didymocystoides pinnicola [Pac]
Didymocystoides submentalis [Pac]
Didymoproblema fusiforme [Pac]
Didymozoon auxis [Eur?]
Didymozoon filicolle [Pac]
Didymozoon longicolle [Pac]
Didymozoon minus [Pac]
Koellikeria globosa [Pac]
Koellikeria orientalis [Pac]
Koellikeria reniformis [Pac]
Lagenocystis katsuwoni [Pac]
Lobatozoum multisacculatum [Pac]
Nematobothrium scombri [Pac]
Neodiplotrema pelamydis [Pac]
Oesophagocystis dissimilis [Pac]
Phacelotrema claviforme [Ind]

Monogenea (gillworms)

Allopseudaxine katsuwonis

Allopseudaxine vagans [Pac]
Caballerocotyla katsuwoni [Pac]
Hexostoma grossum [Pac]
Pricea minimae [Ind?]
Tristomella interrupta [Med]
Tristomella laevis [acc]
Tristomella lintoni [unc]
Tristomella nozawae [Eur,Pac]

Cestoda (tapeworms)

*Nybelinia lingualis**
*Tentacularia coryphaenae**
tetraphyllid*

*Callitetrarhynchus gracilis** [Pac]
*Hepatoxylon trichiuri** [Eur]
Pelichnibothrium sp.* [Pac]
*Pseudogrillotia basipuncata** [Pac]
Rhyncobothrium sp.* [Pac,unc]
Tentacularia sp.* [Pac]

Nematoda (roundworms)

*Anisakis simplex**
Ctenascarophis lesteri
Philometra sp.
Prospinitectus exiguus

Acanthocheilus sp. [Pac]
Anisakis sp. [Pac]
Contracaecum sp. [Pac]
Philometroides sp. [Pac]

spiruroids   *Terranova* sp.* [Pac]
Acanthocephala (spiny-headed worms)
Rhadinorhynchus pristis   *Rhadinorhynchus trachuri* [Pac?]
                                        Raorhynchus meyeri [Ind]
                                        Raorhynchus terebra [Ind]
Copepoda (copepods)
Caligus bonito   *Caligus asymmetricus* [Pac]
Caligus coryphaenae   *Caligus quadratus* [Pac]
Caligus mutabilis   *Lepeophtheirus branchialis* [Ind,unc]
Caligus productus   *Lepeophtheirus salmonis* [Pac?]
Lepeophtheirus bermudensis   *Unicolax reductus* [Pac]
Lepeophtheirus dissimulatus
Pseudocycnus appendiculatus
Pisces (fishes)
                                        Isistius brasiliensis [Pac]
Condition
scombroid poisoning (frequent)   hermaphroditism [IPac]
Anomalies
                                        lacking body stripes [Pac]

Tribe Thunnini - tunas

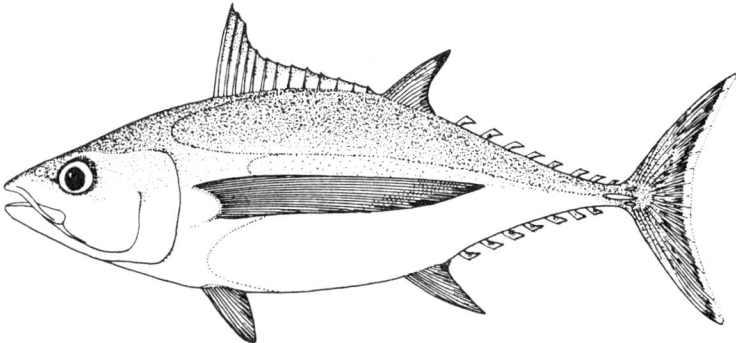

Thunnus alalunga (Bonnaterre) - albacore

Name - Only this fish can be called "white meat tuna". Other tunas, except bluefin, are called "light tuna". It is sometimes called "longfin tuna", "long-finned tunny", *Germo alalunga* (Bonnaterre), *Orcyncnus alalunga*, *T. germo* (Lacepede), and *Thynnus alalunga*.

Diagnostic Characters - All scombrids have small finlets behind the dorsal and anal fins. The pectoral fins are long, extending beyond the light yellow second dorsal and anal fins. The posterior margin of the caudal fin is white, and the anal finlets are dark. The ventral surface of the liver is striated.

Geographic Range - Worldwide in tropical to temperate waters and in all seas, including the Mediterranean. This fish is common in the Caribbean, but not in the Gulf of Mexico.

Food Habits - It eats a variety of fishes, squids and crustaceans.
Ecology - Offshore and oceanic.
Length - Maximum 127.0 cm FL, common to 100.0 cm FL.
Weight - Maximum 40.0 kg, common to 25.0 kg.
Parasites - With 46 parasite species recorded, this host has been at least moderately examined, except in the western Atlantic, where only 13 of these parasites have been found. Indicative of their neglect are the 4 gillworms and 15 tissue flukes not yet found in the western Atlantic. None of these parasites are known to be host specific, but 11 are possibly host specific, 8 genus specific (which is the same as tribe specific in this case), 4 family specific, 1 occurs on tunas and little tunas, 1 on tunas and amberjacks, 3 on tunas and skipjack tuna, and 18 generalists with little host specificity.

Protozoa (protozoans)
Goussia auxidis [Pac]
Hexacapsula neothunni [Pac]

Digenea (flukes)
Hirudinella ventricosa   *Syncoelium filiferum* [Pac]

Didymozoidea (tissue flukes)
Didymocystis lanceolata [EAtl]
Didymocystis macrorchis [EAtl]
Didymocystis philobranchia [Pac]
Didymocystis philobranchiarca [Ind]
Didymocystis rotunditestis [Ind]
Didymocystis thynni [Med]
Didymocystis wedli [Med]
Didymocystoides alaongae [Pac]
Didymocystoides buccalis [Pac]
Didymocystoides opercularis [Pac]
Didymocystoides superpalati [Ind]
Didymonaja branchialis [Pac]
Koellikeria bipartita [EAtl]
Koellikerioides orientalis [EAtl,Pac]
Metanematobothrium guernei [EAlt,IPac]
Nematobothrium latum [EAtl]
Platocystis alalongae [EAlt,Pac]
Univitellodidymocystis lingualis [Ind]

Monogenea (gillworms)
Areotestis sibi [Pac]
Tristomella nozawae [Pac]
Capsala thynni [WAfr,unc]
Hexostoma sibi [Pac]

Cestoda (tapeworms)
*Tentacularia coryphaenae**   *Hepatoxylon trichiuri** [Med,Pac]
tetraphyllid*   *Pseudobothrium grimaldii* [EAlt,unc]
*Sphyriocephalus tergestinus** [EAlt]

Nematoda (nematodes)
Hysterothylacium cornutum   Anisakis sp.* [Pac]
Oncophora melanocephala   Contracaecum sp.* [Pac]
                                   Hysterothylacium aduncum* [Eur]

Acanthocephala (spiny-headed worms)
Rhadinorhynchus pristis   Bolbosoma vasculosum [EAlt]
                                   Gorgorhynchus sp. [Pac]

Copepoda (copepods)
Brachiella thynni   Caligus alalongae [EAlt,Ind]
Caligus coryphaenae   Caligus chorinemi [acc]
Caligus productus   Euryphorus nordmanni [Pac]
Euryphorus brachypterus   Lernanthropus hiatus [?]
Pennella filosa
Pseudocycnus appendiculatus

Isopoda (isopods)
Rocinella signata

Pisces (fishes)
Isistius brasiliensis   Isistius plutodus [Pac]
Naucrates ductor

Neoplasms (tumors)
                                   osteoma [Pac]

Condition
stomach ulcer   mesentary adhesions [SAfr]
scombroid poisoning (rare)

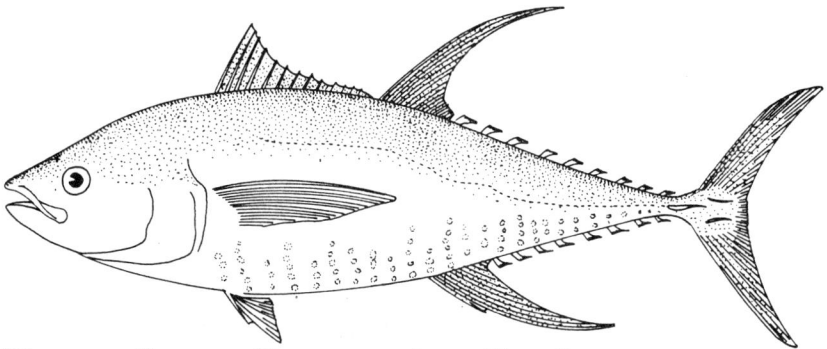

Thunnus albacares (Bonnaterre) - yellowfin tuna

Name - It is sometimes called "Allison tuna", *Neothunnus albacora* (Lowe), *N. macropterus* (Temminck and Schlegel), *N. albacores*, *T. argentivittatus* (Cuvier), *T. macropterus*, *Thynnus albacora*, and *T. macropterus*.

Diagnostic Characters - All scombrids have small finlets behind the dorsal and anal fins. Large fish have a relatively long second dorsal and anal fin, which are more than 1/5 of the FL. The pectoral fins are moderately long, reaching beyond the notch between the dorsal fins. The ventral surface of the liver is not striated.

Geographic Range - Worldwide in the tropics and subtropics.

Food Habits - It eats a variety of fishes, squids and crustaceans.

Ecology - Offshore and oceanic.

Length - Maximum more than 200.0 cm FL, common to 150.0 cm FL.

Weight - Maximum 176.4 kg, common 10.0-46.0 kg.

Commercial Importance - Most canned "tuna" is skipjack tuna, but some comes from this fish.

Parasites - This host appears to have been well examined and supports 85 species of parasites, but only 32 have been found in the western Atlantic. Three of these parasites are host specific; 8 possibly host specific; 18 genus specific (which is the same as tribe specific in this case); 6 family specific; and 1 each occur on tunas and little tunas, jacks and scombrids, tunas and little tunas, and tunas and Atlantic bonito; 1 almost host specific to wahoo; 3 on tunas and skipjack tuna, and 42 generalists with little host specificity. Thirteen species of larval tapeworms must indicate that this fish has a diverse diet of tapeworm intermediate hosts, because the average number among big game fishes is less than 5.

Protozoa (protozoans)
Hexacapsula neothunni [Pac]

Udonellidea (copepod worms)
Udonella caligorum

Digenea (flukes)

Brachyphallus parvus
Hirudinella ventricosa

Cardicola ahi [Pac]
Macradena sp. [Pac]
Phyllodistomum thunni [WAfr]
Plerurus digitatus [Ind]

Didymozoidea (tissue flukes)

Atalostropion sardae
Didymocystis acantyhocybii
Didymozoon longicolle
Koellikeria bipartita
Koellikeria globosa
Koellikeria orientalis
Platocystis sp.

Angionematoborium cephalodonus [Ind]
Dermatodidymocystis vivipara [Pac]
Dermatodidymocystis viviparoides [Pac]
Didymocystis sp. [Pac]
Didymocystis irregularis [Pac]
Didymocystis orbitalis [Pac]
Didymocystis palati [Pac]
Didymocystis philobranchia [IPac]
Didymocystis philobranchiarca [Pac]
Didymocystis rotunditestis [Ind]
Didymocystis spirocauda [Pac]
Didymocystis wedli [Med]
Didymocystoides bifasciatus [Pac]
Didymocystoides oesophagicola [Pac]
Didymocystoides superpalati [IPac]
Koellikeria abdominalis [Pac]

Neophrodidymofrema ahi [Pac]
Univitellodidymocystis lingualis [Ind]
Univitellodidymocystis neothunni [Pac]

Monogenea (gillworms)

Nasicola klawei

Areotestis sibi [Pac]
Caballerocotyla abidjani [WAfr]
Caballerocotyla biparasitica [Pac]
Caballerocotyla verrucosa [WAfr]
Capsala gotoi [Pac]
Capsala neothunni [Pac]
Capsala thynni [Eur,unc]
Hexostoma euthynni [Pac]
Hexostoma sibi [Pac]
Sibitrema poonui [Pac]
Tristomella nozawae [Pac]

Cestoda (tapeworms)

Echeneibothrium sp.*
Grillotia sp.*
*Gymnorhynchus gigas**
*Hepatoxylon trichiuri**
Nybelinia sp.*
*Pelichnibothrium speciosum**
Sphyriocephalus sp.*
Tentacularia sp.*
tetraphyllid*
trypanorhynchid*

*Callitetrarhynchus gracilis** [WAfr]
*Dasyrhynchus talismani** [EAtl,Pac]
Grillotia erinaceus [?]
*Tentacularia coryphaenae** [WAfr]

Nematoda (roundworms)

*Anisakis simplex**
Hysterothylacium cornutum
Oncophora melanocephala

Anisakis sp.* [Pac]
Ichthyostrongylus thunni [unc]
Metanisakis sp. [Pac]
Monhysterides sp. [Pac]
Oncophora albacarensis [Eur]
Philometroides sp. [Pac]

Acanthocephala (spiny-headed worms)

Rhadinorhynchus pristis

Bolbosoma sp. [Pac]
*Bolbosoma vasculosum** [WAfr]
Neorhadinorhynchus sp. [Pac]
Rhadinorhynchus trachuri [Pac?]
Rhadinorhynchus sp. [Pac]
Rhadinorhynchus cadenati [WAfr]

Copepoda (copepods)

Brachiella thynni
Caligus coryphaenae
Caligus productus
Euryphorus brachypterus

Caligus sp. [WAfr]
Caligus asymmetricus [IPac]
Caligus quadratus [Pac]
Caligus robustus [IPac]

Pennella filosa   *Euryphorus nordmanni* [Pac]
Pseudocycnus appendiculatus   *Pennella* sp. [WAfr,Pac]

Isopoda (isopods)

Glossobius impressus[1]

Pisces (fishes)

Isistius brasiliensis
Isistius plutodus
Naucrates ductor
Remora remora

Condition

scombroid poisoning (frequent)
burnt tuna

----

[1]Occurred in the stomach of this host, probably parasitized a flyingfish.

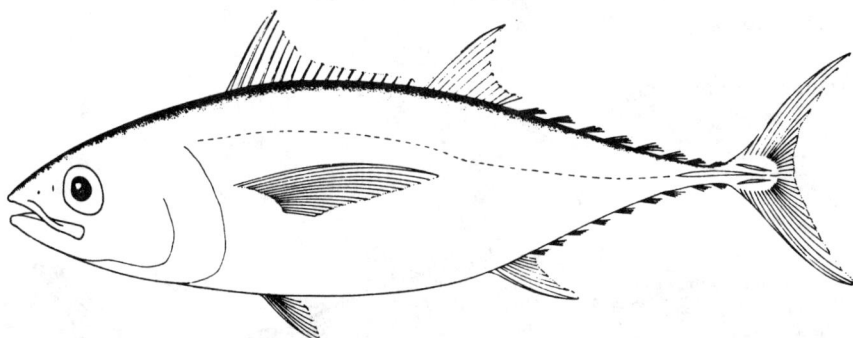

Thunnus atlanticus (Lesson) - blackfin tuna

Name - It is sometimes called "Bermuda tuna" and "black finned albacore".
Diagnostic Characters - All scombrids have small finlets behind the dorsal and anal fins. The pectoral are fins moderately long, reaching beyond the notch between dorsal fins. The right lobe of the liver is longer and the ventral surface is not striated. The finlets are dusky.
Geographic Range - Western Atlantic.
Food Habits - It eats predominantly small fishes, but also squids and larval crustaceans.
Ecology - Offshore and oceanic.
Length - Maximum 100.0 cm FL, common to 72.0 cm FL.
Weight - Maximum 23.0 kg, common 2.3-7.0 kg.
Parasites - This host has been inadequately examined and presumably supports more than 9 species of parasites. None of these parasites are host specific, 3 are genus specific (tribe specific in this case), 1 family specific, 5 are generalists with little host specificity.

Digenea (flukes)
Hirudinella ventricosa

Monogenea (gillworms)
Nasicola klawei

Cestoda (tapeworms)
*Tentacularia coryphaenae**
tetraphyllid*

Nematoda (roundworms)
Hysterothylacium cornutum

Copepoda (copepods)
Caligus coryphaenae
Caligus productus
Euryphorus brachypterus
Pseudocycnus appendiculatus

Pisces (fishes)
Isistius brasiliensis

Neoplasms (tumors)
schwaunoma

Condition
scombroid poisoning (rare)

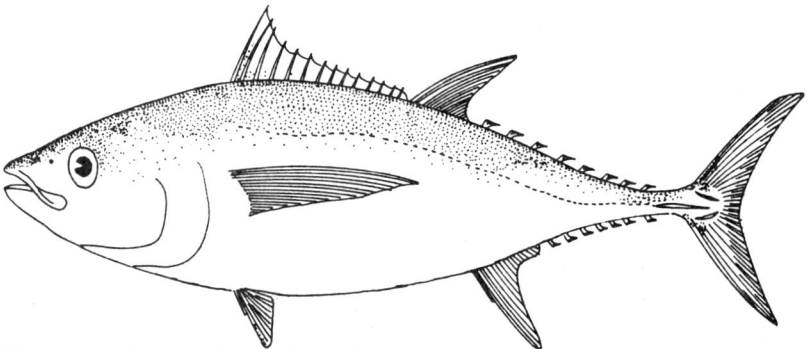

Thunnus obesus (Lowe) - bigeye tuna

Name - It is sometimes called *Parathunnus sibi* (Temminck and Schlegel), *P. mebachi* Kishinouye, *P. obesus*, and *Thynnus sibi*.

Diagnostic Characters - All scombrids have small finlets behind the dorsal and anal fins. The pectoral fins are moderately long, extending beyond the notch between the dorsal fins, in adults 110 cm FL or larger, and are relatively longer in smaller fishes. The finlets are bright yellow and edged with black. The ventral surface of the liver is striated.

Geographic Range - Worldwide in the tropics and subtropics.

Food Habits - It predominantly eats squids, but also a variety of fishes and crustaceans.

Ecology - Oceanic.

Length - Maximum 236.0 cm, common to 180.0 cm.
Weight - Maximum 197.3 kg, common 18.0-125.0 kg.
Parasites - This host has been at least moderately examined since 53 parasite species have been recorded from it, except in the western Atlantic, where only 6 species have been found. Two of these parasites are host specific, 11 possibly host specific, 23 genus specific (tribe specific in this case), 5 family specific, 3 occur on tunas and skipjack tuna, and 9 generalists with little host specificity. We found 25 parasite species which were tribe specific to tunas. This fish harbors almost all of these parasites, possibly indicating that this fish species is older than the other tunas (see Discussion).

Protozoa (protozoans)

Kudoa nova · *Hexacapsula neothunni* [Pac]

Digenea (flukes)

Botulus microporus [WAfr,unc]
Cardicola ahi [Pac]

Didymozoidea (tissue flukes)

Dermatodidymocystis vivipara [Pac]
Dermatodidymocystis vivparoides [Pac]
Didymocystis bifurcata [Pac]
Didymocystis nasalis [Pac]
Didymocystis orbitalis [Pac]
Didymocystis philobranchia [IPac]
Didymocystis philobranchiarca [IPac]
Didymocystis poonui [Pac]
Didymocystis rotunditestis [Ind]
Didymocystoides bifasciatus [Pac]
Didymocystoides pectoralis [IPac]
Didymocystoides superpalati [IPac]
Didymozoon longicolle [Pac]
Koellikeria pylorica [Pac]
Koellikeria retrorbitalis [Pac]
Koellikeria submaxillaris [Pac]
Koellikerioides apicalis [Pac]
Koellikerioides externogastricus [Pac]
Koellikerioides internogastricus [Pac]
Koellikerioides intestinalis [Pac]
Nematobothrium sp. [Ind]
Neonematobothrioides poonui [Pac]
Opisthorchinematobothrium parathunni [Pac]
Orbitonematobothrium perioculare [Pac]
Univitellodidymocystis lingualis [Ind]
Univitellodidymocystis neothunni [Pac]

Monogenea (gillworms)

Areotestis sibi [Pac]
Caballerocotyla biparasitica [Pac]

Caballerocotyla pseudomagronum [WAfr]
Caballerocotyla verrucosa [WAfr]
Capsala gotoi [Pac]
Hexostoma acutum [Pac]
Hexostoma grossum [Pac]
Hexostoma sibi [Pac]
Hexostoma thynni [Med]
Nasicola klawei [Pac,WAfr]
Neohexostoma robustum [Pac]
Sibitrema poonui [Pac]
Tristomella nozawae [Eur,Pac]
Tristomella onchidiocotyle [WAfr]

Cestoda (tapeworms)

tetraphyllid*

Sphyriocephalus sp.* [?]
*Sphyriocephalus dollfusi** [WAfr]
Dasyrhynchus talismani [EAtl,Pac]

Nematoda (roundworms)

Philometroides sp. [Pac]

Copepoda (copepods)

Brachiella thynni
Caligus coryphaenae
Euryphorus brachypterus
Pseudocycnus appendiculatus

Caligus alalongae [WAfr]
Caligus productus [WAfr,IPac]
Euryphorus nordmanni [Pac]

Pisces (fishes)

Isistius brasiliensis
Naucrates ductor

Condition

scombroid poisoning (rare)
burnt tuna

"jelly-meat" [Pac]

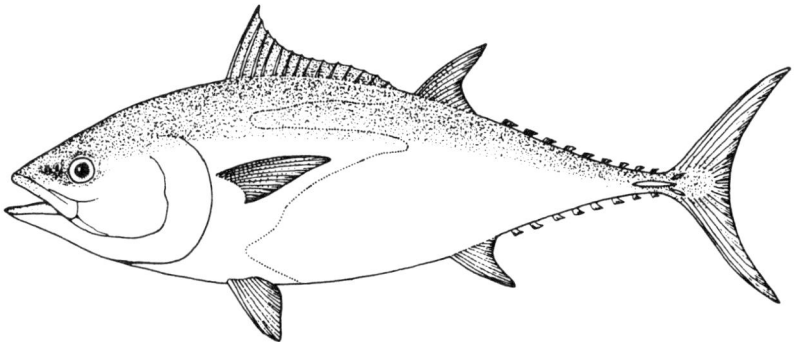

Thunnus thynnus (Linnaeus) - (northern) bluefin tuna

Name - It is also called "horse mackerel", "tunny", *Orcynchus thunnus*, *Scomber thunnus*, *T. orientalis*, *T. saliens*, *T. thunnus* and *Thynnus brachypterus*. It is not a "light tuna" and is not canned, but is highly desired for Japanese raw-fish dishes.

We use the name "bluefin tuna" in the text because it is an established name (Robins et al. 1991). "Northern bluefin tuna" is technically correct because "southern bluefin tuna", *Thunnus maccoyii* (Castelnau), occurs in the southern oceans below 40°S.

Diagnostic Characters - All scombrids have small finlets behind the dorsal and anal fins. The pectoral fins are relatively short, approximately 80% of the head length, and never reach the notch between the dorsal fins. The second dorsal fin is reddish-brown. The ventral surface of the liver is striated. The first gill arches have 34-43 rakers.

Geographic Range - Subtropical and temperate areas in the south and north Atlantic, north Pacific Ocean, Mediterranean and Black Seas. Known from Labrador and Newfoundland down to northeastern Brazil in the Western Atlantic.

Food Habits - It eats a variety of fishes, squids and crustaceans.

Ecology - Oceanic. They do venture inshore in colder waters. Bluefin tuna maintain a body temperature up to 18°F higher (22-30°C) than the surrounding water (5-30°C), allowing them to function more effectively in cooler waters and tripling the power and response of their muscles. They can swim up to 50 miles/hr (90 KPH), but are not the fastest fish in the sea.

Length - Maximum over 300.0 cm FL (rumored 420.0 cm), formerly common to 200.0 cm FL.

Weight - Maximum 682.0 kg (rumored to 700.0 kg), formerly common up to 182.0 kg.

Aquaculture - Bluefin tuna too small to sell to Japan are "ranched" by holding them in net cages or "pounds" in the ocean until they reach marketable size. These must experience parasite and disease problems.

Commercial Importance - Bluefin tuna have become so valuable to the Japanese that a large fish sells for more than the annual salary of a fisherman. This fish is being hunted to extinction (extirpation) in the northwest Atlantic and the international and government agencies appear unwilling to intervene.

Significance to Sport Fishing - Giant bluefin tuna are the highest prized big game sport fish, but unfortunately they may be more highly prized as a food fish in Japan.

Parasites - Only 13 of the 72 known parasites of this fish have been found in the western Atlantic. This suggests that this host has not been adequately examined in our region. This trend is further substantiated by the fact that its 7 species of copepods, which have received worldwide study, have all been found in the western Atlantic. Nine of the 72 species of parasites are host specific, 5 possibly host specific; 6 genus specific (tribe specific in this case); 6 family specific; 4 occur on tunas, little tunas and amberjacks; 2 on tunas and little tunas; 2 on tunas and amberjacks; 3 on skipjack; 1 on little tunny; 4 on tunas and skipjack tuna; and 30 generalists with little host specificity.

Bacteria
Vibrio spp. [Pac]
Protozoa (protozoans)
Kudoa sp. [Pac]
Kudoa clupeidae [WAfr]
Uronema marinum [Pac]
Digenea (flukes)

Hirudinella ventricosa   *Aponurus lagunculus* [Pac]
                                        Bucephalopsis sibi [Pac]
                                        Cetiotrema crassum [Pac]
                                        Lecithaster gibbosus [Med]
                                        *Lecithocladium excisum*** [Eur]
                                        Prosorhynchoides sibi [Pac]
                                        Rhipidocotyle pentagonum [Pac]
                                        Rhipidocotyle septpapillata [RSea]
                                        Sterrhurus imocavus [Med,Pac]
Didymozoidea (tissue flukes)

Koellikeria bipartita   *Anaplerurus thynnusi* [Ind]
                                        Coeliotrema thynni [Pac]
                                        Didymocystis thynni [Eur,Med]
                                        Didymocystis crassa [Pac]
                                        Didymocystis ovata [Pac]
                                        Didymocystis reniformis [Pac]
                                        Didymocystis soleiformis [Pac]
                                        Didymocystis wedli [Med,Pac]
                                        Didymocylindrus filiformis [Pac]
                                        Didymocystoides semiglobularis [Pac]
                                        Didymoproblema fusiforme [Pac]
                                        Didymozoon filicolle [Pac]
                                        Didymozoon longicolle [Pac]
                                        Didymozoon pretiosus [Pac]
                                        Koellikeria globosa [Pac]
                                        Koellikeria orientalis [Med,Pac]
                                        Koellikeria reniformis [Pac]
                                        Lobatozoum multisacculatum [Pac]
                                        Nematobothrium sp. [Pac]
                                        Oesophagocystis sp. [Pac]
Monogenea (gillworms)

Tristomella onchidiocotyle [?]   *Caballerocotyla albsmithi* [Pac]
                                        Caballerocotyla gouri [Ind]
                                        Caballerocotyla magronum [Pac]
                                        Caballerocotyla paucispinosa [Pac]
                                        Hexostoma acutum [Pac]
                                        Hexostoma albsmithi [Pac]
                                        Hexostoma dissimile [Pac]

Hexostoma grossum [Pac]
Hexostoma thynni [Med]
Kuhnia thunni [Pac]
Metapseudaxine ventrosicula [Pac]
Neohexostoma extensicaudum [Eur]
Neohexostoma thunninas [Med]
Tristomella interrupta [Med]
Tristomella nozawae [Eur]
Tristomella onchidiocotyle [Med]

Cestoda (tapeworms)

Lacistorhynchus bulbifer*   *Callitetrarhynchus gracilis** [WAfr]
Tentacularia coryphaenae*   *Grillotia* sp.* [Ind]
tetraphyllid*   *Pelichnibothrium speciosum** [Eur,Pac]
          Tetrarhynchus scomber-thynnus* [unc]

Nematoda (roundworms)

Hysterothylacium cornutum   *Anisakis* sp.* [Pac]
          Ascaris longestriata* [Med,unc]
          Contracaecum sp.* [Pac]
          Heptachona caudata [Pac]
          Hysterothylacium aduncum [Eur]
          Hysterothylacium aduncum* [Eur]
          Oncophora melanocephala [Eur]

Acanthocephala (spiny-headed worms)

          Bolbosoma vasculosum [Pac]
          Neorhadinorhynchus nudus [Pac]

Copepoda (copepods)

Brachiella thynni   *Caligus balistae* [fal]
Caligus bonito   *Cecrops latreillii* [Eur,Med?]
Caligus coryphaenae
Caligus productus
Euryphorus brachypterus
Pennella filosa
Pseudocycnus appendiculatus

Pisces (fishes)

Isistius brasiliensis   *Isistius plutodus* [Pac]
Naucrates ductor

Neoplasms (tumors)

fibroma
lipomas
melanoma
osteoma

Condition

scombroid poisoning (rare)   severe skin lesions [Pac]
          Uronema-like encephalitis [Pac]

Anomalies

vertebral [Eur]

Tribe Scomberomorini - Spanish mackerels

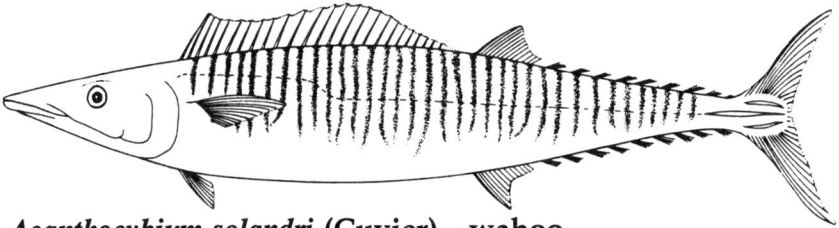

Acanthocybium solandri (Cuvier) - wahoo

Name - It is also called "jack-mackerel"; *A. petus* (Poey) and *A. sara.*

Diagnostic Characters - All scombrids have small finlets behind the dorsal and anal fins. The snout is relatively elongate and pointed. The first dorsal is much longer than the second dorsal fin. The sides of the body are covered with numerous, black vertical bars, which extend below the lateral line.

Geographic Range - Worldwide in the tropics and subtropics, including the Mediterranean.

Food Habits - It eats moderate-sized to large surface fishes and squids.

Ecology - Offshore and oceanic surface waters.

Length - Maximum 210.0 cm FL, common 107.0-140.0 cm.

Weight - Maximum 83.2 kg, common 12.0-41.0 kg.

Parasites - The 18 parasites reported from this important, worldwide host is an amazingly low number. We examined 15 wahoo from Puerto Rico, 4 from the northern Gulf of Mexico, and it has been examined elsewhere including an exclusive study in the Pacific (Iversen and Yoshida 1957). We are forced to conclude that it does not support many parasites. Only 11 of these parasites have been found in the western Atlantic. Five are host specific; 1 is tribe specific to little tunas, but rarely occurs on wahoo; 1 is family specific occurring on tunas, little tunas and wahoo; 11 are generalists with little host specificity. Its parasites suggest that it belongs with little tunas and not with Spanish mackerels (see Discussion).

Udonellidea (copepod worms)
Udonella caligorum

Digenea (flukes)
Hirudinella ventricosa   *Tetrochetus coryphaenae* [acc]

Didymozoidea (tissue flukes)
Didymocystis acanthocybii   *Nematobothrium spinneri* [Pac]
                                      Univitellodidymocystis miliaris [Pac]

Monogenea (gillworms)
Caballerocotyla manteri   *Tristomella nozawae* [Pac]
Neothoracocotyle acanthocybii

Cestoda (tapeworms)
*Hepatoxylon trichiuri**
*Tentacularia coryphaenae**

tetraphyllid*

Copepoda (copepods)

Brachiella thynni

Caligus productus

Gloiopotes hygomianus

Caligus coryphaenae [Pac]

Lernaeolophus sultanus [Ind]

Pennella filosa [?]

Shiinoa occlusa [Pac]

Tuxophorus cybii [Ind]

Pisces (fishes)

Isistius brasiliensis

Naucrates ductor

Remora osteochir**

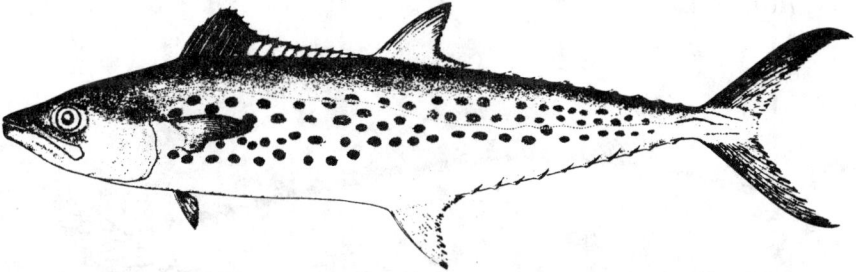

Scomberomorus brasiliensis Collette, Russo and Zavalla-Camin - serra Spanish mackerel

Name - This species was described in 1978, before that time it was confused with Atlantic Spanish mackerel.

Diagnostic Characters - All scombrids have small finlets behind the dorsal and anal fins. The sides of the body have many, relatively small, yellow or bronze spots. The spots extend from the back onto the belly, and surround the pectoral fin. The anterior 2/5 of the first dorsal fin is black, and the highest part of the fin is in the middle of the black region.

Geographic Range - Central and South American coast from Yucatan, Mexico to southern Brazil. It is not found in the insular Caribbean.

Food Habits - It predominantly eats small fishes.

Ecology - Inshore and offshore.

Length - Maximum 125.0 cm FL, common to 40.0-65.0 cm FL.

Weight - Maximum 30.0 kg, common to 13.0 kg.

Parasites - This host has not been adequately or thoroughly examined for parasites. Six parasites are genus specific; 1 almost genus specific, rarely occurring on other hosts; and 5 generalists with little host specificity.

Digenea (flukes)

Rhipidocotyle baculum

Didymozoidea (tissue flukes)

Didymocystis scomberomori

Cestoda (tapeworms)
tetraphyllid*

Nematoda (roundworms)
Hysterothylacium fortalezae
*Hysterothylacium reliquens**
Hysterothylacium sp.*

Copepoda (copepods)
*Caligus mutabilis***
Holobomolochus divaricatus
Lernaeenicus longiventris
Pseudocycnoides buccata
Shiinoa inauris

Isopoda (isopods)
Livoneca redmanii

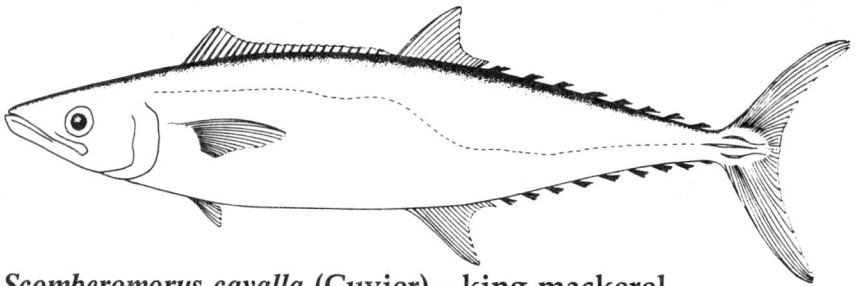

Scomberomorus cavalla (Cuvier) - king mackerel

Name - It is also called "kingfish".

Diagnostic Characters - All scombrids have small finlets behind the dorsal and anal fins. The lateral line turns down abruptly under the second dorsal fin. The sides of the body are plain and lack markings.

Geographic Range - Western Atlantic tropics and subtropics.

Food Habits - It predominantly eats small fishes.

Ecology - Inshore and offshore, not oceanic. This fish tends to be found further offshore than the 3 other species of Spanish mackerels in the western Atlantic.

Length - Maximum 173.0 cm FL, common to 70.0 cm FL.

Weight - Maximum 45.0 kg, common 5.0-14.0 kg.

Parasites - This fish has been well examined for parasites in Puerto Rico and many other localities, but it only supports 23 parasite species. One is host specific, 6 genus specific, 1 almost genus specific, and 15 generalists with little host specificity. The parasites of this host suggests that it differs slightly from the other western Atlantic members of the genus (see Discussion).

Protozoa (protozoans)
Haemogregarina bigemina

Digenea (flukes)

Bucephalopsis arcuata
Lecithochirium sp.
Rhipidocotyle baculum

Hirudinella ventricosa [acc]
Rhipidicotyle capitata [fal]

Monogenea (gillworms)

Gotocotyla acanthophallus
Pseudaxine mexicana
Scomberocotyle scomberomori
Thoracocotyle crocea

Cestoda (tapeworms)

Nybelinia lamonteae*
Otobothrium crenacolle*
Pterobothrium heteracanthum*
Tentacularia coryphaenae*
tetraphyllid*

Nematoda (roundworms)

Hysterothylacium fortalezae
Hysterothylacium reliquens*

Porrocaecum paivai [unc]

Acanthocephala (spiny-headed worms)

Rhadinorhynchus pristis
Bolbosoma vasculosum

Copepoda (copepods)

Brachiella thynni
Caligus mutabilis**
Caligus productus
Holobomolochus asperatus
Pseudocycnoides buccata

Caligus bonito [?]
Caligus elongatus [?]

Isopoda (isopods)

Anilocra acuta

Pisces (fishes)

Petromyzon marinus

Condition

scombroid poisoning (frequent)

Scomberomorus maculatus (Mitchill) - (Atlantic) Spanish mackerel

Name - It is also called "Spanish mackerel" in the USA (see Host Summaries introduction), and "spotted Spanish mackerel" (Fischer 1978).

Diagnostic Characters - All scombrids have small finlets behind the dorsal and anal fins. The sides of the body have few, relatively large, yellow or bronze spots. The spots do not extend onto the belly and do not surround the pectoral fin. The anterior 1/3 of the first dorsal fin is black.

Geographic Range - Western Atlantic from Yucatan, Mexico to Maine, USA,. Not in Bermuda or the West Indies, except possibly in Cuba and south Florida. Previously confused with cero to the north and serra Spanish mackerel in the south.

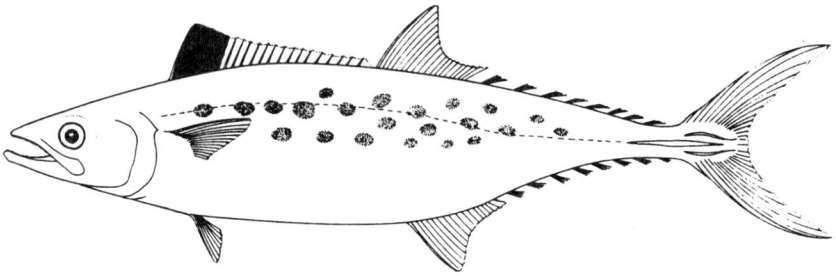

Food Habits - It predominantly eats small fishes, especially anchovies and herrings.
Ecology - In shore and offshore.
Length - Maximum 77.0 cm FL, common to 50.0 cm FL.
Weight - Maximum 5.9 kg, common to 2.3 kg.
Parasites - This fish has been well examined for parasites from many localities, but it is only known to support 24 parasite species. Two are possibly host specific, 10 genus specific, and 12 generalists with little host specificity.

Protozoa (protozoans)

Kudoa crumena

Digenea (flukes)

Bucephalopsis arcuata   *Bucephalus confusus* [acc]
Rhipidocotyle baculum

Didymozoidea (tissue flukes)

Didymocystis scomberomori

Monogenea (gillworms)

Gotocotyla acanthophallus
Pseudaxine mexicana
Scomberocotyle scomberomori
Thoracocotyle crocea

Cestoda (tapeworms)

*Callitetrarhynchus gracilis**   *Dibothriorhynchus speciosum** [unc]
*Lacistorhynchus bulbifer**   *Rhynchobothrium longispine** [unc]
*Nybelinia bisulcata**
*Pterobothrium heteracanthum**
tetraphyllid*

Nematoda (roundworms)

Hysterothylacium fortalezae
*Hysterothylacium fortalezae**
*Hysterothylacium reliquens**
Hysterothylacium sp.*
Philometra sp.

Copepoda (copepods)

*Caligus mutabilis***   *Caligus bonito* [?]
Holobomolochus divaricatus   *Caligus elongatus* [?]
Lernaeenicus longiventris   *Caligus productus* [?]

Pseudocycnoides buccata　　　　　　*Charopinopsis quaternia* [acc]
Shiinoa inauris　　　　　　　　　　*Anuretes heckelii* [acc]
Isopoda (isopods)
Livoneca ovalis
Condition
scombroid poisoning (frequent)

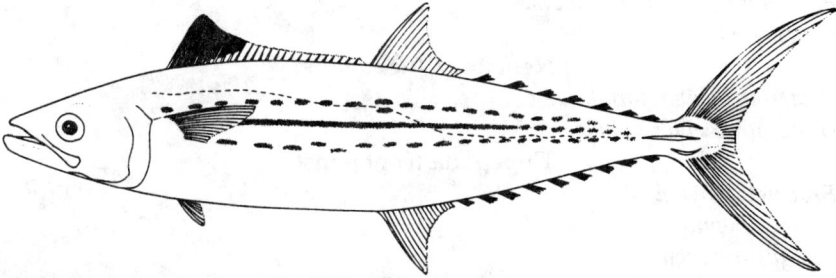

Scomberomorus regalis (Bloch) - cero

Diagnostic Characters - All scombrids have small finlets behind the dorsal and anal fins. The sides of the body have a central line of yellow lines or streaks with a row of relatively small, yellow spots above and below. The anterior 1/3 of the first dorsal fin is black. The pectoral fins are covered with small scales.

Geographic Range - Western Atlantic from Massachusetts, USA, down the Atlantic coast and the West Indies to Brazil. It is not found in the Gulf of Mexico or the Central American and Colombian coast. This fish is most abundant in the West Indies.

Food Habits - It predominantly eats small, schooling fishes, but sometimes squids and shrimps.

Ecology - Inshore and offshore.

Length - Maximum 122.0 cm, common to 45.0 cm FL.

Weight - Maximum 11.8 kg, common 2.0-5.0 kg.

Parasites - This fish has been well examined for parasites in Puerto Rico and from many other localities, but it is only known to support 21 parasite species. One is possibly host specific, 9 genus specific, 1 almost genus specific, and 10 generalists with little host specificity. Heavy to very heavy infections of a tissue fluke, *D. scomberomori*, and heavy infections of an encysted larval roundworm, *H. reliquens*, occurred in this host in a severely contaminated area (Tetra Tech 1992) in eastern Puerto Rico. This appears to be an example of pollution effects increasing the numbers of parasites.

Protozoa (protozoans)
Haemogregarina bigemina
Digenea (flukes)
Bucephalopsis arcuata　　　　　　*Myosaccium opisthonema* [fal]
Rhipidocotyle baculum
Didymozoidea (tissue flukes)
Didymocystis scomberomori

Monogenea (gillworms)
Gotocotyla acanthophallus
Pseudaxine mexicana
Thoracocotyle crocea

Cestoda (tapeworms)
*Nybelinia bisulcata**
*Otobothrium crenacolle**
*Pterobothrium heteracanthum**
tetraphyllid*

Nematoda (nematode)
Hysterothylacium fortalezae
*Hysterothylacium reliquens**

Copepoda (copepods)
Brachiella thynni
Caligus bonito
Caligus productus
Holobomolochus divaricatus
Pseudocycnoides buccata
Shiinoa inauris
Tuxophorus collettei

Isopoda (isopods)
Livoneca redmanii

Condition
scombroid poisoning (rare)

Superfamily Xiphioidea, Family Xiphiidae - swordfishes

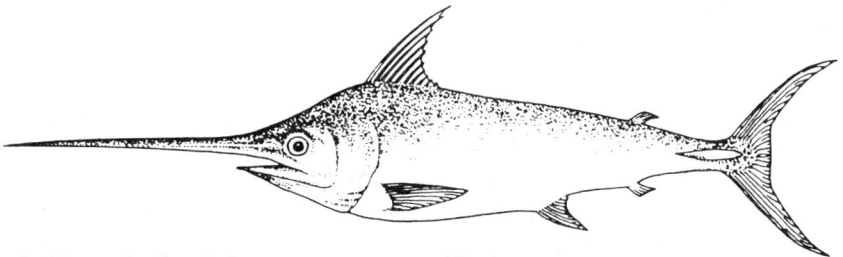

Xiphias gladius Linnaeus - swordfish
Name - It is sometimes called "broadbill swordfish"; *Histiophorus gladius*, *Istiophorus gladius*, and *X. zeugopteri*.
Diagnostic Characters - All billfish have an elongate bill on the upper jaw. The bill of this fish is sword-shaped, wider than thick, and twice as long as the head. It has no pelvic fins. The first dorsal fin is relatively large, the second dorsal small, and they are widely separated.
Geographic Range - Worldwide in tropical and temperate waters.
Food Habits - It predominantly eats small to relatively large fishes, and occasionally squids and crustaceans.

Ecology - Inshore to oceanic. It can swim at a speed of 60 miles/hr [108 KPH].

Length - Maximum 450.0 cm, formerly common to 220.0 cm.

Weight - Maximum 536.4 kg, formerly common 50.0-135.0 kg.

Human Health - Large fish accumulate high concentrations of mercury in their flesh. This discovery caused problems with commercial sales until U.S. Agencies identified the mercury component harmful to humans and adjusted existing regulations.

Commercial Importance - The high prices paid for swordfish has incited over exploitation of this fish.

Parasites - Fourty-nine species is actually a rather low number of parasite species for such an important, worldwide and presumably well studied host. A little more than 1/2 of these species have been found from the western Atlantic. Of the 49 species of parasites, 13 are host specific, 6 superfamily specific, and 31 generalists with little host specificity. The high number of host-specific parasites (26%) indicate that this fish is evolutionarily older than any of the other members of the swordfish-billfish superfamily. This also suggests that it is well isolated and distinct from the others and deserves its own family. This fish harbors 20 species of larval tapeworms, indicating that it has a rich and diverse diet of tapeworm intermediate hosts (the average number among big game fishes is less than 5).

Protozoa (protozoans)
Kudoa musculoliquefaciens [Pac]

Digenea (flukes)
Hirudinella ventricosa	*Cardicola* sp. [Pac]

Didymozoidea (tissue flukes)
Maccallumtrema xiphiados	*Metadidymozoon branchiale* [IPac]
	Nematobothrium sp. [Pac]
	Neodidymozoon macrostoma [Pac]
	Reniforma multilobularis [Pac]

Monogenea (gillworms)
Tristoma coccineum	*Tristoma adcoccineum* [Pac]
Tristoma integrum	*Tristoma adintegrum* [Pac]
	Tristomella laevis [acc]
	Tristomella pricei [Pac]

Cestoda (tapeworms)
*Ceratobothrium xanthocephalum**	*Bothriocephalus claviger* [unc]
*Dasyrhynchus giganteus**	*Bothriocephalus manubriformis* [unc]
Fistulicola plicatus	*Floriceps saccatus** [Eur]
*Grillotia erinacea**	*Gymnorhynchus gigas** [Eur]
*Hepatoxylon trichiuri**	*Nybelinia* sp.* [Ind]
*Molicola horridus**	*Rhynchobothrium ambiguum** [unc]
*Nybelinia bisulcata**	*Taenia* sp.* [Pac,unc]
*Nybelinia lamonteae**	*Tetrarhynchus* spp.* [unc]
*Nybelinia lingualis**	
*Otobothrium crenacolle**	

*Otobothrium dipsacum**
*Phyllobothrium delphini**
*Tentacularia coryphaenae**
tetraphyllid*

Nematoda (roundworms)

*Anisakis simplex**   *Hysterothylacium aduncum** [Eur]
Hysterothylacium aduncum   *Hysterothylacium hanumantharoi* [Ind]
Hysterothylacium corrugatum   *Hysterothylacium petteri* [Pac,unc]
Maricostula incurva   *Hysterothylacium reliquens* [acc]
                                   Oncophora melanocephala [fal]
                                   Paranisakis multipapillus [Ind]

Acanthocephala (spiny-headed worms)

Rhadinorhynchus pristis

Copepoda (copepods)

Caligus coryphaenae   *Caligus chelifer* [acc]
Caligus elongatus   *Chondracanthus xiphiae* [unc]
Philichthys xiphiae   *Gloiopotes huttoni* [IPac]
Pennella filosa   *Gloiopotes watsoni* [Ind]
Pennella instructa   *Lernaeolophus sultanus* [Ind,acc]
                                   Pennella sp. [Ind]
                                   Thysanote ramosa [Med]

Cirripedia (barnacles)

Conchoderma virgatum   *Conchoderma* sp. [Pac]

Isopoda (isopods)

                                   Nerocila californica [Pac]
                                   Nerocila phaiopleura [Ind]

Pisces (fishes)

Isistius brasiliensis
Naucrates ductor
Petromyzon marinus
Remora brachyptera
Remora osteochir

Condition

stomach ulcers

Family Istiophoridae - billfishes

Istiophorus albicans (Latreille) - Atlantic sailfish

[*Istiophorus platypterus* (Shaw and Nodder) - Indo-Pacific sailfish]

Name - It is also called *Histiophorus albicans* (Latreille), *H. americanus* Cuvier, *H. orientalis*, *I. americanus* (Cuvier), *I. greyi*, and *I. orientalis*. The Indo-Pacific sailfish is sometimes combined with it to form one worldwide species of "sailfish".

Diagnostic Characters - All billfish have an elongate bill on the upper jaw. The dorsal fin is enlarged into a broad and wide sail. The pelvic fins are approximately twice as long as the pectoral fins.

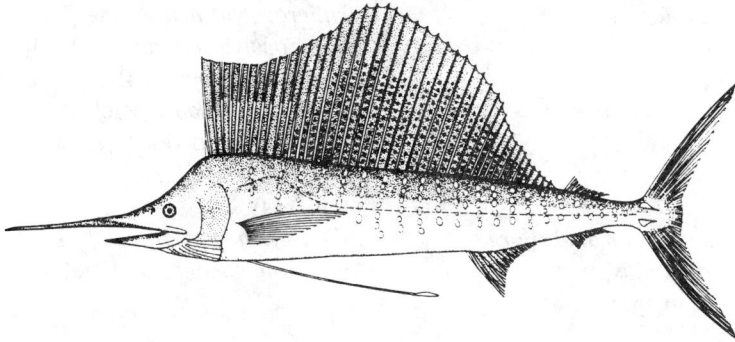

Geographic Range - Tropical and temperate Atlantic.   The Indo-Pacific sailfish occurs throughout the tropical and temperate Indian and Pacific Oceans.
Food Habits - It eats a variety of fishes, crustaceans and squids.
Ecology - Inshore to oceanic. This is the fastest swimming fish. It has been recorded swimming 68 miles/hr [122.4 KPH].
Length - Maximum 315.0 cm, common to 250.0 cm.
Weight - Maximum 79.5 kg, common 12.0-20.0 kg. The maximum for the Indo-Pacific sailfish is 100.2 kg.
Parasites - With only 34 parasite species reported from this host, it appears to have been under examined, particularly in the western Atlantic where only 12 are known. Three of the 34 parasites are host specific, 2 possibly host specific, 1 genus specific, 9 family specific, 5 superfamily specific, and 14 are generalists with little host specificity. These parasites provide little definitive evidence to divide or combine Atlantic and Indo-Pacific sailfish as species.   The 1-2 different host-specific parasites on each fish could be due to regional parasite distribution or specificity. The differences in tissue flukes may be due to under reporting in the Atlantic (see Discussion).

Bacteria

bacterial infection

Protozoa (protozoans)

Haemogregarina bigemina

Digenea (flukes)

Hirudinella ventricosa   *Cardicola grandis* [Pac]
                                           Dinurus scombri [fal]
                                           Parahemiurus merus [Pac]

Didymozoidea (tissue flukes)

Colocyntotrema sp.   *Angionematobothrium jugulare* [Pac]
                                           Metadidymozoon branchiale [IPac]
                                           Nematobothrium sp. [Pac]
                                           Neodidymozoon macrostoma [Pac]
                                           Neodidymozoon midistoma [Ind]
                                           Unitubulotestis istiophorusi [Ind]

Monogenea (gillworms)

Tristomella laevis

Caballerocotyla marielenae [Pac]
Caballerocotyla megacotyle [Ind]
Capsaloides istiophori [Pac]
Capsaloides sinuatus [Pac]
Tristomella ovalis [Pac]
Tristomella pricei [IPac]

Cestoda (tapeworms)

Bothriocephalus manubriformis
*Otobothrium dipsacum**
Tentacularia sp.*
tetraphyllid*

*Callitetrarhynchus gracilis** [Pac]
*Floriceps minacanthus** [Pac]

Nematoda (roundworms)

Maricostula histiophori

Paracanthocheilus striatus [Ind,unc]

Acanthocephala (spiny-headed worms)

Rhadinorhynchus pristis

Copepoda (copepods)

Gloiopotes americanus
Pennella filosa

Caligus quadratus [Pac]
Gloiopotes huttoni [IPac]
Gloiopotes watsoni [IPac]
Lepeophtheirus eminens [Pac]
Lernaeolophus sultanus [Ind]
Pennella biloboa [Pac,unc]
Pennella instructa [Pac?]

Cirripedia (barnacles)

Conchoderma virgatum [Pac?]

Isopoda (isopods)

Nerocila californica [Pac]

Pisces (fishes)

Naucrates ductor
Remora brachyptera
Remora osteochir
Remora remora
Remorina albescens

Isistius brasiliensis [Pac]

Neoplasms (tumors)

liver granulomas

Condition

hyperplasia
stomach and intestinal tumors

Makaira indica (Cuvier) - black marlin

Name - It has also been called *Istiompax indicus* (Cuvier), *I. marlina* (Jordan and Hill), and *M. marlina* Jordan and Hill.

Black marlin are reported in the Atlantic by commercial longline fishermen, but their presence has not been confirmed by the scientific community. They may have inspired great "giant-marlin-that-got-away" stories just off Puerto Rico, but have not been examined for parasites in the Atlantic. Please bring us one!

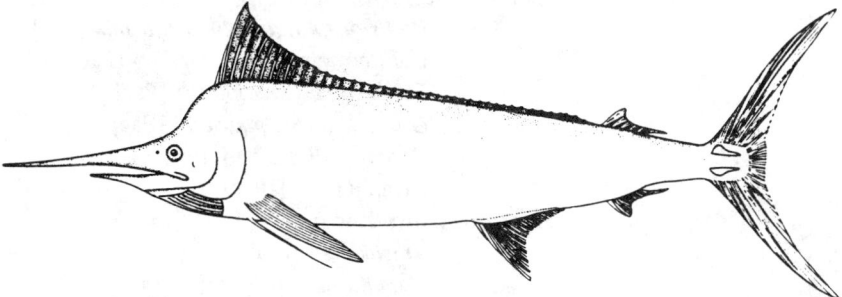

Diagnostic Characters - All billfish have an elongate bill on the upper jaw. This fish is the only billfish with rigid pectoral fins that cannot be folded against the body. The tallest part of the dorsal fin is less than 1/2 the midbody depth.
Geographic Range - Indian and Pacific Ocean, tropical subtropical and sometimes temperate waters, only sporadically in the Atlantic. Rarely reported from the Caribbean and west Africa. Some of the giant marlin hooked, but not landed, off Puerto Rico may be this fish.
Food Habits - It eats squids and pelagic fishes.
Ecology - Inshore to oceanic. This fish is much more abundant in coastal waters than in the open sea.
Length - Maximum 460.0 cm, common to 380.0 cm.
Weight - Maximum 707.6 kg, common to 195.0 kg.
Commercial Importance - This fish is called "white marlin" in Japan because of its white, firm flesh. It commands a high price on the commercial market.
Parasites - This host probably supports more than the 24 species of parasites reported. Too few fish have been examined in the Indo-Pacific, and none in the Atlantic. Two of these parasites are host specific, 10 family specific, 5 super-family specific, and 7 generalists with little host specificity.

Digenea (flukes)
Cardicola grandis [Pac]
Hirudinella ventricosa [Pac]
Didymozoidea (tissue flukes)
Angionematobothrium jugulare [Pac]
Glomeritrema subcuticola [Pac]
Makairatrema musculicola [Pac]
Metadidymozoon branchiale [Pac]
Nematobothrium sp. [Pac]
Neodidymozoon macrostoma [Pac]
Torticaecum sp.* [Pac]
Monogenea (gillworms)
Capsaloides cristatus [Pac]
Capsaloides isiophori [Pac]

Capsaloides tetrapteri [Pac]
Tristomella laevis [Ind]
Tristomella pricei [Pac]
Cestoda (tapeworms)
Bothriocephalus manubriformis [Pac]
*Callitetrarhynchus gracilis** [Pac]
*Floriceps minacanthus** [Pac]
*Otobothrium dipsacum** [Pac]
*Pseudogrillotia zerbiae** [Pac]
tetraphyllid* [IPac]
Nematoda (roundworms)
Anisakis sp. [Pac]
Camallanus sp. [Pac]
Hysterothylacium pelagicum [Pac,acc]
Maricostula makairi [Pac]
Copepoda (copepods)
Gloiopotes huttoni [IPac]
Gloiopotes watsoni [Ind]
Lepeophtheirus eminens [Pac]
Pennella instructa [?]
Pisces (fishes)
Naucrates ductor
Isistius brasiliensis [Pac]
Remora brachyptera [Pac]
Condition
stomach tumors

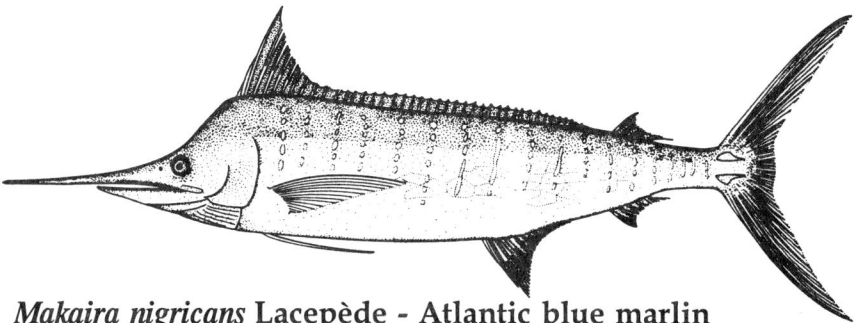

Makaira nigricans Lacepède - Atlantic blue marlin
[*Makaira mazara* Jordan and Snyder - Indo-Pacific blue marlin]
Name - It is sometimes called "blue marlin"; also *M. ampla* (Poey) and *M. marlina*. A "sister species" Indo-Pacific blue marlin is sometimes combined with it to form one worldwide "blue marlin".

Diagnostic Characters - All billfish have an elongate bill on the upper jaw. The pelvic fins are shorter than the pectoral fins; and the tallest part of the dorsal fin is shorter than the midbody depth.

Geographic Range - Atlantic tropical, subtropical and sometimes temperate waters. The Indo-Pacific blue marlin is found throughout that region.

Food Habits - It predominantly eats a variety of small fishes (99%), and some squids (1%). They will rarely eat larger fishes.

Ecology - Offshore to oceanic. It is more abundant in the tropics.

Length - Maximum 400.0 cm, common to 350.0 cm.

Weight - Maximum 636.0 kg, common 80.0-182.0 kg. The maximum for Indo-Pacific blue marlin is 820.5 kg.

Parasites - This host has been well examined, but with only 28 species worldwide, it is a parasite-poor host, and especially so in the western Atlantic where there are only 18. Only 1 of the 28 parasites is host specific, 2 possibly host specific, 8 family specific, 4 superfamily specific, and 13 generalists with little host specificity. Its single host specific parasite and its low total number of parasites, might be due to a relatively short evolutionary history. These parasites provide little definitive evidence to divide or combine Atlantic and Indo-Pacific blue marlin as species.

Digenea (flukes)

Hirudinella ventricosa

Didymozoidea (tissue flukes)

Colocyntotrema sp.

Neodidymozoon macrostoma

Metadidymozoon branhiale [Ind]

Unitubulotestis makairi [Ind]

Wedlia submaxillaris [Ind]

Monogenea (gillworms)

Tristomella laevis

Capsala ovalis [IPac]

Capsaloides nairagi [Ind]

Capsaloides sinuatus [Pac]

Tristomella pricei [IPac]

Cestoda (tapeworms)

Bothriocephalus manubriformis

Nybelinia sp.*

*Nybelinia bisulcata**

*Pelichnibothrium speciosum**

*Prosobothrium armigerum**

Tentacularia sp.*

*Tentacularia coryphaenae**

tetraphyllid*

Nematoda (roundworms)

Maricostula sp.

Philometroides sp.

Oncophora melanocephala [fal]

Acanthocephala (spiny-headed worms)

Rhadinorhynchus pristis

Copepoda (copepods)

Gloiopotes ornatus

Pennella filosa

Pennella makaira

Gloiopotes huttoni [IPac]

Gloiopotes watsoni [IPac]

Lepeophtheirus eminens [Pac]

Cirripedia (barnacles)
Conchoderma virgatum

Pisces (fishes)
Isistius brasiliensis
Isistius plutodus
Naucrates ductor
Remora brachyptera
Remora osteochir

Condition
broken bills
stomach ulcers

Anomalies
malformed bills

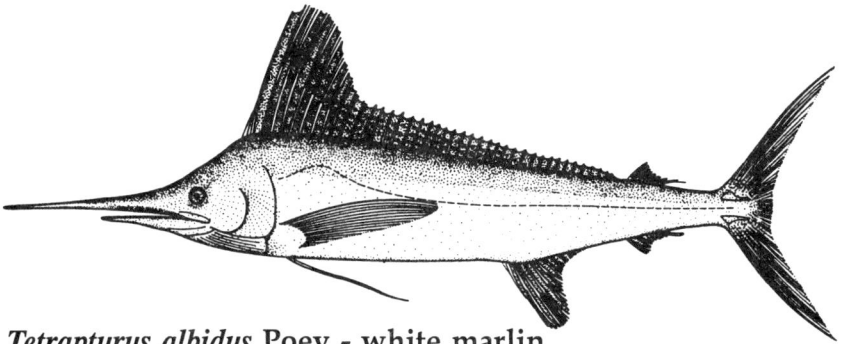

Tetrapturus albidus Poey - white marlin

Name - It is sometimes called "spikefish"; also *Lamontella albida* (Poey), *Makaira albida* (Poey), *T. albidus*, *T. belone*, and *T. imperator*.

Diagnostic Characters - All billfish have an elongate bill on the upper jaw. The pelvic fins are shorter than the pectoral fins; and the tallest part of the dorsal fin is equal to the midbody depth. The ends of the pectoral and anal fins are rounded.

Geographic Range - Atlantic and Mediterranean tropical, subtropical and sometimes temperate waters.

Food Habits - It eats a variety of fishes, squids and crustaceans.

Ecology - Offshore and oceanic.

Length - Maximum 300.0 cm, common to 250.0 cm.

Weight - Maximum 82.5 kg, common 18.0-27.0 kg.

Parasites - The parasites of the white marlin are very similar in number and species to those of Atlantic blue marlin. Only a couple of genus-specific gillworms distinguish this host. The parasites of these 2 hosts suggest that they are so similar that they should be in the same genus. One of these parasites is host specific, 2 genus specific, 4 family specific, 1 superfamily specific, and 9 generalists with little host specificity.

Digenea (flukes)
Hirudinella ventricosa

Didymozoidea (tissue flukes)

Neodidymozoon macrostoma Colocyntotrema sp. [?]

Monogenea (gillworms)

Capsaloides cornutus Capsaloides perugiai [Med]
Capsaloides magnaspinosus
Tristomella laevis

Cestoda (tapeworms)

Bothriocephalus manubriformis
Gymnorhynchus gigas*
Nybelinia sp.*
Otobothrium crenacolle*
Tentacularia sp.*
tetraphyllid*

Nematoda (roundworms)

Maricostula sp.

Acanthocephala (spiny-headed worms)

Rhadinorhynchus sp.

Copepoda (copepods)

Caligus productus
Gloiopotes ornatus
Pennella filosa

Pisces (fishes)

Isistius brasiliensis
Naucrates ductor
Remora brachyptera
Remora osteochir
Remora remora
Remorina albescens

Condition

broken bill
stomach ulcers

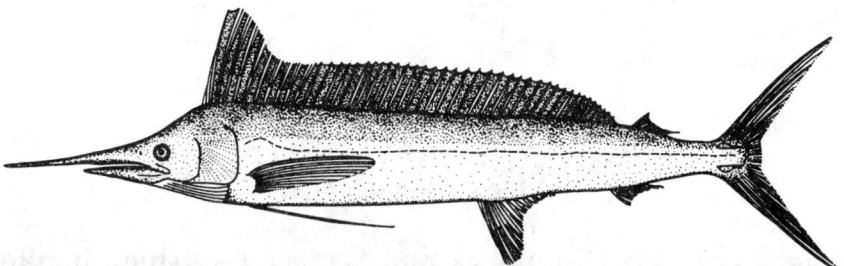

Tetrapturus pfluegeri Robins and de Sylva - longbill spearfish

Diagnostic Characters - All billfish have an elongate bill on the upper jaw.
The pelvic fins are longer than the pectoral fins; and the tallest part of the dorsal

fin is slightly greater than the midbody depth. The anus is also well in front of the anal fin, instead of adjacent as in other billfishes.

Geographic Range - Atlantic tropical, subtropical and sometimes temperate waters. Mediterranean spearfish replaces it in the Mediterranean. This fish overlaps ranges and possibly exchanges parasites with 3 other species of spearfishes in the eastern Atlantic.

Food Habits - It eats primarily pelagic fishes and squids.

Ecology - Oceanic.

Length - Maximum 200.0 cm, more often to 165.0 cm.

Weight - Maximum 45.0 kg, more often to 20.0 kg.

Significance to Sport Fishing - Rarely caught on hook and line. Taken on longlines.

Parasites - We found 8 species of parasites in a single specimen of this host we were able to examine. One fish is hardly an adequate sample. All of these parasites are found in white marlin, as would be expected in hosts from the same genus. None of these parasites is host specific, 2 genus specific, 2 family specific, 1 superfamily specific, and 3 generalists with little host specificity.

Digenea (flukes)

Hirudinella ventricosa   *Dinurus scombri* [fal]

Didymozoidea (tissue flukes)

Neodidymozoon macrostoma

Monogenea (gillworms)

Capsaloides cornutus
Capsaloides magnaspinosus
Tristomella laevis

Cestoda (tapeworms)

Bothriocephalus manubriformis
tetraphyllid*

Copepoda (copepods)

Caligus productus

Pisces (fishes)

Naucrates ductor
Remora brachyptera
Remora osteochir
Remorina albescens

Condition

stomach ulcer

Miscellaneous fish

Sarda orientalis (Temminck and Schlegel) - striped bonito

Atlantic records of this wide-ranging Indo-Pacific fish were in error (Robins et al. 1991).

ACKNOWLEDGMENTS

ASSISTANCE

Our research detailed in this book was supported by the Commonwealth of Puerto Rico Department of Natural and Environmental Resources (DNER) with Wallop-Breaux Sportfish Restoration Funds (Puerto Rico Projects F-28 and F-35) and the University of Puerto Rico, Mayaguez Campus (UPRM) in Puerto Rico; and the Southeastern Cooperative Fish Disease Project, Department of Fisheries and Allied Aquacultures (DFAA), Auburn University, with Wallop-Breaux Funds in Alabama. The Caribbean Aquatic Animal Health Project, Caribbean Stranding Network and the Caribbean Aquaculture Association also provided information and/or support.

We are deeply grateful to Dr. William G. Dyer, Department of Zoology, Southern Illinois University, Carbondale, Illinois, USA, for discussing many points of this work with us, preparing and depositing some of the parasites collecteded in this study, and encouraging our efforts.

We thank the members of the organizations listed above and the big game fishermen at official tournaments and the many people in the organizations noted below who helped collect specimens and cooperated with us in our work, and a small army of high school to post-doctoral students who assisted us in laboratory and field work related to this study, especially: Mickey Tirado, President, Asociación de Pesca Deportiva de Puerto Rico; Arecibo Outboard Club, Club Deportivo del Oeste, Club Nautico de Arecibo, Club Nautico Boqueron, Club Nautico La Parguera, Club Nautico Mayaguez; Aguadilla, Crashboat and La Parguera Fishing Co-ops; Dauphin Island Deep Sea Fishing Rodeo; Iris Corujo-Flores, José Berrios, James Timber, Timothy Churchill, Dr. Craig G. Lilyestrom, Catherine Aliaume, Alfonso Zerbi, Miguel Figuerola, DNER; Dr. Luis R. Almodovar (deceased), Mickey Amador, Aramis Aversa, Robin and Andy Bruckner, Dr. Ileana E. Clavijo, Dr. Patrick L. Colin, Dr. George D. Dennis, Dr. Michael J. Dowgiallo, Dr. Jorge R. Garcia-Sais, Kathy Hall, Dr. Dannie A. Hensley, Nilda Jimenez, Dr. Joseph J. Kimmel, Ed Levine, Ivan Lopez, Uchi Mendoza, Dr. Antonio A. Mignucci-Giannoni, Rubby Montoya, Dr. Debra P. Moore, Edgardo Ojeda, Edgardo Ortiz, Jorge Rivera, Juan Rosado, Marcos Rosado, Victer Rosado, William Rosado, Llena Sang, Dr. Rosa M. Steele, Dr. Richard K. Wallace and Dr. Raymond E. Waldner, Department of Marine Sciences (DMS), UPRM; Sheila Dunstan, Yolanda Lopez and Sylma Martinez de Aymat, DMS Library; Dr. Yolanda Brady (DFAA), Lucy and Dolph Bunkley, Adrian Cooper (Jamaica), Patrick Cotter (Bellairs Research Institute, Barbados), Sherel and Dallas Durrance, Richard Dyer, Antonio Garcia, Marta and Dr. Francisco A. Guzman-Reyes, Froilan Lopez, Juan Muñoz (Punta Betin Marine Laboratory, Santa Marta, Colombia), Dr. Ronald P. Phelps (DFAA), Dr. Doon Ramsaroop and Dr. Max Sturm (Institute of Marine Affairs, Trinidad), Dr. Rand (Bermuda Aquarium), Miguel Rolon

(Caribbean Fishery Management Council) Carol Sanner, Dr. Joseph R. Sullivan (Alaska Fish and Game), Wayne Swingle (Gulf of Mexico Fishery Management Council), Gerard Van Buurt (Department of Agriculture and Fisheries, Curaçao) and Luis Vivoni.
We received unpublished records of tumors, pseudotumors, conditions and parasites from Dr. Harshbarger, copepods from Drs. Hogans and Benz, a remora from Dr. Goldstein, gillworms from Dr. Lester, and a hermaphroditic skipjack tuna from Dr. David Itano, Hawaii Institute of Marine biology, University of Hawaii at Manoa. We received information about ostracodes from Dr. McKenzie, fishes from Dr. Dannie A. Hensley (DMS), and bacteria from Dr. Esther C. Peters. Christoph Schmitt made translations of parts of German articles.
Our parasite samples were deposited and numbers assigned in the following museums: helminths by Dr. J. Ralph Lichtenfels, U.S. National Parasite Collection (USNPC), USDA Beltsville, Maryland; crustaceans by Drs. Thomas E. Bowman (deceased) and Brian Kensley, Division of Crustacea, Smithsonian Institution, U.S. National Museum (USNM); tumors by Dr. John C. Harshbarger, Registry of Tumors in Lower Animals (RTLA); and a reference collection (for local use) by Dr. Jeff Holmquist, Invertebrate Museum (DMS).
We thank Drs. E. W. Shell, Grizzle, Rogers and Plumb (DFAU) and Prof. Edgardo A. R. Ortiz-Corps, Department of Biology, University of Puerto Rico at Humacao for laboratory and office space, library facilities, reference collections and accommodations for completing parts of this work.

ILLUSTRATION SOURCES

Illustrations of the following species were redrawn or further modified from illustrations in the sources listed:

Protozoans: *Trypanosoma* sp. (original), *Kudoa crumena* (Iversen and Van Meter 1967), other protozoans (Lom and Dyková 1992).

Fungi: (Neish and Hughes 1980).

Copepod worm: (Yamaguti 1963).

Flukes: *Brachyphallus parvus*, *Lecithochirium* sp., *Stephanostomum coryphaenae*, *S. sentum* (Siddiqi and Cable 1970); *Bucephalopsis arcuata*, *L. microstomum*, *L. texanum*, *Rhipidocotyle baculum*, *Tormopsolus orientalis* (original); *B. longicirrus*, *B. longovifera*, *Bucephalus varicus*, *S. megacephalum* (Manter 1940a,b); *B. gorgon* (Corkum 1967); *Cetiotrema carangis* (Manter 1947); *Coitocaecum extremum* (Thatcher 1993); *Dinurus scombri*, *R. barracudae* (Schell 1985); *Hirudinella ventricosa* (Gibson and Bray 1977); *Pseudopecoeloides carangis*, *Tetrochetus coryphaenae* (Yamaguti 1970); *R. capitata* (Manter 1944); *S. imparispine*, *Tormopsolus filiformis* (Sogandares-Bernal and Hutton 1959); other flukes (Yamaguti 1971).

Tissue flukes: *Colocyntotrema auxis*, *Didymocystis acanthocybii*, *Neodidymozoon macrostoma* (Yamaguti 1970); *D. wedli* (Madhavi 1982); *D. scomberomori* (Overstreet 1969); *D. thynni*, *Didymozoon longicolle* (original);

Koellikeria bipartita, Nematobothrium pelamydis (Grabda 1991); *Maccallumtrema xiphiados, N. scombri* (Yamaguti 1971); other tissue flukes from the original descriptions.

Gillworms: *Allopyragraphorus incomparabilis, Allopseudaxine katsuwonis, Cemocotyle carangis, Cemocotylella elongata* (Yamaguti 1963); *Allencotyla mcintoshi* (Schell 1970); *Capsaloides magnaspinosus, Protomicrocotyle mirabilis, Tristoma integrum* (original); *Dionchus agassizi* (Rohde 1978); *Helixaxine winteri* (Caballero and Bravo-Hollis 1965); *Pseudochanhanea sphyraenae* (Yamaguti 1968); other gillworms (Hendrix 1994).

Tapeworms: *Bothriocephalus manubriformis* (Yamaguti 1968); *Callitetrarhynchus gracilis, Pterobothrium heteracanthum* (Chandler 1935); *Dasyrhynchus giganteus, Fistulicola plicatus, Gymnorhynchus gigas, Otobothrium dipsacum* (Khalil et al. 1994); *C. gracilis, Eutetrarhynchus lineatus* (Linton 1908, Mac-Callum 1921); *F. plicatus* (Hogans and Hurley 1986); *Ceratobothrium xanthocephalum, Grillotia erinaceus, Hepatoxylon trichiuri, Lacistorhynchus bulbifer, Nybelinia bisulata, P. heteracanthum* (Linton 1897b); *H. trichiuri* (Linton 1941); *L. bulbifer,* (Schmidt 1986); *N. lamonteae* (Nigrelli 1938); *N. lingualis* (Schmidt 1986); *O. crenacolle, Rhinebothrium flexile* (Linton 1905); *Pelichnibothrium speciosum* (Wardle and McLeod 1952); *Pseudogrillotia zerbiae* (Palm 1995).

Roundworms: *Aniskis simplex, Oncophora melanocephala* (original); *Hysterothylacium aduncum* (Berland 1961); *H. cornutum, Maricostula histiophori* (Bruce and Cannon 1989); *H. fortalezae, H. reliquens, Iheringascaris inquies, M. incurva* (Deardorff and Overstreet (1981); other roundworms from the original descriptions.

Ostracod: (Wilson 1913).

Copepods: life cycle stages (Wilson 1905); *Brachiella thynni, Clavellisa scombri, Gloiopotes americanus, G. ornatus, Hatschekia amplicapa, Pennella* sp., *Tuxophorus colletti* (original); *Caligus balistae, C. chorinemi, C. coryphaenae, C. isonyx, C. longipedis, C. wilsoni* (Cressey 1991); *C. bonito, C. mutabilis, C. pelamydis, C. productus; Ceratacolax euthynni, Euryphorus brachyptera, Holobomolochus asperatus, H. divaricatus, Pseudocycnus appendiculatus, Pseudocycnoides buccata, Shiinoa inauris, Unicolax collateralis* (Cressey and Cressey 1980); *C. quadratus, C. spinosus* (Shinno 1959, 1960); *H. crevalleus* (Cressey 1981); *Pennella makaira* (Hogans 1988a); *Philichthys xiphiae* (Kabata 1979); *U. anonymous, U. mycterobius* (Vervoort 1965); other copepods (Yamaguti 1963).

Fish louse: (Yamaguti 1963).

Isopods: *Rocinella signata* (Menzies and Glynn 1968); other isopods (Kensley and Schotte 1989).

Fish associates: *Isistius brasiliensis* and *I. plutodus* (Compagno 1984); pilotfish (Fischer 1978).

Fish hosts: (Fischer 1978).

Other diseases: Pseudotumor drawn from a specimen (RTLA 1895) donated to the RTLA by Walter Kandashoff.

BIBLIOGRAPHY

These citations include literature cited and/or used in this book and additional references which we believe may be useful in the study of these parasites. Due to space limitations, references concerning parasites from outside the western Atlantic are not cited. Popular articles are marked with an asterisk (*).

Amin, O.M. 1985. Classification. Pages 27-72 *In* Crompton, D.W.T. and B. B. Nickol (Eds.) Biology of the Acanthocephala. Cambridge University Press, 519 p.

Anderson, D. 1993. Barnacles, structure, function, development, and evolution. Chapman & Hall, New York, USA, 376 p.

Anderson, R.C., A.G. Chabaud, S. Willmott. 1974-83. CIH keys to the nematode parasites of vertebrates. Commonwealth Agricultural Bureaux, Farnham Royal, Bucks, England, Numbers 1-10.

Anonymous. 1976, 1981, 1989. Registry of marine pathology, volumes 1-3, NMFS Laboratory, NOAA, Oxford, Maryland, USA.

_____ 1980. Proceedings of the 1979 sea lamprey International Symposium. Canadian Journal of Fisheries and Aquatic Sciences 37:1585-2214.

* _____ 1992. Fishes of Puerto Rico [in Spanish and English]. 2nd Edition, Sea Grant Program, University of Puerto Rico, Mayaguez, Puerto Rico, UPRSG-E-43:38 p.

* _____ 1994a. World Record Game Fishes. The International Game Fish Association, Pompano Beach, Florida, 352 p.

_____ 1994b. Evidence for mixing based on parasites. Appendix E and Pages 139-145 *In:* An assessment of Atlantic bluefin tuna. National Academy Press, Washington, DC, USA, 148 p.

Arandas-Rego, A. and C.P. Santos. 1983. Helminths of mackerel, *Scomber japonicus*, from Rio de Janeiro. Memórias do Instituto Oswaldo Cruz 78:443-448.

Barse, A.M. 1988. A contribution to the biology of white marlin, *Tetrapturus albidus*, off the Delaware and Maryland coast (USA) with special emphasis on feeding ecology and helminth parasites. MS Thesis, University of Maryland, 92 p.

_____ and C.H. Hocutt. 1990. White marlin parasites: Potential indicators of stock separations, seasonal migrations, and feeding habits. Pages 41-49 *In:* R.H. Stroud (Ed.) Proceedings of the Second International Billfish Symposium, Part 2.

Bashirullah, A.K.M., N. Aguado, M. Alvarez, I.A. Marcano R. and J.J. Alio. 1995. Preliminary analysis of the parasites of billfishes captured in Venezuela [in Spanish]. Proceedings of the Gulf and Caribbean Fisheries Institute (in press).

_____ and J.C. Rodriguez. 1992. Spatial distribution and interrelationship of four monogenoidea of jack mackerel, *Caranx hippos* (Carangidae) in the north-east of Venezuela. Acta Cientifica Venezolana 43:125-128.

Bane, G.W. 1969. Parasites of the yellowfin tuna, *Thunnus albacares*, in the Atlantic Ocean (Pisces: Scombridae). Wasmann Journal of Biology 27: 163-175.

Benz, G.W. 1984. Association of the pedunculate barnacle, *Conchoderma virgatum* (Spengler, 1790), with pandarid copepods (Siphonostomatoida: Pandaridae). Canadian Journal of Zoology 62:741-742.

* _____ 1994a. Parasitic crustaceans: Back to basics. Pages 76-83 *In:* Regional Conference Proceedings, American Zoo and Aquarium Association, Wheeling, West Virginia, USA, 412 p.

_____ 1994b. Host index to Yamaguti's *Parasitic Copepoda and Branchiura of Fishes* 1963. Journal of Aquatic Animal Health 6:162-175.

Bere, R. 1936. Parasitic copepods from gulf of Mexico fish. American Midland Naturalist. 17:577-625.

Berland, B. 1961. Nematodes from some Norwegian marine fishes. Sarsia 2: 1-50.

Bliss, D.E. (Ed.). 1982-85. The biology of Crustacea. Volumes 1-10, Academic Press, New York, USA.

Bravo-Hollis, M. 1953. Gill monogenea of Mexican coastal fishes [in Spanish]. Congreso Cientifico Mexicano Memoria 7:139-146.

Brown, R.J. 1970. Pathology of pompano with whirling disease and Spanish mackerel with enteric cestodiasis. Proceedings of the World Mariculture Society 1:132-136.

Bruce, N.L., R.D. Adlard and L.R.G. Cannon. 1994. Synoptic checklist of ascaridoid parasites (Nematoda) from fish hosts. Invertebrate Taxonomy 8:583-674.

_____ and L.R.G. Cannon. 1989. *Hysterothylacium, Iheringascaris* and *Maricostula* new genus, nematodes (Ascaridoidea) from Australian pelagic marine fishes. Journal of Natural History 23:1397-1441.

Bunkley-Williams, L., W.G. Dyer and E.H. Williams, Jr. 1996. Some aspidogastrid and digenean trematodes of Puerto Rican marine fishes. Journal of Aquatic Animal Health 8:87-92.

_____ and E.H. Williams, Jr. 1994. Diseases caused by *Trichodina spheroidesi* and *Cryptocaryon irritans* (Ciliophora) ciliates in wild coral reef fishes. _____ 6:360-361.

_____ and _____ 1995. Parasites of Puerto Rican freshwater sport fish [in Spanish]. Department of Natural and Environmental Resources, San Juan, and Department of Marine Sciences, University of Puerto Rico, Mayaguez, Puerto Rico, 190 p.

Burnett-Herkes, J. 1974. Parasites of the gills and buccal cavity of the dolphin, *Coryphaena hippurus*, from the straits of Florida. Transactions of the American Fisheries Society 103:101-106.

Caballero y Caballero, E., and M. Bravo-Hollis. 1965. Fish Monogenea from the Mexican Gulf and Caribbean coasts. I [in Spanish]. Bulletin of Marine Science of the Gulf and Caribbean 15:535-547.

_____ and _____ 1967. Fish Monogenea (Van Beneden, 1858) Carns, 1863, from the Mexican Gulf and Caribbean coasts. III. Anales del Instituto de Biologia de Universidad Nacional Autonoma de Mexico 38:27-34.

Cable, R.M. and J. Linderoth. 1963. Taxonomy of some acanthocephala from marine fish with reference to species from Curaçao, N.A., and Jamaica, W.I. Journal of Parasitology 49:706-716.

_____ and B.A. Mafarachisi. 1970. Acanthocephala of the genus *Gorgorhynchoides* parasitic in marine fishes. H.D. Srivastava Commemorative Volume, p. 255-261.

Causey, D. 1953a. Parasitic copepoda from Grand Isle, Louisiana. Louisiana State University Marine Laboratory Occasional Papers 7:18 p.

_____ 1953b. Parasitic copepoda of Texas coastal fishes. Publications of the Institute of Marine Sciences 3:7-16.

_____ 1955. Parasitic copepoda from Gulf of Mexico fish. Louisiana State University Marine Laboratory Occasional Papers 9:19 p.

_____ 1960. Parasitic Copepoda from Mexican coastal fishes. Bulletin of Marine Sciences of the Gulf and Caribbean 10:323-337.

Chandler, A.C. 1935. Parasites of fishes in Galveston Bay. Proceedings of the U.S. National Museum 83:123-157.

_____ 1937. A new trematode *Hirudinella beebi* from the stomach of a Bermuda fish *Acanthocybium petus*. Transactions of the American Microscopical Society 56:348-354.

_____ 1941. Two new trematodes from the bonito, *Sarda sarda*, in the Gulf of Mexico. Journal of Parasitology 27:183-184.

_____ 1942. Some cestodes from Florida sharks. Proceedings of the U.S. National Museum 92(3135):25-31.

*Cochran, P.A. 1989. Maintaining parasitic lampreys in closed laboratory systems. American Biology Teacher 51:115-119.

Compagno, L.J.V. 1984. Hexanchiformes to Lamniformes. FAO Fisheries Synopsis No. 125, Volume 4. Sharks of the world, Part 1:249 p.

Corkum, K.C. 1967. Bucephalidae (Trematoda) in fishes of the northern Gulf of Mexico: *Bucephalus* Baer, 1827. Transactions of the American Microscopical Society 86:44-49.

_____ 1968. Bucephalidae (Trematoda) in fishes of the Northern Gulf of Mexico: *Bucephaloides* Hopkins, 1954 and *Ripidocotyle* Diesing, 1858. _____ 87:342-349.

Crane, J. 1936. Notes on the biology and ecology of giant tuna, *Thunnus thynnus* Linnaeus, observed at Portland, Maine. Zoologica 21:207-212.

Cressey, R.F. 1967. Genus *Gloiopotes* and a new species with notes on host specificity and intraspecific variation (Copepoda: Caligoida). Proceedings of the United States National Museum 122:1-21.

_____ 1975. A new family of parasitic copepods (Cyclopoida: Shiinoidae). Crustacea 28:211-219.

_____ 1981,1983,1991. Parasitic copepods from the Gulf of Mexico and Caribbean Sea, I. *Holobomolochus* and *Neobomolochus*. II: Bomolochidae. III: *Caligus*. Smithsonian Contributions to Zoology 339:1-24; 389: 1-35; 497:1-53.

_____ and B.B. Collette. 1970. Copepods and needlefishes: a study in host-parasite relationships. Fishery Bulletin 68:347-432.

_____, B.B. Collette and J.L. Russo. 1983. Copepods and scombrid fishes: A study in host-parasite relationships. _____ 81:227-265.

_____ and H.B. Cressey. 1980. Parasitic copepods of mackerel- and tuna-like fishes (Scombridae) of the world. Smithsonian Contributions to Zoology 311:1-186.

_____ and E.A. Lachner. 1970. The parasitic copepod diet and life history of diskfishes. Copeia 1970:310-318.

_____ and P. Nutter. 1987. Reidentification of David Causey's *Caligus* collections (Crustacea: Copepoda). Proceedings of the Biological Society of Washington 100:600-602.

Crites, J.L., R.M. Overstreet and M. Maung. 1993. *Ctenascarophis lesteri* n. sp. and *Prospinitectus exiguus* n. sp. (Nematoda: Cystidicolidae) from the skipjack tuna, *Katsuwonus pelamis*. Journal of Parasitology 79:847-859.

Cuvier, G. 1830. The Animal Kingdom according to their organization in order to serve as a basis for the natural history of the animals and the introduction to their comparative anatomy [in French]. Nouvelle Edition, Volume 3, Déterville, Paris, 504 p.

Davies, A.J. 1982. Further studies on *Haemogregarina bigemina* Lavern & Mesnil, the marine fish *Blennius pholis* L., and the Isopod *Gnathia maxillaris* Montagu. Journal of Protozoology 29:576-583.

Dawes, B. 1968. Trematoda. Cambridge University Press, London, 644 p.

Deardorff, T.L. and R.M. Overstreet. 1980. Taxonomy and biology of North American species of *Goezia* (Nematoda: Anisakidae) from fishes, including three new species. Proceedings of the Helminthological Society of Washington 47:192-217.

_____ and _____ 1981a. Review of *Hysterothylacium* and *Iheringascaris* (both previously = *Thynnascaris*) (Nematoda: Anisakidae) from the northern Gulf of Mexico. Proceedings of the Biological Society of Washington 93:1035-1079.

_____ and _____ 1981b. Larval Hysterothylacium (Thynnascaris)(Nematoda: Anisakida) from fishes and Invertebrates in the Gulf of Mexico. Proceedings of the Helminthological Society of Washington 48:113-126.

_____ and _____ 1982. *Hysterothylacium pelagicum* sp. n. and *H. cornutum* (Nematoda: Anisakida) from marine fishes. _____ 49:246-251.

_____ and _____ 1986. Piscine adult nematode invading an open lesion in a human hand. American Journal of Tropical Medicine and Hygiene 35: 827-830.

_____ and _____ 1991. Seafood-transmitted zoonoses in the United States [of America]: The fishes, the dishes, and the worms. Pages 211-265 *In:* D. R. Ward and C. R. Hackney (Eds.). Microbiology of marine food products. Van Nostrand Reinhold, New York, USA, 450 p.

Delamare-Deboutteville, C. and L. Nunes-Ruivo. 1958. Copepods parasitic on Mediterranean fishes [in French]. Vie Milieu 9:215-235.

Delaney, P.M. 1984. Isopods of the genus *Excorallana* Stebbing, 1904 from the Gulf of California, Mexico (Crustacea, Isopoda, Corallanidae). Bulletin of Marine Science 34:1-20.

Dojiri, M. 1983. Revision of the genera of the Caligidae (Siphonostomatoida), copepods predominantly parasitic on marine fishes. PhD Dissertation, Boston University, 721 p.

Dyer, W.G., E.H. Williams, Jr., and L.B. Williams. 1985. Digenetic trematodes of marine fishes of the western and southwestern coasts of Puerto Rico. Proceedings of the Helminthological Society of Washington 52:85-94.

_____, _____ and _____ 1986. Some trematodes of marine fishes of southwestern and northwestern Puerto Rico. Transactions of the Illinois Academy of Sciences 79:141-143.

_____, _____ and L.B. Williams. 1988. Digenetic trematodes of marine fishes of Okinawa, Japan. Journal of Parasitology 74:638-645.

_____, _____ and _____ 1992a. *Neobenedenia pargueraensis* n. sp. (Monogenea: Capsalidae) from the red hind, *Epinephelus guttatus*, in Puerto Rico. _____ 78:330-333.

_____, _____ and _____ 1992b. *Tristomella laevis* (Verrill, 1875) Guiart, 1938 (Monogenea: Capsalidae) on white and blue marlins from the southwestern coast of Puerto Rico and Desecheo Island. Transactions of the Illinois State Academy of Science 85:183-185.

_____, _____ and _____ 1992c. *Homalometron dowgialloi* sp. n. (Homalometridae) from *Haemulon flavolineatum* and additional records of digenetic trematodes of marine fishes in the West Indies. Journal of the Helminthological Society of Washington 59:182-189.

_____, _____ and _____ 1997. Helminths of the dolphinfish (*Coryphaena hippurus*) in Puerto Rico. _____ (in press).

Eggleston, D.B. and E.A. Bochenek. 1990. Stomach contents and parasite infestation of school bluefin tuna *Thunnus thynnus* collected from the middle Atlantic Bight, Virginia. Fishery Bulletin 88:389-395.

Eldridge, M.B. and P.G. Wares. 1974. Some biological observations of billfishes taken in the eastern Pacific Ocean, 1967-1970. NOAA Technical Report NMFS SSRF-675(2):89-101.

Fernandes, B.M.M. 1970. Occurrence of *Dinurus tornatus* (Rudolphi, 1819) Loss, 1907 in Brasil [in Portuguese]. Atas da Sociedade de Biologia do Rio de Janeiro 14:91-92.

_____, A. Kohn and R. Magalhães-Pinto. 1985. Aspidogastrid and digenetic trematode parasites of marine fishes of the coast of Rio de Janeiro State, Brazil. Revista Brasileira de Biologia 45:109-116.

Finlayson, J.E. 1982. The alleged alternation of sexual phases in *Kuhnia scombri*, a monogenean of *Scomber scombrus*. Parasitology 84:303-311.

Fischer, W. (Ed.). 1978. FAO Species Identification Sheets for Fisheries Purposes, Western Central Atlantic (Fishing Area 31). Volumes 1-7, FAO United Nations, Rome, Italy.

Fischthal, J.H. 1977. Some digenetic trematodes of marine fishes from the barrier reef and lagoon of Belize. Zoologica Scripta 6:81-88.

Franks, J.S. 1995. A pugheaded cobia (*Rachycentron canadum*) from the north-central Gulf of Mexico. Gulf Research Reports 9:143-145.

Garzon-Ferreira, J. 1990. An isopod, *Rocinela signata* (Crustacea: Isopoda: Aegidae), that attacks humans. Bulletin of Marine Science 46:813-815.

Gibson, D.I. and R.A. Bray. 1977. The Azygiidae, Hirudinellidae, Ptychogonimidae, Sclerodistomidae and Syncoeliidae (Digenea) of fishes from the northeast Atlantic. Bulletin of the British Museum (Natural History) Zoology Series 32:167-245.

*Goldstein, R.J. 1988. Offshore fishing from Virginia to Texas. John F. Blair, Winston-Salem, North Carolina, USA, 248 p.

*_____ 1987. Billfish parasites. Sport Fishing (Oct/Nov):58-64.

Grabda, J. 1991. Marine fish parasitology. (English translation, 1981 Polish publication) VCH Verlagsgesellschaft, Weinheim, Germany. 306 p.

Guitart-Manday, D. 1964. Fishery biology of the swordfish, *Xiphias gladius* Linnaeus (Teleostomi: Xiphiidae), in Cuban waters [in Spanish]. Poeyana, Ser. B(1):37 p.

*Hammond, D.L. and D.M. Cupka. 1975. A sportsman's field guide to the billfishes, mackerels, little tunas and tunas of South Carolina. South Carolina Marine Resources Department, Educational Report 3:32 p.

Harding, J.P. 1966. Myodocopan ostracods from the gills and nostrils of fishes. Pages 369-374 *In:* H. Barnes (Ed.) Contemporary studies in marine science, George Allen and Unwin Ltd., London, England.

Hargis, W.J., Jr. 1955,1957. Monogenetic trematodes of Gulf of Mexico fishes. V. The superfamily Capsaloidea. XIII. The family Gastrocotylidae Price, 1943. Transactions of the American Microscopical Society 74:203-225; 76:1-12.

_____ 1956a. Monogenetic trematodes of Gulf of Mexico fishes. XI. The family Microcotylidae Taschenberg, 1879. Proceedings of the Helminthological Society of Washington 23:153-162.

_____ 1956b. Monogenetic trematodes of Gulf of Mexico fishes. XII. The family Gastrocotylidae Price, 1943. Bulletin of Marine Sciences of the Gulf and Caribbean 6:28-43.

_____ 1958. The fish parasite *Argulus laticauda* as a fortuitous human epizoon. Journal of Parasitology 44:45.

Harshbarger, J.C. 1965-1981 (each year). Activities report of the Registry of Tumors in Lower Animals, National museum of Natural History, Smithsonian Institution, Washington, District of Columbia, USA.

Hasegawa, H., E.H. Williams, Jr. and L. Bunkley-Williams. 1991. Nematode parasites from marine fishes of Okinawa, Japan. Journal of the Helminthological Society of Washington 58:186-197.

Hauck, K. 1977. Occurrence and survival of the larval nematode *Anisakis* sp. in the flesh of fresh, frozen, brined, and smoked pacific herring, *Clupea harengus* Pallasi. Journal of Parasitology 63:515-519.

Health, M.R. 1992. Field investigations of the early life stages of marine fish. Advances in Marine Biology 28:1-174.

Hendrix, S.S. 1994. Platyhelminthes: Monogenea. NOAA Technical Report NMFS 121:107 p.

*Hilderbrand, K.S., Jr. 1984. Parasites in marine fishes: Questions and answers for seafood retailers. Oregon State University Sea Grant 79:2 p.

Hogans, W.E. 1985. Occurrence of *Caligus coryphaenae* (Copepoda: Caligidae) on the Atlantic bluefin tuna (*Thunnus thynnus* L.) from Prince Edward Island, Canada. Crustaceana 49:313-314.

_____ 1986. Redescription of *Pennnella instructa* Wilson, 1917 (Copepoda: Pennellidae) from the swordfish (*Xiphias gladius* L.). Canadian Journal of Zoology 64:727-730.

_____ 1987. Morphological Variation in *Pennella balaenoptera* and *P. filosa* (Copepoda: Pennellidae) with a Review of the Genus *Pennella* Oken, 1816 Parasitic on Cetacea. Bulletin of Marine Science 40:442-453.

_____ 1988a. *Pennella makaira*, new species (Copepoda: Pennellidae) from the Atlantic Blue Marlin, *Makaira nigricans*, in the Caribbean Sea. Proceedings of the Biological Society of Washington 101:15-19.

_____ 1988b. Redescription of *Pennella sagitta* (Copepoda: Pennellidae) from *Histrio histrio* (Pisces) in the north-west Atlantic Ocean with a provisional review of the genus *Pennella*. Journal of Zoology (London) 216: 379-390.

_____ 1995. Parasitic Copepoda in the collection of the Atlantic Reference Centre, St. Andrews, New Brunswick, Canada. Canadian Technical Report of Fisheries and Aquatic Sciences No. 2028:6 p.

_____ and J. Brattey. 1982. Parasites of the gills and gastrointestinal tracts of swordfish (*Xiphias gladius*) from the northwest Atlantic Ocean, with an assessment of their use as biological tags. Report to Canada Department of Fisheries and Oceans No. 07SC.FP706-1-CO33:36 p.

_____, _____ and T.R. Hurlbutt. 1986. *Pennella filosa* and *Pennnella instructa* (Copepoda: Pennellidae) on swordfish (*Xiphias gladius* L.) from the northwest Atlantic. Journal of Parasitology 71:111-112.

_____, _____, L.S. Uhazy and P.C.F. Hurley. 1983. Helminth parasites of swordfish (*Xiphias gladius* L.) from the northwest Atlantic Ocean. _____ 69:1178-1179.

_____ and P.C.F. Hurley. 1986. Variations in the Morphology of *Fistulicola plicatus* Rudolphi (1802) (Cestoda: Pseudophyllidea) from the Swordfish, *Xiphias gladius* L., in the northwest Atlantic Ocean. Fishery Bulletin 84: 754-757.

Holliday, M. 1978. Food of Atlantic bluefin tuna, *Thunnus thynnus* (L.), from the coastal waters of North Carolina to Massachusetts. MS Thesis, Long Island University, New York, USA, 27 p.

Howse, H.D., J.S. Franks and R.F. Welford. 1975. Pericardial adhesions in cobia *Rachycentron canadum* (Linnaeus). Gulf Research Reports 5:61-62.

Iles, C. 1971. *Fistulicola plicatus* (Cestoda) and *Tristoma* spp. (Trematoda) on swordfish from the Northwest Atlantic. Journal of the Fisheries Research Board of Canada 28:31-34.

Iversen, E.S. and N.N. Van Meter. 1967. A new Myxosporidian (Sporozoa) infecting the spanish mackerel. Bulletin of Marine Sciences 17:268-273.

_____ and H.O. Yoshida. 1957. Notes on the biology of the wahoo in the Line Islands. Pacific Science 11:370-379.

Iversen, R.T.B. and R.R. Kelley. 1974. Occurrence, morphology, and parasitism of gastric ulcers in blue marlin, *Makaira nigricans*, and black marlin, *Makaira indica*, from Hawaii. NOAA Technical Report NMFS SSRF-675(2):149-153.

Jahn, T.L., E.C. Bovee and F.F. Jahn. 1979. How to Know the Protozoa. 2nd Edition, William C. Brown Company, Dubuque, Iowa, 279 p.

Johnson, G.D. 1984. Percoidei: development and relationships. Pages 464-498 *In:* H.G. Moser et al. (Eds.) Ontogeny and systematics of fishes. American Society of Ichthyology and Herpetology, Special Publication 1.

*Johnson, S.K. 1977. Worm parasites of the edible flesh of Texas coastal fishes. Texas Agricultural Extension Service, FDDL-M1:6 p.

*_____ 1977. Fish worms harmless to humans. Texas Trawler Jan.-Feb. 1977:3-4.

Johnstone, J. 1912. *Tetrarhynchus erinaceus* van Beneden. I. Structure of larva and adult worm. Parasitology 4:364-415.

Jolley, J.W., Jr. 1977. The biology and fishery of Atlantic sailfish, *Istiophorus platypterus*, from southeast Florida. Florida Marine Resources Publication No. 28:31 p.

Jones, E.C. 1971. *Isistius brasiliensis*, a squaloid shark, the probable cause of crater wounds on fishes and cetaceans. Fishery Bulletin 69:791-798.

Jones, J.B. 1991. Movements of albacore tuna (*Thunnus alalunga*) in the south Pacific: evidence from parasites. Marine Biology 111:1-9.

Jones, S. 1962. The phenomenal fish mortality in the Arabian Sea in 1957--A speculation on the possible identity of the species concerned. Symposium on Scombroid Fishes, Marine Biological Association of India, Part II:713-718.

Justine, J.-L., A. Lambert and X. Mattei. 1985. Spermatozoon ultrastructure and phylogenetic relationships in the monogeneans (Platyhelminthes). International Journal of Parasitology 15:601-608.

_____ and X. Mattei. 1987. Phylogenetic relationships between the families Capsalidae and Dionchidae (Platyhelminthes, Monogenea, Monopisthocotylea) indicated by the comparative ultrastructural study of spermiogenesis. Zoologica Scripta 16:111-116.

*Kabata, Z. 1970. Crustacea as enemies of fishes. T.F.H. Publications, Inc. Neptune City, New Jersey, USA. 171 p.

_____ 1979. Parasitic Copepoda of British Fishes. Ray Society, London, England, 468 p., 2030 figs.

_____ 1988. Copepoda and Branchiura. Pages 4-127 *In* L. Margolis and Z. Kabata [Eds.] Guide to the parasites of fishes of Canada. Part II Crustacea. Canadian Special Publications of Fisheries and Aquatic Sciences 101:184 p.

Kawahara, E., J.S. Nelson and R. Kusuda. 1986. Fluorescent antibody technique compared to standard media culture for detection of pathogenic bacteria for yellowtail and amberjack. Fish Pathology 21:39-45.

Khalil, L.F., A. Jones and R.A. Bray (Eds.). 1994. Keys to the Cestode Parasites of Vertebrates. CAB International, Oxford, England, 751 p.

Kensley, B. and M. Schotte. 1989. Marine isopod crustaceans of the Caribbean. Smithsonian Institution Press, Washington, DC, 308 p.

*Klemm, R. 1984. Cookie cutter shark. Sea Frontiers 28(2):9.

Koratha, K.J. 1955. Studies on the monogenetic trematodes of the Texas coast. II. Descriptions of species from marine fishes of Port Aransas. University of Texas Institute of Marine Science Publication 4:251-278.

Lee, J.J., S.H. Hutner and E.C. Bovee (Eds.). 1985. An Illustrated Guide to the Protozoa. Academic Press, Lawrence, Kansas, 629 p.

Lester, R.J.G., A. Barnes and G. Habib. 1985. Parasites of skipjack tuna, *Katsuwonus pelamis*: Fishery implications. Fishery Bulletin 83:343-356.

Lewis, A.G. 1967. Copepod crustaceans parasitic on teleost fishes of the Hawaiian Islands. Proceedings of the U.S. National Museum 121:1-204.

Llewellyn, J. 1956. The host-specificity, micro-ecology, adhesive attitudes, and comparative morphologies of some trematode gill parasites. Journal of the Marine Biology Association of the United Kingdom 35:113-127.

_____ 1957. The mechanism of the attachment of *Kuhnia scombri* (Kuhn, 1829)(Trematoda: Monogenea) to the gills of its host *Scomber scombrus* L., including a note on the taxonomy of the parasite. Parasitology 47:30-39.

Linton, E. 1897a. Notes on larval cestode parasites of fishes. Proceedings of the U.S. National Museum 19:787-824, 8 pl.

_____ 1897b. Notes on cestode parasites of fishes. _____ 20:423-456, 8 pl.

_____ 1900. Fish parasites collected at Woods Hole in 1898. Bulletin of the U.S. Commission on Fish and Fisheries 19:267-304.

_____ 1901. Parasites of fishes of the Woods Hole region. _____ 19:405-492.

_____ 1905. Parasites of fishes of Beaufort, North Carolina. Bulletin of the U.S. Bureau of Fisheries for 1904. 24:321-428, 34 pl.

_____ 1907. Notes on parasites of Bermuda fishes. Proceedings of the U.S. National Museum 33:85-126.

_____ 1908,1910. Helminth fauna of the Dry Tortugas. I. Cestodes. II. Trematodes. Carnegie Institution of Washington Publication 102:157-190; 133:11-98.

_____ 1924. Notes on cestode parasites of sharks and skates. Proceedings of the U.S. National Museum 64:1-114, 13 pl.

_____ 1940. Trematodes from fishes mainly from the Woods Hole region, Massachusetts. _____ 88:1-172.

_____ 1941. Cestode parasites of teleost fishes of the Woods Hole region, Massachusetts. _____ 90:417-441, 3 pl.

Lom, J. and I. Dyková. 1992. Protozoan Parasites of Fishes. Elsevier Science Publishers, Amsterdam, Netherlands, 315 p.

Love, M.S. and M. Moser 1983. A checklist of parasites of California, Oregon, and Washington marine and estuarine fishes. NOAA Technical Report NMFS SSRF-777:576 p.

MacCallum, G.A. 1913. Notes on four trematodes parasites of marine fishes. Centralblatt fur Bakteriologie Parasitenkunde und Infektionskrankheiten., 1 Abteilung Originale 70:407-416.

_____ 1915. Some new species of ectoparasitic trematodes. Zoologica 1:393-410.

_____ 1917. Some new forms of parasitic worms. Zoopathologica 1:43-75.

_____ 1921. Studies in helminthology. _____ 1:137-284.

_____ and W.G. MacCallum. 1916. The family Koellikeriadae (Didymozoidae). Zoologische Jahrbuecher Abteilung fuer Systematik 39:141-168.

Madhavi, R. 1982. Didymozoid trematodes (including new genera and species) from marine fishes of the Waltair coast, Bay of Bengal. Systematic Parasitology 4:99-124.

*McClane, A.J. (Ed.). 1974a,b. McClane's field guide to salt water fishes of North America. [and] McClane's New Standard Fishing Encyclopedia and International Angling Guide. 2nd Edition, Holt, Rinehart and Winston, New York, USA, 283 p.(a), 1156 p.(b)

McIntosh, A. 1934. A new blood trematode, *Paradeontacylix sanguinicoloides* n. g., n. sp. from *Seriola lalandi*, with a key to the species of the Family Aporocotylidae. Parasitology 26:463-467.

McKenzie, K. 1983. The selection of parasites for use as biological tags in population studies of bluefin tuna. ICCAT, Collected Volume of Scientific Papers 18:834-838.

McMahon, J.W. 1964. Monogenetic trematodes from some Chesapeake Bay fishes. Part II: the superfamily Diclidophoroidea. Chesapeake Science 5: 124-133.

Mamaev, Y.L. 1982. Monogeneans of the subfamily Grubeinae Price, 1961 (family Mazocraeidae) [in Russian]. Parazitology 16:457-463.

Manooch, C.S., III and W.T. Hogarth. 1983. Stomach contents and giant trematodes from wahoo *Acanthocybium solanderi* collected along the south Atlantic and Gulf coasts of the United States. Bulletin of Marine Sciences 33:227-238.

_____, D.L. Mason and R.S. Nelson. 1984. Food and gastrointestinal parasites of dolphin *Coryphaena hippurus* collected along the southeastern and Gulf coasts of the United States [of America]. Bulletin of the Japanese Society of Scientific Fisheries 50:1511-1525.

Manter, H.W. 1931. Some digenetic trematodes of marine fishes of Beaufort, North Carolina. Parasitology 23:396-411.

_____ 1940a. Digenetic trematodes of fishes from the Galapagos Islands and the neighboring Pacific. Alan Hancock Pacific Expeditions, Volume 2: 329-497.

_____ 1940b. Gasterostomes (Trematoda) of Tortugas, Florida. Papers from the Tortugas Laboratory of the Carnegie Institution of Washington 33:1-19.

_____ 1947. The digenetic trematodes of marine fishes of Tortugas, Florida. American Midland Naturalist 38:257-416.

_____ 1970. A new genus of trematode (Digenea; Gorgoderidae) from the ureter of tuna fish (*Thunnus thynnus maccoyii*) in Australia. Transactions of the Royal Society of South Australia 94:147-150.

Margolis, L., Z Kabata, and R.R. Parker. 1975. Catalogue and synopsis of *Caligus*, a genus of Copepoda (Crustacea) parasitic on fishes. Bulletin of the Fisheries Research Board of Canada 192:117 p.

_____, J.O. Corlis, M. Melkonian, D.J. Chapman (Eds). 1989. Handbook of Protoctista. Jones and Bartlett, Boston, USA, 914 p.

Menzies, R.J. and P.W. Glynn. 1968. The common marine isopod crustacea of Puerto Rico. Studies on the fauna of Curaçao and other Caribbean Islands 27:1-110.

Mignucci-Giannoni, A.A. 1996. Marine mammal strandings in Puerto Rico and the United States and British Virgin Islands. PhD Dissertation, University of Puerto Rico, Mayagüez, Puerto Rico, 247 p.

Millemann, R.E. 1956. Notes on the genus *Hexostoma* (Monogenea: Hexostomatidae) with a redescription of *H. euthynni* Meserve, 1938. Journal of Parasitology 42:316-319.

Murchelano, R.A., L. Despres-Patanjo and J. Ziskowski. 1986. A histopathologic evaluation of gross lesions excised from commercially important North Atlantic marine fishes. NOAA Technical Report NMFS 37:14 p.

Muroga, K., T. Nakai and T. Nishizawa. 1994. Viral diseases in Japanese seawater pen culture. Page V-2 *In:* International Symposium on Aquatic Animal Health, Abstracts, Seattle, Washington, USA, 298 p.

Nahhas, F.M. 1993. Some acanthocephala and Digenea of Marine fish from Grand Cayman, Cayman Islands, British West Indies. Journal of the Helminthological Society of Washington 60:270-272.

_____ and R.M. Cable. 1964. Digenetic and aspidogastrid trematodes from marine fishes of Curaçao and Jamaica. Tulane Studies in Zoology and Botany 11:167-228.

_____ and K. Carlson. 1994. Digenetic trematodes of marine Fishes of Jamaica, West Indies. Hofstra University Marine Laboratory, Ecological Survey of Jamaica Publication 2:60 p.

_____ and R.B. Short. 1965. Digenetic trematodes of marine fishes from Apalachee Bay, Gulf of Mexico. Tulane Studies in Zoology and Botany 12:39-50.

Nasir, P. and J.L. Fuentes Zambrano. 1983. Some Venezuelan monogeneans [in Spanish]. Rivista di Parassitologia 44:335-380.

Neish, G.A. and G.C. Hughes. 1980. Fungal Diseases of Fishes. TFH Publications, Neptune City, New Jersey, 159 p.

Nigrelli, R.F. 1938. Parasites of the swordfish *Xiphias gladius* L. American Museum Novitates 996:1-16.

_____ 1939. *Didymocystis coatesi*, a new monostome from the eye muscles of the wahoo, *Acanthocybium solanderi* (C. and V.). Transactions of the American Microscopical Society 58:170-178.

_____ and H.W. Stunkard. 1947. Studies on the genus *Hirudinella*, giant trematodes of scombriform fishes. Zoologica 31:185-196.

Nikolaeva, V.M. 1968. Studies of the helminth fauna of *Thunnus albacroes* and Histiophoridae in the Gulf of Mexico [in Russian]. Pages 150-157 *In:* Z. B. Yankovskaya (Ed.) (Studies of Central American Seas). Kiev: Nankova Dunka (2).

_____ 1985. Trematodes--Didymozoidae fauna, distribution and biology. Pages 67-73 *In:* W.J. Hargis, Jr. (Ed.) Parasitology and pathology of marine organisms of the world ocean. NOAA Technical Report NMFS 25:135 p.

_____ and A.M. Parukhin. 1968. Study of the helminths of fish in the Gulf of Mexico [in Russian]. Pages 126-149 *In:* Z.B. Yankovskaya (Ed.) (Studies of Central American Seas). Kiev: Nankova Dunka (2).

Norris, D.E. and R.M. Overstreet. 1976. The public health implications of larval *Thynnascaris* nematodes from shellfish. Journal of Milk and Food Technology 39:47-54.

Olsen, L.S. 1952. Some nematodes parasitic in marine fishes. Publications of the Institute of Marine Science, University of Texas 2:173-215.

Ortiz, E.A.R., E.H. Williams, Jr., and L. Bunkley-Williams. 1995. A record of paper nautilis (*Argonauta argo* and *Argonauta hians*) in Puerto Rico. Caribbean Journal of Science 31:340-341. [in a dolphin stomach]

Overstreet, R.M. 1969. Digenetic trematodes of marine teleost fishes from Biscayne Bay, Florida. Tulane Studies in Zoology and Botany 15:119-176.

*_____ 1978. Marine maladies? Worms, germs, and other symbionts from the Northern Gulf of Mexico. Mississippi-Alabama Sea Grant Consortium MASGP-78-021:140 p.

_____ and G.M. Meyer. 1981. Hemorrhagic lesions in stomach of rhesus monkey caused by a piscine ascaridoid nematode. Journal of Parasitology 67:226-235.

Palko, B. J., G. L. Beardsley and W. J. Richards. 1982. Synopsis of the biological data on dolphin-fishes, *Coryphaena hippurus* Linnaeus and *Coryphaena equiselis* Linnaeus. NOAA Technical Report, NMFS Circular 443, FAO Fisheries Synopsis 130: 28 p.

Palm, H. W. 1995. Study of the systematics of tapeworms (Cestoda: Trypanorhyncha) of Atlantic fishes. [in German]. Berichte aus dem Institut für Meereskunde an der Christian-Albrechts-Universität, Kiel, Nr. 275:238p.

Parker, R.R. 1969. Validity of the binomen *Caligus elongatus* for a common parasitic copepod formerly misidentified with *Caligus rapax*. Journal of the Fishery Research Board of Canada 26:1013-1035.

Pearse, A.S. 1949. Observations of flatworms and nemerteans collected at Beaufort, N. C. Proceedings of the U.S. National Museum 100:25-38.

_____ 1951. Parasitic crustacea from Bimini, Bahamas. _____ 101:341-372.

_____ 1952a. Parasitic crustacea from the Texas coast. Institute of Marine Science, Publication 2:5-42, 151 figs.

_____ 1952b. Parasitic Crustaceans From Alligator Harbor, Florida. Quarterly Journal of the Florida Academy of Sciences 15:187-243.

Perez-Vigueras, I. 1935. *Tristomum poeyi* n. sp. (Trematoda) a parasite of *Makaira ampla* Poey (Pisces) [in Spanish]. Memorias de la Sociedad Cubana de Historia Natural 9:43-44.

_____ 1942. Helminthological notes [in Spanish]. Revista de l'Universidad de Habana (40-42):193-223.

_____ 1958. Additions to the Cuban helminth fauna [in Spanish]. Memorias de la Sociedad Cubana de Historia Natural 24:17-38.

Pillai, N.K. 1971. Notes on some copepod parasites in the collection of the British Museum (N.H.), London. Journal of the Marine Biological Association of India 11:149-174.

Pinkus, G.S., C. Coolidge and M.D. Little. 1975. Intestinal aniskiasis: First case report from North America. American Journal of Medicine 59:114-120.

Plumb, J.A. 1994. Health maintenance of cultured fishes: principal microbial diseases. CRC Press Boca Raton, Florida, USA, 254 p.

Price, E.W. 1938. North American monogenetic trematodes. II. The families Monocotylidae, Microbothridae, Acanthocotylidae and Udonellidae (Capsaloidea). Journal of the Washington Academy of Science 28:109-126.

_____ 1939. North American monogenetic trematodes III. The family Capsalidae (Capsaloidea). Journal of the Washington Academy of Science 29:63-92.

_____ 1951. A new North American Monogenetic trematode *Capsala manteri*, n. sp. Proceedings of the Helminthological Society of Washington 18:24-25.

_____ 1960. The giant marlin, *Makaira marlina* Jordan and Evermann, a new host for *Capsala pricei* Hidalgo, 1959, with a review of the subfamily Capsalinae. Libro. Homenaje al Dr. E. Caballero y Caballero, Mexico, p. 237-244.

_____ 1961. North American monogenetic trematodes. VIII. The family Hexostomatidae. Proceedings of the Helminthological Society of Washington 29:1-18.

_____ 1962. North American monogenetic trematodes. X. The family Heteraxinidae. Journal of Parasitology 48:402-418.

*Prince, E.D. 1984. Don't throw back recaptured tagged billfish or tuna-- SAVE IT FOR SCIENCE. Marlin Magazine 3(2):50-54.

Ragan, M.A., C.L. Googin, R.L. Cawthorn, L. Cerenius, A.V.C. Jamieson, S.M. Plourde, T.G. Rand, K. Söderhall and R.R. Gutell. 1996. A novel clade of protistan parasites near the animal-fungal divergence. Proceedings of the National Academy of Sciences 93:(in press).

Raju, G. 1960. A case of hermaphroditism and some other gonadal abnormalities in the skipjack *Katsuwonus pelamis* (Linnaeus). Journal of the Marine Biological Association of India 2:95-102, 5 figs.

Rand, T.G. 1996. Fungal diseases of fish and shellfish. Pages 297-313 *In:* Howard/Miller (Eds.) The Mycota VI. Human and animal relationships. Springer-Verlag, New York, USA, 399 p.

Raptopoulou, F.A. and R.H. Lambertsen. 1987. Parasite-associated pathology of the dolphinfish, *Coryphaena hippurus* L., from Florida waters. Journal of Fish Diseases 10:379-384.

Rees, G. 1969. Cestodes from Bermuda fishes and an account of *Acompsocephalum tortum* (Linton, 1905) gen. nov. from the lizard fish *Synodus intermedius* (Agassiz). Parasitology 59:519-548.

_____ 1970. Some helminth parasites of fishes of Bermuda and an account of the attachment organ of *Alcicornis carangis* MacCallum, 1917 (Digenea: Bucephalidae). _____ 60:195-221.

Robins, C.R., R.M. Bailey, C.E. Bond, J.R. Brooker, E.A. Lachner, R.N. Lea and W.B. Scott. 1991. Common and Scientific Names of Fishes from the United States and Canada. 5th Edition, American Fisheries Society, Special Publication 20:183 p.

Rohde, K. 1978. Monogenea of Australian Marine Fishes. The Genera *Dionchus*, *Sibitrema* and *Hexostoma*. Seto Marine Biological Laboratory 24:349-367.

_____ 1994. Ecology of marine parasites. CAB International, Wallingford, Berkshire, England, 298 p.

_____ 1987. *Grubea australis* n. sp. (Monogenea, Polyopisthocotylea) from *Scomber australasicus* in southeastern Australia, and *Grubea cochlear* Diesing, 1858 from *S. scombrus* and *S. japonicus* in the Mediterranean and western Atlantic. Systematic Parasitology 9:29-38.

_____ 1989. *Kuhnia sprostonae* Price, 1961 and *K. scombercolias* Nasir & Fuentes Zambrano, 1983 (Monogenea: Mazocraeidae) and their microhabitats on the gills of *Scomber australasicus* (Teleostei: Scombridae), and the geographic distribution of seven species of gill Monogenea of *Scomber* spp. Systematic Parasitology 14:93-100.

_____ 1991. Size differences in hamuli of *Kuhnia scombri* (Monogenea, Polyopisthocotylea) from different geographical areas not due to differences in host size. International Journal of Parasitology 21:113-114.

_____ and N. Watson. 1985. Morphology, microhabitats and geographic variation of *Kuhnia* spp. (Monogenea, Polyopisthocotylea). International Journal of Parasitology 15:569-586.

Rose, C.D. 1966. The biology and catch distribution of the dolphin, *Coryphaena hippurus* (Linnaeus), in North Carolina waters. PhD Dissertation, University of North Carolina, 153 p.

Ruszkowski, J.S. 1932. Studies of the life cycle and structure of marine cestodes. The life cycle of the tetrarhynchid *Grillotia erinaceus* (van Ben., 1858) [in French]. Académie Polonaise des Sciences et des Lettres, Comptes Rendus Mensuels des Séances Mathématiques et Naturelles, Cracovie (9):6.

Saunders, D.C. 1958. Blood parasites of the marine fishes of the Florida Keys. Yearbook of the American Philosophical Society, p. 261-266.

_____ 1958. The occurrence of *Haemogregarina bigemina* Laveran and Mesnil and *H. dasyatis* n. sp. in marine fish from Bimini, B.W.I. Transactions of the American Microscopical Society 77:404-412.

_____ 1959. *Haemogregarina bigemina* Laveran and Mesnil from marine fishes of Bermuda. _____ 78:374-379.

_____ 1964. Blood parasites of marine fish of southwest Florida, including a new haemogregarine from the menhaden, *Brevoortia tyrannus* (Latrobe). _____ 83:218-225.

_____ 1966. A survey of the blood parasites of the marine fishes of Puerto Rico. _____ 85:193-199.

*Schell, S.C. 1970. How to Know the Trematodes. William C. Brown Company Publishers, Dubuque, Iowa, 355 p.

_____ 1985. Handbook of Trematodes of North America North of Mexico. University Press of Idaho, Moscow, Idaho, 263 p.

*Schmidt, G.D. 1970. How to Know the Tapeworms. William C. Brown Company Publishers, Dubuque, Iowa, 266 p.

_____ 1986. CRC Handbook of Tapeworm Identification. CRC Press, Boca Raton, Florida, 675 p.

Schwartz, F.J. 1977. Effects of sharksucker, *Echeneis naucrates*, disk on scaled and scaleless fishes and sea turtles. American Society of Biologists Bulletin 24:84.

Scott, T. and A. Scott. 1913. The British parasitic Copepoda. Volumes I-II, Ray Society, London, England, 256 p., 72 pl.

Shaffer, R. V. and E. L. Nakamura. 1989. Synopsis of biological data on the cobia *Rachycentron canadum* (Pisces: Rachycentridae). NOAA Technical Report NMFS 82 and FAO Fisheries Synopsis 153:21 p.

Shiino, S.M. 1959. Copepod parasites of eastern Pacific fishes [in German]. Report of Faculty of Fisheries, Prefectural University of Mie 3:267-333.

_____ 1960. Copepods parasitic on the fishes collected on the coast of Province Shima, Japan. Report of Faculty of Fisheries, Prefectural University of Mie 3:471-500.

Siddall, M.E., D.S. Martin, D. Bridge, S.S. Desser, and D. Cone. 1995. The demise of a phylum of protists: phylogony of Myxozoa and other parasitic Cnidaria. Journal of Parasitology 81:961-967.

Siddiqi, A.H. and R.M. Cable. 1960. Digenetic trematodes of marine fishes of Puerto Rico. Scientific Survey of Porto Rico and the Virgin Islands 17:257-369.

Silas, F.G. 1962. Parasites of scombroid fishes. Part I. Monogenetic trematodes, digenetic trematodes, and cestodes. Pages 799-875 *In:* Symposium on Scombroid Fishes, Marine Biological Association of India, Part III: 799-1236.

_____ and A.N.P. Ummerkutty. 1962. Parasites of scombroid fishes. Part II. Copepoda. Pages 876-993 *In:* _____ Part III:799-1236.

Simmons, D.C. 1969. Maturity and spawning of skipjack tuna (*Katsuwonus pelamis*) in the Atlantic Ocean, with comments on nematode infestation of the ovaries. U.S. Fish and Wildlife Service, Special Scientific Report Fisheries 580:1-17.

Sindermann, C.J. 1990. Principal Diseases of Marine Fish and Shellfish. 2nd Edition. Academic Press, San Diego, California, USA. Volume 1, 521 p., Volume 2, 516 p.

_____ 1993. Interactions of pollutants and disease in marine fish and shellfish. Chapter 16, Pages 451-482 *In:* J.A. Couch and J.W. Fournie (Eds.) Pathobiology of marine and estuarine organisms. Advances in Fisheries Science. CRC Press, Boca Raton, Florida, USA.

Skinner, R.H. 1978. Some external parasites on Florida fishes. Bulletin of Marine Science 28:590-595.

Smith, J.L.B. 1950. The sea fishes of southern Africa. Central News Agency, Capetown, South Africa, 550 p.

Sniesko, S.F. (Ed.). 1970. A Symposium on Diseases of Fishes and Shellfishes. American Fisheries Society, Special Publication No. 5:526 p.

Sogandares-Bernal, F. 1959. Digenetic trematodes of marine fishes from the Gulf of Panama and Bimini, British West Indies. Tulane Studies in Zoology 7:70-117.

_____ and R.F. Hutton. 1959. Studies on helminth parasites from the coast of Florida. IV. Digenetic trematodes of marine fishes of Tampa, Boca Ciega Bays, and the Gulf of Mexico. Quartly Journal of the Florida Academy of Sciences 21:259-273.

Speare, P. 1990a. Relationships among black marlin, *Makaira indica*, in eastern Australia coastal waters, inferred from parasites. Australian Journal of Marine and Freshwater Research 45:535-549.

_____ 1990b. Parasites of the Pacific sailfish (*Istiophorus platypterus*): A preliminary investigation of their useful in stock discrimination. Pages 95-102 *In:* R. H. Stroud [see Barse and Hocutt 1990].

Sproston, N.G. 1945. The genus *Kuhnia* n. g. (Trematoda: Monogenea). An examination of the value of some specific characters, including factors of relative growth. Parasitology 36:176-190.

Steele-Llinás, R.M. 1982. Some parasitic copepods of marine fishes of Puerto Rico and other adjacent areas of the Caribbean. MS Thesis, University of Puerto Rico, Mayaguez, Puerto Rico, 88 p.

Strasburg, D.W. 1959. Notes on the diet and correlating structures of some central Pacific echeneid fishes. Copeia 1959:244-248.

_____ 1959. An instance of natural mass mortality of larval frigate mackerel in the Hawaiian Islands. Journal of Conservation 24:255-263.

Sumner, F.B., R.C. Osborn and L.J. Cole. 1913. A biological survey of the waters of Woods Hole and vicinity. Section 3. A catalogue of the marine fauna. U.S. Bureau of Fisheries Bulletin 31:545-794.

Tetra Tech, Inc. 1992. Characterization of Use Impairments of the U.S. Virgin Islands and Puerto Rico. Final Report to Marine and Wetlands Protection Branch, USEPA, New York, 428 p.

Thatcher, V.E. 1959. A report on some monogenetic trematode parasites of Louisiana marine fishes. Proceedings of the Louisiana Academy of Sciences 22:78-82.

_____ 1993. Neotropical Trematodes [in Portuguese]. Instituto Nacional de Pesquisas da Amazônia, Manaus, Brazil 553 p.

Vervoort, W. 1965. Three new species of Bomolochidae (Copepoda, Cyclopoida) from tropical Atlantic tunnies. Zoologische Verhandelingen, Leiden 76:3-40.

Vigeras, P. 1935. *Tristomas poeyi* n. sp. (Trematoda) parasitic on *Makaira ampla* Poey (Pisces) [in Spanish]. Memorias de la Sociedad Cubana de Historia Natural 9:43-44.

Wallace, D.H. and E.M. Wallace. 1942. Observations on the feeding habits of the white marlin, *Tetrapturus albidus* Poey. Publications of the Chesapeake Biological Laboratory 50:3-10.

Walters, V. 1980. Parasitic copepoda and monogenea as biological tags for certain populations of Atlantic bluefin tuna. ICCAT Collection Volume Science Papers IX(2):491-498.

Ward, D.R. and C. Hackney. 1991. Microbiology of marine food products. Van Norstrand Reinhold, New York, USA, 450 p.

Ward, H.L. 1954. Parasites of marine fishes of the Miami region. Bulletin of Marine Science of the Gulf and Caribbean 4:244-261.

Ward, J.W. 1962. Helminth parasites of some marine animals, with special reference to those from the yellow-fin tuna, *Thunnus albacares* (Bonnaterre). Journal of Parasitology 48:155.

Wardle, R.A. and J.A. McLeod. 1952. The zoology of tapeworms. The University of Minnesota Press, Minneapolis, Minnesota, USA, 780 p.

Watertor, J.L. 1973. Incidence of *Hirudinella marina* Garcia, 1770 (Trematoda: Hirudinellidae) in tunas from the Atlantic Ocean. Journal of Parasitology 59:207-208.

Watson, C., R.E. Bourke and R.W. Brill. 1988. A comprehensive theory on the etiology of burnt tuna. Fishery Bulletin 86:367-372.

Williams, E.H., Jr. 1978. *Conchoderma virgatum* (Spengler) (Cirripedia, Thoracica) in association with *Dinemoura latifolia* (Steenstrup and Lütken) (Copepoda, Caligidea) a parasite of the shortfin mako, *Isurus oxyrhynchus* Rafinesque (Pisces, Chondrichthyes). Crustaceana 34:109-111.

_____ 1982. Disease factors which should be considered in fish kill investigations. Pages 42-43 *In*: D.K. Atwood (Ed.) Unusual mass fish mortalities in the Caribbean and Gulf of Mexico. Atlantic Oceanographic and Meteorological Laboratories, Miami, Florida, 46 P.

_____ 1983. New host records for some nematode parasites of fishes from Alabama and adjacent waters. Proceedings of the Helminthological Society of Washington 50:178-182.

_____ and T.E. Bowman. 1994. *Lironeca* Leach, 1818 (Isopoda, Cymothoidae): proposed conservation as the correct spelling. Bulletin of Zoological Nomenclature 51:224-226.

_____ and L. Bunkley-Williams. 1994. Four cases of unusual crustacean-fish associations and comments on parasitic processes. Journal of Aquatic Animal Health 6: 202-208.

_____ and _____ 1995. Book Review: Keys to the cestode parasites of vertebrates, edited by L.F. Khalil, A. Jones, and R.A. Bray. 1994. CAB International, Oxon, United Kingdom, 751 p. Fisheries Review 40:574.

* _____ and _____ 1997a. Fish parasitic isopods. Chapter *In*: G.L. Hoffman (Ed.) Parasites of North American Freshwater Fishes. Cornell University Press (in press).

* _____ and _____ 1997b. Marine major ecological disturbances: Destructive indicators of global changes? Chapter *In*: B. McKay, Greenpeace (Ed.) Global Changes. Oxford University Press (in press).

_____, _____ and T.G. Rand. 1994. Some copepod and isopod parasites of Bermuda marine fishes. Journal of Aquatic Animal Health 6:279-280.

_____, _____ and C.J. Sanner. 1994. Some copepod and isopod parasites of Colombian marine fishes. _____ 6:362-364.

_____, _____, M.J. Dowgiallo and W.G. Dyer. 1991. Influence of collection methods on the occurrence of alimentary canal helminth parasites in fish. Journal of Parasitology 77:429-431.

_____ and J.L. Gaines, Jr. 1974. Acanthocephala of fishes from marine and brackish waters of the Mobile Bay region. Journal of Marine Sciences of Alabama 2:135-148.

_____, R.R. Lankford, G. van Buurt, D.K. Atwood, J.C. Gonzalez, G.C. McN. Harvey, B. Jimenez, H.E. Kumpf and H. Walters. 1982. Summary report of the IOCARIBE steering committee for developing regional contingencies for fish kills. UNESCO, Paris, Report Number CARI/FK/-1/3, 20 p.

* _____ and C.J. Sindermann. 1992. Effects of disease interactions with exotic organisms on the health of the marine environment. Pages 71-77 *In*: M.R. DeVoe (Ed.) Introductions and Transfers of Marine Species,

Achieving a Balance Between Economic Development and Resource protection. South Carolina Sea Grant, Charleston, South Carolina, 204 p.

_____ and L.B. Williams. 1986. The first association of *Conchoderma virgatum* (Spengler)(Cirripedia: Thoracica) with a euryphorid copepod in the mouth of a fish. Galaxea 5:209-211.

* _____ and _____ 1987. Caribbean Mass Mortalities: A problem with a solution. Oceanus 30(4):69-75.

Williams, H.H. and A. Jones. 1976. Marine helminths and human health. Commonwealth Institute of Helminthology Misc. Publication No. 3:47 p.

Wilson, C.B. 1905. North American parasitic copepods belonging to the family Caligidae. Part I. The Caliginae. Proceedings of the U.S. National Museum 28:479-572.

_____ 1908. North American parasitic copepods: New genera and species of Caliginae. _____ 33:593-627, pl. 49-56.

_____ 1911. North American parasitic copepods belonging to the Family Ergasilidae. _____ 39:263-400.

_____ 1917a. North American parasitic copepods belonging to the Lernaeopodidae with a revision of the entire family. _____ 47:565-729, 29 pl.

_____ 1917b. North American parasitic copepods belonging to the Lernaeidae with a revision of the entire family. _____ 53:1-150, 20 pl.

_____ 1932. The copepods of the Woods Hole region. Massachusetts. U.S. National Museum Bulletin Number 158:1-635.

_____ 1935a. New parasitic copepods. Smithsonian Miscellaneous Collections 91(19):1-9.

_____ 1935b. Parasitic copepods from the Dry Tortugas. Papers from the Tortugas Laboratory 29:329-347, 6 pl.

Yamaguti, S. 1939. Parasitic copepods from fishes of Japan, part 5: Caligoida, III. Volumen Jubilare Pro Prof. Sadao Yoshida 3:443-487.

_____ 1959-1963. Systema Helminthum, Vol. II, 1959. The Cestoda of Vertebrates (860 p.). Vol. III, 1961. The Nematodes of Vertebrates (1261 p.). Vol. IV, 1963. Monogenea and Aspidocotylea (699 p.). Vol. V, 1963. Acanthocephala (421 p.). 1963c. Parasitic Copepoda and Branchiura of Fishes (1104 p.). Interscience Publishers, New York, USA.

_____ 1968. Monogenetic trematodes of Hawaiian fishes. University of Hawaii Press, Honolulu, Hawaii, USA, 288 p.

_____ 1970. Digenetic trematodes of Hawaiian fishes. Keigaku Publishers, Tokyo, Japan, 436 p.

_____ 1971. Synopsis of digenetic trematodes of vertebrates. Vols. 1-2, Keigaku Publishing Company, Tokyo, Japan, 1074 p.

_____ 1975. A synoptical Review of Life Histories of Digenetic Trematodes of Vertebrates: With Special Reference to the Morphology of Their Larval Forms. Satyu Yamaguti, Kyoto, Japan, 590 p.

Young, R.T. 1954. A note on the life cycle of *Lacistorhynchus tenuis* (van Beneden, 1858), cestode of the leopard shark. Proceedings of the Helminthological Society of Washington 21:111.

INDEX

When more than one number occurs after a name, the number in bold face indicates the location of the general description of the parasite, disease, etc. Scientific names and authors of big game fishes appear in the Host Summaries as indicated. Those of other animals appear in their first use in the text. Big game fish hosts are not indexed from the parasite descriptions because these can be more easily found in the Host-Disease Checklists.

ABOUT THE AUTHORS

Cutting-edge science thrives on mysteries, and **Dr. Ernest H. (Bert) Williams, Jr.** finds an ample supply at the crossroads between Caribbean Aquatic Animal Health and Worldwide Disturbances. Bert received his doctorate in Fisheries Management from Auburn University in 1974 and has been a Professor in the Department of Marine Sciences UPR ever since. His interests include not only fish parasites but large-scale marine ecological disturbances.

Bert was an Officer in the Alabama and Puerto Rico Army National Guards. He is a Member of the Board of the Global Coral Reef Alliance and the Caribbean Stranding Network, a Member of the U.S. National Research Council Non-Indigenous Marine Species Panel, Headed a UNESCO/United Nations Committee on Caribbean Fish Kills and is a Cofounder and Country Representative of the Caribbean Red Tide and Mass Mortality Network. He was Coordinator of the Marine Ecological Disturbance Information Center (unfunded at present), and Executive Director of the Association of Marine Laboratories of the Caribbean for 15 years (1977-91). Bert is an Associate Editor of the Journal of Aquatic Animal Health, and is on the Review Board of the Caribbean Journal of Science. A fluke, copepod and isopod have been named in Bert's honor; and he received an honorable mention in the 1993 Rolex Awards for Enterprise for his work with marine ecological disturbances.

Dr. Lucy Bunkley-Williams completed her Doctorate in Fish Pathology at Auburn University in a near record pace of 2 years by 1984. She supported herself as a Research Associate in DMS from 1987 until 1995 when she became an Assistant Professor in the Biology Department, and continues to support her research at UPR with external research grants. In 1991, she completed a Shrimp Disease Course at the University of Arizona with Sea Grant support to make this expertise available in Puerto Rico.

Lucy is an award-winning underwater and scientific photographer. Her photographs are on display in the Smithsonian and have appeared around the world in books and magazines, and her underwater video footage has been used in national and international TV programs. Lucy has been honored as one of the Outstanding Women Graduates of Auburn University, by being featured in a U.S. News and World Report article, and by having 6 new species named for her (protozoan, fluke, spiny-headed worm, copepods, isopod).

Recent emergencies for Lucy and Bert included investigating massive kills of coral reef fishes in Barbados, mortalities of sea urchins throughout Puerto Rico and south Florida, and dying tilapia and shrimp in aquaculture facilities; diagnosing a scoliosis condition in local largemouth bass, *Micropterus salmoides* (Lacepéde), which may infect humans; isolating and naming a new primary pathogen which causes Tilapia-Wasting Disease, describing the new disease, and tracing its origin and international distribution in hopes of stopping its spread; and responding to a plan submitted to the government, to import a new exotic fish, with recommendations to protect Puerto Rico from its diseases. Despite this typically frantic but productive schedule, they have found time to characterize the parasites and diseases of local freshwater fishes in books in English and Spanish to make this information available in a friendly and useable format for everyone.

Lucy and Bert also solve aquatic animal health problems for sport fishermen, the Department of Natural and Environmental Resources (DNER), the University of Puerto Rico (UPR) and the local public; and represent Puerto Rico in international fish kill investigations as part of the Sportfish Restoration Project DNER/UPR. They have solved disease problems for aquaculture projects under separate grants, and for the Caribbean Stranding Network. They have "Doctored" all sorts of creatures from microscopic fairy shrimp to whales. Lucy has known the frustration of having a beautiful Atlantic spotted dolphin, *Stenella frontalis* (Cuvier), she was trying to save, die in her arms; and the joy of rehabilitating and releasing marine mammals and sea turtles.

Lucy and Bert have published more than 180 scientific papers and they have also written popular articles explaining coral reef bleaching, mass mortalities and fish isopods. They are preparing a chapter about marine ecological disturbances for the Greenpeace volume on "Global Change". Their work has been featured in a marine biology textbook, a children's science book, in numerous national and international newspaper and magazine articles and TV programs, and they were featured in a national "Network Earth" television program filmed in La Parguera, Puerto Rico. Future endeavors include a textbook "Marine Major Ecological Disturbances" (MMED), and a guidebook to isopod parasites of world fishes.

Bert and Lucy have "buddied" on more than 2500 hours of underwater research scuba dives throughout the West Indies and parts of the Pacific. Bert has known the terror of going "nose-to-nose" with a 2000 pound great white shark in open mid-water. Lucy is preparing a popular book describing their experiences living and working underwater, as Co-principal Investigators and Aquanauts, on 5 week-long Hydrolab Undersea Habitat, NOAA research missions (1979-85), in St. Croix, U.S. Virgin Islands.

Bert and Lucy were Visiting Foreign Researchers at the Sesoko Marine Science Center, University of the Ryukyus, in 1985-86, where they conducted underwater studies around Okinawa and many adjacent islands, that resulted in 20 scientific publications about fish parasites, fish associates, fishes and birds. They also visited almost every fisheries and marine sciences lab. in Japan to examine isopod parasites of fishes.